Author unknown

falling in Love...rising in radiance

By Greg Benner

Author unknown
by Greg Benner

Printed in the United States of America

ISBN 9781619967465

www.xulonpress.com

"Hang on...this book is fixin' to give you hurricane hair"
Bud

Contents

Foreward

I first met Greg when he randomly showed up at my church while on his second Trans-American walk across the country. With a wide grin, a firm handshake, and an unmistakable joy in his eyes, he introduced himself and went into his spiel about who he was and why God had called him to such a unique trek. As he was wrapping up his story I thought, "This guy is crazy...but I like him!" Over the course of the next three days we spent hours together engrossed in cultural and theological discussions that usually ended with us praying for our country and the churches that dot our land. I got to know who Greg was, where he was from, and what he was about. I saw in him a sincerity for God and a heart to obey even the smallest whisper of the Holy Spirit. Though distance soon separated us, our relationship began to deepen as we stayed in touch via phone and e-mail. Since that time we have developed a life-long friendship, and I have found that my first impression of Greg was correct. He lives a life that would be deemed "crazy" by many, for when he hears God speak he obeys without question - regardless of the consequences. This level of obedience takes a tremendous amount of faith yet to those who live by it there is an - quality about them that draws the hungry and the humble near to them.

And that is why this book is so powerful; it draws you in and asks you to look at life through the lens of faith's hope and love's radiance. In following God's voice Greg has been given the unique opportunity to see the heart and hands of the American church; not just one denomination but rather the church as a whole. It is from this vantage point that he pens out the heart of this book...a heart of pain, loss, life, and hope. The reality of a how God can take a broken heart, a broken life, a broken country and bring it to the place of healing and wholeness. So if you are one of the lost, the lonely, the left out; the broken, the wounded, the jaded - then this book is for you. For it tells the story of a life that was broken before God and how He supernaturally orchestrated the path (for Greg over 6,000 miles of it) that brings peace, understanding, and the fulfillment of God's perfect will.

While we are all on a journey through life, many hesitate to take such a path of blind obedience. But when we do answer God's call and step out into the unknown, something powerful happens... something supernatural. As you read this book I pray that you are encouraged to step out into the realm of faith as you hear the cry behind each page, each paragraph, and each word. It is the savage cry of a Savior who longs for us to know Him and reciprocate His love for us. It is a cry of sincerity that permeates the heart of God and the core of *Author unknown*. May you embrace God's cry and be forever changed as you answer the call to be with Him.

Todd Schumacher
Lead Pastor
Church of the King
Lake Charles, LA

Preface

This work is a milepost punctuating a journey of years, challenges, discoveries, adventures, and continents. Its navigation delivered me home...halfway around the world...before the famous...to the broken...inside foreign compounds...for tea with presidents-to-be... and deep into my own soul. The saga sprouted in rural America, passed through metropolitan masses, landed in third world war zones, and jumped into weaponized enemy territory in both the physical and unseen worlds. Along the way, I have been privileged to encounter people possessing from bottom-to-top statures within diverse cultures in amazingly unique settings. In the midst of it all, my reality was rocked, ignorance confronted, worldview stretched, horizons expanded, and my life was radically changed. No matter where I've been or who I've met – people are simply traveling life's journey from birth toward enlightenment while discovering themselves, pursuing dreams, raising families, and preparing for the life-to-come...

Author unknown's message flows out of love's insincerities, vision's eccentricities, affliction's brutalities, and mercy's redemptive qualities as portrayed in the lives of those I've met as well as my own. My journey tapped its roots in mid-to-late 1800's Germany, drove another stake in early 1900's America, and traced its path across geography and generations to drive destiny's peg deep in my life's soil from the time I was a child. Though oblivious, I was in fact a world-changer-unawares with nary-a-soul nearby selflessly willing or equipped to join my quest to uncover all I was created to be. Going it alone – I asked hard questions, suffered their traumas, stayed my course, and gained insights empowering me to color outside the world's lines, live beyond religion's box, and stand among milling multitudes alone – with purpose. My message was forged and gained its voice as I rose out of the achievable into the impossible to experience the supernatural in this life. Cutting through tradition to reach revelation is a lonely place as vision beckons beyond yesterday's miracle to cement today's decision in its stretch toward tomorrow's unknown.

My pathway was incited by impropriety, driven by necessity, and compelled by destiny within the scope of God's inconceivability. The more I dug to escape religion's rubbish and the harder I tugged to see God's face – I realized that He's as close as a whisper, mightier than a hurricane, more tender than a lover, and faithful as a friend. Despite life's fallout dear friend – God is in love with us, always at His post, and able to merge our mortal mess with His masterpiece in moments. Author unknown is about love, loss, liberty, and launching resurrected life victoriously. Though I have my own fears, I refuse to let them master me. Though I can tussle with theology, I'm into love's serendipity. I simply have no time for religion's aristocracy, while people around me crumble in today's reality. Like you – I'm just a guy who's been a place-or-two, puts his pants on one leg at a time, hungers for truth, experiences God, and has a story to share with those listening...

Greg Benner – Steward
BattleCry Ministries

Acknowledgements

Thank you for pouring out to bring this vision to reality...

My ever-loving, merciful, and faithful Lord Jesus Christ...

Those who loved me through God's transformation...

Those who prayed to hold my arms up in battle...

Those who trusted and shared their story...

Todd for his friendship and Foreward...

Josh for wonderful cover design...

Those who read my writings...

Those who gave to God...

Bless you in Jesus...

Introduction
Author unknown
By Greg Benner

What this book IS NOT
Author unknown IS NOT typical, IS NOT an interpretation of Scripture, and IS NOT my attempt to indoctrinate you with my views. Instead, Author unknown poses Scripturally-based revelation which God has granted to me as basis for us all to ask Him deeper questions which reveal His loving heart. Likewise, this book IS NOT based on human performance, intellectual knowledge, or theology. Instead, Author unknown is based on one's personal, hungry, wholehearted, and undying pursuit and embrace of God's character and Love.

What this book IS
Author unknown IS written and punctuated in prophetic progression, contiguous thoughts, and word pictures used to portray and fully communicate important concepts without fragmentation. Though some sentences may seem long, they are penned to avoid misconception. This work is written to communicate its intent, not appease grammatical structure at the expense of the message. The prior statement was not intended to disregard, it was merely my effort to help you grasp how to read this work in light of the fact that I'm not perfect. Author unknown is written based on God's timeless principles mined from Scripture which apply to many of life's current situations. This book makes no effort to fit the grid of strict intellectually-based theological methodology. God's truth is simple enough for a child as though His thoughts are higher than our thoughts (Isaiah 55:8-9). PLEASE UNDERSTAND, Author unknown is written to encourage us to let God teach our spirits in lieu of man indoctrinating our minds (Matthew 5:6, 11:25-27; John 4:23-24, 6:44-45; 1 Corinthians 1:26-2:16). Man may be able to help us know about God, but only God can teach to know Him face-to-face.

Book Premise
Author unknown reveals the vast difference between knowing about God versus knowing God personally. This work's premise is

based on John 16:1-15 especially verse 3 which says, "They will do such things because they have not known the Father or me." In a nutshell, all of us began our spiritual journey in pursuit of God in unique places under unique circumstances. In truth – we entered the process, rose through religious teachings, and have arrived to our current stature of spirituality in God's sight whatever that means. Some of us continue to pursue and grow, while others choose to be immobilized in religious form having a form of godliness without power (2 Timothy 3:1-5).

Contrast

Author unknown is a contrast between God's Law versus man's opinion, God's reality versus man's perversity, God's truth versus human justification, relationship versus religion, practice versus knowledge, mercy versus legalism, restoration versus judgment, revelation versus deception, and life versus death. I present this contrast through the only means I have – my personal relationship with Jesus Christ, reasonable knowledge of His word and example, and my life-changing experiences with His love, forgiveness, and mercy.

Purpose

Author unknown IS written to display how to hear God's voice...how His voice sounds and what the process looks like...what it means to test the Spirits, embrace one's call, and apply what is heard in daily life...and how the whole picture comes together while in the middle of being re-created in Jesus Christ each day (2 Corinthians 5:17-20). It is my hope that readers will see themselves, recall things they've heard and experiences they've had, and will recognize what it looks like to sort it all out, step into it with faith, and stay their course as they consider my personal journey, flaws, and victories. Remember dear friend, God responds to hunger, wholehearted pursuit, and to those willing to settle their Gethsemanes (Jeremiah 29:13; Matthew 5:6; Mark 14:36). This book is written to encourage those God created and called to be last day warriors, members of Christ's bride, and those in search of personal identity and their King.

The assertions made in Author unknown are not about people's origins, cultures, creeds, or religions – this book is about knowing, experiencing, and pleasing God. Some of you may feel a need to challenge or debate what I propose for the purpose of prayerful consideration – you are welcome to your opinion (Philippians 3:12-16; 2 Timothy 2:23-26). I have no desire to indoctrinate you with my views. In my presentation, I simply portray a very real distinction which exists between the expression and realization of God's Love and revelation VERSUS man's misguided and misappropriated version of God's Law found in fallen human practice and religion (2 Timothy 3:1-5). My effort does not constitute a line of division – it merely provides you with a contrast for the purpose of our individual Christ-centered consideration, revelation, and transformation. It is within my grasp to make this statement as I do my utmost, with God's help, to unify all tribes, tongues, and nations who are known as either the natural or in-grafted of the true Israel under the dominion of One Lord, One Lawgiver, One Law, One Love, and One Messiah through One Promise of eternal life and liberation (Romans 9:6-8). To do so, Author unknown draws insights and perspective from both Jewish-and-Gentile based Scripture as communicated through the Bible, Torah, Talmud, and Tanakh while in the presence of the Holy Spirit.

Perspective

It is my prayer that God will compel us all to dig deeper in our personal consideration of His timeless principles, historical facts, and current world events indicating the season of Christ's return (Matthew 24:32-46). All I have written herein is easily verified through one's time and simple research available to all who possess the unction to enter a personal quest to identify and discern spiritual issues relevant to the kingdom season we have recently entered. Some may take issue with my vantage points, challenge my non-traditional assertions, or even label me as miss-guided in their effort to justify personal view. But, please realize we are all created with a unique identity, purpose, and relationship with God within the scheme of His unfolding plan. I extend you freedom to be yourself with God's help, please give me the same...

Framework

Within Author unknown, I have provided you with a framework of well-founded facts gathered from Scripture and history for your consideration. Respectfully, many calling themselves Christians have grown lazy and complacent as they expect others to do the study and prayer on their behalf while sitting back to eat unearned snack lunches on their way to heaven. It doesn't work that way... Simply put, it's time that we who are created in God's image, fearfully and wonderfully made, called according to His purpose, inhabited by His Spirit, and listed in His book do our own hard work to chase Him with whole hearts (Jeremiah 29:13; Matthew 10:6-39, John 4:32-38, 5:17, 9:4, 14:12, 17:4-26; 2 Corinthians 4:8-12, 6:3-13; 1 Thessalonians 5:12-24; Hebrews 5:11-14). If the Holy Spirit has not illuminated your understanding on those issues which He has helped me grasp through extraordinary trial, travail, and travel...there is simply nothing I can say or do to reveal them to you. Though my comments above may seem a bit terse to you, I assure you that they are ventured in love for your benefit and the expansion of God's kingdom before it is too late. We live in the most urgent hour in human history. Look around you...

Voice

Author unknown is written in the eternal voice through which God speaks, Jesus acts, and timeless principles handed down millenia ago still intervene to redeem. All activities conducted by Jesus Christ herein are related in present voice because He is alive, still acts, and ever will be (John 14:12, 17:25-26). Meanwhile, I have chosen to personify all satanic forms and forces in possessive language to portray them as real entities that have been dispatched against God's people with authorized destructive purpose. Though we know that Christ's authority is eternally superior to satan's, the fact remains that forces of darkness gain real power in people's lives as the result of personal sin. In such cases, these evil entities are identified as demons, minions, or spirits (i.e. greed, anger, lust, hate, etc.). My personification of these forces DOES NOT grant them increased power. Instead, it merely helps readers better understand that those evil forces dispatched against them by their adversary...have recognizable identities, are weaker than God, and can be easily defeated in Jesus' name.

Content

Stories and events related in Author unknown are original to me and are based on real experiences I've had and people I've met while chasing God…praying dangerous prayers…rising through my humanity…walking continents…surviving car wrecks…traveling internationally…and doing my best to become God's man of the hour. Though numerous events in my life certainly reveal "what not to do" along the way, it is my hope that you will be encouraged by how God redeemed my failures, trained me for battle, and empowered my created purpose for His glory. Whatever happens, I'm at peace knowing that I only answer to my Loving Lord and King Jesus Christ – alone. Thanks for your grace in advance…

God's Law of Love

Author unknown reveals and portrays the practical differences between God's Law of Love and man's fallen judgment-based administration of it. Though I have been aware of this reality for many years…it was only during the composition of this book that God gave me a clarifying insight on how to express that contrast to those He sends my way. Eight months into this book's creation, the Holy Spirit revealed this contrast to me as: God's Upper Case Law of Love and death's lower case law of hostility. This revelation emerged after my careful consideration of "all" references to God's Law found in Matthew, Mark, Luke, and John. God's Law of Love is portrayed in the following passages (Matthew 22:37-41; Mark 12:30-31; John 13:34, 14:15-26, 15:12-17; Romans 13:8-10; 1 Corinthians 13:1-13; 1 John 3:16-24, 4:7-21). You will find glimpses and an elaborate presentation of these opposing administrations as you read. Meanwhile, you will find snapshot references throughout Author unknown to sharpen your recognition of genuine and pervasive expressions of God' love as displayed in people's lives and circumstances related within this writing. I believe these clarified character qualities regarding God's Law of Love potentially represents a thinking patter or Bridge Theology capable of helping span the divide between Jews and Gentiles (Ephesians 2:14).

Other Important Book Information

Other bullet-point things you need to know about this book before jumping in are as follows...

1. All references to God are capitalized to honor my King.

2. satan's junk is never capitalized because he's a loser.

3. I'm not a theologian, religionist, or grammar & punctuation guy. I am a well-informed man of God doing what I'm called to do.

4. My writing and punctuation are in connected thoughts, concepts, and word pictures – not MLA or ALA format. I am sharing the message God gave me, so please relax as you read.

5. The names of some people have been changed in the real encounters shared in *Author unknown* to protect their privacy.

Reasoning Together

Though I choose not to lock horns in debate over vantage points I have related in Author unknown, I will entertain any genuine, heartfelt, and honest question or perspective from anyone who fosters unity and life. None of us have all the answers. We need each other in our journey from this life into the presence of God. Therefore, if you would like to communicate on any matter related to building and advancing God's kingdom in people's lives, please feel free to communicate with me as shown in the contact information page at the back of the book.

My Reality

Like Paul, I related to feeling like the chief of sinners as I continually realize just how much I've been forgiven and how dependent upon Christ I am for life. My vantage points and words may reveal a stature of man within my life which you do not know how to relate to or cannot find agreement with because I'm very real in my presentation of self. However, it is in my ongoing pursuit of God amid my failures and His redemption that I have learned what I now share. What you do with it is up to you. I am merely responsible for how I steward my life, God's transformation, and the destiny He has entrusted to my care (Ezekiel 33:1-20).

Hope and Blessings!
Therefore, I pray that the above clarification of book format and style have enlightened and better equipped you to benefit from Author unknown's message which has extracted its price from my own life. In a way, Author unknown is both an autobiographical collection of highlights from the path I've traveled and my personal testimony to God's love, mercy, and transformation in my own world. Thank you for taking time and giving me a chance to encourage and help you become all God created you to be...

Greg Benner – Friend
BattleCry Ministries

Dedication

I give my work to Jesus, those I love, and all He knows are His…

"We must walk the impossible to experience the miraculous"

Greg Benner -2005

Premise

"They will do such things because they have not known the Father or Me"

John 16:3

"You disowned the Holy and Righteous One…You killed the Author of life…"

Acts 3:14-15

Jesus knocks at our door waiting to be invited in...

Chapter 1
At the Door

"Even so, when you see all these things, you know that it is near, right at the door" (Matthew 24:33).

Loving people God's way can be challenging...sometimes even painful. Yet, His love compels us to guard the eternal welfare of others far above our personal comfort and popularity (Philippians 2:3-5). Let me pull from the perils of parental perplexities to paint you a picture...

Surrounded by shredded paper, ribbons, and a sea of gifts just garnered at his fifth birthday party – your son Johnnie tornadoes through cardboard to gain his grubby grip on the plastic picnic table and Play Dough inside his latest target as you catch your husband's over-his-glasses glance. Caught somewhere in the crossfire between flying gift wrap and a imagined narrative balloon appearing over your husband's head in which he silently wonders if he will have to assemble his son's plastic monstrosity – you re-focus your motherly attentions on Johnnie... Hours later, after all the fallout has landed, the table has risen from the pieces, and its residential parking place determined – you drag the contraption out the back door to the patio's edge beneath the awning with Johnnie shadowing your steps. Running around the table swinging his legs across the seat and spinning into position, Johnnie blurts, "Mom, let me have my Play Dough please!" Caught up in his excitement, you proceed to put his assorted colors on the table before him, telling him to jump in and have fun. Suddenly, your phone rings from the living room calling you indoors as you tell Johnnie to stay out of trouble... A bit later as you tell your caller farewell, you meander through the kitchen toward the patio door just in time to catch a glimpse of Johnnie playing quietly by himself with play dough stuck to his forehead... Parental pride rises within as you clasp your hands over your heart, swell with adoration, and gloat tearfully over your darling little buckaroo's wondrous demeanor. Beside yourself, you run outside and throw your arms around and praise him for the joy he brings...

A few days later, just after swabbing the backroom toilet...you wander back to your living room only to discover the patio and front doors wide open with your knee-high rascal nowhere in sight. As you frantically scan the area for your pride and joy, he's nowhere to be found. With intuition rising within – you whirl around just in time to spot the pint-sized whirlwind through your front window playing quietly at his picnic table with play dough...smack in the middle of the busy four lane street whizzing past your house! In a flash; you bolt through the air onto the street in a single bound flapping, trapping, and dragging Johnnie in one hand and his misplaced table in the other, out of harm's way. Regaining your composure moments later as you step out of slow motion back into current reality...Johnnie's horrified face crumbles to confusion, clueless how he fell from favored to failure in a blink of your eyes. Just days before – he enjoyed the spotlight as your wonderful well-behaved little boy engulfed in your praise. Now, he found himself an outcast for playing quietly with play dough by himself. Puzzled, demoralized, and wondering why...Johnnie simply doesn't get all that is wrapped up in your protective love (1 Corinthians 13:7-8). Though his demeanor had been quiet and sublime, his place of choice to indulge his freedom was, life-threatening...

Why the story? Today's world is busy doing marginal-to-good things in wrong places, rather than good-and-moral things in God places. Both people and statistics are challenged-at-best, whether inside or outside what calls itself the Church. Hunger, heartache, and horror dominate our television screens. Indecency and perversion permeate our reading material. And, greed's materialism pollutes our integrity as selfish manipulations plague our relational realities... Yet, these are mere symptoms indicating the existence of deeper problems-at-large. In the interest of regaining God's view of His unfolding plan to save us from ourselves...it appears high time to delve deeper into those issues unraveling the world around us at an ever-increasing pace during this eleventh hour in human history...

The birth-to-maturity process in people's physical and spiritual lives is developmentally identical in structure, though rooted in different realms. When children are born, they communicate their desires and exert their will without manners or concern for the imposition on others. As they move through childhood into adolescence, they emulate their parent's nature and wrestle their way toward independent self-rule. At the onset of young adulthood, they venture away from home, armed with their parent's faith to define, solidify, and discover their own potential. As they desert childishness, encounter responsibility, investigate autonomy, define spirituality, and embrace maturity rightly within their own faith... Jesus Christ's indwelling presence and transformational character gains stature and speaks into an out-of-control world through those genuinely submitted to Him. Their resulting reality, experience, and life satisfaction will be defined and immortalized by their views, decisions, and chosen path – God's way, or their own. Most people do their best to yield their lives to Jesus as newborn believers by going to church, reading their bibles, and making their own mistakes while investigating their individual purpose and destiny. Next, they launch out to do what they learned only to discover who they were truly created and called to be. And finally, if they make God's decision, they rise to become the man or woman of He created them to be amid the goings-and-comings of His redemptive plan which was designed to love a wayward humanity back to Himself before it is too late...

One day, many years ago, I asked one of my sons to do his weekly chore of mowing the lawn. The lawn mower we had at the time was old, ran when it felt like it, and generally complicated and made it a real pain to cut the grass. Recollecting my own experience as a young boy mowing my grandfather's lawn-from-hell with a dull less-than-cooperative reel-style mower...I had mercy on my son and bought a brand new Honda self-propelled rotary mower with four gears... We jumped in my truck and headed for town to pick it up at the local Honda dealer that late spring afternoon scurrying home immediately afterwards to assemble it – together. As the grass-munching monster rose to resemble a mower before our very eyes and we only begrudgingly consulted the instruction manual thereby preserving our mutual rise to manhood – my son could hardly wait to pull the rope and cut grass! We checked the oil, filled the tank, and set the wheels to what seemed a pretty good grass length and he gave it a yank. It sputtered, smoked, and caught its wind to purr like a kitten as we all excitedly looked on. He glanced around, charted his course, and hit the grass running.... It was amazing to watch the wind blow through his hair as he did end-run spins at the yard's edge with his lips growing weary from sporting a smile which stretched from ear-to-ear. He was in heaven, the grass got mowed, enthusiasm swallowed chagrin, and his world was a great place. Our lawn got mowed five times in the first two weeks as it silently cried out for mercy against the coming wrath of Honda wheels and size 10's... Finally, I could relax without having to threaten in-house slave labor who was more enticed by wearing leg-irons than embracing their outdoor freedoms of mowing the grass. Time passed as my world returned to its normal sun-up-to-sundown pace, letting now-resolved yard details slip into the shadows of my mind...

A month later while leaving for work early one morning, I poked my head in my son's room and said, "Please mow the yard today" to which I received a curtain-pulled, pillow-covered "Uh-huh." So, I hopped in my truck and headed off to work. When I got home later that afternoon I noticed the lawn remained un-cut and our almost new lawnmower parked next to the shop. Curious as I walked up to and looked down upon the silent machine, I noticed a small shiny spot on the mower's deck just beneath the engine oil filler spout. I surmised... Standing to my feet, I turned and walked down the sidewalk coming face-to-face with son's motherly protector who said, "He couldn't mow the lawn because the mower is low on oil." I replied, "I just checked it this morning before I left...it's brand new." Not understanding mechanics well...not knowing what was at stake...not seeing through a once-son-but-now-father's eyes... my wife gently stood up for our son. I gave her a hug, shot her a grin, and walked into the kitchen... Have you ever had one of those parental visions pop into your head, which causes you to fully understand something you could not possibly know, but make kids shudder when you do? Well, I had one! I sauntered over to the sink, grabbed a glass of water, leaned against the countertop, paused momentarily, and headed for my son's room... Peering over the edge of his comic book at me doing his best to muster a studiously compliant look he said, "The lawnmower's low on oil." I replied, "Let's go check it out...come on." We chuckled about stuff on our way up the sidewalk toward the grass grinder where I crouched down, pulled the dipstick, and sure enough...it was low on oil.

Pausing momentarily, surmising a bit more, and then looking up into my son's eyes I asked him, "Did you run it for awhile?" He said, "No...it was low on oil." "Hmmmm," I said mentioning that I had checked the oil earlier that morning on my way to work. So, I asked him, "Do you have any idea how it could possibly be low on oil if it was okay this morning and you never started it?" By now, the heat was on with his eyes darting from one place to another as he avoided making direct contact with mine. I let the question linger...silence...more silence...he offered no answer. So I said, "Let me tell you what I think happened." He said, "Okay." "You rolled the lawnmower around the back side of the shop, took off the oil cap, tipped the lawnmower up on its side to pour its oil out on the ground in the weeds, and dropped it back down on all fours. When it hit the ground, a drop of oil dripped from the engine oil spout down onto the mower deck right here where you see this shiny spot caused by you wiping off the oil. See...the rest of the lawnmower is dusty...all except...that little shiny spot below the oil spout." His shoulders fell, his head dropped, and his sigh deflated like an ole' tire as he toed a dirt clod with his shoe and asked, "How'd ya know?" Looking him in the eyes I replied, "Never kid a kidder...I was your age once too." Then I said, "Please mow the yard" and off he went. Father's just know things... My son and I never had that conversation again...

Just like parents do with kids...God sometimes pulls us to the edge of life's lawn in His Fatherly wisdom to reveal sin's back story, reflected by the shiny spot in life's dust when illuminated by His loving light (John 3:19-21). We often spend hours, days, weeks, months, and even years trying to escape a five minute, unavoidable decision that calls us to simple obedience in Jesus' name. At those strategic moments, immersed in His love, God the Father pokes His head into our room, takes us for a walk, grants us perspective, and says, "please mow the yard" amid the issues of life. As my son and I experienced...obedience restores unity and ends strife. Yet, if we, as God's people resist His purpose...we will find ourselves on another walk engaged in another conversation on ever-intensifying turf, until we yield our independence beneath His Almighty and loving hand (1 Peter 5:6-7). Those heart issues we face in life before a holy God never change...they simply take on new faces, extract higher prices, and leave deeper scars the longer we wrestle with God for control. If we do not learn our lessons young by following the instruction manual, we will suffer unduly as our rebellion goes from pulling our cat around by his tail...to smoking our first cigarette...to dragging our friends into crime ...to seducing a partner into immorality...or, leading the lost to their destruction. God draws us to Himself trying to teach us how to live because He loves us, not because He wants to control us. Our Father in heaven wants us to live free and fantastically filled with joy, not heartache. How we respond to His lesson-of-the-hour however, will chart our course either good or bad...

God has been declaring His existence, dominion, love, and unfolding plan to both the physical and spiritual worlds throughout the whole of eternity...man is without excuse with regard to knowing that "God exists" (Romans 1:18-32). Sadly, we do not listen well or yield to His input readily, unless we are first faced with uncomfortable circumstances. And yet, God is portrayed as Love reaching to a wayward world with forgiveness and mercy, at the cost of His own Son (1 John 4:16-21; Luke 23:26-49). Besides His Son and Himself... the greatest gift God has ever given to pave our way toward eternal life...is the Holy Spirit who emulates the Father, upholds the Son, and testifies to His people about what is yet to come (John 14:26, 16:8-15). In light of Scripture, God's love, and pressing world events – are we listening, do we trust, will we yield and obey for His glory and our own good? I invite you to consider if any of the following excerpts sound vaguely familiar as you rub elbows with life, interact with people, or watch the news each day...

"You will hear of wars and rumors of wars...nation will rise against nation and kingdom against kingdom...there will be famines and earthquakes in various places. At that time many will turn away from the faith and will hate and betray each other, and many false prophets will appear and deceive many people. Because of the increase of wickedness, the love of most will grow cold, but he who stands firm to the end will be saved (Matthew 24:6-13)."

"There will be terrible times in the last days. People will be lovers of themselves, lovers of money, boastful, proud, abusive, disobedient to their parents, ungrateful, unholy, without love, unforgiving, slanderous, without self-control, brutal, not lovers of the good, treacherous, rash, conceited, lovers of pleasure rather than lovers of God – having a form of godliness, but denying its power (II Timothy 3:1-5)."

"For since the creation of the world God's invisible qualities – his eternal power and divine nature – have been clearly seen, being understood from what has been made, so that men are without excuse. For although they knew God, they neither glorified him as God nor gave thanks to Him, but their thinking became futile and their foolish hearts were darkened. Although they claimed to be wise, they became fools and exchanged the glory of the immortal God for images made to look like mortal man and birds and animals and reptiles. Therefore God gave them over in the sinful desires of their hearts to sexual impurity for the degrading of their bodies with one another. They exchanged the truth of God for a lie, and worshiped and served created things rather than the Creator. Because of this, God gave them over to shameful lusts. Even their women exchanged natural relations for unnatural ones. In the same way the men also abandoned natural relations with women and were inflamed with lust for one another. Men committed indecent acts with other men, and received in themselves the due penalty of their perversions. Furthermore, since they did not think it worthwhile to retain the knowledge of God, he gave them over to a depraved mind to do what ought not to be done. They have become filled with every kind of wickedness, evil, greed and depravity. They are full of envy, murder, strife, deceit and malice. They are gossips, slanderers, God-haters, insolent, arrogant and boastful; they invent ways of doing evil; they disobey their parents; they are senseless, faithless, heartless, and [sic] ruthless. Although they know God's righteous decree that those who do such things deserve death, they not only continue to do these very things but also approve of those who practice them (Romans 1:20-32)."

Not sure about you, but the above sounds pretty relevant in our world today – doesn't it? Simply put, no one can scare or intellectualize people into the kingdom of God. If someone does accept Jesus based on fear, their conversion is usually shallow and fleeting as it later leaves them disenchanted, disenfranchised, and dead within... Yet, our awareness of what the bible and Holy Spirit tells us is coming upon the earth during the season of His return should either compel us to give our lives to Him as a loving God through personal relationship with Jesus Christ...or motivate us as believers to sacrifice our personal comfort and rights to extend our lifestyle salvation message to others at more intensified level than ever before. The bible invites people who do not know God personally to seek Him while He may still be found (Isaiah 55:6). Jesus communicated and extended both warning and invitation through His parable of the ten virgins, which strongly portrayed that there is a time coming soon when our entrance into Gods presence will fall beyond our irresponsible reach – forever (Matthew 25:1-13).

Likewise, Scripture encourages those of us who have accepted Jesus Christ as both Lord and Savior to gain His life-giving character in ever-increasing measure as we make our selfless preparations to arrive, as members of a radiant Church (bride of Christ), to the wedding feast of the Lamb (2 Peter 1:3-11; Ephesians 5:25-27). Jesus described creation's last day events as immediately preceding and intimately surrounding His second arrival to earth as "...the beginning of birth pains" (Matthew 24:3-8). We later find John the revelator's reference to the bride of Christ making herself ready thereby revealing the purification process we must all undergo if we are to be found faithful in His God's sight at the time of His return (Revelation 19:7). Obviously, unparalleled events and deteriorating perspectives already rampant around the world are escalating as Scripture's metaphorical child-birth process intensifies the closer to its conclusion becomes. Likewise, it is obvious that our only hope remains in preparing ourselves, at a level necessary in God's eyes, to enter His eternal presence. As eluded to in the birth-to-maturity process of human and spiritual development as portrayed throughout the whole of Scripture, God calls us deeper into His presence and service each day in our personal relationship with Him through His only Son, Jesus Christ. Please consider the following story of birth, preparation, and decision from everyday life...

A bit more than a year ago, I became aware that a young married couple I know and love were expecting their fifth child. What biological bravado Jon and Kelly have! Please understand however, this brave, one-flesh team already had four sons under age seven who operate more like whirling Tasmanian devils, buzzing their ways through tree stumps in a Bugs Bunny cartoon, than as cuddly little critters. Their names are Noah, Elijah, Isaac, and David. This time around however, the doctor joyously announced the arrival of their first girl! Excitement was off the charts as Kelly was soon to be delivered from being the only girl in the house, while Jon looked beyond non-stop puppy dog tails to some sugar and spice. Preparations for the new arrival commenced with the nursery being equipped with female faire, while the house acquired a new bathroom and windows in the basement. Every time I called Jon to chat...he was up to his neck in toilet rings or ceiling tiles working into the wee hours of the night...getting ready. Jon, being my best friend...was suddenly otherwise detained on what he glibly called "more important things" than talking to an old cuss like me. Caught in a senior moment, I fondly wandered down my own parental corridors of thought which were filled with Gerber's carrots, Huggies, mud pies in the back yard, missing teeth, hospital visits, a Doberman wearing sunglasses, paying for pantyhose, graduation ceremonies, and feeling displaced by my daughter's new husband – all rich memories. With reality resurrecting me from nostalgia's grasp...I left Jon to his honey-do list and hung up.

As trimesters passed and Kelly's jeans were hi-jacked by comfort-fit clothes more in keeping with family expansion, indicators of the approaching birth intensified. At the same time, Jon was working overtime at his second attempt to ring a cantankerous toilet during early morning hours; going to doctor visits mid-day to be sure all with his lady was on track, and returning home to choke down his dinner before resuming his husbandly duties at hand. Meanwhile, arrangements were made to house the boys, Kelly's last minute outlet mall excursions were accomplished and checked off, laundry was done, bills were processed early, phones were charged, gas tanks kept filled, and their house was put in order. Finally, delivery was at the door! They got up early, farmed the boys out, and headed for the hospital where Kelly was prepared for c-section and Rachel was born. Following delivery, Kelly hemorrhaged and landed back in the operating room having an unplanned hysterectomy. On the heels of surgery and following recovery, her blood levels dropped so severely that they had to take her back to surgery a third time in less than 30 hours to seal internal bleeding. I was 2,500 miles away on the road walking America and could only offer prayers. Post third surgery, Kelly continued to decline as her body began to shut down. Doctors contemplated flying her to a trauma center 150 miles away, but were concerned she would not survive the flight. I waited anxiously, updated my prayer list, and we prayed. Decisions were made regarding the course to take as Kelly lay there silently retreating into her inner sanctum with God, making her peace...just in case.

Despite the best laid plans, extensive preparations, and following doctor's directives leading up to birth, death came knocking at their door to make its unjust bid for a man's wife and five children's mother... Jon called, I updated my prayer list again, and we all hit our knees in Jesus' name. Everyone was on pins and needles as the clock ticked away the time moment-by-moment... What else could have been done? In retrospect; they had done all in their power to guard Kelly's health, to attend all doctor appointments, to work out family logistics, to read the right books, and get their – house in order. Yet, an everyday scenario turned tragically wrong as hell hammered at their door. As is usually the case, prayer broke through and Jon called, sighing with relief, saying Kelly's levels were back on the rise, finally putting her on the road to recovery. Over the next few days...Kelly rallied...levels stabilized...reality normalized...a husband was spared tragic loss...a mom's guiding light preserved... and death had been swallowed up in victory in new and renewed life... Because of conception, right living, diligent preparation, seasoned leaders, prayerful decisions, enduring faith, and God's mercy – Kelly, Jon, Noah, Elijah, Isaac, David, and Rachel received the gift of life. In the shadows of their experience, we hear reality whisper that life is precious, fleeting, and dependent upon our view and embrace of all God foretold...

Spanning history, we see theologians and ardent believers alike pressing ever-toward Jesus' return based on divergent scenarios charting the prophetic course of God's culminating reach to mankind. The bible tells us that this apocalyptic season will be ushered in by indicators like the recreation of Israel in 1948, intensifying wars, earthquakes, disasters, famines, plagues, persecution, and moral decline we are already encountering on an escalating basis each day. Other interpreted matters on the subject...often spoken of in absolute tone by self-appointed theological formula followers ... remain intellectually pondered at best. While misguided religionists, denominationalists, and antagonists conjure heresy into existence while playing demonically-driven mental chess over their personal views on security, baptism, healing, ministry, divorce, rapture, dates, and the Holy Spirit's indwelling presence – God weeps as those lost outside His kingdom listen to the bickering and reject His love as a result (2 Timothy 2:14-26)... In spite of us however, Jesus reassuringly declares that we can know the season of His return as His Holy Spirit leads us into all truth and tells us the things to come (John 16:13). We can make our best eternal investment pursuing God with whole hearts and growing in right relationship with Jesus Christ as we complete heaven's work by doing the Master's business until He comes (Jeremiah 29:13; Matthew 24:45-46; John 15:15, 17:4-19). Sadly, too many calling themselves Christians spend more time concerned over rapture arrival theories fueled by their selfish desire to escape persecution, than fulfilling Christ's great commission to love and forgive others at all costs. Theology focused on self incites heresy, while theology focused on preserving others embodies mercy... Though other over-spiritualized opinions surrounding the season of His return seem interesting...only obedience will find us wise and faithful when Jesus arrives (Matthew 24:45-51; John 15:15-17) ... In this light, please journey ahead with me to consider all it means to truly know, love, obey, and romance the Lord of Glory...

Based on bible passages and imagery, Jesus Christ is clearly portrayed as Heaven's Bridegroom Who shall return to gather, marry, and consummate with His radiant bride (Church) at the wedding feast of the Lamb on a day at an hour only God His Father knows (Matthew 24:32-39; Ephesians 5:21-33; Revelation 19:7-9). Day-by-day, it grows increasingly apparent that our world's downward spiraling social, moral, spiritual, governmental, and fiscal attitudes mirror those prophetically foretold in Scripture at a level never-before-equaled in human history. We live in a perilous, yet exciting hour! Perilous for those adrift in their faith and relationship to God – exciting for those rightly positioned in Jesus Christ and prepared to stand firm to the end, come what may (Matthew 24:4-13). In my own world, I was enlightened while working with people on technical and spiritual pursuits for 38 years across America, the Middle east, and parts of the UK...while engaged in youth, evangelistic, or prophetic activities on varied levels for 21 of those years...while walking and preaching across America two times...while knocking on over 3,000 churches, sitting at length with nearly 1,000 pastors representing more than 60 plus doctrinal stances, and speaking hundreds of times in churches, jails, missions, schools, campgrounds, organizations and finding myself portrayed in newspapers, hosted on radio, and interviewed on television along the way. In reality dear friend, we as the Church are not relevant, ready, or radiant to the degree necessary to take our seat at heaven's wedding feast. Instead, we lack eyes to see, ears to hear, or hearts that understand that our culture, creeds, and Christianity are cast adrift on a sea of delusion bound in spiritual blindness...

Though you may take issue with my assessment of westernized spirituality...I only report what I see while motivated by God's love as defined within Scripture and based upon observable facts, personal experience, and the vantage point I gained through pursuits few have engaged or paid the price to acquire (Matthew 10:1-42, 28:19-20; 1 Corinthians 13:7-8). As little Johnny's mom experienced while extending love's terse touch to protect her son in the story above – caring about people gets guys like me in hot water as I reach into situations uninvited to pull the unsuspecting off hell's highway. Western world Christians have grown un-bridled, complacent, detached, fragmented, deceived, rebellious, and sadly religious – boasting a form of godliness, but denying its power (2 Timothy 3:1-5). If we keep doing what we have always done...we will be who we've always been. Yet, Jesus is coming back for a radiant church without stain or wrinkle or any other blemish holy and blameless before Him – not a wayward woman of the faith... Religion is dead and relationship is life! Unless we blow past Old Testament law through New Testament grace to plunge into personal, purposeful, and passionate intimacy with Jesus our King...we will die shackled to hell's gate by the chains of head-based theology. We must prepare...we must be washed...we must be made whiter than snow if we're to become clean instruments useful in the Master's hands to do all good works (2 Timothy 2:21).

One's lifestyle of either life or death is a choice...a decision to be made! We were created in His image according to His purpose to do good works He prepared in advance for us to do (Ephesians 2:10). Will we pay the price and embrace His work for His glory and the good of others (John 5:17, 14:12)? Or, will we sit back on our laurels marking time thinking we have our ticket to heaven punched only to hear "...away from me I never knew you" (Matthew 7:22-23)? Truth is eternal, Truth is a person, Truth has a voice...will we listen? If yes, how and to whom do we listen? Jesus lived, died, rose, and ascended back to the right hand of His Father so He could send us His Counselor – the Holy Spirit. Some of the Holy Spirit's key jobs in our lives as believers are to guide us into all truth and tell us about things yet to come (John 16:13). As an Old Testament type of Christ and predecessor of the Holy Spirit – even Moses gave the Israelites a weighted choice between life and death...blessings and curses (Deuteronomy 30:19). Likewise, Jesus made it clear that our decision to either enter or avoid God's light will be determined based on our desire to pursue Him or go our own way (John 3:19-21). God is patient and loves us not wanting any of us to perish, but to come to repentance so we can experience eternal life with Him (2 Peter 3:9). Sadly, many will drift away on the waters of lukewarm Christianity to suffer eternal consequences outside the grace of

God as Christ's return pounds heavy on history's door (Revelation 3:14-22)... Considering the global events or groans of child birth foretold in Scripture now continually intensifying all over the world, how are we to truly recognize the season of HIs return...

Everywhere I go... people of all cultures and backgrounds are keenly aware of an underlying sense of pending chaos lurking in history's shadows upon the earth. People sense an unexplainable and unspoken apprehension that disaster is coming though they do not know what it is...they just feel it! Though many caught in life's cross-currents are not Christians...they have an innate sense of an imminent unknown and desire to flee just as animals do before an Earthquake. Despite people's inability to identify or quantify the scope and magnitude of what is coming, they are uncomfortably aware. The bible tells us what signs to look for, those circumstances under which they will occur, and how many will be caught blindly off-guard by their occurrence in the last days...

Jesus says, "Now learn this lesson from the fig tree: As soon as its twigs get tender and its leaves come out, you know that summer is near. Even so, when you see all these things, you know that it is near, right at the door. I tell you the truth, this generation will certainly not pass away until all these things have happened. No one knows about the day or the hour, not even the angels in heaven, nor the Son, but only the Father. As it was in the days of Noah, so it will be at the coming of the Son of Man. For in the days before the flood, people were eating and drinking, marrying and giving in marriage, up to the day Noah entered the ark; and they knew nothing about what would happen until the flood came and took them all away" (Matthew 24:37-39).

Now what? Have I penetrated your skin, become a burr under your saddle, or generally dismantled your composure? I pray so because I care! Whether we like it or not, two opposing powers are knocking at our heart's door...one crouching around the corner waiting to break in and destroy...and a redeemer waiting to be invited in to deliver heaven's bread of life (Genesis 4:7; John 6:35; Revelation 3:20). Who will you let in...who will you give dominion to...who will you serve (Luke 16:13)? I realize western world inhabitants have been overwhelmed, inundated, and generally desensitized to almost everything in life. As a result, people ramble, reason, and reject that which saves them in exchange for that which destroys. Do you find me too persistent...maybe verbose...a bit annoying...or a pain in the butt? Like little Johnny, I would rather have you mad at me and make it, than forever dead. Do you really care about those people God has entrusted to your care...really (John 17:6-19)? Will you be among those concretely positioned in Jesus Christ the Living Truth, or scoffing away seasonal indicators declaring His return (John 14:6, Galatians 2:20; Ephesians 2:6-10; 2 Peter 3:3-5). I imagine some of you may feel the same toward me as those who previously discounted Noah's message before they found themselves outside pounding on the ark's closed door when it began to rain (Genesis 7:5-24)...

Years ago, I met a woman named Sara who grew up in a somewhat dysfunctional, rural home surrounded by bickering parents and wayward siblings bent on going their own way. Sara's home life and upbringing left her prematurely burdened with adult responsibilities as her folk's work outside the home spurred independence at an early age, rather than healthy maturity. Searching for identity... Sara married an alcoholic young man, had a daughter, divorced, and jumped into second marriage with an even more troubled young man named Jim. Coming from a broken home with alcoholic parents himself...Jim entered relationship with Sara weighed down by insecurity, anger, addictions, and other instabilities lurking within. As the next ten years came and went, Sara and Jim were blessed with two sons in addition to the daughter Sara brought with her from her prior marriage. Over time...spending sprees, gambling, unpaid bills, yelling, drinking binges, infidelity, drugs, abuse, and middle-of-the-night moves pierced their rattled reality over-and-again without mercy. It was not uncommon for unsavory, gun-packing characters to pound at their door demanding money for under-the-table business deals conducted or drugs secretly consumed in the growing shadows tracing of Jim's life...

Sara was a wreck as she worried about her children's welfare, her own survival, and Jim's explosive mood-swings that ripped her apart without warning. Life was in uproar and spinning hopelessly out of control... Suddenly, Sara's world crumbled as life pressures, bitterness, anger, and opposing views dealt their death blow. It was early evening...finances were gone...and kids were screaming as Sara and Jim yelled-and-argued their way back to their bedroom and slammed the door! Anger rose, hatred bellowed, and fists flew as Jim knocked Sara to the floor, unconscious, before fleeing the scene... A while later, Sara came too, hauling herself to the edge of their bed where she stared out the window through blood-mixed tears pierced by desperation and crying, "I don't know if you are real God, but someone is going to die if you don't do something fast." As Sara collected herself making sure the kids were okay, she retreated into her room to clean and dress her wounds... Later, mustering every ounce of strength within her – Sara cinched her robe's belt, walked out of her room, and put the kids to bed. She flipped off the TV and turned out the lights as she made her way back to her own bed where she hoped to escape what lay behind...

With tears tracing their path across Sara's throbbing cheeks, she finally drifted off into a deep but tormented sleep during early morning hours with Jim, still not home... As if only moments had passed, Sara gasped as pounding at her door pulled her through the nightmare into a pain-ridden, startled reality. She shot a glance at the nightstand clock through swollen eyes, suddenly realizing it to be just a bit past 7:00 a.m. Now engulfed by last night's events... Sara was unnerved by not knowing who was at her door or what they could possibly want at this hour. "Who's after Jim now?" Sara thought to herself. Gathering courage, she pulled herself out of bed, cinching her robe once again and making her way to the front of the house where she inquired through the door, "Who is it?" "Police," the voice replied. Carefully, Sara opened her door to find two homicide detectives standing on her steps... They introduced themselves, gave Sara their cards, and asked if they could come in to have a word with her. Relieved that no immediate threat existed – Sara stepped aside, motioning them into the dining room where they sat down to talk. Asking if Sara was okay first, one of the men gently informed Sara that her husband Jim had been found in a back alley behind a dumpster in a nearby town dead of a Heroin overdose... Unable to breathe as her earlier prayer for intervention by an unknown God echoed off the walls of her mind, Sara knew that He had heard her and allowed life to shift... As reality in the aftermath of Jim's death penetrated Sara's being over subsequent months, she yielded her life to Jesus Christ at church one Sunday and began her journey as a new creation... Determined to unravel the impact of prior decisions...Sara forged ahead day-by-day to weave new threads into her fabric of experience in life. And yet, only God knows what Jim transacted during those fleeting moments of existence on earth as he passed from this life...

Though we may have opinions based on the outward appearance of another person's life decisions, actions, and demise...the bible tells us that only God is capable of seeing into or weighing the motives our hearts, men cannot (1 Kings 8:37-40; Proverbs 21:2; Romans 2:2-11). Though we often by-pass our own moral and spiritual responsibilities in a blink of an eye...God will not allow us to hide in life's shadows while turning our skewed self-righteous version of truth's spotlight on another based on our perception of their sin (Matthew 21:31-32; Luke 7:36-50; John 8:1-11). God's "Romance Theology" challenges us to withdraw pride's pointing finger selfishly directed at others – while gazing deeply into the mirror of His Spirit to uncover our own shortcomings on our path toward Christ-likeness instead (Romans 8:28-30). As believers in Jesus Christ, we are told to work out our own salvation with fear and trembling...not meddle in someone else's destiny (Matthew 7:3-5; Philippians 2:12-13). Why? Because we will all stand before God to receive that which is due us for things done while in this life – whether good or bad" (2 Corinthians 5:10). It is mere human nature for us to tear others down in our carnal effort to elevate, or project attention off of ourselves when our own actions cause repercussions or heartache we wish to avoid. God's word tells us clearly that we are to take a serious look within ourselves if we're to administrate the faith He gave us for His glory, rightly (Romans 12:3).

Our Lord defies the religious and indwells the common. Religionists stood on law, while ordinary men spent time with Jesus and their irrefutable faith stood next to them healed in a now-seeing man, once born blind (Acts 4:13-14). God is not a vacation destination... He is our Loving Lord that we only come to know in the working out of our salvation along life's way... Destinations may fuel our imagination, but process provides the fire and produces the heat necessary to melt away our dross to reveal – pure gold. As Jonah knows, anyone can be swallowed by a whale... Yet, whirlwinds only engulf those champions of the faith who lockstep with Jesus to honor their King (I John 2:6).

Each day I'm alive, my own flaws remind me of how undeserving of God's grace and dependent upon Him I really am for my salvation. The more I live, the more pierced I am by what I do not understand and how my human attempts at righteousness are but filthy rags (Isaiah 64:6). It is our human inclination to compare ourselves to others as we seek some form of temporal validation. And yet, we stand before God called to do that which is found noble in His sight, not men's. Just because God has called, equipped, and sent me to uncommon places to do out-of-the-ordinary things for Him...does not make me superior, more spiritual, or special. I am simply a man who gets up with bed hair and morning breath to shower and put my pants on one leg at a time like everyone else. So, please forgive me if my attempts to reveal my process and tell my stories and illustrate what God has revealed to me for your benefit sound grandiose or out-pacing to your own. I have no control over all He God created me to do, where He called me to go, or what He ordained for it to produce. Please understand that I do not tell my story to wow or impress... Instead, I tell my story because it is all I have to offer as my very best tool to encourage others that God will do the incredible if they will simply "go" when He calls. Meanwhile, I am doing my best to survive its rigors and get it done...

To give you a few highlights and a bit of insight into my vantage point acquired over the past ten years – this book has been penned after walking and preaching 3,900 miles across America on faith... navigating a 50 day fast and praying at America's east and west gates for God's people to return to home...almost dying in an auto accident...leading others to Christ...driving more than 450,000 miles…traveling to Afghanistan twice…almost being kidnapped in Pakistan…doing research in England…closing a 3 year prayer loop bowed at Jerusalem's Wailing Wall…traveling to procure supplies for a 30 million dollar foreign project…sitting down over tea with Middle Eastern presidents-to-be...surviving God's seven year season learning of coming tribulation…growing 417,000 apple trees…completing my second walk across America at the onset of Rosh Hashanah 2011 on a Florida beach…helping indigent widows survive…monitoring recent earthquakes, storms, and intensifying prophetic events surfacing through qualified news sources from all over the world…and turning age 55 to boot…

During this same time period – America has experienced 911's tragedy, breached privacy, war on terror, conflict in Iraq, presence in Afghanistan, family disintegration, historical revisionism, economic Recession, same-sex marriage, agricultural regulation, oppressed prayer privileges, Hurricane Katrina, extreme flooding, banned ten commandments, legalized euthanasia, intensified earthquakes, religious limitation, governmental invasion, water shortages, political abuse, gun control, moral suicide, social profiling, citizen monitoring, corporate failures, mismanaged bailouts, ecumenical compromise, unparalleled foreclosures, erratic stock markets, rampant unemployment, compounded pharmaceutical sales, increased hunger, biological threats, growing homelessness, snowballing deficits, out-of-control cancers, spiraling debt, reduced world influence, and overt power grabs by now-out of the closet, elitists…

In general terms and on a worldwide scale since January 1, 2011 – there have been 77 earthquakes between the magnitude of 6 and 9 worldwide with widespread increases in storms, flooding, droughts, disease, hunger, poverty, and conflict. Japan's nuclear power capacity was decimated by earthquake and the wake of its Tsunami lapped at California's shore as I stood and watched. Extreme Islam has expanded its boundaries, Sharia law has gained its footing in the United States, and our own president is sympathetic with its cause in the shadows of 911's tenth anniversary. Revolution occupies Wall Street and more than a thousand other cities throughout the world as self-focused idealists perpetrate destructive agendas upon the earth... Hollywood releases apocalyptic movies, comets appear in the heavens, and Jews were burned at the stake in Mexico for practicing their faith exactly "69 sevens" earlier (483 years-see Daniel 9:25-27). Europe reels trying to save EU currency now infused by staggered IMF, America's dollar and global credit rating have diminished with deficits looming large on the world's horizon, China tightened its lending criteria, and a world currency is being called for... Palestine makes its United Nation bid for statehood... the Oval Office implements troop withdrawal from Iraq...Israel faces increased attack...Cyber warfare multiplies...United States pressures Israel to divide the promised land...Iran races and declares its intent to become a virulent Nuclear power...and Syria kills citizenry and threatens regional firestorm. US decommissions its largest nukes... China increases its naval fleet...Hezbollah and Hamas gain strength... European and US forces half-heartedly prepare for Middle eastern war...Russia threatens US with military action...Superpower fleets are dispatched to Israel's coast...Iran captures US drone, exchanging its technology for military support and nuclear arms with Russia and China...Israel postures to destroy Iran's nuclear program...US withdraws support from Israel via imposed demands...czars are appointed to empower America's presidential executive decisions without congressional approval...all while economic, social, moral, and spiritual chaos erupt amid compounding anti-Semitism all over the world. Yet, four year old kids like Jon and Kelly's son Isaac run through the house fighting an imaginary battle with their swords drawn yelling, "Get ready, the battle is coming" as those around them who claim to be spiritually enlightened yawn blinded with delusion and immobilized by disinterest...

Tragically, God's people sleep in the light distracted by the cares of this life and blithely forgetting that God is not adding extra days to His culminating plan to compensate for man's complacency as ecumenicalism launches Chrislam's new world religion...crosses are removed from churches...technologies counterfeits God's presence... impatience shortcuts the burning bush...infidelity prostitutes divine marriage...political views pollute pulpits...denominations re-package truth...compromise halts transformation...and castaways drift toward destruction while God looks toward birth once again as an expectant father waiting, weary, and weeping as History's contractions tighten their grip on humanity's doorknob...

Based on people you've known, places you've been, things you've done, and decisions you've made – who will come pounding at your door, when will they arrive on your doorstep, and what news will they bring?

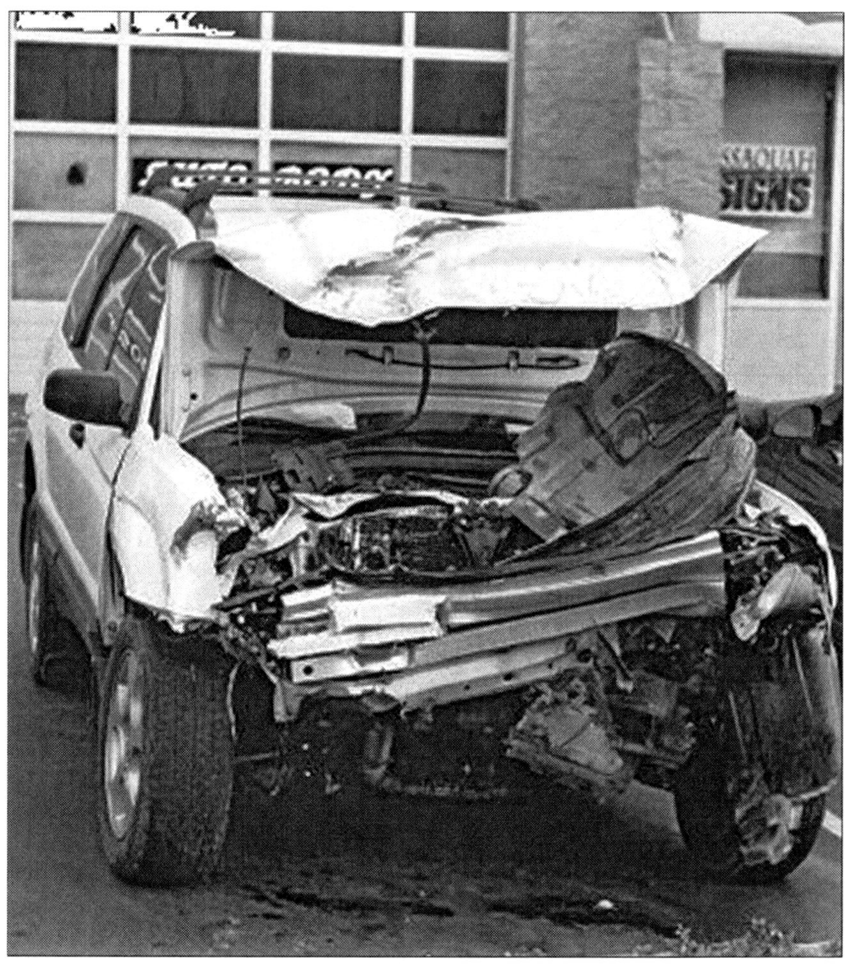

My near-fatal 63 MPH tangle with a semi-truck – 2004

Mom and Dad being themselves...

Chapter 2
Romance Theology

"This is My command: Love each other" (John 15:17).

Growing up on the farm is a great place for kids to be kids and to learn about work, responsibility, and how to drive long before turning sixteen. I was no exception to the unspoken rule as dad gave me surprised me with my first motorcycle at age thirteen after I had been driving tractors, the pick-up, and moved the truck from time-to-time. Just imagine thousands of acres of dirt, sagebrush, apple orchards, gravel roads, and rock piles right outside my door and forest-lined foothills within less than 5 miles. When you take all that and add a dirt bike, fun and adventure are limitless for roughneck like me with an aptitude for mischief. Meanwhile, I was up to my typical inventive self always looking for ways to port a cylinder, trim a rotary valve, or shave a cylinder head to coax a few more RPM's and horsepower out my ride. When I first got the bike, I stayed studiously close to home within the boundaries of our ranch. Soon, I was riding between ranches early in the mornings to change sprinkler pipe before breakfast. Like everyone, the grass always looked a bit greener, the dirt a bit richer, the hill a bit higher, and the adventure a bit bigger on the other side of the line dad told me not to cross... As time passed, I found myself astride the rocket-on-wheels over forty hours a week by the time I was fifteen and had made my way through life into the ninth grade as a freshman in high school...

On one particular day, dad caught me off guard when he said I could ride my dirt bike to school "if" I promised to stay off the highway and get there through orchards and on back roads. I gave him the appropriate nod as adrenaline coursed my veins at the mere thought of sliding into school in front of the crowd and looking cool. Being the compliant sort that I am, I gave my bike a kick...dumped it in gear...gave her some throttle...and let a rooster tail fly as I catapulted out through the field with nary-a-care. Soon coming to the edge of our property, I was presented with an optional choice called a highway, on which I was not to travel, but offered alluring, fast, and stupendous ride... The wheels in my mind began to spin as I looked across the road at my well-worn path and...I pondered...I looked both ways...I contemplated...I pursed my lips...lowered my goggles...twisted the throttle...grabbed a gear...hung a left...and hit the asphalt blowing through the gears engulfed in freedom as wind blew up my sleeves, bugs hit my chest, and I laid into the turns. Coming to the stop sign across from the school, I looked carefully to be sure I was unnoticed, and made my way through the lot and around back where I parked next to the Ag shop. I was so puffed up at my accomplishment that I could have passed for an over-stuffed kernel of Puffa-Puffa rice on field day... I navigated my classes in another world completely side-lined as I zeroed in on the greatness of my upcoming departure from school that day...

Finally, the last bell rang and I headed for my bike, cranked her up, rode around the school, and did my best to look nonchalant as I headed for the exit in full view of the world. I seem to have heard a little voice inside saying, “Stay off the highway,” but was sure I was mistaken as adrenalin rose within again. I rolled up to the stop sign, looked both ways, hung a left and hit the open road... With no prior plan, I pulled the front end off the asphalt and rode through the gears on one wheel disappearing over the rise out of my classmate’s sight. Being that my bike was for off-road only, I had no lights, speedometer, or signals because it was built for speed. As I laid into the throttle and leaned into one turn and then laid her hard into the next shooting through the draw and up over the next rise coming to my home road. As I rounded the curve, I caught a glimpse of something white to my left glancing just in time to spot the local State Patrol car which I later discovered had been on my tail since leaving the school. In a flash, I made one of those split decisions that one knows better than to make before dropping a couple of gears and bounded out through the orchard down the gulley, through the trees, and into the pear orchard where I ditched my bike next to a tree. I made my way through the orchard and walked toward the house. As I came into the back yard feeling a bit smug that I had not only made it to-and-from school on the highway, but had pulled a wheelie extraordinaire and outrun a State Trooper all in the same day. As I rounded the corner of the house, to my chagrin I had arrived just in time to see my dad, the head bus driver, and the State Trooper standing in the yard talking...

Have you ever had one of those sinking feelings when you realized your goose was irreversibly cooked – well, I had one. Before I could duck or dodge, my dad said, "Hey, there's someone here to talk to ya." My chin dropped, my lungs deflated, and my shoulders sagged as I wandered toward likely execution at the hands of three old guys... The Trooper asked, "Do you know how fast you were going?" "No sir," I replied a bit sheepishly. "You were doing 70 in a 50 zone. Where's your bike?" "In the field sir," I replied. "Can I see your license?" he asked. "Don't have one sir," I whispered as the frog climbed further up my throat. "Hmmm," he said turning to my dad saying, "I'll have to write him a ticket, he may not get his license till he's eighteen now." "Well, sometimes lessons are hard," dad replied. "Well son," the officer said, "I'm going to have you come into the office so I can make a report." "When sir?" I asked. "Tomorrow," he said. "Okay," I whispered sweating bullets... When I left his office the next day, I was expected to have no more problems of a similar nature for 90 days or my driver's license would be delayed for two more years... And then I thought, "It was only four miles of highway and a little clean fun," But, it was I who had considered my options, traveled my own course, and hit the highway to cross the law's line...

God provides us with all we need in life to be happy and blessed. And yet, our experience will be determined based on the vantage point we have, options we choose, and risks we take in response to His guidelines of love. If we choose rightly, we will remain enlightened, empowered, and emancipated from the imposed turmoil of life. But, if we make the wrong decisions, we will wander through this life trying to find our way while filtering life through blinded eyes, hardened hearts, and weary souls. It was choice exercised by those whom God gave His Law of Love to at Mount Sinai, which resulted in their vision being clouded, perception of God's love diluted, and ultimately opened death's door for lifeless law and religion to reign over His people for thousands of years. Though I will not take time to develop it here, there is a stark contrast between the pure Law of Love God gave us in His effort to bless and liberate us versus man's sinful perspective and wrongful administration of God's Law of Love upon the earth. In this light, I will make occasional references to God's Upper Case Law of Love and death's lower case law of hostility. When you see these terms or references to them, you will know that God's Upper Case Law of Love refers to His perfect unpolluted love toward us versus man's fallen religious practice known as death's lower case law of hostility. Please keep this awareness tucked under your hat as you read on...

Please note, that Scriptural patterns cited in this chapter portray Spirit-led understanding that beckons us beyond traditional theological views based in head knowledge alone. Passages referenced below are located next to a word or concept addressed in that bible passage and join together to express a collective vantage point – not biblical interpretation. The following lifestyle-based application of Scripture God has given me to communicate is called Romance Theology. Our practice of its principles calls us to shift our style of life, from knowing to doing...from self to others... from judgment to compassion...and from striving to peace. So, please open your heart, grab a cup of coffee, sit back, and dig in...

Seated at Starbucks engulfed in thought's overstuffed corner chair drifting from work worries through mind mazes to distant destinations...your eyes scan, land, and crystallize on human perfection sitting across the room. Your nerves buzz, palms sweat, and pulse pounds as heart happenings and inspired imaginations brush color into dreams. Wondering if your doo is done, smile is smashing, and car is clean...you unravel within. Now caught in the crossfire of crumbling confidence, escalating emotion, and rushing reality...hope hauls you heavenward only to ask, "What will I say... what will I do...what will I feel?" Paralyzed precariously, pondering perspective, and pending pursuit...you watch on helplessly as the door opens, a hand extends, and perfection is whisked away by another who loved actively thereby leaving your focus on self sucking wind... What just happened before your very eyes? It's obvious that thinking on self loses, what reaching to others wins. Mere thought leaves one lacking, when taking action gains ground. It's important to realize that one's basis for beliefs and their corresponding actions scratch a line in life's sand somewhere between defeat and victory. How we form and what we do with our life values and motivations will greatly impact our own life experience and the legacy we leave in the lives of others...

Throughout history...man has approached and viewed God through human eyes rooted in a mindset of intellectual understanding called theology. By definition – theology is the study of religious faith, practice, and experience; especially the study of God and His relation to the world (Merriam-Webster). Yet, how is it possible for an incomprehensible God to be defined or contained within limited human understanding? Since its inception, traditional theology has been defined by and built upon Scripture's historical context, original language, syntax, and other grammatical principles greatly detached from God's heart. Sadly, this knowledge-based method of reading, studying, and knowing about God quenches Spirit-led learning virtually altogether. But, Jesus says that "...the Father seeks those who worship Him in Spirit and truth (John 4:23-24)... that no one can come to me unless the Father who sent me draws him...and it is written in the prophets: they will all be taught by God (John 6:44-45)." The Apostle Paul weighed in on the matter too, saying "...we are no longer to conform to the pattern of this world, but are to be transformed by the renewing of our minds so that we may test and approve God's good, pleasing, and perfect will" (Romans 12:1-3). Therefore, God obviously intends for us to be enlightened by the love-filled mind of Christ through the eyes of a child, not mere intellectual interpretation alone (Mark 10:15). Why is this so important?

By iself, intellectual theology imposes judgment, rather than actively loving life and peace back into others (Romans 8:6). Why? God's unconditional love-based reach to us glues Scripture together in a manner that supersedes human reason and comprehension as typically produced by traditional theological approach. God's selfless theology knits Scripture together based on His loving heart toward a dying world... In my own life experience with His truth, love, and mercy – I have been a recipient of His grace beyond measure. It is though these eyes dear friend, I call God's love language to humanity Romance Theology... Romance theology is only discovered, lived, and experienced through intimate one-on-one personal relationship with Jesus Christ. God's loving worldview cannot be gained through one's mental quest for knowledge while simply living on a path of religious form. The bible tells us that Jesus is coming back as Heaven's Bridegroom to marry and become one with His radiant church known as the bride of Christ (Ephesians 5:25-32). The entire Bible is about the romance of marriage-style relationship from cover-to-cover as Jesus reaches to meet His bride at the ultimate wedding ceremony of all time. Based on prophetic and human factors foretold in Scripture indicating the season of Christ's return – it is crucial that we, His wayward bride, make ourselves ready to take our seat at the wedding feast of the Lamb before our opportunity is gone (Revelation 19:7)! Are you gripped and compelled by a sense of romance that intimately, passionately, and wholeheartedly loves and pursues Jesus at any cost? Or, are you back to counting the cost after the honeymoon ended, simply trudging through religious duty day-by-day? Without romance, your relationship with God and those He has given to your care – will die.

Theology is to religion what romance is to relationship. In other words...knowledge only talks what love actually walks. Jesus drove this point home to the religious, saying, "You diligently study the Scriptures because you think that by them you possess eternal life. These are the Scriptures that testify about me, yet you refuse to come to me to have life...I know that you do not have the love of God in your hearts" (John 5:39-41). The Apostle Paul said it this way, "Knowledge puffs up, but love builds up" (I Corinthians 8:1). Knowledge gained by intellectual study has a form of godliness, but denies God's power (2 Timothy 3:5). Yet, learning from God face-to-face while chasing Him with a whole heart radically alters us in His presence and leaves us in love with our King (Isaiah 6:5-8; Jeremiah 29:13; John 6:44-45, 14:15; 1 Corinthians 13:7-8; 2 Corinthians 5:17; I John 4:19-21). Jesus told us that we would follow His example as evidence that we have faith in Him – if our faith truly exists (John 14:12). What is Jesus still doing (Matt 22:37-41; John 17:26)? Simple – He is spending time with His Father, doing what He sees Him doing, and still completing the work His Father gave Him to do for the welfare of those He was given – that's us (John 17:4, 6-10; Hebrews 7:25). The life of Jesus embodies the two greatest commandments of loving God and loving people with all His heart, mind, and strength (Matt 22:37-41; Mark 12:30-31). Romance theology is God's love letter to our struggling world... What language is your personal theology speaking?

Intellectual theology rises out of flawed human logic to indoctrinate, while romance theology flows through love-soaked Holy Spirit inspiration to liberate. Romance theology joins Scripture to champion God's heart and communicate His love to and through one person to another with action...not empty words (James 2:14-17; 1 John 3:16-20). I remember walking out of the hills of Tennessee on my first trek across America back in 2001-02 when the Holy Spirit whispered, "second Timothy two fifteen." I tipped my head back, squinted, and suddenly saw the passage scroll before my mind's eye, "Do your best to present yourself to God as one approved, a workman who does not need to be ashamed and who correctly handles the word of truth (2 Timothy 2:15)." Without skipping a beat...God's still small voice continued, "Too many theologians are more concerned about whether their interpretation of Scripture is right, than if their view extends My loving heart to a dying world. They make the bible and idol, but do not know Me. The bible is merely an introduction to Me, its Author. The bible is simply a skeleton of understanding that helps you recognize Me. Yet, knowing Me face-to-face puts meat on its bones so My people can rise, live, love, and walk in My likeness with power!" When we live and love like Jesus – we touch heaven and change earth one life at a time...

Several years ago, I learned of a pastor whose daughter had been raped and murdered. The loss ripped both he and his wife's lives and hearts apart without warning or mercy. Time ticked by as the pastor and his wife pushed through rejection, anger, acceptance, and arrived at peace – still shaken by the loss. One year tumbled to another as the pastor loved his people through his own brokenness... While sitting in his study one afternoon deep in prayer many years later, his phone rang, cleaving the silence, and drew him in. He picked up the receiver and said, "Hello, Pine Crest Community Church." A weighty silence lingered before a trembling voice spoke from the line's other end. "Who's calling – may I help you?" the pastor asked. Seconds turned into moments until the voice on the other end of the line finally said, "This is Tom...I need to speak with you about an important matter...may I come see you?" "Just a moment please, let me check my schedule," the pastor replied. After the brief delay of thumbing through his calendar the pastor said, "It seems my schedule is open this afternoon, how soon can you be here?" Tom replied, "I can be there in half an hour or so." The pastor replied, "That will be fine, we'll see you soon...goodbye" and hung up the phone... As silence returned to his hiding place, the pastor sat back, sinking deep into his chair, pondering what Tom could possibly want to discuss that was so urgent...

Thirty minutes passed...no one. Forty minutes passed...no one. Fifty three minutes after he had hung up the phone, an older cream-colored Plymouth Valiant rolled to its temporary resting place in front of the church as the pastor gazed curiously through his study's shadow-laced glass to see who would emerge. The car door opened and a middle-aged man climbed out turning to make his way across the weathered asphalt as his frame seemed to bear a heavy load. The man plodded somberly toward the door, never lifting his eyes to glance within... Rising from his chair and making his way to the building's front entry to receive his guest, the pastor opened the door with an ease to inquire, "Tom?" as the man neared the door. Lifting his eyes to meet the pastor's he replied, "Yes sir, that's right." Pastor said, "Come in...come in...my office is just around the corner" motioning to his still unknown visitor. Doing his best to muster a smile-of-sorts, Tom followed the church leader to his refuge. As the pastor walked in the room around his desk before sitting...he motioned Tom toward a chair on the desk's opposing side and said, "Have a seat, please make yourself comfortable." In silence, Tom seated himself and fixed his eyes on a bronze of Calvary's empty cross stationed in the dust at the desk's edge...

Finally, the pastor asked, “How can I help you, what is it that you need to talk to me about?” Silence became palpable as it filled the room... Quietly, Tom cleared his throat and his voice whispered to life asking, “Do you remember me?” The pastor looked at Tom, closed his eyes, retraced the corridors of his mind, and reopened them to say, “No, should I?” Silence filled the room once again as Tom’s look fell back to the desk and tears swelled in his eyes... Silence resumed as Tom’s looming burden squeezed life from the room’s refuge. Tom’s eyes rose with uncertainty...tears fell to his shirt below as his eyes finally locked with pastor’s and he said, “I came to ask for your forgiveness.” Puzzled, the pastor replied, “I don’t even know you Tom, what could you have possibly done to need my forgiveness?” As tears flowed freely, Tom’s nose began to run, and a tear threatened to drip from its tip, he answered, “I’m the man who killed your daughter...please sir...please forgive me for what I did.” Feeling as if he’d been hit by a freight train, the pastor crumbled in his chair and wept... Time passed, tears finally subsided, and speech became possible once again...

“My son,” the pastor said quietly, “I forgave you so long ago... and have prayed for you all these years.” Pierced to his core by unmerited favor, Tom’s voice broke as he asked, “Why sir...why would you do that for me after what I did...why? The pastor replied, “Being angry was not going to bring my girl back to life, son.” Tom spoke up and said, “Your prayers must have worked because I gave my life to Jesus Christ in prison and have been reading my bible for many years.” For the next few hours the two men talked, wept, prayed, and thumbed through the pastor’s well-worn bible together sharing special passages that had carried them individually through their dark nights of the soul. Now mid evening, the pastor’s phone rang...he answered...and was greeted by his wife’s voice as he nodded his head as if in silent reply as he listened before saying, “I’ll be home in a while dear...we’ll talk later...everything’s fine.” As the pastor returned the receiver to its cradle, Tom rose slowly to his feet and said, “I suppose I should be going...thank you for taking time...for extending mercy...and for...forgiving me.” As Tom moved toward the door, the pastor said, “Tom, church starts at 11:00 AM Sunday morning...why don’t you come? I would be honored if you join us for worship." In response, Tom replied, "Well, if you're sure it's okay, I'd like that." Tom showed up that Sunday and many thereafter. As time passed, the two men became great friends...

One day about six months later – a member of the church stopped by to talk with his leader, "Pastor, where's Tom from?...what does he do?...have you known him for long?" Pastor replied, "It's a long story, but yes...I've known him to varied degrees off-and-on for years." Over subsequent weeks, a buzz began to grow among the congregation until one Sunday after church another man who had been a member for more than 40 years cornered the pastor in the entry and menacingly said, "I hear Tom's the man who killed your daughter...is it true?" Now, surrounded by what seemed to be half his fellowship, the pastor looked down, paused, lifted his gaze to lock eyes with his opponent and said quietly as Tom stood aside, "Yes, it's true." Coming to her husband's side and moving closer to Tom, the pastor's wife locked arms with her man and stood her ground alongside their new friend... Chaos erupted as churchgoers gasped, whispered, rolled their eyes, and some stormed out the door while those remaining to watch withdrew to the room's edge before the fellowship's Pharisees cut their line deep in the wine-colored carpet...

Finally, the man who caused the ruckus retorted, "How could you invite the one who killed your own flesh-and-blood to church... what in the hell's the matter with you?" Without warning, it was open season as others chimed in and said, "Yeah pastor, how could you? We don't need his kind here...how could you forgive a murderer...he killed your daughter?" Moving silently to the side of the room...staring off into the distance...and pulling at the edge of God's garment in prayer as he stood protectively next to Tom...the pastor lingered waiting for his people to silence...and finally said, "I simply see a picture of my Jesus on the cross dying to forgive me after all I've done... How could I ever refuse to forgive someone else? In Luke chapter seven verse forty-seven, Jesus teaches if we have been forgiven much, we are to love much in return." Turning amid the free-for-all to stare out the window once again...the pastor prayed. A few moments later...he turned, raised his hand calling his people to pause, and challenged, "You who are without sin...cast the first stone" as he took his stand next to his brother... Over the next half hour...one-by-one...their accusers walked away until just the three of them remained. As the pastor and his wife turned to look in Tom's eyes and hold his hand...the pastor said, "We love you Tom, we'll see you Wednesday night for bible study." "I'm so sorry for all I've caused the two of you," Tom whispered. "It's water under the bridge Tom...Jesus makes all things new" as the three of them touched heaven, changed earth, and chose life – forever...

Theology without love always controls others through legalistic pride (Luke 11:46). Yet, romance theology bows with God's humility to accept, forgive, and love at any price (Matthew 26:36-46; Philippians 2:3-5; James 3:6-10). Our reach to others is defined by our concept of God and the character of love our vantage point lets us experience in our relationship with Him. Our concept of God is shaped by core beliefs either built on intellectual knowledge or Christ Himself...we choose. "If" our concept of God leans on human understanding and traditional theological methods, our empty version of God's love will fall to the ground void long before it ever woos a wayward heart... When we do as Jesus is still doing, life flows through us to others relative to whatever level of spiritual transformation we have experienced ourselves up to that moment in time (John 14:12, 17:26). Have you been radically altered in the presence of the Living God? When He said "go"...did you? If not...why not?

Unapologetically...intellectual theology is hell's hard rock miner, blasting its complex maze of carnal corridors through hearts of stone with explosive force primed by human assumption, extrapolation, and justification. Intellectual theology defines the unknowable, imposes the unlovable, and absolutes the unlivable. The contrast between intellectual and romance theology is life-altering for both the unwitting theologian and the one driven by love's passion. Where intellectual theology assumes the worst, romance theology believes the best. When intellectual theology draws a line, romance theology builds a bridge. What intellectual theology destroys, romance theology restores. Intellectual theology is a tragedy, while romance theology remains heaven's remedy. I experienced both the intellectual tragedy and the romance remedy in a matter of hours through a chain of events along my path one day...

As I prepared to move from one town to another...a man who became my dear friend made arrangements for me to park five days at a large church in the next city I was moving toward. On the day of my departure after saying my good-byes and before hitting the road...I called the church ahead to get directions, ask who I was to connect with upon arrival, and told them when I planned to be there... While on the line with the church receptionist assuming I would need to make an appointment to see the pastor amid his schedule demands, I made my request with her telling me she would call me back when she had confirmed a time. I thanked her, started the engine, and pointed my RV eastward in their direction... Exiting the freeway an hour later and traveling the prescribed route, I rolled into the church driveway and looked up the gentleman whose name I had been given. We chatted for a few moments in the parking lot before he mounted his runabout and led me to my landing spot where I would park while there... As I hooked up my main power cord however, I felt the urge to leave my other cable and hoses in the storage bay for some unknown reason... Once parked, I hopped in my tow rig and went to explore the city to discover churches most likely scattered throughout... Later that evening, I returned to my motor coach and retired for the night. The next morning as I navigated my daily custom of spending time reading my bible and in prayer, I was jolted from my serenity when the phone rang and I answered to find the church secretary I had spoken to the day before on the other end of the line. "The pastor can meet with you this morning at ten if you're available," she said. "That would be wonderful!" I replied hanging up after she told me where the office complex was...

Climbing out of the shower, getting dressed, and making my way toward the church a few minutes early to meet the pastor, I encountered a middle-aged woman in the foyer behind the welcome center who beamed with the love of God. Passing a few moments in easy conversation...we gave each other a snapshot of our passion and calling in Christ before it was time for me to move on... I walked down the long corridor around the corner through a set of double doors and hung a right where I landed in front of the secretary's desk whom I'd spoken to by phone the day before. "Good morning, the pastor is ready for you," she said motioning me toward an open door. "Thanks," I said as I stepped through the doorway to be greeted by the pastor now rising behind his desk. As I approached, he stuck out his hand and said, "Good morning" while rounding his desk and inviting me to join him at the conference table... Both pulling our chairs out to take our seats, he turned momentarily to close the door to the outer office, and we sat down to make ourselves comfortable. He asked about me, where I was from, and what God had called me to accomplish that carried me through the area. I filled in the blanks for him reciprocating to inquire about his church, how long he'd been pastor there, and what he saw God doing in his congregation. Our conversation continued with a pleasant tone, soon moving to an even deeper plane as we both began sharing key aspects of our individual journeys along life's way...

Over the next hour, we revealed our personal visions in ministry, experiences with people, and observations which had emerged during our time involved in mainstream Christianity. Topics wandered one-to-another as we slowly-but-surely discovered our common ground. As our discussion turned a corner and we began relating more of our personal vantage points, I said, "I'm amazed how many churches go through religious motions, give pep talks, or cultivate an experience during service causing people to laugh, dance, shout, weep, and leave thinking they encountered God's when He wasn't even there. So many wander through their weeks making no effort to read, pray, confess, or repent...come to church getting caught up in the action only to walk out the door emotionally charged...and live the same defeated life that was killing them before they came to church that day. We spend so much time wearing the right clothes, looking the part, and conjuring up yesterday... that we overlook doing what it takes to obey God today so He can transform our tomorrows!" As the last few words rolled off my tongue...the pastor's gentle smile disappeared, his hand reached for the doorknob, and he said, "I have another appointment to get to." In seconds, his entire demeanor changed as he leaned forward in his chair and shut things off...

In response to the unexpected change in atmosphere I said, "Well, thanks for taking time...may I pray for you?" "No!" he said abruptly. "Is there a reason?" I asked. "You're messed up man," he said emphatically. "Can you please tell me what you think I'm messed up about?" I asked. Silence filled the room... Finally he said, "I believe we both hear God and have the Holy Spirit...but, you're messed up!" "I'm puzzled...you say we both hear God and have the Holy Spirit which means we're listening to the same voice....but, you won't let me pray for you?" I said. "I don't want you talking to my people, I won't let you preach, and I want you gone from the church parking lot by tomorrow morning" he retorted. "I never asked to preach...we were simply talking," I responded. More silence... "I'll just go ahead and leave today since I'm not welcome," I offered. "I didn't say you weren't welcome," he shot back. "It seems that you invited me to park here for 5 days...I came to meet you and connect...you tell me I'm messed up without explanation... and you're telling me to be gone by morning after inviting me for five days...I don't feel very welcome," I explained. "I didn't say you weren't welcome," he defended. "It's no problem pastor, I'll go wind up my cord and find another place while it is still light out," I said as I headed for the door. Walking out of the office together into the outer hallway, I stopped and turned toward him holding my hand out and said, "Thanks for letting me stay the night, I'll go ahead and take off." As I prepared to leave...I shared with him that God had given me Matthew chapter ten verses five through sixteen as a pattern for how I'm to work with God's people who I encounter along my path. His face took on an even more troubled expression... "Thanks again" I said, turning and heading down the long corridor where I passed by and smiled at the kind lady I had met on my arrival.

After exiting the building – I got in my rig and rolled down the street to grab a bite to eat before I rolled up my cord and went to look for another place to park. I found an IHOP restaurant a few blocks away and went inside where I took my place at a back table contemplating what had just transpired with the pastor. Here I was, a preacher walking across America on faith to encourage others while asking for nothing, now some 2,500 miles from home, and I was just thrown out by a brother in Christ without explanation. I had known for more than two months that the issue I had been observing in that denomination would come to a head, but had not quite envisioned that it would happen in the manner it did that day – religious spirits are unpredictable... Saying, "Father forgive them" within my own soul, releasing it into His hands, and keeping myself stayed on Him...a little black waitress named Jessica stepped up to my table. "What would you like?" she asked. "I'll have three orders of crispy bacon and a large orange juice" I replied. She smiled, turned, and disappeared before returning a few minutes later to set my food before me. "That was fast," I said. She smiled again, asked if I needed anything else, and walked away to help other patrons... Suddenly, my phone rang drawing me into a call that encompassed my entire meal. Jessica walked by from time-to-time mouthing silent words to see if I needed anything...our smiles would meet with me nodding my head from side-to-side...and she continued on by to return a bit later for another pass... Eventually, my call ended and I asked Jessica for my ticket. She reached deep into her apron pocket to retrieve it...wadding up straw wrappers she found lingering within...and handed me the paper I requested with a smile...

I approached the register where I found another young black lady ready to ring me up... As she took my ticket and began to run it through the till, I heard the Holy Spirit say, "Give Jessica that last hundred dollar bill you've been saving." "Okay Lord," I whispered out loud. Reaching into my belt pouch...I pulled out the bill, folded it, and held it in my hand waiting for Jessica to come to the front of the restaurant. A moment later, she passed by other side of a dividing wall and I approached her saying, "I don't know what you need this for, but God told me to give it to you" holding out my hand to place the folded Franklin gently in her palm as privately as possible. She said, "Thank you" without looking at what I handed her and turned to walk away as I spun back toward the cashier. Seconds later I heard a squeal behind me followed by, "I've been going to church and asking God all week...!" Jessica sputtered. About then, the cashier called past the people in front of her to Jessica saying, "See, you got your blessing!" Without skipping a beat, the cashier turned to me and asked, "Do you go to people's homes and pray for them?" I said, "Sure!" The electricity between us buzzed as I handed her my card, invited her to call, and walked out of the building to my waiting vehicle...

Back on the street reminiscing over that morning's events...I prayed, "Lord, where should I go now...I need a place to park?" "Straight ahead," He replied within me. So, on I went before hearing the Holy Spirit say, "Turn right." I hung a right, traveled a few blocks, and heard, "Turn left." I pulled a left and right before my eyes...a church sign was painted on the side of an older movie theatre. I made my way down the block and turned into the parking lot where I came to rest in a birth of my own between angled white stripes... Strolling across the parking lot and up the steps...I looked for an entrance... I noticed a door standing ajar to my left and walked down the concrete to-and-through the entrance where I found a couple of young men who appeared in their mid-thirties chatting... one in an over-stuffed chair and the other buried in an under-sprung couch. On my way through the door I heard the Lord say, "Authenticity" before silence resumed. Then I said, "Hi, I'm Greg from BattleCry walking and preaching my way across America for the second time...I didn't learn the first round." "My name's Josh... I'm one of the pastors...and this is Blake...a member of our church" he replied as they both leaned forward to offer me their hands. I pulled up a nearby folding chair, sat down, and joined hearts as we journeyed into one another's lives... An hour later – Pastor Josh said, "Why don't you come to church tonight and meet our head pastor...his name's Todd." "I'd like that" I replied. We all had places to be, so I asked, "Do either of you gents know of any local RV parks that are affordable?" Blake pulled a Google search on his smart phone, gave me a couple numbers, and off I went telling them I would see them a bit later that evening...

As I sat in the third row following worship that evening at church listening to another of their pastoral team give the message – I locked eyes with Josh with him glancing back and pointing toward his head pastor so I'd know who he was after service. The congregation was comprised of young people and families in their late twenties and thirties with few in their forties as children scurried about everywhere. The message soon ended, an invitation was given, and prayer for those in need unfurled... Not wanting to interrupt the pastors as they embraced their people, I waited for the building clear before walking up to short-haired Pastor Todd, also in his mid-thirties, to introduce myself. He looked straight at me through his smiling eyes and said "Josh and Blake told me about you" as he held out his hand with a grin. "It's been great to meet all of you today!" I said. "It's awesome to see such a young crowd of believers and their kids in a church that worships, preaches the simple truth, stands for marriage, and loves people!" I added. "Thanks, we want to change lives and reach our community for Jesus," he replied. "Would you have any time to sit down and visit over the next day or two?" I asked. "Sure, I'll call ya in the morning when I figure out my schedule and we can spend some time together in the afternoon," he responded. "Great," I replied. We parted company that evening as I returned to my RV to get some sleep after an eventful day...

About 9:30 a.m. the next morning as promised, Pastor Todd called and said, "Why don't you drop by my office about 2:30 and we can talk then." "That will give me time to finish my walk details...I'll be there," I replied. Rolling up to the curb a few hours later just minutes before we were to meet, I jumped out of my vehicle in time to catch a glimpse and wave at Josh on my way into the church. As I passed through the door...again, I heard the Holy Spirit say, "Authenticity." I loitered in the foyer for a moment-or-two before Pastor Todd rounded the corner in his button-down-the-front shirt, blue jeans, and bare feet in flip-flops to say, "Hey man, how are ya today?" "Great...thanks for taking time," I responded. "Follow me," he said as he bounded up the stairs...through the theatre's old administrative area...into his office. I felt at home immediately as I scanned to find well-marked planners on the wall, vision statements and ministry goals scrawled on glass in doctor-like form with dry-erase markers, a somewhat orderly desk, a big couch, and a love-filled grin on Todd's face... He said, "Have a seat" waiving me to the couch and handing me a bottle of water in one fell swoop. He pulled up his chair and our conversation commenced with initial introductions, cursory life details, and then...it was all Jesus from there on. Our hearts cemented as we dove into the unknown that day, soon-to-emerge and incredible and irreversible friendship that he later assured me would last forever... As we continued, I learned much more about his education, personal life, local fellowship, church affiliations, and his theology through how he lived and loved...

Over months-to-come, I was privileged to meet and befriend another thirteen pastors associated with Todd who embraced my life, spent time getting to know me, and honored me with freedom to address their people in Jesus' name... The course of events that began not-so-good in one pastor's office, bridged the gap on crispy strips of bacon, and delivered me into a second pastor's presence compelled by love – spoke wholeness into my world as it opened doors of blessing in-and-through my life to others... In retrospect and without malice, I experienced the tragedy of intellectual theology, responded based on my own theology, and found my remedy in a brother who gets romance theology...

Head-based theology is nothing more than a religious idealism, while romance theology incarnates the One Who personifies truth, embodies love, bleeds mercy, resurrects hope, and grants eternity (Luke 23:34, 42-43, 24:13-49; John 1:1, 3:16, 14:6, 15:1-17, 20:10-23; 1 Timothy 1:15-16). Romance theology is not just a belief... Romance theology...IS...He Who reaches the unreachable, loves the unlovable, forgives the unforgivable, pardons the unpardonable, and redeems the unredeemable by paying the unimaginable to accomplish the unfathomable. All freedom is paid for in blood by those who die on distant battlefields or...an old rugged cross. Words are cheap, but God's romance for His wayward bride suffers silently to protect, trust, hope, and persevere with the one He loves because...romance theology never fails (Matt. 27:13-14; 1 Corinthians 13:7-8; Heb. 5:9-10; James 2:14-17)!

What cultivates, challenges, and catapults romance theology past our head to our heart with authenticity? Simple! Romance theology rises from human ash as one chooses to see the selfish through God's eyes, hear the hardened through God's ears, and love the lost through God's heart because one has been forgiven much (Luke 7:47). Romance theology wrestles with human dignity when one is scourged by schoolmates, abandoned by authorities, defined by demographics, exploited by employers, marginalized by morons, crushed by critics, harassed by hotheads, plundered by partners, and raped by religion for standing alone in adversity armed with created purpose. Romance theology overwrites human character as one reveals personal weakness to strengthen people's hope...spends personal time to communicate people's worth...risks personal reputation to erase people's shame...gives personal resources to meet people's needs...yields personal rights to restore people's freedom...and pays a personal price to empower people's purpose.

The heart behind our theology reveals itself in the way those God has given to us respond (John 17:6-10). This truth pierced me unexpectedly while behind bars on one of many days when I was there to speak to an entire cell block of men locked away for drug trafficking, assault, rape, armed robbery, and other aggravated crimes... Arriving into the block just in time to hear the Chaplain say to the men again, "I do not trust you, I do not respect you..." leaving me troubled within. As I came forward, he yielded the floor to me and I prayed before speaking to the men about the unconditional love of God. The Holy Spirit settled with a hush as tears flowed and men were changed during a time of one-on-one prayer. Afterwards, I dismissed them to carry out their other duties and rejoined the chaplain now standing soberly at the side of the room. As I stepped up to him, being sure no one was listening, I asked "How do you justify not trusting the men based on love's character found in First Corinthians 13:7?" He replied, "I don't want to be played for a fool!" In response, I said, "Simple people stumble through ignorance and fools fall because they reject truth they already know...but, you are bound by pride." I told him he was more worried about looking bad than loving the men God gave him. You could see his eyes narrow and jaw tighten as he listened... By now I was on heaven's roll up yonder and continued...

I told him that nothing worth having is free. Helping people rise from their failure requires that we risk all in faith, knowing that God will protect us as we step into battle. I reminded him that love always protects, trusts, hopes, and perseveres....love never fails (I Cor. 13:7-8). Then I said, notice that the bible does not say love trusts when convenient or when you feel like it...it just says "always." I explained that telling the men he did not trust them sent the message that they are already defeated in his eyes, giving them no reason to try. Likewise, I reminded him that the men were already in prison and aware of their wrongs...they did not need a human holy spirit. Then I said, "What they really need is hope that they can win in life." Then, I zeroed in saying "If we extend trust to someone before they earn it...we give them a chance to succeed. To extend that chance, we will have to risk our own reputation and welfare with humility, knowing they may hammer us in return. If they take advantage of our gesture and we get offended...they will see us as the offender and walk away self-justified beyond God's reach. Yet, if we respond to their injustice with love trusting Jesus as our defender...our gentleness will release His Spirit on them to convict. Though it may take a day, a week, or longer after walking away...they will wake up in the wee hours of the night staring at the bottom of the bunk above wondering why we didn't fight back. At that moment of realization, the Holy Spirit will break them and send them back to us seeking forgiveness with tears... Then, I asked him "Which one of us really deserves the unearned trust Jesus gave us at the cross when He died for our salvation? Loving and trusting others who are unworthy can extract a high price, I said. Now looking deep into the Chaplain's troubled eyes, I asked "Are you willing to pay that price to save the men God gave you...or, Are you still worried about being played for a fool?" Suddenly, he stood to attention leaning into my face and snapped "I'll have you removed" loud enough for others to hear. Then, I leaned even closer and quietly said, "God will not leave you here to oppress these men... you will be gone in less than a year." He turned and stormed out...

Immediately, the cell block erupted into chaos as the word spread and men threatened to riot if he pulled me out. I held up my hands and asked my men to be seated so I could speak to them. With every man's eyes on me...I said, "You have a choice to make this day... You can either revert to back to the same animals you were with behaviors which put you in here...or, you can be the men of God I know you to be and honor the Chaplain's authority beneath the Lordship of Christ. In truth, men...he can only do to me that which God allows." At that moment, the cell block door buzzed and swung open as the Chaplain accompanied by 2 officers, strode in. They walked up to me, said that they were there to escort me off premises, and motioned me toward the exit. Turning to the men with tears...I waved and told them I loved them as I yielded to the officer's direction. As I walked toward the exit and the Chaplain took his position at the front of the group where I had just preached the unconditional love of God, he stood speechless as the once-enraged men sat composed with bibles-in-hand to honor him. What really happened? The Chaplain had become jealous because the men always wanted to talk to me, but rarely to him because of his harshness. Eight months after-the-fact...this Chaplain whom oppressed the very men God had dispatched him to love...was removed from his long-term post. Again, what just happened? In a nutshell, this dear man of God knew enough "about" God to fuel his legalism, while my personal awareness of my own failures and God's forgiveness stirred me to love others out of appreciation for all my Lord gave me (Luke 7:47). The above story reveals a sharp contrast between two different administrations of theology...one intellectual and one romantic. Ultimately, our theology reflects how much access and permission God has been given within us to transform all we have ever lived, loved, or lost into His image. So, if you find yourself explaining your faith from a safe distance without living it at the risk of personal loss for the benefit of others, romance theology has likely eluded your grasp...

Romance theology chases God with a whole heart...falls facedown in His presence, undone...is a new creation forever changed...does nothing out of selfish ambition...puts the needs of others first with the same attitude as Jesus...stands silent before accusers...prays for its persecutors...yields to authority and settles its Gethsemanes... casts reputation aside to protect the downcast...completes its work and sanctifies itself..keeps loving and forgiving while nailed to a cross...and takes those dying next to it into paradise without baptism (Isaiah 6:5-8; Jeremiah 29:13; Matthew 27:13-14; Mark 14:4-9, 36; Luke 23:23, 34, 42-43; John 17: 4, 19; 2 Corinthians 5:17; Philippians 2:3-5). True romance flows from loving and chasing the Author of Life...and intimately knowing Him. Romance theology steps on religion as it steps up to being real. Talking religion or changing the world flows out of two different realms...one temporal and the other...eternal. Romance theology is all about God's glory... Romance theology walks into bars, hugs panhandlers, pays power bills, rescues prostitutes, defends the fatherless, restores the wounded, helps widows, eats with prisoners, challenges theologians, and gets judged by religion. Romance theology is rooted in the two greatest commandments raising the challenge to "Love the Lord your God with all your heart, mind, soul, and strength...and your neighbor as yourself (Matthew 22:37-41; Mark 12:30-31).

Intellectual theology crucified the Lord of Glory – romance theology died on a cross for a wayward bride who seduced, wounded, divorced, deceived, and committed adultery against the Son of Man in return for love. Intellectual theology is safe, prudent, predictable, legalistic, and power-based as its knowledge puffs up those who wield it to exert control, while refusing to do what Jesus is doing...in faith...for the welfare of others (John 14:12). Intellectual theology has a form of Godliness, but denies love's power. Romance theology emerges through intimacy with one's King and rises from the depths of one's soul with gratitude for all He did to seek, save, transform, empower, and release us with a mercy we could never earn or deserve. Those who have been forgiven much will be proven as they love God and others...much (Luke 7:47). If you were arrested and put on trial for your theology, would enough evidence exist to convict you in heaven's courtroom for a crime of passion known as "romance in the first degree?"

References helpful in letting God stir His heart in us

1 Kings 19:11-13; Isaiah 61:1-3; Jeremiah 29:13; Proverbs 9:10, 11:5, 20, 20:7; Matthew 5:6, 6:14, 33, 22:37-40, 24:10-13, 28:18-20; Mark 12:30-31; Luke 4:18-19; John 14:26, 15:12-17, 16:8, 13-14, 17:3-26; Romans 12:3-8; 1 Corinthians 12:7-11, 13:7-8, 14:1; 2 Corinthians 7:10; Galatians 5:16-26; Ephesians 1:4, 5:1-33; Philippians 2:9-11, 4:8; Colossians 3:1-2; 1 Thessalonians 5:17-18, 23-24; 2 Timothy 2:21; Hebrews 7:26-28, 11:1, 6; James 3:17-18, 5:16; 2 Peter 1:8, 3:14; 1 John 1:9, 3:17

Walking highways of Topeka, KS on first USA Walk – 2001

Chapter 3

Burdens and Brokenness

"Carry each other's burdens, and in this way you will fulfill the law of Christ" (Galatians 6:2).

Burden takes on many forms...gymnasium weights, heavy cargoes, wind loads, growing debts, lost jobs, racial tensions, marital fights, fleeting memories, terminal illnesses, old addictions, unbridled fears, shattered hopes, unsaved friends, and hidden sins. Burden, either good or bad, is unavoidable in life. Our perspective and response to burden will determine if it fuels us up or weighs us down. Our understanding and management of burden becomes our hinge point between victory and defeat. When properly understood, shared, and applied...burden produces life, love, and liberty in us and others on whose behalf we assume it. Burden is not merely meant to be drug laboriously forward...it is to be lifted upward, shouldered, and shared. Moving merely forward in life portrays a flat line similar to death on a hospital heart monitor, while moving upward implies that we're rising on our way toward life. As believers, we are called heavenward...not merely forward (Philippians 3:14). We will only produce in others what we own within ourselves and are willing to pay the price to communicate through action. Let me paint you a practical picture from personal experience...

During my first walk across America in 2001-2002 from the coast of Washington State to Charleston South Carolina and north to the White House...I learned that I walk 6/10 of a mile per hour faster when I carry hand weights than I do without. I know it sounds crazy since most hikers make extreme efforts at great expense to trim weight and lighten their loads. Though most would never guess it true, I found throwing my weight-laden hands forward stretches my stride length to increases my speed substantially...especially up hills. The whole concept came about because I wanted to maintain balance between upper and lower body strength... So, I decided to carry a properly managed burden consistently to strengthen my stamina and increase my speed by using timeless principles (Matthew 11:28-30; Luke 11:46; Galatians 6:2; I Peter 5:7). Every time I left my weights behind...my pace slowed, my rhythm wandered, and my daily miles decreased.

About halfway through my second walk across America from Los Angeles, CA to Jacksonville, FL in 2010-2011...I was picked up by new friends one day as I finished walking and given a ride to their home to hang out. When I walked in, I purposely laid my weights by the door to be sure I would not forget them when I left. We talked for the next few hours, until it was time for me to leave. We jumped in their car and they took me back to where my RV was parked. When I got ready to walk again the beginning of the next week, I realized that I had left my weights at their home despite my efforts not to do so. Nuts! So, I rattled off an email asking if my weights were there and received a prompt "yes" in reply. Attached to my friend's reply however...was their comment, that God may be trying to talk to me about laying down a couple of life's burdens. They admonished me to leave my weights and pray, assuring me that they would send them to me later if I needed them. I agreed and headed eastward... Through that interchange, challenge, and subsequent prayer...I eventually wrote back sometime later to share what God revealed to me about the positive effects of managed burden and shared load.

As days fell by the wayside along my path, I was quickly reminded how much it slows me down when I do not carry weights. Then, the Holy Spirit whispered that those burdens God gives to and shares with us are essential to our training, effectiveness, and productivity for Him (2 Peter 1:8). Next, I saw a vision of my two walks side-by-side with the first going from sea level in Washington State to high Colorado mesas up over 13,000 foot Rocky Mountains descending onto the front range before settling into the Midwest elevations toward the South Carolina coast. My second trek journeyed from ocean's edge in California slightly upward through Arizona's low-to-moderate altitudes sloping toward Texas hill country downward to and along sea level shores toward Jacksonville, Florida. My first walk built uniform muscle mass and increased endurance from head-to-toe because of undulating topography. My second walk developed a more one-sided muscle profile because its path was predominantly flat in nature. In this light, God revealed that the ebb-and-flow of adversity in life trains us to be stronger, more resilient, and better balanced than taking the more appealing line of least resistance. Then, the Holy Spirit paraphrased Paul's words saying that everyone who wants to compete trains hard to win a trophy. But, believers are to train, run, and fight as they help others live forever in a manner that does not disqualify the coach from competition after telling everyone else what to do (1 Corinthians 9:25-27). Obviously, God thinks burden and hard work go hand-in-hand to train real winners. So, I bought another pair of hand weights and resumed my prior pace as I trained to win the victor's crown.

For years, I read biographies, autobiographies, and other available materials to discover what pillars of the faith had in common. There were people like Tyndale, St. Francis, Luther, St. Augustine, Wesley, Edwards, Spurgeon, Finney, Moody, Bonheoffer, Mother Teresa, Chambers, Sunday, Olson, Wigglesworth, Elliott, Lake, Bonnke, and others. Great intercessors like Rees Howells, John Hyde, Andrew Murray, A. W. Tozer, E.M. Bounds, Derek Prince impacted untold lives through time on their knees. It was icing on the cake to read about the reformation, great awakenings, and revivals that swept entire regions as God's people humbled themselves and prayed. Whether a person or move of God – they all shared whole-hearted devotion, repentance, humility, obedience, selflessness, faith, and they chased God before touching things of this world. Souls were first and self was second. And yet, their individual quests to impact the world around them for Christ left them outcasts, targets, martyrs, and immortalized in ways similar to the One they serve. In a nutshell, they all pursued Christ-likeness through unconditional surrender, abstract brokenness, extreme obedience, and selfless assumption of burden on behalf of others at the cost of their own lives...

We all struggle to gain freedom from our selfish nature as the law of sin bombards us over the course of our lives during the days

God gave us (Psalms 139:16; Romans 7:21-25). Too often, we get caught up in life's daily details that weigh us down, pollute our values, sap our energy, and break our grip on all God created us to be. Consequently, those He ordained for us to reach, touch, and impact with His love fall through life's cracks because of our choices. Though our fleeting realization of this sober situation is troubling to some degree at various times...God's suffers the ultimate agony through tears as those created in His image for His good pleasure drift dying beyond his grasp, lost and alone. The essence of God's protective love cries out our willing assumption of burden on behalf of others who are not able or willing to help themselves (1 Corinthians 13:7-8). Yes, I said, "Even those not willing." Many will take on the task of helping someone who appears unable to help themselves. Yet, only real Christians share the load to liberate the willful, defiant, and hardened-of-heart (Romans 5:7-8; Matthew 20:26-28). Did Jesus go to the cross for some, or did He die for all? Did He tells us that we will do what He is doing if we're His disciples (John 14:12)? Thought so...

In God's economy...biblical burden calls us to carry the self-or-otherwise imposed load of another while being wholly invaded by humility's Gethsemane decision, suffering's sweet fellowship, and death's plundered sting (Mark 4:36; I Corinthians 15:55; Philippians 3:10). Remember, dear friend, perseverance equals *endurance with joy* (James 1:2-4). As the Holy Spirit whispered one day...we gain the victory when we "stand resolutely, praise Him, and gather the miracles." God's people...heaven's warriors...must stop hiding passively in life's shadows waiting for the devil to bring his fight to us...and start standing aggressively in God's burden to take His fight to the devil! We are called heavenward in Christ Jesus, to love one another, to stand, to strain ahead, and to go and make disciples – not converts (Matthew 28:19-20; John 13:34-35; Ephesians 6:13; Philippians 3:14, 4:13). Jesus never taught us to ask the two diagnostic questions, tally statistics, and generate quarterly reports for headquarters to gain brownie points. Instead, He called us to produce fruit that lasts (John 15:16-17). We are commissioned to make lifestyle disciples impassioned to love others and change the world at all costs. As His friends, Jesus calls us to make real disciples by loving real people, expending real time, paying a real price, suffering real heartache, living real freedom, portraying real truth based on the real Lord to authorize heaven's focal point (John 15:15). "Go into the world and preach the gospel and when necessary...use words" (St. Augustine). Mere hearer-of-the-word converts cannot produce real doer-of-the-word disciples. Jesus taught us to reproduce true disciples trained to go the distance by walking side-by-side with the unlovable amid the unlivable to produce the impossible. God does not send court jesters to train knights (John 15:16). He creates and commissions real warriors to reproduce more warriors who win wars for God's glory and the welfare of others! Bearing burden God's way is essential to being and making disciples. God's burden is built on brokenness and is only gained as the Lord of Glory pulverizes our personal preoccupations into morally modified and merciful meditations (Psalms 51:17; Mark 14:22-24; 15:22-39). Let me tell you a bit of my story...

My life represents a transition generation... My great grandfather emigrated from Germany to America as a 17 year old preacher in the 1880's to plant churches in both Oregon and Washington between the early 1890's and 1900's. Five of those works, or their extensions, still hold services today more than 110 years later. Due to emerging communication barriers occurring as his growing congregation's language transitioned from German to English...my great grandfather left ministry to enter agriculture as discouragement defeated his resolve. As a fourth generation fruit grower, the only son who could take over the farm, and the first in four generations drawn toward ministry...I received my own call to preach at age 15 while weeping at a church camp altar in eastern Washington in 1971. I went home glowing and told my buddies, who thought I had lost my marbles. I was hurt, rattled, and lacked the guts to withstand their ridicule. So, I grew my hair to my shoulders, jumped into party life with them, and never looked back...until I married and had kids of my own. On January 1, 1980, I made the only New Year's resolution I ever kept – to stop smoking pot, to get back in church, to pursue Jesus Christ, and to love my family God's way. My burden had shifted that day from myself to others... I never partied again, ever. I had been raised in church, but wandered away searching for the wrong things in all the wrong places. Following my decision however, my wife and I started attending church, made new friends, and watched life change...

In 1984, after having our third daughter, achieving financial stability, and reducing my work hours from over 100 down to 50 per week, God reached in and began inciting my pursuit of Him... Now, at age 28, at the helm of four commercial companies I built from the ground up in custom tree production, heavy equipment repair, controlled explosives, and technical consulting...my 4:30 AM's shifted from processing paperwork to reading the bible and time in prayer. Early one morning while journaling..."I asked God to break me and make me His." I had no clue what I set in motion that day. I was still growing fruit with my dad, running my companies, and regaining a sense of God's call on my life as rural farm life was being swallowed by agri-business in a meat grinder of a rising one-world government, marketplace, and economy. I had no interest in being devoured by expanded regulation, reduced margin, increased capitalization, and demoralized demands. I had a family to grow, a life to live, and a call to discharge in full view of a Loving yet Holy God. Pressure was everywhere... Yet, my sense of burden had shifted from worry to faith...from accomplishment to obedience...from possessions to people...and from temporal to eternal. Breaking free from one life to lay hold of another always comes at a price (Matthew 10:35-39; Mark 10:29-31).

I knew God was speaking to me in those early morning hours while journaling my prayers. What could I possibly say to my third generation farming father to help him grasp that God was calling me from plowing dirt and growing apples to producing fruit that lasts? One evening while out to dinner with my wife, she looked across the candle-lit table at me and said, "You've changed...things don't affect you the same anymore." I was encouraged... Without asking, God's transformation in my life had become visible to another. What I did not understand that evening and would only later learn, was that she was really telling me "You've changed and...I don't like it." Fueled by different perspective...I pressed in, dug deeper, and pursued God even more. Several months later, amid a squabble, I went out the back door of our home toward my diesel shop to work. While up to my elbows in an engine I had torn down, the Holy Spirit began to speak... I knew His voice; so I stepped away from the truck, washed my hands, and headed down to the house to pursue peace. When I got there, no one was home. So, I headed back for the shop thinking that my wife had simply gone to town for groceries based on prior conversation. A few hours later, the school bus went by and my little girl didn't get off. Again, I wrote it off in my mind as my wife having picked her up at school, as was common. Dinner time came...still no one... I drove to town by one route and returned another, thinking she may have had a flat tire. Please keep in mind that this all occurred before the onset of cell phones. Upon my return home, I sank into my easy chair growing more concerned, waited, and finally dozed off not waking up until early the next morning. I called her mom, whom had denied seeing her the day before, and was now told that my wife had taken the kids and gone. I did not know where she was or where she had taken my children...I had no way to reach them. In moments, I was reduced to rubble, broken before God....

Our church had been in an interim period between pastors. Several months before, God had spoken to me about tithing on our annual income and I spoke to my wife about it. Together, we decided to give and dropped the check in the offering plate the following Sunday. Later that afternoon, the Holy Spirit impressed on me that I was to have those funds we had just given, specifically designated to bring the new pastor to our church. I knew nothing about him... The only thing God told me was that this new pastor would become my best friend. Before knowing it was inappropriate to direct the tithe, I called the church administrator late that evening making my request at God's direction and was told it would be done. So, I forgot about it and woke early the next day to spend time with the Lord. Resuming my prior story line... Facing a dilemma with my wife and children gone, myself in shambles, and unable to protect my family...I needed someone to talk to. I called our church and asked when the new pastor was to arrive. The secretary told me he had pulled in that day and gave me his number. So, I called him late that night around 10 PM. The phone rang, connected, and an unfamiliar voice spoke from the other end. We introduced ourselves, I filled him in on what had happened, and he told me I was his first prayer request since his arrival. His nickname was Fletch... Over subsequent months, he became my dearest friend as we spent untold hours together talking, laughing, crying, and praying. Meanwhile...I withdrew from business temporarily...went to work for one of my largest clients...charted my course through Scriptural counseling...disassembled my world like a pile of blocks pushing the rejects aside...and re-stacked the ones left into a strong tower based on God's word.

Over subsequent months I devoured the bible day-and-night, having God draw me into a 40 day fast with revelation flowing like water. He reminded me of His call when I was 15, assured me of his forgiveness for the wandering path I had chosen, and filled my heart with fresh vision. Then, God compelled me toward baptism as I sat early one morning journaling my prayers. Though I had been dedicated as a child and baptized as a young boy at my parent's decision...I yielded to God's voice and called Fletch to see when it could be done. The following Sunday, I went beneath the waters of baptism as a skilled young man able to do anything I put my hand to with excellence and I emerged with a passion to preach burning in my bones. People around me said it would go away, but it only grew stronger each day. God's burden is birthed out of brokenness...not taught. A few early mornings later while journaling my prayers... God led me to thumb back through my past journals as if He had me looking for something. Suddenly, the words "...break me and make me yours" leapt off the page and crystallized before my eyes and, I wept. God had not only heard me that day-gone-by, but had answered my prayer. I fell to my knees in front of my chair that morning and promised my Lord that I would do what He told me to do, go where He told me to go, and love those He told me to love... at any cost. He heard and answered that prayer too...

Two years later, on the heels of resumed business, I prayed another dangerous prayer. I said Lord, "I want to obey, but don't know how to get out of business to do what you ask. Please help me." Two months later, over the course of a week's time, I heard the Holy Spirit say "You're going to lose everything in the winter." He said over-and-over throughout the week. I told several people I knew and then forgot about it... On December 12, 1989, winter temperatures plummeted from a preceding low of +17 degrees above to -38 degrees below zero in 30 hours. My nursery looked like a wildfire had blown through it... Without remedy, I went from international to almost homeless overnight as 280,000 fruit trees were severely damaged and business stopped in its tracks. A few months later, I began working with youth while navigating the aftermath. Over the next year, all was lost and yet another prayer had been answered... As I climbed out of the trenches through other winter-related battles, the Holy Spirit drew me into another 40 day fast. This time, He told me that I would preach all over America...

Youth and other ministry work continued over the next several years, until God brought me to another whirlwind in 1995 which involved my being the first in four generations to move out of state. Through a course of miracles, like being paid more than asking price on remaining equipment...selling a home to the first person who looked after raising the price $20,000 at the Lord's direction... and closing on the first house looked at...the move to Colorado Springs was made. Along the way, I reminded God that He would have to give me a double portion if He planned to use me for His glory... One day, while attending a well-known large church there...I responded to a message on the Holy Spirit, simply wanting all God has to give. With a couple hundred other people, I went to the altar when invited. The pastor went down the line praying and laying hands on each person one-by-one. When he came to me...he laid hands on me, prayed, and went down the line... Now several people away...he suddenly looked up, came back, and prayed for me again. I was the only one who got prayed for twice that day. Several months later, Reinhardt Bonnke spoke on the power of the Holy Spirit inviting everyone to come to the altar and be prayed for. Again, I jumped up and went to the altar with 300-400 others wanting all God has to give. The same scenario repeated itself. He went down the line laying hands on and praying over people one-by-one. He came to me...laid his hands on me, prayed, and went down the line. When a few people away…he suddenly looked up, came back, and prayed for me again. This was the second time in a matter of months I was the only one to be prayed for twice by two great men of God. My burden for people increased again. God was answering another prayer…

By now, I was starting to travel and speak as opportunities presented themselves. My next dangerous prayer was, "God show me your tears." The challenges came… My next prayer was, "God please show me your heart." And brokenness came… Now, ten years since that 40 day fast in which He had told me I would preach all over America…after moving back to Washington in 1998…the Holy Spirit led me back to Colorado to pray for a sick friend. As I walked into the world prayer chapel alone, a woman prophesying at the piano began speaking out of my journals, while I was 1,500 miles from home and had never met her. Three months later, Trans-American walk 2001-02 began, finished some 3,900 miles and 14 months later, and left me standing in ocean waters, alone… As I said earlier, breaking free from one life to lay hold of another always comes at a price (Matthew 10:35-39; Mark 10:29-31). There are even deeper seasons yet to be told of more dangerous prayers…50 day fasts…praying at America's east and west gates…getting delivered to Jerusalem's wailing wall miraculously…a seven year season learning of coming tribulation… and living out heaven's word picture revealing Christ's weeping heart to His wayward bride while walking across America for my second time, alone. For now, I will set my story aside and resume it again later in the book. As you can see thus far – God's burden is borne and forged through brokenness, not taught…

Until we yield to brokenness under God's Almighty hand in humility, He cannot transform us into His likeness as new creations through His Son (I Corinthians 5:17; 1 Peter 5:6). Until we are broken…until we are recreated…until we are wholly yielded to Jesus Christ… we cannot bear burden for God's glory. Until we bear burden for God's glory…we will never cry out through silent sacrifice and whole-hearted obedience to God on behalf of those dying around us (Matthew 27:12-14; John 5:17, 19). Until we cry out through selfless sacrifice and open obedience...we will never embody faith able to pray God's heart into existence through our lifestyle (Hebrews 11:1-2, 6; James 2:14-17). Until we pray God's heart into existence through our lifestyle...we will never live the impossible or experience the miraculous. Until we live the impossible and experience the miraculous...our lives will never truly declare God's marvelous deeds to our troubled world with power (Psalms 71:17, 78:4, 96:3, 145:6; Matthew 5:14-16; Revelations 15:3). Until our lives declare God's deeds through His supernatural display of manifest miracles that shock people's sin-mesmerized world from its slumber...our message is dead, proving we only possess a form of godliness without power, otherwise called religion (Romans 13:11-14; 2 Timothy 3:5). If our best efforts expose mere religion...we still lack real brokenness-based, burden-bearing relationship with Jesus Christ... Oh God...help us die so you that may live, love, and liberate others You love, through us...

Throughout the bible – we see the earth created, names changed, Isaac born, bushes burn, seas parted, armies routed, giants slain, kings anointed, idols removed, villains executed, prophets commissioned, lions silenced, walls rebuilt, visions interpreted, the Messiah born, fishermen called, religion exposed, eyes opened, lepers cleansed, prostitutes honored, demoniacs delivered, dead raised, betrayers hung, disciples restored, Pilate troubled, love exemplified, Pharisees transformed, angels dispatched, prisoners freed, wardens saved, Stephen stoned, churches disciplined, letters written, glory defined, forgiveness promised, prayer modeled, minds renewed, marriage structured, vessels purified, faith honored, brides prepared, and heaven entered when God's people did things, His way.

Through Scripture we see Jesus lifted up in Sinai's desert, confirmed by a Psalmist, foretold by tortured prophets, born of a virgin, brought up through humanity, opposed by the religious, handed over to the government, crucified by the chosen, entombed by the righteous, raised by God's power, and seated by the Father – ALL SO those created in His image, called by His purpose, filled by His Spirit, and empowered by His name can still do even greater things (Numbers

21:4-9; Psalms 16:9-11; Isaiah 61:1-3; Matthew 1:23, 12:14, 27:2; Luke 2:21-52, 11:53-54, 19:47-48, 23:50-51; John 3:14, 12:32, 14:12, 19:12-18, 38-39; Acts 2:22-24; Ephesians 1:18-21). How do I know this is true? Jesus remains the same yesterday, today, and forever (Hebrews 13:8). He is still doing what He always did to liberate those He always loves (John 17:26). God's stance on love has never changed...His payment for sin has never floundered...and His miraculous power has never ended (Mark 9:23; I Corinthians 13:8; Hebrews 7:26-28). And, all of it happened through ordinary everyday people who lived broken, burdened, transformed, commissioned, anointed, and dispatched lives anointed with God's heart, fueled by spending time with Jesus (Acts 4:13). Go figure... Got any spare time on your hands? Oh yeah, I forgot American idol's on... Why endure to eternal life, when you can have fleeting fantasy now, right?

During my high school years, I recall hanging out at my friend's house for inordinate amounts of time after school, wrestling matches, and other unmentionable activities... His home was built by his grandfather long ago during the Great Depression and had remained in the family over subsequent years. As typical with many projects planned by amateurs and slated for construction on a shoestring, there were a few things about my friend's home that left a bit to be desired, politely speaking. Reminiscent of one occasion, I will never forget that one of those less-than-desirable items in the house was a not-so-strategically located bathroom just to the side of main living space. Though usable, this indoor version of an outhouse was not down a hallway or even tucked around a corner out of sight. Instead, it was just on the other side of a wafer-thin door which had been erroneously stationed in the living room's side wall. As a momentary aside, I think most of us have realized that people grow far less aware or concerned with the natural details of everyday life the older they get. And yet, to the young, suave, and still self-perceived debonair...some things deemed "private" are simply not acceptable for public display within the confines of human dignity and reputation. On one particular evening...while at my friend's house having blast in a packed room full of people...one of those less-than-desirable events occurred...

Now, please try to imagine the evening's setting through the eyes of my friend. His living room was filled to over-flowing with people of all ages including his grandpa and grandma, mom and dad, siblings, and our much-coveted crowd of buddies and babes from school... Conversation's crescendo was gaining momentum...TV had just been shut off...the last song on the 8-Track tape was done... and white noise had been over-shadowed by activity's voice. As mid evening landed and without warning...grandpa grumbled to his feet, made his way across the room flopping once-shouldered suspenders to his side, and disappeared inconspicuously inside the previously described poorly-placed restroom's door as no one looked on. Laughter...spirited interchanges...flying loveseat pillows...with Billy Bob's soda on the hearth being blown off its feet by incoming cushions...and time froze as foolhardiness hit the floor. Without warning from a parallel dimension amid the silence...an unknown, unwelcome, and unmentionable beyond-white-noise sound pierced the air from behind the bathroom's door soon followed by a sigh of relief from within... Chaos erupted as one friend groaned, another laughed, three rose to leave, parents launched a new subject, and my friend's cheeks hit their flashpoint. Like machine gun fire, his entire social future flashed before his eyes with visions of himself being publically scorned in stocks at the city square, paraded across the high school football field at half time in a dunce hat, and wandering aimlessly through life's streets as an old man zipped in a canary yellow jump suit with the word "loser" across his back. Already convinced that his life was over, the plot thickened...

Suddenly, the toilet flushed...the bathroom doorknob turned...and out strolled grandpa patting his beyond-boundary belly with one hand and clutching his newly discolored newspaper in the other. He looked around appearing as though he had just been liberated from prison and was ready to live once again as he waved, sauntered off through the kitchen, and made his way down the hall... A noxious cloud of oppression hung heavily over the room as those who remained had nothing to say. One-by-one, people filtered out into the night as my friend sat alone shell-shocked by the bomb which had just been dropped on his fleeting reputation. Looking at the floor while wringing his hands, he declared himself hopelessly undone. All he could imagine was the persecution most certain to come as he passed the school halls come Monday. Then, walking innocently into the room on her rounds to turn out the last lights, his mom spotted him sitting in self-imposed ashes of reputation's ruin as he said, "Grandpa just flushed my world."

While in this life...things will happen, difficulties will rise, and troubles will come (John 16:33). How we perceive them, respond to their impact, and exercise our choice to overcome determines the lasting mark they will leave upon us. Our adversary always comes against us with offense, rejection, fear, and anger to rattle our peace and disturb our sense of acceptance in front of the world. Even though burden can be imposed and persecution can wield its sword, solid personal identity and character rooted in Jesus cannot be crushed... As I look around in life, one of the most troubling faces of burden comes within the atrocities of what is known as persecution. It's stories plague our television screens as we witness genocides, fill global political arenas as tyrants manipulate their masses, plays out on our streets as gangs assault the powerless, cries out as selfish revolutionaries impose idealisms which demoralize freedom, and invades our homes as mates and children grapple for power in an upside down world. Persecution is simply not as narrow as being punished or martyred for one's religious faith as many believe. Instead, persecution includes any and all forms of oppression where destructive power or domination is imposed by one person, group, or force upon another with intent to control or destroy...

Though persecution has existed since the onset of human history as those determined to define the world and reality on their terms extract their toll at the expense of others, persecution's burden upon those who are indeed persecuted has incited uprisings which finally stop, turn, stand, and fight tyranny's injustice. Power's persecution of those considered powerless has provided the very spark which has ignited wildfires of human uprising and is responsible for some of mankind's greatest physical, intellectual, and spiritual advancements ever chronicled. Because of persecution's weight, nations have risen to ward off their oppressors, patriots have risked their lives to gain freedom, and spiritual warriors have forfeited their lives to champion their King's cause. The dilemma we face when persecuted however, is whether or not our view of injustice and our chosen response is rooted in reality and truth, or a lie. Persecution comes in many forms which emanate from different realms whether physical or spiritual. In the physical realm, persecution comes through people who are wrongly emboldened with pride and power's preoccupation with controlling others. Yet, persecution begins in the dark spiritual realm with an ugly intent perpetrated by the enemy of our souls to dispatch evil forces whose mission is to manipulate power-addicted people among men who are willing to oppress peers for personal gain. Persecution is rooted in evil, rises from rebellion, and opposes the heart and love of God as hell makes its bid to destroy those created in His image.

Greg training war-torn men in Eastern Afghanistan – 2006

It was persecution's burden that scattered New Testament believers throughout the world to advance the gospel and expand God's kingdom. It was persecution that inspired those in the free world to assume the burden and champion the cause of oppressed people who could not defend themselves. And it will be persecution's burden that will cause a one-world system to search out, identify, and confront last day believers in Jesus Christ with a choice to either take the mark of darkness or suffer the price to stand in their faith to the end (Matthew 24:4-13). Though unfortunate, it is none-the-less true, that most people in life simply refuse to make their choice between life and death until heartache and persecution comes. Sadly, many sell out to a lie to secure temporary personal relief from difficulty at the expense of those they claim to love, while making eternal decisions that will destroy their own souls. So, you see, burden comes in all shapes and sizes. It's simply a question as to how we will respond to that burden or suffering when it comes...

Standing in line at a local Starbucks waiting for my turn to order morning Joe...I ventured an off-the-cuff comment to a man sporting on an Iraqi fire department emblem on his shirt as he stood in line ahead of me. I asked, "Were you in Iraq?" He replied as he turned to pay for his drink saying, "Yeah, I was there for eighteen months when we took Felucia" He stepped away to await his drink at the other counter as I ordered and paid for my own cup of mud before rejoining him. As we both stood waiting for our coffee, he distractedly punched out a text message to a recipient unknown to me. As I casually looked on, he finally looked up to meet my gaze and cracked a half-hearted grin. The barista slid his coffee to the counter's edge followed almost immediately by mine and we headed for the sugar and crème bar before finding our seats. He walked to a table, pulled out his chair, and put his coffee down. I walked by and turned asking if he had time to chat. He took a sip of coffee, winced at his torched lip, and motioned me toward an empty chair on the opposing side of the table through coffee-induced still-watering eyes. We both sat...trundled through the small talk...and introduced ourselves. I said, "Hi, my name's Greg... what's yours?" He replied, "Joe" as he warily-eyed his steaming cup with well-founded suspicion trying to decide if he should risk another swig. I asked him how long he'd been in the military and he said, "I've been in for 17 years and will be out in another 3 weeks if they don't mess up my paperwork again." We both relaxed and leaned back in our chairs as I stretched out my legs and he pushed his hat back on his head. As I probed a little deeper into his Middle-eastern excursions...Joe's countenance fell as he soberly glanced beyond as if trying to fix his focus on a re-run reality...

Over the next hour...we dug deeper into the desert sands of Joe's past as he lobbed one-word grenades of agony that pierced my soul. His mental movie became palpable as he transported us back into enemy crossfire, driving convoys deep into hostile territory, feeding hungry children unknowingly recruited to slap C-4 under US hummers, trying to identify herdsmen from could-be-terrorists, and the explosive force of IED's leaving fragmented friends grounded, bleeding, and dismembered, languishing toward death's elusively open grave as he watched on, powerless...in tears. There are many disclosed details I will not share...but suffice it to say that Joe's military path had carried him through other disturbing combat theatres during his career. By now in the conversation, I had been drawn to the edge of my spectator's seat as Joe's tear-filled eyes glanced to the ground... Silence settled, thoughts raced, and composure clamored to climb out of Joe's foxhole we had both jumped in. I was moved, Joe was stirred, and all I had to offer him was genuine interest, a listening ear, a different vantage point, open-hearted time, and God's love... After a moment, Joe stood to say, "Let me grab another cup of coffee and we can talk some more. I've enjoyed the conversation. But, we'll have to go outside to sit cause' I need a cigarette."

He flicked a match, took a puff, and charted our course deeper into enemy territory at an umbrella-donned outdoor table bombarded by the crossfire of passing pedestrians and traffic's trajectory. We took our seats, leaned back, and Joe hit the play button again, picking up where he left off without skipping a beat... He said, "...watching friends die all around me...good men, family men, honorable men...hardened my heart and filled me with hate. How could God let such good friends die? Where is His mercy? I went from caring about life to putting enemy soldiers in my crosshairs and deciding which one of them went home or dropped in the desert that day. I stopped sorting between those trying to feed families and terrorist threats...I didn't care...I pulled the trigger. What had previously been a moral determination between the life and death of another...had degraded to a one-sided autonomic decision already made. On the battlefield, we decided between life and death...who needed God? Later, while home on furlough, my mom encouraged me to pray and ask God for help. I told her there is no God, there is no mercy, and on the battlefield...I'm God." Finally, the Holy Spirit began to speak as I said, "Joe, God loves you. He cares, and you are receiving mercy right now as He reaches to heal your heart. I know it seems like there is no God amid the hell and suffering you've seen, but God is and always will be. When you get a chance, read Isaiah 57:1 and you'll find why a loving God lets bad things happen to good people." At that moment, Joe said "I've read that verse before...interesting you would bring it up." He then told me he'd been in therapy for a couple years and that progress had been slow at best. I gently told him that therapy may help think about things over-and-over, but only God can heal the hell and make one whole again.

I went on saying, "Though you feel God has no mercy...those people at home on US soil...Iraqi men, women, children, and families who have new chances to live...those you did not shoot...all received mercy because you were there. I know it's hard to see God's mercy when He has chosen you as the hammer in His hand to win freedom and extend mercy to others while you wade through the blood of friends. Yet without you, God's mercy to those people your presence has preserved may have likely left them dead, discarded by empty idealisms. Your presence there declared God's existence and extended His mercy to a dying people and to others back home, clueless as to what it means to buy freedom with blood. Yes, you made decisions for wrong reasons, but based in pain. Yet, there is One who knows the burden and brokenness you feel because He too spilled His blood to free wounded and wandering wayfarers at the cost of His own life on a cross long ago..." Through tear-filled eyes and trembling words, Joe said, "Thank you, no one has ever helped me see myself that way." He sat more erect, life filled his chest, and his eyes brightened as value's purpose flooded his soul. Then Joe said, "My dad was stern, but fair... We boys always knew he loved us as he worked hard and sacrificed for his family. He's a good man!" And then Joe said, "I was called to preach when I was

15 and read my bible day-and-night for many years. After I joined the service and saw people dying in combat...I slowly hardened and withdrew finally not reading at all. My mom tells me she is praying for me and encourages me to read each time I come home. Until now, I couldn't see the point."

As the Holy Spirit rose within me...I told Joe, "It's an urgent hour! The time is short and God is raising His army to fight for those dear to His heart. He is raising warriors whose hands have been trained for battle, to win. Though your journey until now left you weary and war-torn, filled with hatred, believing there was no God or mercy... you understand war, what it costs, and how to fight. God needs warriors, not wimps. If you will lay down hatred, acknowledge God, and yield to His plan for your life...He will heal and restore you with His unconditional love, forgiveness, and mercy will flood your soul. You see Joe, I believe God allowed you go where you went and experience what you did to grant you the privilege of feeling the pain of others, so you could lead them toward mercy in Jesus' name. Rights are demanded and privileges are earned. Rights feed self, while privilege is selflessly rooted in opportunity and responsibility, inseparably married. First, you must experience the transformation within and own it yourself before you can lead others there. God's people need you to rise into your destiny and to lead His warriors toward victory as the world around us comes unglued. You are a man of war, now positioned to surrender your inner fight to God so He can use your transformed heart and life to take His fight to the enemy. Are you willing?" He replied, "I would do it all again to fight for people's freedom." In response I said, "Even if you or I were the only ones....so would our King."

Now three hours in, moving to my RV, and sitting back with a glass of water in-hand...the Lord compelled me to share a bit of my own life story filled with agony...common passion...and seasoned willingness to defend others at any cost. As we prayed together I looked deep into Joe's eyes and said, "You're a warrior...God is re-calling you, war is at hand, and the choice is yours. Will you re-enlist in His army?" He looked back at me in silence as his wheels turned within... Joe now knew that God exists, loves him, grants mercy, and has called Him back to Himself. Likewise, Joe now understood the purpose of bearing burden God's way, because he carries it for others. And, Joe certainly knows the cost of brokenness, because he survives its savagery. Bearing burden built on brokenness bathed in blood on behalf of others, buys freedom. Jesus paid it on Calvary's cross compelling us to carry our own each day... As Joe stepped out my door onto the sun-baked asphalt in the church lot where I was parked, he grinned and said "I never go to Starbucks man, but today I just felt like I needed coffee and met you..." With tears dried, smile back, and leaving his indelible mark on my life...Joe left a different man that day, armed to change the world God's way...

If I had never navigated life's battlefields, invited brokenness, said yes to burden, and landed in hell's desert reaching to souls...I would not have owned God's grit, given God's compassion, shared God's time, conveyed God's interest, and acted as God's friend to Joe that day. As one called forth in heaven's battle – there is a price to be paid, it will be extracted, and victory will prevail if we love one another. If I had remained in life's barracks, bantered over theology, worried about money, and deserted the downtrodden... my decision would have stirred God's heartache, caused angels' silence, robbed heaven's warriors, and plundered humanity's hope to whatever degree Joe's impact was diminished. That dear friend would be treason on high...

Seven year old boy in Jalalabad, Eastern Afghanistan

Along the Jalalabad Road Eastern Afghanistan – 2006

Chapter 4
Whales to Whirlwinds

"As they were walking along and talking together, suddenly a chariot of fire and horses of fire appeared and separated the two of them, and Elijah went up to heaven in a whirlwind" (2 Kings 2:11).

Have you ever been suddenly engulfed by a set of circumstances or carried away by a chain of events you could do nothing to stop? Life has a way of swallowing us whole or drawing us into whirlwinds... some days both. Without a doubt, most of us can easily recall those days which disintegrated from bad-to-worse the moment our eyelids peeled back in the morning until we later collapsed in bed that night. Other days, however, momentum grew out of nowhere as seemingly unrelated situations joined by our corresponding decisions to chart an unstoppable course into the unimaginable. In both cases, whether bad or good...we found ourselves wholly unable to stem the tide of ensuing outcome.

Whales

Situations that swallow us whole typically represent life challenges into which God allows us to be drawn in order to confront waywardness and re-direct our path, if we're willing. For example... we saw Aaron's staff become a snake and swallow those produced by a hard-hearted Pharaoh's magicians, the earth open up to swallow Korah, Dathan, Abiram, and other leaders for insolence and rebellion against Moses, and a whale swallow Jonah for disobedience as God got the attention of each and re-directed their paths to reflect His will...not theirs (Exodus 7:8-13; Numbers 16:28-33). Jonah's roundabout story reveals my point...

The word of the Lord came to Jonah telling him to go to Nineveh and preach against it because of its wickedness. But, Jonah hopped a ship in another direction, running from God because he was irritated at the Lord's likely extension of compassion toward the ungodly. After setting rebellion's sail, a storm with violent winds rose and the sea raged, threatening to dismember the ship board-by-board. As the crew's fear mounted, they chucked cargo over the side not knowing that Jonah slept below deck without concern amid the storm. Suddenly, the ship's captain found Jonah crashed out in the hold and rousted him to call on his god. Beside themselves with fear, the crew cast lots trying to discover who had caused the tempest. Finally, Jonah stepped up to tell them for a second time that he was running from God, instructing the crew to throw him overboard to calm the seas... Afraid of bearing the guilt for killing an innocent man, however, the crew by-passed Jonah's directive and rowed toward shore. It was futile... Out of options, the oarsmen cried out to their gods while throwing Jonah overboard and the raging seas became calm. In response, God sent a whale to swallow Jonah whole and carry him into the depths... Over the next three days; Jonah looked within himself, cried out to God in his distress, turned his heart from rebellion, and promised to obediently fulfill his vows to the Lord. Without delay, God sent him to the surface and spewed him out on the shore in a pile of who knows what. Can you imagine what Jonah looked like after three days in the deep?... bleached white by stomach acid, face unshaven, plankton between his toes, salt-soaked toga, slimed-out-hair, seaweed around his head, and smelling like whale breath... Ever been there?

Then, the word of the Lord came to Jonah a second time: "Go to the great city of Nineveh and proclaim to it the message I give you" (Jonah 3:1-2). Jonah listened to the Lord, obeyed what he was told, and went without delay or question. Just as Jonah knew God's message through him would produce, however...Nineveh turned from evil and repented with sackcloth and ashes from the King down to the last animal and received God's mercy. Jonah was outraged and told God that he fled the first time because he knew He would have compassion if Nineveh turned from their sin. Enraged by injustice, Jonah wanted to die more than share God's heart with others. At that moment, the Lord asked his struggling prophet if he really had the right to be mad just before drawing him into one of those divine word pictures using Jonah's concern over a common vine that sprang up one day only to die the next. In light of Jonah's concern for the vine, God asked him if He should not care more for Nineveh's 120,000 people than for a fleeting vine. What a contrast... On one side we see God's messenger run in pride's rebellion to block God's compassion to the lost...while on the other side, we see an entire wayward and godless city cease their rebellion with humility, thereby receiving God's mercy (Jonah 1:1-4:11). It seems rather obvious here that our chosen view, attitude, posture, and love toward God and others impacts our course and future. God grants us choice in almost all situations we find ourselves in each day as we chase our desires...or fulfill His purpose (Exodus 7:3; Joshua 11:20; Romans 9:16-18; John 12:37-43). The above account of God's call, human response, divine re-direction, and man's ultimate submission – suggests that our expression of free will operates in cooperation with God's redemptive plan. If we look carefully and conclude honestly...we see snapshots of God's sovereign reach into individual lives based on his purpose as displayed through the stories of others who've gone before us...

God's Sovereign Purpose

As I've stated throughout this writing – my intention is not to interpret Scripture or indoctrinate people's minds. Instead, I merely hope to call you beyond traditionally-taught and intellectually-held doctrines to discover God's true heart on issues that have divided the body of Christ for centuries. If we're to hope that we possess capacity to achieve the God-sized task of helping heaven's wayward bride of Christ (Church) rise from sin to a position of holy radiance necessary for her to gain entrance to the wedding feast of the Lamb, we must know and labor God's way (Romans 12:1-2; Ephesians 5:25-27; Revelation 19:7-10). Though some driven by other persuasions will take issue with my approach, I am at peace knowing that the Holy Spirit compels me to challenge unproductive dogma in exchange for helping God's people enter heaven's classroom to be taught by the Counselor...not men (John 6:44-45, 14:26, 16:8, 13-14). Though many have been taught that God does not violate man's expression of free will, the bible shows otherwise. God is sovereign and answers to no man as He asserts His all-knowing, ever-present, and eternally-existent character as...I AM! God is God and does as He chooses because His ways are above our ways and His thoughts are above our thoughts (Isaiah 55:8-9). If we are so arrogant as to assume that mortal clay can reduce an incomprehensible God to the confines of futile human understanding...we are perilously adrift, to put it mildly. Therefore, in light of Scripture, I submit to you that God's level of intervening direction in our lives remains eternally focused on His glory, His love, His purpose, man's redemption, and His unfolding plan...not ours.

Both Old and New Testaments clearly communicate that God created us in His image, foreknew us before physical birth in creation, fearfully and wonderfully made us, wove us together in our mother's womb, marked out our days before any of them came to be, called us according to His purpose, predestined us to conform to Christ's likeness, and subsequently justified and glorified us through His Son alone – not religious form (Genesis 1:26-27; Psalms 139:13-16; Romans 8:28-39). This distinction is critical because it wrenches control from religion's grip and restores our right view of God's sovereignty, dominion, and role as He lovingly redirects our lives formerly bound by futile intellectual theology. Likewise, this distinction is critical to an individual believer's freedom to hear and obey God consistent with the bible and without the judgment, interference, and the perversion of those around them who are addicted to legalistic, head-based control.

Now; with regard to God's sovereignty, foreknowledge, predestination, and situational intervention in our expression of free will...let's consider a few Old and New Testament examples in conjunction with the words of Jesus Himself. First, we see that God hardened the heart of Egypt's Pharaoh multiple times according to divine purpose...the Pharaoh was powerless to resist (Exodus 9:15-21). Next, we see God destroy Israel's enemies by turning them against each other as God's people looked on, did nothing, and won

(2 Chronicles 20:22-24). Likewise, we find God dispatching Isaiah to speak spiritual blindness, dullness, and confusion over Israel for a season to promote His purpose (Isaiah 6:9-10). Excluded by a crowd, four men lowered a paralytic through a roof to the floor below where Jesus forgave the man's sins and made him walk based on the faith of those who brought him (Mark 2:1-12). Next, we see Jesus deliver a violent demoniac from Gerasenes whose binding spirits begged the Lord not to torture them, but send them into a heard of pigs. It was only after Jesus delivered this man that he spoke and acted on his own behalf with a restored mind (Mark 5:1-20). In another scene, we watch Jesus deliver a demon-possessed boy brought to Him by a troubled father struggling in his faith (Mark 9:14-29). Jesus brings His triune perspective to bear on man's fallen definition of free will in response to His disciple's asking who had sinned, regarding a man before them who had been born blind. Jesus clearly stated that the man's infirmity was not the result of sin, but an opportunity for God's power to be displayed through healing the man. To drive his sovereign point home, Jesus made holy mud and restored the man's sight without even being asked (John 9:1-12).

And to prove God's intervention in human free will did not stop after Jesus' death, burial, resurrection, and ascension back to the right hand of His Father...take a look at Saul's conversion. On the heels of breathing out murderous threats against the Lord's disciples, Saul left for Damascus to persecute and imprison those who were part of the Way. During his journey there however, the risen Christ confronted Saul, blinded him with light, and laid him out in the dirt...temporarily blind. Then, Jesus instructed Saul to go have Ananias lay hands on him, to pray for him, and that he would be told what to do. Meanwhile, Jesus told Ananias that Saul was His "chosen instrument" who would suffer much for His name in his mission to the Gentiles. Here we see God's direct intervention, imposed confrontation, sovereign selection, prophetic instruction, and supernatural transformation...all without Saul's desire, request, or decision (Acts 9:1-19). As clearly shown...all of these life travelers were foreknown by God, created in His image, specifically designed, born at strategic junctures, thrust onto history's stage, healed or converted at God's discretion, and subsequently dispatched to testify to Christ and display God's glory. Free will had nothing to do with any of these. All of them were either healed, delivered, converted, or dispatched based on someone else's faith, at another's discretion without asking, amid complaining, while possessed, or in the act of opposing God – none of them exercised free will. And yet, God had his way. But PLEASE HEAR THIS... despite God's sovereign invasion of our lives to accomplish His purpose...we all remain called, commissioned, and accountable to live and administrate God's character and love toward others based on Christ's example, biblical truth, and the drawing and teaching power of the Holy Spirit.

Why did I take the above side trip from this chapter's main subject matter? Answer: because it is important that all of us consider and embrace God's sovereign imposition of responsibility in our individual lives when chosen by Him to do His bidding (Proverbs 19:21; John 15:16-17; Romans 8:33-35; Ephesians 1:11; 1 Peter 1:1-2; Revelations 17:14). As the Lord raises His last day army... many warriors-to-be have been caught and cut down in religion's crossfire, dying prematurely on life's battlefield. Their demise occurs because an incomplete message is being preached by intellectual expositors lacking revelation of God's word and without enlightened compassion for His "called out" people. Though I will suffer for writing this book challenging lifeless religious paradigms...I know what God has revealed to me and called me to do. I will give an account to Him on that day, not to men (Ezekiel 33:1-9).

Please understand...all are called, but few are chosen (Matthew 22:1-14; John 13:18). There are two kinds of being chosen: (1) As one of God's everyday people who live in relationship with Jesus Christ based on His terms, and (2) As one called to accomplish specific God-ordained tasks that incite, propel, and display God's perfect will upon the earth as He determines (John 14:12; Romans 12:3-

8; Corinthians 12:11; Ephesians 4:11-13). Being called to specific tasks does not make any of us superior, more spiritual, or special... Being called to strategic tasks simply calls one to a different type and level of obedience relative to that person's created purpose in God's plan. Obedience is obedience whether praying for a lost neighbor across the street or converting a king halfway around the world. We all have liberty to exercise our free will in life subject to God's foreknowledge that we belong Him...that He already knows what we will choose because He's all-knowing...that He inserted our lives at strategic points in time based on His foreknowledge of our related impact on others...and in light of His sovereign intervention because He's God...we're not. We are the created, not the Creator. Theologians may bark and bite...but God still reigns over all the earth and those upon it. Just as God's plan will not be thwarted by our expression of free will, He will not impose Himself upon us "unless" it declares His glory and does us good (Job 42:1-6). If we truly trust Him to love us unconditionally because He knows what is best for us...we will not fret about His compassionate invasion of our lives. Though Jesus calls us all to work as cooperative members of one body, motivated by His unconditional love and forgiveness based on Truth in submission, one to another, out of reverence for Him...we ultimately answer to our Savior for our administration of His work, not to man (John 14:12; John 17:4-5, Hebrews 7:26-28). In light of Jonah's prior story and now being better equipped to recognize God's sovereign direction in our individual lives through His eyes – let's get back to whales and whirlwinds...

A night-and-day contrast differentiates between those life scenarios that either swallow us (whales) in devouring circumstances or catch us up in miraculous events (whirlwinds)... This night-and-day contrast exists within the compelling motivation and resulting chain of events associated with two diametrically opposed pathways portrayed by whales and whirlwinds. These contrasts find their voices between deception and truth, pride and humility, rebellion and obedience, hate and love, selfishness and selflessness, our way...or God's. Being swallowed whole by devouring circumstances is ultimately escapable through our willing embrace of love, humility, and obedience (Deuteronomy 28:1-13; Psalms 97:10-12; John 14:23; 1 Peter 5:6). Relative to God's purpose and plan, being caught up in heaven's whirlwinds in response to humility, obedience, and being centered in His perfect will – is unstoppable. Whirlwinds are God's perfect storms...

Whirlwinds
Just as God lets life's whales swallow us whole to re-direct our waywardness...He engulfs our yielded lives in heaven's whirlwinds to give credence to His character and display His glory through us (2 Kings 2:9-12; John 9:1-4, 17:4, 10; Acts 1:1-9). His character can only be forged within us as we lay our lives down for others as our act of worship toward Him (Mark 12:3-31; Romans 12:1; 1 Corinthians 13:7-8; Luke 23:34; John 14:15, 15:13-17; 1 John 3:16-24; 2 John 1:6)...in humility (Matthew 27:12-14; 1 Peter 5:16; James 4:6-10)...in obedience (1 Samuel 15:22; John 14:12, 15:10-11, 17:4; Luke 14:36; Hebrews 5:8-9; 1 Peter 1:1-2)...and, in faith (2 Kings 19:14-37; 2 Chronicles 20:1-30; Romans 4:17; Hebrews 11:1-6). As we give our lives in obedience to pursue Him with whole hearts... He redeems us, delivers us, and releases us to complete His work granting us victory over darkness that earlier whale-bellies equipped us to fight (Psalms 34:17-22, John 6:13, 17:4-19). This reality finds basis through Enoch, who walked with and pleased God and "was no more" (Genesis 5:21-24)...Elijah, who was caught up in heaven's whirlwind after doing all God called Him to accomplish (2 Kings 2:1, 11-12)...The Counselor Who arrived on the scene to an upper room in a violent wind (Acts 2:1-3)...and John the revelator who was moved on the wind of God's Spirit to pre-record His-story in advance (John 3:8; Revelations 1:9-19). Just as God uses whales to wash away willfulness...He uses whirlwinds to verify His presence, display His power, and love His people as they carry out the work He gave them to do...

Being caught up in one of God's whirlwinds does not just magically happen... Being wholly engulfed is in keeping with God's purpose and our individual calling, decision, obedience, faith, and His divine timing. Being caught up in God's whirlwind follows an established pattern of encountering, yielding, integrating, discharging, and completing the work God gave us for His glory (John 17:4-19). First, we must encounter God and His plan face-to-face at its ordained inception (season of change – point of decision). Second; we must yield to God and His plan whole-heartedly when faced with unknown (expression of faith – foundation of action). Third, we must integrate with God's plan according to His purpose amid growing momentum (state of immersion – awareness of God's timing). Fourth, we must discharge God's detail diligently even when we do not understand (path of humility – power of agreement). And fifth, we must do our best to complete God's work His way with His heart to bear His fruit for His glory (evidence of Lordship – quality of fruit). Obviously, we all fall short, especially me, in our attempts to hear and obey God while bombarded by life...

Regardless of whom we are or how long we have been chasing God, we all simply miss it sometimes. It is the unsolvable reality connected to being human, despite what theologians say... And yet, that does not give us license to presume upon God's forgiving grace. Jesus only requires our best with His help, realizing that no one is perfect – no not one. He is far more concerned with our heart motives than our whiz-bang execution and stellar performance. Typically, most "doers" find it far easier to extend grace to others who have blown it than to themselves. Realize however...there is a fine line, dear friend...but huge difference...between extending grace to ourselves...and...wrongly excusing our complacent or willful negligence at another's expense. In light of our human process of trying to cooperate with God...whirlwinds are like hurricanes which start small, escalate, and then take us by storm! Once they are upon us, there is nowhere to run! Where being swallowed by whales takes us deeper with time...God's whirlwinds carry us through vision to a reality beyond the impossible to experience heaven's miraculous. Be warned however...the vision-to-whale-to-whirlwind process is an ever-intensifying cycle that repeats itself throughout our lives, taking us deeper, further, and higher in Christ as we pursue the Father with whole hearts for His glory alone (Jeremiah 29:13). If you will permit me, I would like to make this more personal...

I was raised on a farm in a Christian home by a mom and dad who love God and each other. As a small boy; I was inquisitive, persistent, and full of imagination as my curiosities repeatedly disassembled my tricycle to see how it worked at ages 3 through 5. My growing inquisitions tore old clocks which were gleaned from grandma's gaggle of old girls, apart leaving their misplaced gears for mom's feet to discover in the darkness of night at ages 6 to 8. I swiped grandma's silver dollars, broke with guilt, and ran to her soaked with tears at age 9...deciphered compound mechanical advantage for my dad's machinery using my closet rod, a pencil, and string at age 10. Then, I joined cub scouts, climbed Mount Clemens, rode my first motorcycle, flew in a helicopter, and saw my first Playboy Magazine by age 11 as I shot slingshots, BB guns, and flipped green apples off a stick at my buddies through dad's orchard at ages 12 and 13. As I grew, I went to youth group, spent time at camp, rebuilt a dirt bike engine on my bedroom carpet when mom wasn't looking, and kissed my first girl at age 14.... The next year, God called me to preach while kneeling at a church camp altar next to a pro quarterback-to-be in Washington's evergreen forests at age 15. When I came home and told my friends what God said...I got hammered by rejection, grew out my hair, and began smoking pot at age 16 before being swallowed whole by life's converging whale through my descending decisions... It took seven years for me to surface in the sea of God's grace... Though God does not cause sin... He allows it and uses its trauma, lessons, and transformation to forge His character in those called according to His purpose. My personal journey has navigated a labyrinth of ancestry, youth, surroundings, decisions, and discovery on God's divine course through life detours essential to God's message finding voice through my life. Caught in the crossfire between destiny and desire, I looked beyond God's purpose to create Him in my image to my own peril, rather than conform myself to His likeness (Romans 8:29-30). As is true with everyone, we can only do our best to ask God questions, listen for His answers, and do what He calls us to do with His help...the rest is up to Him. Our purpose and pathway are unique by God's design and inseparably-linked to His plan, which is anchored to His glory as a lifeboat to others...

Though we often do not share the same vantage point or travel the same course as another...God draws, teaches, and dispatches each of us differently as He carries us upon His Spirit to test, approve, and do His will in sync with His reaching return (John 3:8; Romans 12:1-2). It is not our job or right to judge one another's pursuit of God (Luke 6:37-38; Romans 14:4). We may observe things in another person we do not understand or agree with... Yet, we must remember that judging fruit in another is not possible, until that life has been lived. Though mortals see through eyes dimly... only God knows the heart face-to-face (Psalms 44:21, 139:23-24; Proverbs 17:3, 21:1-2, 24:12, Jeremiah 17:9; 1 Corinthians 13:12). Meanwhile, Jesus commands us to extend love, grant forgiveness, and pursue complete unity for the sake of those He has given to us as He continues to do (Matthew 6:14-15; Mark 12:30-31; John 14:12, 17:6-19, 23). Though we are individually unique and called to tasks of different magnitudes, we hold equal value in God's eyes. Since we do not fully grasp the heart intent or nature of God's call on someone else...we must honor and help each other in love (Romans 12:3-8). Our personal view, internal attitude, chosen posture, and love for God and His people defines our course. Amid your battles...please know that you are not alone and that your life matters because God created you in His image to rise victorious in a time such as this (Esther 4:14).

Greg looking the world in the eye – 1957

The following narrative from my story resumes in 2003 after walking 3,900 miles, while being broken within, during a 50 day fast, and just before hearing God say He was hemming me into a seven year season to learn of coming tribulation before sending me to preach it... He never teaches me from a textbook. Instead, He pulls me through living word pictures I'll never forget. Please understand, telling my story makes me vulnerable to scrutiny that is rarely loving or kind... Though judgments are many, few are willing to put on my boots... God wrote my story line, not me. I'm just doing my best to live it with His heart to encourage those of you rising to heaven's destiny during this urgent hour when few grasp the intensity of your unorthodox inner world which God designed with purpose. I pray that my experiences will help illustrate patterns and life settings within which God's whirlwinds seem to emerge, while also revealing the level of detail He discloses to lead us in our quest...the escalation of heaven's momentum...that prophetic action precedes manifestation...and a glimpse of what it extracts from His agents-of-change who play by His rules (2 Timothy 2:5). Please be aware dear friend, chasing God with a whole heart, knowing the season of His return, and embracing His perfect will is a contact sport – not a time to go AWOL.

Resuming my prior story line from "Burdens and Brokenness"...

Just eleven months after drying my sea-drenched cross-continental boots which had been soaked in sovereign surf while surrounded by beachgoers unaware...God's seventh wave of revelation education washed over my life's jetty. Wind warnings had been issued, hatches had been battened, and personal evacuation had been considered as brutal blasts hit my world at gale force... Squalls of disillusion, isolation, and brokenness flooded my soul with agonies untold as God's guiding hand delivered me from deep waters onto distant deserts up to my neck in Son-parched sands. Reaching deep into my storm chest, I pulled out a 50 caliber fast, Living Armor, and laid siege to all assaulting me as I clothed myself with Christ (Galatians 3:26-27). In a twinkling of an eye, heaven's hurricane sucked me out of life's drifting dory and cast me into hand-to-hand combat with survival itself... Surrounding sands shifted from breaker-beaten to fire-fueled... Still awash in the aftermath of a continent's traverse, my battle transmuted into one-on-one war with the enemy of my soul. Day after day...I rose early to feed on God's word while pillaged by sleepless nights, untold tears, and dreams upon my bed (Daniel 7:1). Revelation flowed like water and descended like dust. I prayed...wept...and warred as I touched heaven to change earth... My phone rang all hours of the day and night as brothers and sisters in Christ yielded confirmations from afar. God's hand was at my heart's canvas as He spoke to my spirit and portrayed His plan. Everything in and around my life stopped... I was on God's clock and marching to a different drum. Days wore on, pounds fell off, and journals took form as flesh gave way to spirit and lies tumbled to truth. I had entered God's grid and there was no way out without completion...

To help you better understand the onset of what I call a whirlwind... please consider the following highlights from 82 pages of detailed journal related to my 2003 fast. For the sake of already-lost brevity, much detail has been left out. God was indeed catching me up in one of His whirlwinds...

NOTE: The following entries are written in the "present journal voice" as lifted off of my journal pages...

<u>Journal Entry (August 20, 2003)</u>
Jack called from Ireland. I sense God is preparing me for travel to Chicago for a season of strategic prayer. Over the next five days... the Holy Spirit defines reason, location, and pattern for prayer at America's East Gate on the shores of Lake Michigan with upcoming time at West Gate not yet defined.

<u>Journal Entry (August 26, 2003)</u>
Purchase airline tickets for Chicago in preparation to fly out at God's dispatch. Continue in prayer...

<u>Journal Entry (August 27, 2003)</u>
Holy Spirit leads me to downtown Chicago web-site revealing Old Triangle District with the Masonic Lodge on one corner, Reebe

Storage and Moving representing Egyptian Revival Architecture on another, and St. Michael's Church stationed on final corner. NOTE: St. Michael's Church one of the few buildings to escape total destruction in the October 1871 fire that ravaged North Chicago. NOTE: John Hancock Tower stands to side of the Triangle District... NOTE: John Hancock was both signer of US Constitution and High Mason from Massachusetts. Revealed detail amazing! Thanks God! NOTE: Chicago layout portrays striking resemblance to Jerusalem and nearby Kidron Valley...amazing! Holy Spirit now defining specific actions, wind directions, Scriptural recitations, and resulting repercussions associated with task and experience while there...amazing!

Journal Entry (September 4, 2003)
Receive package from South Carolina with a hand-made prayer sash and cloth edged in gold thread, anointed with oil, and prayed over by east coast prayer team in preparation for and to accompany me on my solitary quest.

Journal Entry (September 7, 2003)
Now 43 days into my fast...Fly from Seattle to Chicago arriving on time making my way to St. Michael's Church. Meet Father John Schmidt there, who gave me permission to park and sleep in church parking lot tonight. Thanks Jesus! Statue of Michael the Archangel with sword-in-hand and foot-on-the-serpent stands in front of the church entrance...confirmation. Attend evening mass 7 PM St. Michael's. Father Schmidt speaking from Mark 7:31-37 about opening the ears and mouth of a deaf mute. Father Schmidt's timely reading significant as God led me to same passage prior to flight to Chicago.... confirmation now 2,000 miles from home through Catholic Priest.

Importance of passage four-fold: (1) 7:34 shows Jesus declaring "Ephphatha" which means "Be opened." (2) God sent and mandated me to shoot Lord's arrow of victory through "east window" (2 Kings 13:10-19) praying that archangels Gabriel and Michael fight and defeat princes of Persia and Greece to "Open East Gate" to prepare way for God's people to go home (Daniel 7:1-10:21). God promises to gather His people from wherever they have been scattered and return them home once and for all (Zephaniah 3:10-20), (3) Tyre and Sidon indicated as second destination I'm to pray at upon my return to Washington. Located in Friday Harbor on San Juan Island in Washington's Puget Sound, (4) Chicago's Triangle District correlation to Kidron Valley...similar to correlation of Tyre and Sidon imagery to Friday Harbor provided me is equally consistent as overlay of my current second destination prayer path. Scriptures revealed by Holy Spirit on Ferry between Anacortes and Friday Harbor:

Journal Entry (September 8, 2003)
Chicago. Start all night prayer vigil at sundown on shore of Lake Michigan. Security states all parks close at 11:00 PM. Find prayer site. Police stop and grant me permission to pray through night.

Journal Entry (September 9, 2009)
Sunrise...throw prayer staff in water as instructed... Spread prayer cloth and pray for God's people. Breeze reverses direction against prevailing wind just as God promised would occur. Head for airport, board, return to Seattle. Spend night at Steve's. Drive to Friday Harbor early in morning.

Journal Entry (September 10, 2003)
Leave for ferry at 5:00 AM to board first boat. Asking God where to pray once I arrive. Holy Spirit leads me to following passages while en-route on Ferry to Friday Harbor destination:

"I will gather all of you...I will bring together the remnant of Israel...One who breaks open the way will go up before...they will break through the gates...the King will pass through before them" (Micah 2:12-13 NIV). "...They...came to the iron gate leading to the city. It opened for them by itself, and they went through it" (Acts 12:10 NIV). "...The reeds and rushes will wither, also the plants along the Nile, at the mouth of the river" (Isaiah 19:6b-7). "...he set my feet on a rock and gave me a firm place to stand" (Psalms 40:2b). "In that day there will be an altar to the Lord...and a monument to the Lord at its border...it will be a sign and a witness to the Lord...when they cry out to the Lord because of their oppressors, He will send them a Savior and will rescue them...in that day there will be highway..." (Isaiah 19:19-23 NIV).

IN LIGHT OF ABOVE SCRIPTURE TRAIL, I found the following upon my Ferry docking at Friday Harbor:

(September 10, 2003): Ferry ramp dropped and was confronted by large "iron gate" all cars exiting ferry must pass through. Holy Spirit reminds me the Lord is going through before me. Next, I travel around harbor at Holy Spirit's direction down side road and arrive at University of Washington Marine Biology Center. Park, go up to door to discover "owl" etched in glass. NOTE: Owl significant of unclean night demons in Scripture and is widely associated with Canaanite god Moloch to which children are sacrificed (refer to Bohemian Grove for current American involvement/ancient mysteries of Egypt). Enter biology center, explain I am there to pray for America, and request to look out back of building...permission granted. Walk out back door to discover large "rock" outcropping to put my feet on. Walk over rock to discover "memorial bench" under tree. Walk down to shoreline to find bare stone without "reeds or rushes." Look to right to find "mouth to river." This river wound 10 miles through Island to originate several hundred feet from prayer focus. Speechless at what I found in light of Scripture. Amazing!

NOTE: This comment has been inserted in the journal's time line at time of this book's writing.

"AS YOU CAN SEE by the above detail, God leads us specifically in our work for Him."

Starting to rain...crud! Go buy raincoat. Begin prayer vigil at sundown. Pray in rain through night into morning of 09-11-2003.

<u>Journal Entry (September 11, 2003 / 911)</u>
Early AM, Finish all night prayer in rain on NE rim of Friday Harbor behind University of Washington Marine Biology Center. Amazing... breeze stops and reverses to blow against prevailing winds at sunrise just like Chicago. Grab car, Ferry back to land, return Steve's car, and return to Yakima...collapse in bed. NOTE: Holy Spirit tells me I will close this 3-site prayer loop at the WAILING WALL IN JERUSALEM on

my 50TH BIRTHDAY three (3) years later on October 26, 2006. No clue how, sounds like God.

END OF CURRENT JOURNAL EXCERPTS
FAST-FORWARDING TO RESUME MY STORY IN MID 2006...

Early July 2006, I received and e-mail asking me to consider traveling to eastern Afghanistan to provide technical assistance to an impoverished nation. The e-mail mentioned that a friend had recommended that this Non-governmental Organization (NGO) contact me, so I gave the inquiry serious thought. I was unusually drawn by this out-of-the-ordinary request, though uncertain as to why. On August 12, 2006; after upgrading my passport, having my will prepared, and securing necessary supplies...I boarded my plane in Seattle bound for Jalalabad, Afghanistan...alone. My flight carried me from Seattle to Frankfurt onward to Dubai, finally landing in Kabul, Afghanistan after multiple plane changes around the Globe. Landing in Kabul, I was intercepted by the NGO's young indigenous agent who gathered my bags and transported me through narrow, people-plagued streets criss-crossing a sprawling war-torn city...

The atmosphere was surreal as horns honked...donkey carts merged... Chinese bicycles darted...exchange agents counted...military Hummers encroached...and unlikely pedestrians chattered on cell phones. My eyes scanned and gathered third-world snapshots as my nose caught a savory whiff of local food hanging heavy beneath open-air canvas draping the cobble-stoned street. Hungry young peddlers thrust their wares through our open windows inciting our driver's wrath and his get-out-of-my- face wave. We wound our way past rough-poured buildings rising from rubble...monuments to fallen regimes...pungent street latrines...make-shift embassies... local tea shops...camouflaged peacekeepers...and veiled women charting their course home. Finally, we arrived to our iron-gated destination surrounded by sun-baked walls topped with razor-wire's coiled crowns as our driver tooted the horn...gate opened...and we rolled past the compound's AK-armed guard securing the gate behind... I stepped from the car to be greeted by an unknown host's hug before being ushered to my upper-level room inside. Once settled…I washed up, descended the stairs, and was introduced to the awaiting compound staff and those they served. Unexpectedly, I came face-to-face with a gentleman I later learned was positioned to be president of Afghanistan just prior to Karzai taking office. Braving Kabul's inner city streets the next day together in his old Mercedes, I discovered who he was and that two of his brothers had been assassinated by the Taliban, one being the former Vice President. He too was a target of political retaliation… As time permitted an hour here and a couple-hours-there…we sat and talked over tea probing subjects like culture, family, politics, suicide bombers, Shiites, Sunnis, religion, and his thoughts on Jesus Christ…

Two days later, I hopped a small United Nation's plane from Kabul to Jalalabad dropping into the US military outpost at the NGO's direction to avoid kidnapping by resistance forces, which would be otherwise probable if driving the relatively short section of desert highway known as "the Jalalabad Road." I draped my carry-on over my shoulder and hit the rag-tag runway plowing my way toward the waiting reception team with rolling suitcase wading gravel behind me… One dark-skinned gent chucked my bags in the back and motioned me to my seat. Four of us in all…we made our way to a concrete compound built by Russian forces thirty-some years prior during their unwelcome occupation of Afghanistan. Our shortwave-equipped vehicle contained a driver who did not speak English, another Afghan NGO staff member who did, an armed guard packing an AK-47, and myself, taking it all in. Our wheelman fixed his eyes on the road, dodging potholes and giving wide berth to on-coming olive drab 6 X 6 trucks before ducking in and stopping at an unnoticed gate… Two sentries scanned beneath our Rover for bombs with up-turned mirrors on rough-hewn handles before raising the yard-arm and waving us in… We strolled past giant Eucalyptus trees, pulling to a stop in front of a short-stack of sandal-laced stairs as sun-borne dust sifted by. Piling out of our ride, the compound door swung wide as the NGO's director, whom I had only met by phone, extended his hand before showing me to my room…

This unlikely desert oasis was surrounded by many different types of cultivated flowers, shrubs, fruits, vines, and more…all within ten clicks of Osama Bin Laden's deserted terrorist camp... What more could a man ask for?...sand, machine guns, Guava, barb-wire, lamb kabob, bombs, sunrises, Russian compounds, and a chance to teach local agriculturalists how to grow food, instead of dope. I was in my element as the next day landed me squarely on top of Osama's old camp to assess soil, water, topography, crop possibilities, and the course ahead... As I gathered information and ventured recommendations, the director quickly recognized my big-picture vision with extreme attention-to-detail capacity. One night while talking together one-on-one in his personal quarters...he asked me to spearhead the design, supply, and direction of an upcoming 3,000 hectare 7,500 acre, thirty million dollar planting project comprised of pomegranates, blood oranges, and paper shell almonds. I paused, ran it past my internal grid, and said, "I'm interested." We shared more conversations over the next two weeks on the matter while out-and-about or at the dinner table being fed like kings. Our kind-hearted smiling cook rose from the ranks as a former Mujahedin freedom fighter who faced death to liberate his people in years-gone-by. Finally, it was decided that I would take on the upcoming project if they were able to secure funding...

Bin Laden's pool turned to Mosque – Eastern Afghanistan

I finished my stint there...jumped a plane landing in a seat next to a lovely lady UN Financial officer from England on her way to Tehran while flying between Jalalabad and Kabul onward to Dubai...then I sat next to a disheartened young Israeli man named Nimrod from there to Germany...drank coffee with a Tennessee gent heading home to the US from Laos during my layover...and pondered trip events from Frankfurt to Seattle between snippet conversations, jet lag, and engulfing zZzZz's. As usual, my eyes slammed open a hundred and fifty miles out as we blew through Seattle's territorial spiritual power boundaries just before landing in Starbucks' hometown surrounded by cheeseburgers as if I'd never been gone... On that August 28, 2006...I snagged an Americano, grabbed my car from long-term parking, hit the freeway, and made my final 150 mile leg home to collapse in bed after 3 disjointed days and 30 hours in the air.

Please recall God's promise to get me to Israel's Wailing Wall on my 50th birthday to close the 3 year prayer loop...

NOW, GOD'S WHIRLWIND GROWS...

Journal Entry (October 10, 2006) / 16 days prior to my 50th birthday
Receive phone call from NGO director Afghanistan confirming project funding and needing me back in Middle East to locate vendors, gather supplies, and kick things into motion ASAP... Tell him I will come right away....need tickets. He asks where? My response: Seattle to London, England to Tel Aviv, Israel back to London, London to Islamabad, Pakistan to Jalalabad, Afghanistan back to Islamabad, Pakistan to London, and London to Seattle. Also need ticket to Los Angeles to secure new Pakistan visa in person... short timeline. Director says NGO will finalize travel itineraries immediately...

Journal Entry (October 11, 2006)
Director e-mails project contract...both domestic and international airline ticket confirmations. Need new Pakistan visa, Afghanistan visa, and second passport before Seattle departure to Middle East on October 23, 2006.

Journal Entry (October 15, 2006)
Fly Seattle to Los Angeles for Pakistan visa....take cab to hotel...go to

Pakistan consulate next morning...

Journal Entry (October 16, 2006)
Gather things and re-pack bags...take cab to Pak consulate downtown LA... Arriving inside the Pakistan consulate...I was greeted by a full room of foreign-speaking men, women, and children of all ages... it was chaotic. I approached the window and told the agent I was there to get a last-minute visa, handed him my papers, and took my seat. People around me chattered in languages I did not understand. The wall clock ticked away time as I settled into my hardwood chair. Office traffic between the seating area and the barred agent window seemed non-stop... Mid daze, I snapped back to reality as I heard the groan of dry hinges and my name being called quietly from behind me. I stood, turned, and wandered through the door-left-ajar where I was promptly introduced to and seated across the desk from Pakistan's Consulate General who had been the right arm to their President for 8 years. He asked me the nature of my business and why I was traveling to Pakistan on such short notice. I explained my need to locate, secure, and supply tractors, plants, fertilizer, irrigation, chemicals, and other items to an Eastern Afghanistan project I had been contracted to oversee. He picked up his phone, called an aide to his side, asked for my passport, and sent the man on a mission after saying a few words to him first...

As we conversed...the consulate general pulled out his business card and jotted down his cell number telling me he would like to show me around LA later that day. About 20 minutes later, his aide returned with my passport and scurried away... The general reviewed it and handed it to me...amazing...a 1 year visa in less than 20 minutes! I stood extending my hand after concluding our business...tucked his personalized business card away...and left his office treated like a king. Upon exiting the building, I found my first FedEx drop box, slipped my updated passport and its accompanying explanation letter in an overnight envelope, addressed it to the Afghanistan Consulate in New York, and dropped it in the box...

Now noon and faced with an extra day of allotted time due to not knowing how long the Pakistan visa process would take...I hailed a cab and headed downtown to kill time... I vacated my hotel earlier planning to sleep in the airport that night to wait for my late afternoon flight the next day. Around 4:00 PM, I pulled the Consulate's card from my pocket and called to thank him for his help. He answered and asked, "Where are you?" I told him I was downtown kicking around the mall passing time. He said, "Stay there and I'll be right down to get you." Fifteen minutes later, he screeched to a halt in front of me... I jumped in and we ventured toward a Middle Eastern restaurant of his choice. The waitress seated us; we scanned our menus, ordered, and began to talk. Our conversation re-convened on the project I was working in Afghanistan finally migrating to a more personal note as time wore on... He asked about my professional skills, my family, and my personal life. Eventually, his questions drew a passing comment out of me with regard to walking across America a few years before. He was immediately intrigued and asked me why I had done it. I told him that God sent me to call America's church out of empty religion into living God's real love toward people around us...

God had opened the door and I shared how Jesus pulled me from sin into His arms of love so many years before... With eternal things now spread across the table before us, I asked him about his own life sitting back to listen. He leaned forward with his gaze growing a bit distant an began to tell of his wife and children...how long he had been in the US...reflecting on his long time working next to Pakistan's President...and about his dying brother not allowed in America for chemotherapy based on his country of origin. He gazed at the table in silence momentarily before looking up with tear-filled eyes. Then he asked, "Can you pray for my brother?" I said, "Sure" and we bowed our heads. As prayerful moments melted away he said, "I would like you to come stay in my home next time you're in LA...my family needs to hear what you have to say." I told him I would be honored... He pulled a piece of paper and pen from his pocket to jot something down as he said, "I own a hotel in Islamabad...I'll give you a free room as my guest while you're there." I said, "Thank you...I appreciate that" as he paid the waitress and we wandered toward his car...

On our way toward LAX airport he asked, "How come you're going to sleep in the airport tonight?" I explained that, "Everything we need is in place when we do what God wants us to do... He probably has someone in the airport He wants me to meet and talk to about Him." Appearing a bit troubled, he continued toward the airport driving into the evening. As we rolled under the awning at LAX, I caught a flash in his eyes as he leapt from the car and ran! I spun in my seat, pulled the handle, swung the door open, and lifted my gaze just in time to see him throw his arms around another man with excitement! As I approached...he turned to me with eyes dancing said, "you just told me that if we do what God wants us to do, everything we need is here in place for us. This is my dear friend...we have not seen each other for years...he is one of the head men here for United." Then his friend chimed in both asking-and-saying, "So you want to get home early huh...you just missed the last flight for the day...but, I'll put you on the first one in the morning" as he pulled something from his pocket. Pinning an extracted business card against a pillar with one hand, he wrote down his cell phone number with the other while saying, "Call me anytime 24/7...I can fly you anywhere in the world for $200." He pushed the card into my hand, grabbed my bags, and led me inside with the General in tow before trundling away... The General and I shook hands, hugged each other, and parted new friends that night...God is amazing!

Throughout the night...the General's friend brought me water, chattered, and kept me company intermittently until I headed through security the next morning. I cleared the scanners, boarded my plane, and arrived back in Seattle a little before 1:00 PM. I deplaned...snagged an Americano...made my way to the parking garage...paid my parking toll...and cruised through the discharge gate to I-5 North toward the Federal Building downtown. A car pulled out of its parking spot, I pulled in, and I scrambled inside to an elevator where I made my vertical trip to the ninth floor. Exiting the elevator, hanging a sharp right...heading down the hall...I strolled through the Passport Office door, coming face-to-face with an armed guard... I explained to him that I did not have an appointment, was flying in a few days, and needed a second passport without Islamic stamps ASAP to avoid being denied access in Israel upon arrival. He sauntered across the room, chatted with the agent, and waved me to window as I explained my situation again to the lady who was looking down at her watch and saying, "We close in 15 minutes, hon." Before I could say a word, she continued "Run up the street, have your photos taken, and get back here quick!" I bolted out the door, jumped down the elevator shaft head first (not really), ran up the hill to say "Cheese," and arrived behind my pumping heart to a locked Passport Office door 8 minutes after they closed...harrumph! I knocked with fingers crossed hoping, and waited... After a moment, the door cracked... they eyeballed me...and I was ushered back to the window where I handed over my mug shots and laid my money down before fleeing the scene... On my way across the courtyard heading back to my car on this sunny October 17th day...I called the General in LA and said, "Hi!" We spoke for a few moments as I snagged another cup of mud on my way past Starbucks...and hit the long road home...

Journal Entry (October 18, 2006)
Receive FedEx from New York with new Afghanistan visa...good, have both new visas. Receive second FedEx letter from Seattle Passport office with new passport inside...yea! God is good!

Journal Entry (October 19, 2006)
Buy new suitcase...dinner with Mike...update my Will...pack for Afghanistan...

Journal Entry (October 20, 2006)
More packing...get new Blackberry...grab Americano...dinner with mom and dad...more packing...

Journal Entry (October 21, 2006)
Crossed off last item on list...don't forget gas for car...load bags...call kids in Seattle...set time to say good-bye.

Journal Entry (October 22, 2006)
Drive to Seattle...meet kids for dinner...ice cream...watch David Letterman...call director in Afghanistan...send e-mails...hit the rack...

Journal Entry (October 23, 2006)
Sleep in...call remaining friends...arrive SEATAC...fly out of Seattle for London at 3:30 PM...arrive London 9:00 AM next day on October 24...board plane for Tel Aviv, Israel 6:00 PM...arrive Tel Aviv 1:00 AM on October 25...all luggage except one bag lost in London at Heathrow...double-crud...picked up by Tax, sent by Amiad Filtration

arriving to Kibbutz in northern Israel 5:00 AM on October 25...must replace lost travel supplies...pray lost bags will arrive before I leave and they get lost again:-D

After arriving bag-less with luggage lost somewhere between Heathrow and Israel...I waited for the Taxi being sent by an irrigation company transporting me toward Northern Israel to a location immediately across the border from Lebanon when Hezbollah was blowing it apart. Blurry-eyed and melting down as the cab pulled up, I jumped in. I was infused with unseen energy as we passed along the Palestinian wall, beyond Nazareth, and past Galilee arriving to the Kibbutz where the Amiad factory was located before being dropped at my quarters. By now, I was running through the cracks and grabbed an hour's sleep, jumped up, showered, and got ready just in time to answer my host's knock at the door. We toured their factory, drank coffee, and said our farewells as Plastro Irrigation's Taxi arrived to escort me to their drip irrigation production facility before convening for lunch. I was amazed, sitting across the table from Raphi in Israel as he reminisced over times he had been to my hometown in Washington State...small world. We finished lunch and made our jaunt back to tour their plant for the remaining afternoon. At our tour's conclusion, I was collected by a third Taxi sent by Netafim, who pioneered drip irrigation in 1961...and I was then taken to meet Ami their President for a personal one-on-one tour of their state-of-the-art automated production line.

Now looking more like a destabilizing bowl of Jell-O than human as mid evening rolled in...I waited for my fourth and final Taxi of the day that would carry my crumbling constitution several hours back toward Jerusalem on one hour's sleep in 2 days. I only remember waking up to the driver's call as we arrived to my hotel one hour after midnight on October 26, 2006, my fiftieth birthday and Golden Jubilee. After 6 hours sleep, a hot shower, and Israeli coffee...I made my solitary trek to and through Old Jerusalem's Jaffa Gate past a neon "Authorized Money Changer" sign, through the Muslim Quarter, the Armenian Quarter, into the Jewish Quarter, and to the Wailing Wall...

At the Wailing Wall on my 50th birthday October 26, 2006

I stepped up to a public table and wrote my prayers on Rabi-provided paper, folding it multiple times on my way toward The Wall where I stuffed my heart's cry deep into the cracks of time with untold others... I leaned forward resting my head on sacred stone, thinking back on America's East and West Gates several years before, with the moment's weight descending on me in the tears of God as I wept my way through the work He'd given me to do. As I broke prayer's communion with the West Wall and ascended overlapping slab steps to walk on pathways and up stairs, past shops, through corridors, around perimeters, and back through history's gate...I could not help but wonder if my feet had tread where Jesus walked on His way to die for me... As I cleared the gate, reality set in; reminding me of the shofar I had borrowed from Ken back home. I whipped out my phone, glanced at my watch, scrolled through the list, and hit SEND... His wife answered and I asked her to tell Ken that I would have his horn back to him upon my return. She replied, "He's not here...he's in Israel." Twenty minutes later, my phone rang with Ken on the other end saying, "Come on down to the King David Hotel and join us for dinner." I reached in my pocket, pulled out my Jerusalem-by-numbers map, and wound my way there on foot. Upon arrival, Ken met and escorted me to the "Banquet Hall" where I was seated next to some of Jerusalem's leaders in the midst of 50 Americans there on tour. While at the podium and without warning...Ken stopped his speech and introduced me to the group as he led them to sing Happy Birthday to me halfway around the world spreading God's frosting on heaven's cake... Even now, as I write of the events almost five years later, it makes me weep...

From there, I traveled back to London, onward to do business in Pakistan, drove to meet engineers over the Khyber Pass in Afghanistan, drove back to Pakistan, flew back to London, and soared back to Seattle, arrested by God's adventure before steering my car toward home. While in the whirlwind...I met, spoke, and traveled with world-class agronomists, pathologists, director generals, tribal leaders, presidential candidates, customs directors, former freedom fighters, scientists, pump manufacturers, reigning aristocracy, armed escorts, police, United Nations officials, German Consultants, East Indian Engineers, and noble everyday people from many walks of life. And God always gives the baker's dozen... because...I got paid to "Go into the world" in Jesus' name.

Though your journey will be different, dear friend...that is the way a whirlwind starts, how a whirlwind looks, and what a whirlwind costs, in my world. Yet, I'm no better than you and my call is no bigger than yours – just on a different path in the plan of our King... Our faith is not about what we know or what we do. Our faith is about Whom we know and if we are willing to do what He is doing... Whether God called you to be a cool breeze to those in life's fire or tornado of truth to warn those off-course, jump into the whirlwind of His Spirit and blow however, whenever, and wherever He calls you to blow in Jesus' name...

Hurricane hair is around the bend...Get ready! — Bud

Gala apples hanging on Eastern Washington tree...

Chapter 5
Fruit That Lasts

"You did not choose me, but I chose you and appointed you to go and bear fruit – fruit that will last" (John 15:16).

Being raised on the family farm where we grew, packed, and sold different types of apples and pears...I gained a deep appreciation for life principles related to soil, plants, weather, work, and producing fruit that lasts (John 15:16). Members within both sides of my family emigrated from Germany, somewhere near Belarus, and Ireland – to the United States between the 1880's and early 1900's with a companion blend of German, Irish, and Jewish blood coursing their veins. Though my great grandfather on my mother's side originally immigrated to America as a seventeen year old preacher planting churches in Oregon and Washington between 1893 and 1905... both my father-and-mother's families engaged in fruit production as a way of life through which their individual journeys played out... With me being born later in 1956 as a fourth generation fruit grower rising from such heritage...my ever-changing leaves of experience, perspective, and vision were colored by seasonal breezes sifting their way through the branches of my tree row in life...

Simply put: I was an inquisitive, adventuresome, and spontaneous red-blooded American boy with an energy level akin to the Energizer Bunny...a boldness that could plunge off a rock onto my belly in a puff of dust between clumps of sage brush, bunchgrass, and buttercups... and an imagination engulfed somewhere between conquest and romance, soaring on impossibility's wind high overhead, gazing into the blue-skied unknown. There was no greater place on earth for a lad to grow, ponder, and discover the realities of life, than trudging through knee-deep orchard grass, slingshot dangling from a pocket behind...apple branch-dubbed-walking stick in-hand...unbridled imagination locked in high gear...and one's faithful dog sniffing too-and-fro for pheasants and gophers in the same breath. On a given day – there was no shortage of mud, mischief, or motherly inputs with regard to the misalignments of boyhood and its proper integration with more refined manners in life. Though the clash between bathtub rings associated with such young dust busters like me and parental oversight ensued...I always enjoyed my times hanging out at our family's fruit packing and storage warehouse...

What a great place – noise, honking horns, forklifts, floating apples, soap machines, people, hydraulic pumps, fruit inspectors, wind tunnels, box makers, bin piles, big trucks, tools, Freon compressors, and cold rooms chuck-full of ice cold apples and their aroma filling the crisp 33 degree air... The packing room wall next to the cooler was covered with old fir one-by-twelve's and lined with ten-foot-high cardboard box piles upon which my trusty dog Casper and me dared to climb for afternoon naps high above conveyors and the concrete floor...at age 5. My excitement grew as years passed with dad letting me drive our old electric forklift around at night as I swept the packing room and sorting shack floors and emptied cull bins after everyone had gone home. As the sun rose-and-set and seasons passed, my curiosities and mechanical aptitudes ushered me into compressor, cold, and electrical rooms where I gave dad a hand fixing refrigeration, replacing electrical controllers, silver-soldering copper pipe, and standing high atop a forklift in an empty bin 20 feet above the floor to repair condensers or replace light bulbs. We cleared ground, dug footings, poured concrete, built buildings, graded driveways, installed well pumps, climbed bin piles, shot squirrels, and pulled out the occasional flatlander-turned-truck driver who slid down the hill in front of our warehouse sideways, frozen by fear as he hung on to his white-knuckle express in snow storms crossing our path. To a visionary, inventive, and curious young whippersnapper like me...the warehouse was a dream-come-true in my quest to go where no farm boy had gone before...

Most mornings around the farm came early as we slapped roosters from their slumber on our way out to move sprinkler pipe at dawn, came back in to eat breakfast, and later returned to the field unexcited to cut suckers, hoe around trees, and contemplate mowing our monstrous yard if it just happened to be that day of the week... I always looked forward to supper frequented by beef stew, homemade potato soup, fried chicken, mashed potatoes, and a leftover noodle-casserole-catchall my mom haphazardly referred to as – slumgullian. Though money did not grow on trees around the farm when I was young, good food, hard work, freedom's fun, and lots of love were everywhere at home. Over the years, I made my life's traverse through the eyes of a curious toddler, grit-under-his-fingernails seven year old, pudgy fourth grader, adolescent inventor, motorcycle riding teenager, and love-struck sixteen to twenty year old phases, all dotting my path toward farming and running the family's fruit packing and storage plant with my dad. Just a few years earlier, I had begun my first business at age fifteen growing apple and pear trees for other orchardists as my high school agricultural project. My tree growing efforts soon excelled and expanded over the next few years, making my burgeoning schedule full as it merged with family fruit-growing pursuits working alongside my dad...

My boyhood years fell beneath the feet of approaching manhood calling me beyond teenage freedoms and motorcycle riding to shoulder growing responsibilities associated with marriage, parenthood, and business. As my personal and professional abilities, duties, and opportunities grew...I diversified business pursuits, simultaneously operating my four company's focused on tree and rootstock production, diesel repair and fabrication, controlled explosives and construction, and technical consulting services. By age twenty-eight, expanding workloads and re-orienting spiritual values dictated that I hire full-time employees on several fronts to slash my professional demands in half to spend more time with my wife and kids. Changing gears in this fashion shifted my mode of operation from very hands-on to a more logistical, technical, and international style, zeroed in on locating and networking with various experts all over the world. Doing so would later redefine my life options and future in ways I did not comprehend as I unwittingly prepared to collide with life-altering unknowns in response to my prayers .... There was an unspoken awareness within me that transition was coming... Yet, I had no clue when or how it would occur with God's hand at the wheel. I simply knew that what had once been known by prior generations as a family-friendly lifestyle called farming was quickly being swallowed by a people-eating meat grinder called agri-business as an era ended never to rise again. Where children once roamed freely to climb trees, drive farm trucks at age 14, and swim ice cold irrigation canals on a 100 degree days...farm managers, no trespassing signs, and governmental regulations – took over. With my visionary awareness on high alert – I was simply not interested in trading in my straw hat and farm boots for a briefcase and board meetings. After all, I was a farmer destined to grow things...

Though largely unaware of all the strings God was and would eventually pull to order my steps in life, my unfolding path equipped me with an extensive diverse technical knowledge base with skills rooted in numerous specialized fields, unleashing vision and my ever-ready adaptability. Consequently, I became quite capable at growing, nurturing, and harvesting crops, trees, fruits, businesses, networks, and people. That said, my life composition and core constitution obviously find their basis in and have their impact through timeless principles that govern both physical and kingdom realm aspects of soil, plants, and production... Whether in this world or the kingdom of God – my curiosities have been ever-intrigued by all involved in growing and preserving fruit that lasts for profit and the benefit to those God entrusted to my care in life. Simple-to-grasp, difficult-to-balance factors impact the quality and ultimate storability of fruit – some real and others environmental. Before we move forward to consider those factors in the production equation considered as real however, let's take a brief look at the first-of-two environmental factors...

Weather

In farming, one can do everything right in preparing soil, planting good seed or plants, nurturing their crop, and bringing it successfully to harvest, only to be suddenly wiped out by weather conditions like wind, hail, or frost without warning. The likelihood of such catastrophic loss can be greatly minimized or even removed altogether based on the site or location the farmer chooses to grow his crop upon when the known weather patterns that effect those individual locations are considered. If one wants to produce a crop that cannot survive cold temperatures...growing in a temperate area removes risk. If one hopes to bring a crop susceptible to wind damage successfully to harvest...a sheltered location is the right choice. Or, if one wants to grow a crop that does not do well in a water shortage...choosing a site next to a river with deep soil works well.

According to the bible – any good farmer or builder chooses the best seed to plant or site to build the foundation of their crop or building upon. In one story Jesus told, we find a farmer sowing good seed only to have an enemy scatter weeds on top of the farmer's work in the middle of the night when no one was looking. After the seeds began to sprout and grow, one of the farmer's servants noticed there was a problem as weeds popped up everywhere making the difference between good and bad seed apparent to all (Matthew 13:24-30). In a different parable, we find the contrasting choices and results realized by the wise or foolish builder who chose to build on either rock or sand. When the rains came down, the stream rose, the wind blew, and beat against the house of the wise builder – it stood unscathed upon the rock. But, when the weather went from bad-to-worse hammering against the house built on sand by the foolish builder, all was lost in a great crash (Matthew 7:24-27). So, obviously dear friend – choices matter!

From the principles of farming and building...we find our key to surviving an enemy's attack or weathering the storms of life successfully! Our victory comes through sowing the good seed of God's word within our hearts, minds, and spirits as we build our lives upon the Rock, Jesus Christ. Whether one is a farmer, business person, husband, wife, parent, pastor, boss, or friend...we will all reap a harvest, either good or bad, based on the type of seed we sow, site we build on, and our response to the environment we encounter in life (Galatians 6:7-9). Over the years, I learned the importance of minimizing risk through buying quality seed or plants, choosing the right growing site, and being prepared to protect my crop against unexpected harm... It was during the 1989-90 winter when our tree nursery business was destroyed, that my site selection was less-than-ideal due to land shortages, environment was unseasonably extreme, and we were mere months from building storage facilities that would allow our trees to be dug in the fall rather than spring. As it was, the afore-mentioned factors converged, leaving destruction in their wake... And yet, none of these events surprised God, Who lovingly re-directed my life pursuits out of growing apples and trees into producing His fruit that lasts. Now that we grasp the idea that outside forces beyond our control heavily influence our outcome in producing fruit – let's roll up our sleeves, climb understanding's ladder, and look behind the leaves on the tree of life...

Fruit

Just what is fruit anyway? In reality, fruit is something different in all realms it occurs within. Let me explain... In farming, fruit is the fleshly product of a tree or plant that contains seeds and can be eaten for food (i.e. apples, pears, etc.). In work, fruit is the by-product or outcome of our labors (i.e. completion, paycheck, recognition). In human reproduction, fruit is the by-product of a woman's womb following conception, gestation, and birth (i.e. baby). In spirituality, fruit comes forth through different types of behavior within our lives, revealing God's character through the way we live and act (Galatians 5:22-23). Another aspect of spiritual fruit occurs within God's kingdom as we do the work necessary to reproduce our personal relationship with Jesus Christ, within the life of another person, through our lifestyle extension of love, selflessness, and true discipleship (Matthew 28:19-20).

Honeybee pollinating apple blossom during full bloom...

In basic terms - fruit is the finished product of a tree, investment, relationship, or decision resulting from design, purpose, process, labor, time, and necessity. Without fruit, life or those sustaining activities related to it...is not sustained...nor can it exist. Fruit is both the reason to live and – the means of staying alive. Hoeing the soil of inner thought, I find it very interesting that the production of fruit requires interaction or intercourse between flower (female) and pollen (male), effort and outcome, man and woman or... people and God. Whether that interaction or intercourse occurs between flower and pollen on the wings of a honeybee...between salesperson and customer wrangling to close a deal...between husband and wife during tender times of love's intimacy...or, between people and God engulfed by circumstance in the presence of others or the Holy Spirit – fruit production is a team effort built on cooperation and agreement between those essential to the process. It is likewise interesting, that life's fruit production occurs based on cycles. In farming – fruit rises out of a cultivating, planting, developing, and nurturing cycle that occurs throughout the spring, summer, fall, and winter seasons. In work – fruit rises out of an idea, strategy, effort, and completion cycle. In relationship – fruit rises out of an introduction, attraction, love, and marriage cycle. In reproduction – fruit rises out of an intercourse, conception, gestation, and birth cycle. In spirituality – fruit rises out of an awareness, surrender, obedience, and transformation cycle. And in life – fruit rises out of heaven's governing birth (spring), adolescence (summer), adulthood (fall), and old age (winter) cycle. Whenever fruit is mature – harvest comes as that fruit either goes in an apple bin...a bank account...a common pursuit...a parent's arms...or, a grave – in this world. Apples will be eaten, money will be spent, love will be challenged, children will be raised, and loved ones will be released as their different types of harvest slip into the shadows of this life to either rise or fall – in or excluded from – the presence of God in the life to come. So you see, there is design and continuity in the operation of God's creation (Romans 1:20). In light of fruit's intricate beauty and obvious value to God and man – let's dig into another real factor that provides foundation upon which we produce fruit...

Soil

While cultivating daily life amid the dust of this world – the Holy Spirit continually piques my awareness with regard to principles of the soil. For example, we find Jesus painting the imagery of farming through His Parable of the Sower where we see a farmer going out to plant seed in his field. As he goes, he misses the field altogether as some of his seed falls along the path, nowhere near its intended target. Traveling a bit further to the rocky edges of his field, he prematurely chose to sow another portion of his seed on a less-than-desirable area having too little soil for plants to take root. Continuing onward, he cast a bit more of his seed on good... but weed-infested...soil that lacked proper preparation for planting. And finally, he arrived at the prime seedbed to venture his most productive planting effort in well-tilled weed-free productive soil able to produce an abundant harvest (Matthew 13:1-9). As we read on in other related passages, we discover that "seed" refers to the word of God and that different types of soil represent various life circumstances and heart conditions under which people hear and respond to eternal truth (Luke 8:11-15). Sliding our finger back up the sanctified page in our unfolding story, we find the farmer reaping varied levels of planting success that range from zero to a hundred times that which was planted relative to the different types of soil he chose to plant. God's eternally immutable kingdom principles of the soil have never and will never change – ever! Soil selection and pre-plant preparation play make-or-break roles in a given soil profile's crop quality potential. We find this same eternal principle at work in making disciples for Jesus Christ, when we shift our view from physical world dynamics to spiritual realm realities associated with cultivating soil and producing fruit that lasts in people's lives... Remember, one can only reproduce that which they have gained themselves, nothing more...

In farming terms...soil is the medium comprised of smaller organic particles in which roots penetrate, expand, establish, anchor, feed, and eventually supply the overall plant structure with soil borne food. When soil quality or quantity is poor or even non-existent...its capacity to produce is greatly diminished relative to its composition. Spiritually speaking...the hardened, bitter, stubborn, or deluded soil within our hearts has little-to-no ability to receive, support, or produce life. Before we can experience life transformation through Jesus Christ, our heart's hardened exterior must be plowed, cultivated, and softened through conviction of our need, confession of our sin, submission of our will, and declaration of our allegiance to Jesus as Lord and Savior over our individual lives. The soil quality represented by our heart condition will largely determine our eternal future and world-changing impact within the lives of others for God's glory while we're in this life. Please let me share a story of an encounter I had during one of my adventures...

Approximately 650 miles into my first walk across America, I happened into a small hole-in-the-wall sized town criss-crossed by aging streets and the occasional blinking 4-way light from yesteryear... Concluding my trek for the day, we made our way up one street and down the next knocking on church doors eventually bringing me face-to-face with a kind, young mid-thirties aged pastor named Dennis. We introduced ourselves and he invited me into his office where we shared a bit about our lives with each other after he asked me to sit down in a comfy chair on the opposite side of his over-stacked desk. He ventured a few questions and I reciprocated. Once past our initial pleasantries, I asked him to tell me about his town, how long he had been a pastor there, what his vision for ministry was, and what he saw God doing in his local community. It did not take long to discover that Dennis' father happened to be the regional evangelism director for the western half of the United States in his denomination... So enlightened, I already knew by default that my young new friend would likely declare his main focus concerning God's appointed task for him to accomplish in his community would revolve around...evangelism. Sure enough, he turned the key starting the engine on the subject as he went from first-to-high gear in a single shift with the smell of enthusiasm's fuel soon permeating the air around us. He said, "We started with twenty people in our first semester of outreach and led forty people to Jesus Christ. The next semester, we started with thirty people and saw another fifty two people saved." Finishing his story, I inquired "May I ask you a question?" He said, "Sure!" Then I said, "A year after-the-fact...how many of those who were saved through your efforts are still in your church?" His gaze plummeted to the floor like one's little brother falling out of the top bunk in the middle of the night... "Over ninety percent of them are gone," he quietly replied. Then I asked, "Do you know why?" He paused, stared at his hands folded in his lap, and sighed before saying, "I'm not sure...but, I have really been praying about it." In the next breath He asked me, "Why do you think so many have left?"

In gentle response trying to handle his discouraged heart with kindness I offered, "Producing fruit is hard work!" "And heartbreaking at times too," he added. "Why is it so hard to reach people?" he asked. "It takes strong trees, quality soil, hard work, and the right environment," I said. "Can you explain?" he asked. I replied, "First, someone who only knows about God (convert) cannot make a disciple like Jesus commissioned us to do in Matthew twenty-eight. Before a person can help somebody else, they must actually know God One-on-one themselves. We cannot lead where we have never been or produce what we have never become, ourselves. Like farming...plants only produce their own kind...apple trees do not grow lemons and pepper plants don't grow pears... Second, everything Jesus did was built on committed personal relationship with those he helped and loved. He wasted no time on short-term acquaintances – He was all-or-nothing in His long-haul quest to love people. And yet, most of today's packaged evangelism programs send people out to ask strategic questions...to share their salvation experience in nutshell version...to call those before them to decision...to take their new follower through an 8 week basic bible study of John...and then to hand them off to a stranger for discipleship training. It's nuts...we indoctrinate their minds with religion and crush their hearts with unwitting insincerity as we put them through spiritual divorce like intellectual religionists have taught us in organized Christianity... People long to be loved and valued, not assimilated," I said.

"Would you want to hang out with people who drew you in, involved themselves in the most important decision of your life, and then cast you aside without warning?" I asked. "No, I guess not," he replied. "If you'll notice...Jesus never bailed on friends, He was committed to the end at any cost. He knew His purpose, was devoted to His Father, and stuck closer than a brother to those He was given." Then Dennis asked, "How do we pull that off when working with a wide variety of people and when so many of those we reach too change churches or move away?" I replied, "As a leader, it's important that you spend time getting to know your people well enough to identify if they are disciples themselves before you send them out. Once their spiritual maturity is determined, there are two basic questions they must consider and answer within their own hearts before they are recruited or dispatched by your church to approach anyone in the name of Jesus Christ." "What questions?" Dennis inquired. "The first question is...are you willing to make a life-long commitment to those you visit...and the second is... are you willing to invite them over, laugh and cry with them, and share your resources with them even when it's inconvenient – really get to know them? If your person's answer is no, they should postpone their involvement until their answer and passion changes" I said. "Why's that?" he asked. I replied, "When you climb deep into people's grid, involving yourself in eternal issues rising from and essential to the core of their being – your potential to wound, offend, and permanently estrange them from God based on their perception that you violated them is huge! Remember, we'll all give an account for what we do while in this life." Dennis weighed in saying, "I never thought through it at this level. We just followed the program and learned the hard way that it doesn't work." I asked, "Do you know why?" He replied, "No." Then I said, "Loving people God's way is not a program – it is a choice, a commitment, a privilege, and what we are called to do out of appreciation for all Jesus did for us, it's others-based. People know the difference between evangelism-by-numbers and someone truly caring about their life. It's not about statistics, performance, attaboys, or putting our thumbs under our religious suspenders, Dennis...it's about loving other people the same way God loves us – with joy! Freely we have received...freely give." Now looking me straight in the eyes with strength filling his previously deflated frame, Dennis said, "Things are going to change around here! From now on, we're going to love people into God's kingdom His way, not ours!"

The issues found in my encounter with Pastor Dennis that day were by no means an isolated occurrence within the Church-at-large.

Simply put, expanding God's kingdom fruitfully requires our personal transformation and Christ-centered application of unconditional love, forgiveness, commitment, authenticity, understanding, and motivation. As you tuck the above word picture in your overall's pocket, it's time to consider other factors that co-labor with principles to compel God's heart and govern His creation...if...we're to grow fruit His way...

Trees

Like people – trees (plants) are complex living organisms sustained by physical, chemical, biological, or environmental processes used to collect, metabolize, and generate compounds like carbon dioxide, oxygen, water, or minerals as they transport food, build structure, replenish reserves, and produce fruit. A tree is a living factory that assimilates, assembles, and announces its product in an unimaginable array of seeds, cones, flowers, and fruit. A tree can be a challenge to grow, a structure to train, a place to land, a sight to see, a factory to run, a material to erect, and eventually – a fuel to burn. Trees can either sprout from seed or be custom-grown to meet orchard and market demands by grafting a desired root (bottom) selection possessing known size and fruiting characteristics onto a fruiting variety (top) of choice. Like people, the choices made in the root-and-top variety selection process will determine the quantity and quality of fruit that tree grows...

Work

I learned another valuable skill on the farm – hard work (2 Chronicles 15:7; Proverbs 13:4). It always amazed me how God empowered me to grow superior crops using older equipment, smaller budgets, and less-than-desirable growing sites than my well-to-do neighbors who had abundant manpower, brand new tractors, and state-of-the-art technology. How? I paid attention to the details and applied good ole' elbow grease! It's not a matter of how new the iron in your machine shed is...whether you sport a company logo on your shirt...or, how recognized you are in the community – success comes through diligence and focused effort! There are many things I am not good at...like running fast, drawing pictures, surfing, or winning door prizes. But, I can literally grow or build anything based on abilities and vision God gives me, with excellence! The reason I am able to do such things well is due to the existence of – passion. Simply put, one must know their identity, purpose, capabilities, and source of strength for passion to exist and prosper. Sadly, most people today are like a runaway trailer loaded with apples speeding down a hill backwards after coming loose from Grandpa's tractor... they lack Christ-centered wisdom, motivation, direction, and self-control. Anyone can go through the motions, do their time, or spin their wheels while expecting all the benefits without doing the work at the expense of the one in charge. Yet, only those who have invested themselves in the process of identifying who they were created to be, what God designed them to do, who they are called to impact, and for whose benefit it is to be done – change the world with eternal impact. As I've had the "privilege" (opportunity and responsibility are inseparably married) to work alongside some of the greats within various industries, those already proven or yet destined-to-become-great shared several common, but noteworthy traits – personal identity, clarity, humility, and integrity...

By-passing the human however, let's go to the root of reality planted in the One Who not only understands farming better than anyone... but, also designed and birthed the entirety of all creation within which farming happens – Jesus Christ. If anyone in the whole of human history ever knew His identity, it was Jesus Who embodied and personified His Father in heaven. Throughout the four gospels of Matthew, Mark, Luke, and John – we see Jesus defining and keeping Himself in step with His Father's heart as He proclaimed the message and did the work He'd been given (John 5:17, 19, 9:4). Jesus knew the work He was called to do, what it would cost Him to do it, who it was designed to touch, and the One it was to glorify (John 17:3-26). Without exception – Jesus functioned with absolute clarity, avoiding distractions as He humbled Himself under His Father's almighty hand through obedience, thereby giving evidence of His integrity before God and man as our example (Matthew 4:1-11; Luke 9:51, 62, 22:42; Hebrews 5:8-10). And finally, He wrapped it all in one very neat, easy-to-understand package clear enough for children to grasp when He said that we who have faith in Him will do what He is doing (John 14:12). In a nutshell my friend, we must only look at the life of Jesus to know what we should be doing as believers in Him...

Production

Now that we better understand the importance and impact of weather, fruit, soil, trees, and work...please let me describe growing a crop of apples through the eyes of a farmer... Once we realize that our goal is to produce fruit with superior taste and storage quality on good soil by farming the best trees amid unknown weather potential through lots of hard work – we are rightly positioned to grow fruit that lasts. Growing apples is a job, a passion, and even – an art. Some people go to the grocery store and imagine Johnny Appleseed skipping through the countryside slinging seed...trees leaping out of the ground from sapling-to-monstrosity...big red apples falling off into boxes loaded on a magical train...and landing in the hands of movie a star who bites them with a big, juicy, slow-motion – crunch! In reality, it simply doesn't work that way...

Though many romanticize farm life and growing fruit akin to TV commercials showing Jim-Bob in his straw hat trundling in from a sunlit valley on his old John Deere with his red handkerchief trailing out of his back pocket and a load of apples in tow...actually producing quality fruit in the real world is much harder work! I believe it common for most people lacking farm experience to think that growing a crop of apples starts in the spring when little green fruit appear on the trees, but not so. Producing next year's crop starts on the heels of gathering last year's harvest. As I've talked to people along the path of life, I've discovered the existence of a common misconception held by many who believe that farmers go out, pick their apples, haul them to the warehouse, get a big check, go to the bank, and kick back drinking hot apple cider for the winter, on vacation. Once the prior season's crop is picked, however, it is more accurately time for the farmer to shift into high gear thereby applying nutrient sprays to trees and fertilizer to soil before cold temperatures freeze the leaves and seal the ground. It's a race of man and machine against – Mother Nature. Why the hurry? Simple...

Leaves on a tree have fleeting ability to absorb nutrients while they are green and supple before freezing. Once frozen, they no longer transport nutrients from the leaf surface where they were applied through that leaf and into the tree where they were destined to go. This makes application of these products potentially expensive, ineffective and a general waste of money if one's weather window is missed. Likewise, soil only has the biological capacity to break down and convert ground-applied fertilizers into usable forms available to the tree for immediate use "before" the soil profile's temperatures drops below 55 degrees F. If timely post-harvest ground fertilizer applications are made – converted nutrient availability will provide the tree with food critical in terms of expanding roots, re-vitalizing tissue, building fruit buds, and boosting vascular energy during the heaviest tree demand of the production season– spring bloom. If post-harvest ground fertilizer applications are delayed until after soil temperatures drop below thresholds, however, applied nutrients will remain unused, trees unfed, spring bloom unsupported, and crop quality, quantity, and ongoing consistency – tragically compromised. If weather holds however, the farmer takes care of business, and all gets done on time – pruning trees during the winter season comes next...

Pruning

Pruning is somewhat of an obscure phase of production to most people who are unfamiliar with fruit farming. Yet, it is highly important to the end result as it plays several significant roles. First, a tree is pruned to get rid of damaged, dead, or over-crowded twigs and branches. Second, farmers prune for the purpose of opening up the tree's structure to facilitate air movement and light penetration deep into the tree for thereby promoting tree efficiency, fruitwood formation, disease control, fruit color, and ease of access by harvesters. Sunlight's deep penetration and uniform distribution are essential to tree vitality and fruit formation just as the light of God's Son, Jesus is essential to dispelling darkness and enlightening one's heart (John 3:19:21; 1 John 1:5). Sunlight is essential to plants for photosynthesis – the process of synthesizing food from carbon dioxide and water in the presence of sun-generated light for that plant's subsequent use. In humans, sunlight is essential to our body's assimilation of vitamin D which is of key import in the absorption of other elements like calcium, potassium, or the production of neurotransmitters like, serotonin. Without sunlight, we spiral downward into depression and ultimately death, if our deprivation of light is not quickly corrected. So, both photosynthetic plants and humans need light to exist and produce their crops. Why? God is portrayed as light, life's light, or as the light of men making the link between man's existence and light absolutely essential to our victory over darkness – whether physical or spiritual (Matthew 6:22-23; John 1:4-5; 1 John 1:5-7). Third, farmers prune trees to maintain balance between root and top, fruit exposure and protection, and leaf-to-fruit ratios necessary to spur consistent annual crop loads year-after-year.

Pruning season usually lasts through winter months leading up to spring bloom. If post-harvest nutrient applications were made on time, pruning was properly performed, and God is smiling – a farmer can watch fruit buds begin to fatten on the tree's twigs as spring bloom grows closer each day... About now you're probably thinking..."Finally, we get to talk about little green apples!" Well, not quite yet...we must apply early spring pre-bloom sprays to control bugs, diseases, and boost trees with another nutritional shot in the arm... Spring spray applications to the tree contain natural and low-impact chemical ingredients that kill insect eggs, eradicate mildew spores, and spoon-feed tender emerging buds, leaves, and shoot tips to keep the tree from depleting its internal nutrient reserves necessary to maximize spring bloom strength. Again, why is this important? Simple! At the point spring bloom flowers open (attraction), bees cross-pollinate flowers (intercourse), and tiny fruits are set (conception) – cell division rate is established (gestation). This is a critical juncture in the production of fruit that lasts! Why? Cell division rates that are established at fruit set (conception) remain relatively constant throughout the entire production cycle leading up to pre-harvest fruit maturity. An apple that starts well finishes well to become a prime-sized, well-formed, nicely-colored piece of fruit. Conversely, apples that start slow under adverse conditions typically finish last as sub-standard, low-quality pieces of fruit.

Thus far in production cycle many did not even realize existed – it is imperative that we grasp the make-or-break impact of strategically timed, diligent, and targeted inputs have on a farmer's fruit growing success. At the same time spring tree sprays are put on, farmers also apply weed control agents that keep noxious plants in check beneath and between trees down the row. Ever since the Garden of Eden, weeds have plagued mankind, increasing his toil (Genesis 3:17-19). And still, the above process has not even factored weather's variables into the equation... That said, we arrive to the conclusion of spring bloom marked by emerging little green fruits hanging on the tree during mid spring – the phase most who are unfamiliar with fruit production likely consider to be the onset of growing apples, yet now you know better... During the season of spring bloom through fruit formation phase – unwelcome cold weather patterns land without warning and hit full-tilt. Frost protection season is one of the most perilous and potentially expensive mileposts in the entire production pathway as seemingly powerless farmers go toe-to-toe with Mother Nature's heartless brutalities. As a side-note – I recall a particular never-to-be-forgotten season many years ago when my dad and I stayed up 21 nights straight to run wind machines, fire orchard heaters, and run frost water only to lose our crop to plummeting temperatures just before dawn the final night. We were tired, spent in more ways than one, and pondering what it would take to navigate and survive the loss until next year without a crop... Moving beyond that nightmare, past post-harvest nutrient applications, winter pruning, early spring sprays, and little fruit phases – farmers kick into high gear for the rest of the summer leading up to harvest... Crop demands marry those of us crazy enough to farm to our crop day-and-night as we keep pace with irrigation, tree training, maintenance sprays, miscellaneous repairs, fruit thinning, nutrition assessment, load management, disease prevention, sunburn protection, and more. From the time little green fruits appear – farmers manage and monitor their crop as apples grow, wind storms blow, sun scalds, hail destroys, banks bail, and harvest comes when fruit heads for the warehouse into someone else's care. Breathing a sigh of relief after braving nature's elements, growing our crop, and surviving an obviously technical job now well done...we come to the other environmental factor which effects how long our fruit will keep...

Controlled Atmosphere (CA)

One of the most interesting things I ever encountered around my family's warehouse was that of controlled atmosphere storage (CA) in which we lowered the oxygen and monitored CO^2 content in the air within the storage to levels able to "put apples to sleep" for prolonged periods of time on a controlled basis. By reducing the apples' respiration rates through lowered oxygen levels...we slowed their conversion of starches-to-sugars, making it possible to bring them back into normal atmosphere 8 months later, let them sit in storage for a week to re-acclimate, and have them taste as though they were just picked off the tree yesterday – amazing! If we monitored and maintained atmospheric conditions within the rooms based on established guidelines...realized benefits were tremendous! If we got distracted, too busy, or neglected taking daily oxygen and carbon dioxide readings however...levels could either rise out-of-bounds to diminish storage benefits...or...plummet without remedy to suffocate and destroy our fruit. I find the benefits and risks associated with controlled atmosphere storage, and its ability to preserve fruit quality and flavor for one's enjoyment, directly parallel to those benefits and risks tied to the Holy Spirit's preservation of one's life and impact before God and man in a dying world (Galatians 5:19-26)... If we keep our eyes on Jesus and live by the Spirit, we rise to life. If we yield to our human desires and get snared by the cares of this world however, we will suffocate and die.

Growing Trees

Several years ago, a gentleman I had gone to high school with contacted me about growing 417,000 apple trees for his company that were needed to establish several hundred acres of new commercial fruit orchard. Though I had grown large quantities of trees commercially off-and-on for more than 35 years, his last minute request made the timeline tight and pulling it off more demanding than usual... Being a visionary armed with faith, knowing my own capabilities, and enjoying a chance to do the impossible...again...I entertained the challenge and engaged in project negotiations with him and his partners. I told them I would have to secure plant material in an over-sold environment, acquire machinery of all types, lease land, and hit the ground running with the 2.5 million dollar project within 60 days to achieve it – assuring him I was able. Before the deal closed, I began searching for 60 acres to lease along the west coast anywhere between the Canadian border and northern California. I contacted plant suppliers and was fortunate enough to locate an unknown stash of much-sought-after rootstock adequate to do the job and placed the order before someone else beat me to the punch.

As I drove the highways and backcountry roads to follow up on leads, talk to farmers, kick dirt, poll real estate agents, consider water sources, and assess government soil maps – negotiations continued. Spring was coming, daylight was burning, and I had no time to waste despite my uncertainty if the deal would even come together. As I began to get my arms around project scope and its sure-to-be-demanding logistics...I ventured tree price quotes based on project demands, increased costs generated by last minute dynamics, and my level of long-term expertise empowering me to get the job done. While I scurried to-and-fro on a...maybe...trying to achieve the impossible for his potential benefit...amazingly...the price game between us began.

Sitting across the desk from one another with my written proposal before him, he offered me half the profit margin I quoted, telling me that the order size was going to generate substantial revenues, and that I should be satisfied with a smaller percentage. In response however, I said, “It has taken me 35 years to acquire the knowledge, experience, and network capable of pulling this project off. If I have to work for free, I’ll go fishing.” So, I stood my ground as I went on to explain that producing a quality tree takes investment, balanced nutrition, timely labor, and strong attention to detail. Then he asked me, “How do other nurseries grow their trees cheaper?” I replied, “Anyone can grow a tree that looks reasonably good. Yet, not everyone grows a tree that actually, is good. Most nurseries grow their stock using excess nitrogen because it’s cheap and makes a big impressive-looking tree. Sadly, a tree grown in that manner has large cells, soft wood, and does not withstand environmental extremes like heat or cold temperatures very well after the nursery delivers it to the farmer for planting in his field. Quality trees require more expensive nutritional inputs and technical production methods necessary to build tighter cell structure, increase wood density, withstand future weather extremes, and offer proper branching characteristics necessary to farm success. In other words, you get what you pay for." Appearing as though he was being sold a bill of goods, he looked over the rim of his glasses at me with a gaze that implied, "You're blowing smoke." Despite his opinion however, I was doing all in my power to protect his interests and provide him with a tree that would be cheaper for him in the long run...

Days fell by the wayside as I continued pursuing property, scanned ads for equipment, and upheld my price amid the barrage. Since my suppliers were the only source of rootstock, I was the only one willing to engage the project, and they needed the trees to achieve their goals...they conceded and agreed upon my original price. We signed contracts... set up accounts...transferred funds... and commenced the next day as land was located...tractors were purchased...plants confirmed...fertilizer ordered...irrigation designed...manpower was hired...and ground was renovated in the next few weeks... Over the next twenty-one months...the project landed, trees grew, money was consumed, other nurseries watched, challenges were navigated, beautiful trees emerged, autumn leaves fell, digging season came, tree delivery occurred, and their new orchard was established...

The coming fall, America's Pacific Northwest was prematurely hammered by unseasonably cold fall temperatures severely injuring many nurseries and orchards throughout the states of Washington and Oregon... As I monitored weather conditions, talked to my client, and waited to see what spring and summer weather conditions would unleash in the form of damaged plants...I watched how many trees from various nurseries died as a result of winter injury. Spring came and summer unfolded with horror stories circulating within the apple industry regarding orchard devastation and tree loss. Several months later, I called my customer to chat one afternoon. As we talked about fruit prices, crop size, and other issues related to apples – we landed on the subject of tree growth. He said, "Less than a thousand trees you grew for us died due to winter damage...your trees look the best out of all we purchased. Yet, we lost high percentages out of those trees grown for us by other nurseries that same year." Then I asked, "Do you recall when we spoke up-front about how it costs more to grow quality trees capable of withstanding environmental extremes?" He replied, "Yes, but I didn't believe you when you told me. Now, I can see it with my own eyes. Your trees grew and survived better than everyone else's and the bank who financed the project loves them!" Again I said, "You harvest what you plant...quality takes time and costs more." After navigating the entire tree production cycle with these gentlemen, they proved to be some of the most ethical men I have ever worked with in my life. Like all people coming to the table to do business together first time, we had all simply done our part at the onset to be responsible businessmen. In the midst of it all however, we gained deep respect for each other, became good friends, and ended up in a good place. Whether growing trees, apples, or people – the process demands seasoned experience

One field of 260,000 apple trees in my nursery – 2008

(relationship), good soil (maturity), healthy roots (truth), good decisions (wisdom), real commitment (love), hard work (devotion), and simple faith (trust) to grow fruit that lasts...

Quality Control

Bringing an apple or tree crop to market is a demanding task as you can see. Yet, in addition to all that has been said above...tree and fruit quality assessments are performed both internally by the farmer...and externally by those qualified nurseries, agencies, or buyers positioned to supply and certify new trees, to inspect and validate crop quality, or purchase a farmer's fruit for retail distribution to the general public through grocery stores. It is critically important for tree and fruit inspectors to perform their duties at proper times throughout the entire process consistent with established rules and under the right conditions. Doing so helps them avoid making unfounded, misinformed, and inappropriate judgments with potential to discredit a tree, diminish a crop, or undermine a market – without basis. Any inspector who is out-of-step with his job description, the production cycle, or in excess of his qualifications has potential to destroy a tree or crop's value and future – prematurely. We find this same violation on the loose through its misapplied spiritual counterpart – as misinformed, misguided, and unqualified people calling themselves Christians judge others based on misappropriated Scripture and flawed theologies that miss the mark and grieve the heart of God (Matthew 7:16-20, 22:37-41; John 15:1-2).

Let me explain... Jesus said we could judge a tree by its fruit while otherwise making it clear that both guidelines and consequences exist for doing so (Luke 6:43-45). Sadly, many people pull His statement out of truth's grid and use it as a license to judge others by imposing standards on them that the self-appointed judges do not live, themselves (Deuteronomy 25:13-16; Proverbs 20:10; Matthew 7:1-2). It is human nature to focus on the perceived flaws within another to avoid looking into the mirror of God's Spirit and into the light of His word – ourselves. In reality, the bible teaches us that only God truly knows and has the ability to see into the human heart with eternal clarity...man himself cannot (1 Kings 8:39; Romans 2:2-11)... So, when we wrongly exercise our freedom to judge another person's heart or life through human eyes...we, in essence...install ourselves on God's throne in His place executing judgments only He is qualified to make (1 Peter 2:16-17). By doing so – we convict ourselves as committing the same sin that cast satan out of heaven (Isaiah 14:12-15). That is why God's warnings to us with regard to judging another person's life are so stern. In addition, there is an often overlooked and equally destructive issue regarding assessment of another person's heart standing before God and man – that of premature judgment. Once again, please let me revert to farm jargon...

Premature judgment

As an apple farmer, there are many opportunities to judge the visual appearance or external quality of fruit throughout the production cycle. For example – if I were to approach a Red Delicious apple tree two to three weeks after spring bloom and consider that tree's quality based on the little green apples I saw hanging all over it, I would wrongly conclude the tree to be bad. Why? It is very hard to sink my teeth into hard small green apples...they are starchy and bitter...and they will give me a stomachache. But, if I were to wait another month on the heels of a big wind storm scuffing the tree's apples against its branches and were to judge the tree's quality then...I would again wrongly conclude the tree to be sub-standard because its apples were rough in appearance. Likewise, if I were to wait two more months until the apples were much larger, taking shape, but beat up by yesterday's hail storm...I would wrongly assume once again that the tree was bad. Why? Its apples are still green, covered with cuts and bruises from hail damage, and still lacking in color. And finally, if I were to wait until two weeks before harvest as the tree's apples go from green to red, workers have removed all damaged fruit, and internal starches have still not yet converted to sugar...I would likely believe that the tree is bad because I am still unable to find fruit that satisfies my expectation.

If I chose to assess tree quality at harvest time when apples are well colored, internal starches have turned into sugar, and workers have removed all damaged fruit from the tree however...then...and only then...would be able to see the finished outward appearance of that tree's final product (fruit). Now comparing apples to a person's life from a human standpoint...if I were to judge a person's life quality or destiny based on mistakes, decisions, or even sinful tendencies prior to Christ's transformation...very probably, I would conclude they were a wayward soul without potential. Yet, I would still remain incapable of seeing into the other person's heart to know their motives, the price their efforts had cost them, or what they had truly learned up to that juncture in life. Sadly, many people judge those around them through fallen human eyes as they assess the other person's life prematurely "before" has been given full opportunity to complete its production cycle. As with apples, judging the quality of another life (tree) before it reaches harvest time (death)...will always lead to wrong conclusions that destroy that person's image, credibility, potential, and ultimate productivity before God and man. If I were to plant an orchard and ponder the quality of my trees in this manner...I would be ever making wrong judgments, cutting down trees before they matured, and destroying their ability to produce fruit that lasts. This principle represents one of the most sinful violations committed by people calling themselves Christians as they point wagging fingers at others, but never consider, with God's help, what goes on within their misguided hearts... How will we ever reap God's harvest for His glory and the welfare of others if we're constantly cutting His trees down in heaven's orchard before their harvest comes?

In 1979, following our rise out of party life, my wife and I met an educator I'll call Tom for the sake of this story and his spouse at a local church where we began attending in response to a friend's invitation. We were expecting our first child and trying to get our lives on-track as we prepared to take on the parental responsibilities associated with our soon-to-arrive newborn. Tom taught a Sunday school class of "boomers" comprised of pipe fitters, janitors, nuclear facility employees, housewives, school teachers, mechanics, farmers like me, and other professionals too. It was commonplace for our group to have parties in people's homes, join each other in the mountains for a class camp-outs, or dream up other holiday-related activities in keeping with the season-at-hand. As time passed, my wife and I grew more involved in church, getting closer to several in the class including Tom and his wife. Some six years and several children later, our class arrived at our place to help us stand the walls and hang the ceiling rafters on a much-needed new addition to our single-wide mobile home to make room for our fourth child... Through subsequent years and events, Tom observed the ups-and-downs of my unfolding life to which one day he commented, "Greg, you will probably never be in ministry because of your past." Pausing for a moment to ponder his words...I simply replied, "Well, the Jesus I know forgives whether people do or not."

As our pathways diverged traveling in different directions, more years melted away as God heard my prayers, answered them in ways I never imagined, and I found myself navigating a disjointed road in life plagued by potholes that appeared to be detours. Nearly 23 years later after meeting this dear gent and wife...getting to know each other...losing touch as ministry pursuits called my wife and me out-of-state...losing everything...and walking America the first time – he broke, wept, and retracted his words from long ago as we prayed. He said, "Oh God, this is not the same man I once knew" recognizing the transformation that had occurred in my life. Despite his once diminished view of my potential in the hands of God, what had happened? Simple... God foreknew and predestined me to conform to the likeness of His Son compelling my heart, inspiring my prayers, hearing my cry, and using life, circumstance, and passion in keeping with His design to deliver me from death to life for His glory...

Though we may have opinions based on the outward appearance of another's life decisions, actions, and untimely defeat...the bible tells us that God weighs the motives of a human heart...not men (Proverbs 21:2). "Romance theology" challenges us to pursue God, love others, and look within ourselves to discover and change our own shortcomings with His help. As believers, we are told to work out our own salvation with fear and trembling, not someone else's on their behalf (Matthew 7:3-5; Philippians 2:12-13). Dear friend... God is patient and loves us not wanting any of us to perish, but to come to repentance so we can experience eternal life with Him (2 Peter 3:9). Sadly, many around us will choose to do their own thing and suffer eternal consequences outside the grace of Almighty God as Christ's return pounds heavy at history's door... As we consider the global groans of child birth intensifying all over the earth, we must realize that humans beings only see the impact of a person's passing life on others whom they've spent time with through eyes dimly (1 Corinthians 13:12). As one very aware of my own shortcomings and frailty, I encourage you to err on the side of grace, rather than judgment. There is a key but subtle difference between facing truth and judging another... Are we truly in love relationship with Jesus Christ...and...fully prepared to stand blameless before Him?

Though this book encompasses many years of my life experience... upon my pathway, I have encountered intensifying spiritual blindness, delusion, legalism, protectionism, and appeasement as people continue their own way with little concern for issues dear to God's heart. There is an extreme and visible social, moral, and spiritual decline apparent to those who are looking through God's eyes, listening through God's ears, and discerning through God's heart... Unfortunately, this decline will only be conquered and surmounted by those who heed and apply the red-lettered words and example of Jesus Christ in the way they live toward God and those around them... Over the past few days amid penning this chapter, I met a dear Muslim gentleman and his wife from Iran while seated in the early December southern California sun at Starbucks. As we visited and shared increasingly more personal areas of our lives with one another, they invited me to go with them to look at a potential business site and venture they were thinking about kicking into motion nearby.

We arrived at their location, spent time together dreaming out loud, jumped back in their car, and returned to the parking lot just outside the coffee empire's door. By now, our rapport had grown and communications between us were kind and relaxed... Curious with regard to their vantage point on the matter, I asked both of them about their personal and cultural perspective on Israel, God, and last day events unfolding all over the world. I must say – his response was genuine, transparent, balanced, and open. Both he and his dear wife shared their perspectives of being in relationship with God, who Christ is, and what it takes for all of us to make our way to heaven. When they had finished relating their views and faith, I shared my own thoughts on who Jesus is and all He has done for me. An hour after arriving to the parking lot as our conversation and time together were coming to a close I said, "Though I have my own view of God and Who Jesus is...it is not my right to impose it on anyone. Instead, it's my job to know Jesus Christ personally at a level that frees Him to use my life to love others as the Holy Spirit draws them to Himself." He replied, "You're different than many

Christians we know." Then I added, "I simply realize how much God has forgiven me when I least deserved it. How can I love others any less than He loves me?" In truth, we can only give others what we have ourselves...

As I mentioned earlier, fruit is both the reason to live...and...the means of staying alive. Life comes from Christ, man comes from dust, and fruit comes from intercourse between God and His creation (Genesis 3:19). Fruit comes from the womb and rises out of destiny's tomb... Simply put, producing fruit requires that a seed fall to the ground and die before a plant can sprout, a stalk can emerge, a head can form, and a kernel can ripen to produce a harvest whether it occurs in farming, human reproduction, or the spiritual realm (Mark 4:26-29; John 12:23-26). Before any of us can truly live – we must be crucified, dead, and buried in this life to rise through temporal harvest into the presence of God through eternal life... This same principle affects and ultimately governs those created in God's image, the expansion of God's kingdom, and the whole of God's creation – without exception. This fact is humanly inconceivable and forever unavoidable. In the scheme of eternity, however, fruit remains the apple of God's eye...the creation of God's hand...the object of God's love...the passion of God's heart...and the product of God's mercy as Eternity's Bridegroom waits, weeps, and woos His wayward bride to heaven's wedding table to marry, dance, consummate, and produce fruit that lasts...

My kids: Crystal, Brooke, Melody, and Casey – 2010

WA Monument at 5:30 am on Repent America Walk – 2002

Chapter 6
Two or More

"For where two or three come together in my name, there am I with them" (Matthew 18:20).

It was 5:00 am one early November Palm Desert morning when I made my way to read and pray in the secluded hot tub at an RV Park on my second walk across America. The star-ridden sky glistened atop a gentle breeze, swaying palm trees rising from the desert floor to surround the bubbling waters yielding their steam into vanishing twilight... Engulfed by deeper truths gleaned from my prior journey through Scripture...I looked somberly eastward toward the rising sun with head tipped back to rest on red adobe bricks symmetrically edging the pool of water in which I sat, alone. As morning rose red in declaration of its dominion over night's black expanse...the sun's rays broke the horizon's brow, piercing the darkness to announce the new day's glorious birth... Within moments, heaven flipped a switch calling people forth from their slumber, delivering an elderly, but spry man of 87 years, who stepped down into the waters on the pool's opposing side. We exchanged glances, a few cursory words, and finally introduced ourselves through the chlorinated mist... I reached across the tub with outstretched hand saying, "Hi, my name's Greg, what's yours?" Looking me straight in the eyes with a quiet confidence and unspoken authority he said, "My name's George."

Over the next hour...George and I bantered back-and-forth about social issues, political boondoggles, and personal experiences, trading stories one-after-the-other. It soon became obvious that we shared much in common with regard to character, vision, tenacity, and out-of-the ordinary adventures in life. As our conversation deepened amid laughter and international sarcasms – George mentioned he was a retired full-bird colonel who navigated three consecutive tours of duty in two different branches of the American armed services. His first stint was spent on an earlier-model weaponized submarine during the Korean war...his second tour was on an upgraded atomic sub fitted with intercontinental ballistic missiles armed with nuclear warheads...and his third charge was in the cockpit as an Air Force fighter pilot dropping napalm over Vietnamese jungles. George was full of tales of what it was like to be submerged underwater for months, trying to stay mentally and physically fit on-board, and finding himself part of clandestine stealth operations-of-the-day... Listening to him was like being immersed in epoch war movies like "The Bridges of Toko-Ri" and "Apocalypse Now." Following a decorated completion of his final military tour over Viet Nam... he became a civilian jet fighter test pilot working for an American arms manufacturer, which provided more than ample opportunity to encounter the unpredictable side of life's adventure...

Now, about two hours into our dialogue...I asked George, "Can you tell me some of your most memorable experiences from testing never-before-flown fighter prototypes?" He wiped sweat off his face and squinted through a chlorine-tinged eye saying, "Sure," and he continued painting a portrait of a flight test he'd conducted over western US deserts many years before. His rendition came complete with the emotions, smells, and goose bumps untold... George began, "It was a typical early morning take-off, maneuver, and landing sequence during which I was to take a new fighter through its paces. The engineers wanted me to gather data so they could make their refinements. I hit the pilot's quarters, donned my jumpsuit, grabbed my helmet, and threw my flight bag over my shoulder before cutting a path across the runway's cool morning concrete to climb the ladder and wedge myself into the plane's cockpit. As I nestled into my seat, gained my bearings on newly appointed instruments, and cinched myself into the harness hooked to the jettison module into which I was strapping myself...I flipped the switch and fired my engines. As they were coming up to temp, I ran through my pre-flight checklist glancing at different recording instrument read-outs for post-flight engineer review. After engine temps were up to snuff, I lowered the canopy, gave her some boost, turned the nose wheel, and made my way from the Tarmac down the ramp to grab my spot in line at the runway's end for take-off. I pushed the throttle forward and multiplying G's pushed me deep into the seat as ground speed mounted and engines roared firing me down the runway and shooting me skyward. Tucking my landing gear into the wings...I snatched a look at my altimeter, boost pressure, temps, and righted my horizon. I banked upward into a sweeping left arc gaining altitude fast, everything felt solid. It was customary for me to take a new plane through a series of banked turns, rolls, climbs, and dives, giving design flaws a chance to declare themselves.

About half an hour into my run, it was time to take her higher to get a feel for plane stability and engine performance in colder outside temperatures and low oxygen conditions. Leveling out at 28,000 feet and soaring across the early morning desert sky...all was well with my soul as performance levels fit guideline grids... With a sudden and unexpected boom, I found myself hanging in thin air 28,000 feet over nothing strapped to my falling seat with my plane nowhere in sight... I knew I wasn't supposed to pull my parachute rip cord at that elevation in low oxygen and cold temp conditions, but gave it a yank anyway while stunned by shock's crossfire... Man, I about froze to death on my way down! I closed my eyes and retreated into my mind, watching instant replays within. One minute I was on a routine run and the next minute – my reality took a radical turn from in-plane to a plummeting pilot on his way down... It's wild to wrap my head around a disappearing plane that felt so solid just moments before...that just disintegrated, leaving me speeding toward earth through an unfriendly atmosphere low on options... Because the plane disintegrated, the cause remained a mystery."

What causes things around us to disintegrate? In some cases, outside forces beyond our control reach in unexpectedly to destroy that which is near to us without warning. Yet, most things disintegrate before our eyes because their foundation lacks structural integrity due to their engineer's misunderstanding, miscalculations, design, workmanship, or application...

Foundation and Truth

As Christians, there is only one foundation upon which we can build our beliefs, lives, and eternities – Jesus Christ the Risen One and Great I AM (Genesis 1:1; Exodus 3:14-15; John 1:1-5, 10:30, Ephesians 2:19-22; Colossians 1:15-20; Hebrews 13:8; Revelations 22:13). We know that the government of all kingdoms, domains, and powers are upon the shoulders of Jesus Christ – not men's (Isaiah 9:6). Having identified and established our sole foundation...we must continue building with a second essential stone found only within the person, heart, and example of Jesus Christ Himself Who embodies this eternal character quality known as "truth" – not upon the philosophies of men (John 8:31-32, 14:6; 1 Corinthians 3:11-23). Now, that we have established Jesus Christ as the Chief Cornerstone, foundation, and the eternal standard of truth He incarnates...it becomes obvious that human misunderstanding and its resulting waywardness only occurs in the absence, distortion, misappropriation, or misuse of truth due to one's ignorance, impropriety, or insubordination toward God Himself (Romans 8:6-8; Galatians 5:16-25; Ephesians 2:19-22). Likewise, it is only possible for a design's structural integrity to be perfected and duly established when its blueprint for construction and its subsequent assembly rises from a solid foundation while held together by principles of established truth (Matthew 7:24-27; I Corinthians 10:23-24; 2 Timothy 2:19).

Another key factor affecting an article's durability is found in the quality of workmanship with which that item is produced or built. As God's people, we are in fact His workmanship, created in Christ Jesus to do good works He prepared in advance for us to do as active members of His body and a royal priesthood (1 Corinthians 12:12-31; Ephesians 2:10; 1 Peter 2:9-10). When we reject God's foundation, truth, and design at any level – we estrange ourselves from Him, proudly and defiantly adulterating His workmanship to build life our way in futility that causes structural instability as we labor in vain (Psalms 127:1; Romans 1:18-32; James 4:1-8). Finding ourselves able to say, "I did it my way" as Frank Sinatra once sang...reveals a crumbling foundation, distorted truth, fallen design, and wrong application in our pursuit of, relationship to, and dependency upon Jesus Christ, which is essential to salvation and His intervention in the affairs of man (Psalms 11:3; Luke13:22-30). These foundational truths deeply impact the individual and corporate freedoms considered to be "unalienable" by most republic-or-democracy-based societies. Remember, life's options rise from yesterday's actions, present today's choices, and change tomorrow's realities when we agree with God...

"I tell you the truth, whatever you bind on earth will be bound in heaven, and whatever you loose on earth will be loosed in heaven. Again, I tell you that if two of you on earth agree about anything you ask for, it will be done for you by my Father in heaven. For where two or more come together in my name, there am I with them" (Matthew 18:18-20).

The importance of "two or more coming together in His name" to experience His presence and blessing will grow more obvious as you read on...

Agreement

The subject and power of scriptural agreement between people in prayer and God is one of the most misunderstood concepts in the bible. People everywhere seem mystified when two or more come together to pray for a white Mercedes in Jesus' name and nothing happened when they said, "Amen." Why did their prayer go unanswered? God's version of agreement is a bit more involved than simply praying for whatever we want in Jesus' name, standing back, and watching God snap His fingers and go "boom" as a white Mercedes magically appears at no cost to ourselves. Please remember, God's loving gift of eternal life to save mankind incurred opposition, suffered heartache, and nailed Jesus to the cross, we were bought at a price... When Jesus prayed, heaven and earth shook, storms stopped, and waters calmed because He sacrificed His own desires and life to be in agreement with His Father in heaven through humble obedience (Matthew 4:1-11). As Christians, we must remember all that Jesus exampled and realize that the evidence of our faith is established, only when, we do what He is still doing – end of subject (John 14:12). He was a pure sacrifice without stain, blemish, or sin – wholly blameless before His Father (1 Peter 1:17-23).

As His followers, we too are called to live blamelessly before God through repentance to experience the benefits of our position in Christ (Ephesians 1:4, 2:1-9; 2 Peter 3:9). There are no free lunches in life as we pursue our desired answer through God's deliverance, provision, or blessing while in genuine agreement with Him. In brief, the power of scriptural agreement is only realized when our entrance into it is rooted in vertical relationship with Jesus Christ, horizontal relationship with man, alignment with God's purpose, and supernaturally empowered by God's motive, approached with God's method, and focused on God's outcome. Many believing amiss that they are praying in agreement; sidestep one or more of the above factors in God's equation through unwitting omission or ignorance, only to become disillusioned with Him as their prayers seemingly go unanswered. Now that we understand right foundation, truth, and agreement – let's take a look at authority...

Authority

Next on the list – we must define, understand, and consider our level of cooperation with the eternal institution of authority God created and entrusted to Jesus Christ His Son to administrate over all creation. God's institution of authority remains an unchanging eternal structure which resembles a vertical ladder (hierarchy) with the servant role (man) positioned beneath the leader role (Christ) ever-stationed at the top (head). Though authority's structure and principles remain eternally unchanged, their expression and application within the context of humanity changes tone case-by-case. Please let me explain... In the Old Testament, God led and governed His people through eternal law administrated by human leaders, kings, and high priests. Under the law, God's people approached Him in fear out of law's obligation with a sense of duty as human high priests offered repetitive sacrifices to atone for their own sins and those of others without lasting effect (Hebrews 7:26-28). In the New Testament, however, Jesus changed everything when He died on the cross as Heaven's Sacrificial Lamb to pay the price for all sin in-full – forever (Matthew 26:28; 2 Corinthians 5:17-21; Hebrews 7:26-28).

When Jesus took His position as the Perfect Sacrifice of all time, He exerted absolute, unending dominion over sin's penalty against members of the human race. In so doing, He transformed people's prior obligation-based, duty-motivated approach toward obeying God the Father...into an attitude of joy-filled appreciation for being given the gift of eternal life they could never earn or deserve.

Though the eternal structure of God's institution of authority did not change, its redemptive reach into the hearts of men, women, and children all over the earth throughout history rose from rules to rejoicing when Jesus' immortal words "It is finished" were spoken into existence and shook the earth (John 19:30). In this single transaction, authority's expression went from imposed, law-driven leadership typically stirring strife...to...submissive, Christ-centered, marriage-style cooperation, inspiring peace. Please let me illustrate with simplicity...

In the Old Testament and illustrative terms – a lamb obeyed the child, a child obeyed the mom and dad, a wife obeyed the husband, a husband obeyed the Priest, a Priest obeyed the High Priest, and a High Priest inquired of and obeyed God directly. Old Testament authority operated like an insensitive regimented military chain of command. In the New Testament however – all members of the body (Bride) of Jesus Christ (Bridegroom) are co-equal and called to submit one-to-another out of reverence for Him to honor of His role as Eternal High Priest, forever (Ephesians 5:21-33; Hebrews 7:11-28). New Testament authority functions like a marriage, in which different members of the body rise or bow as led by the Holy Spirit, acting in reciprocal submission to each other to honor Jesus the High Priest Who is Lord over all. Sadly, many marriages, homes, churches, and ministries cling to Old Testament, law-based authority and theologies which are bound in legalism that's fully incapable of releasing the biblical freedom New Testament submission-based authority was designed to extend. This reality is easily confirmed as heavy-handed fathers, husbands, pastors, and religious leaders impose a self-righteous and judgmental form of authority that binds and destroys without grace...while conducting their own lives...based on different standards than they extend to those they lead. Where Old Testament authority adhered to structure, New Testament authority breeds cooperation within the body of Christ and kingdom of God...

Kingdoms

God's kingdom is eternal, infinite in nature, and governed by immutable laws, not man's darkened understanding or level of agreement with Him. Conversely, satan's domain is a doomed, fallen kingdom limited by reduced time, space, and influence subject to God's unchanging laws, sovereign authority, and absolute supremacy. God is no respecter of persons or angels... He's God. Until we, as those who claim to be His people, choose to humble ourselves under His Almighty hand, both our individual and combined lives will fail to experience His deliverance, blessing, or abundance in life (1 Peter 5:6-7; John 10:10). Where God has the capacity to weigh our heart motives and know our unspoken thoughts – satan does not (Psalms 139:4; Proverbs 16:2). Therefore, we must resist the external pressures, thoughts, immoralities, and other sinful inclinations if we're to stand blameless before a holy, all-knowing God on that day...

Dominion

Authority, by definition, is the power to enforce laws, exact obedience, command others, determine, or judge...whereas dominion is merely the position of control gained by exerting that authority according to kingdom law. God's sovereign authority, supreme dominion, and eternal kingdom law ultimately validates who does or does not have the preeminent right to exert secondary dominion over others in a given sphere of influence. God's dominion through Jesus Christ is eternally supreme, absolute, and subject to no one (Philippians 2:9-11). Man's dominion is relative to and only limited by his level of scriptural agreement with God as outlined above. Yet, satan's dominion remains fully subject to God's sovereign authority, man's rightful assertion of positional power in Jesus' name, and the limited sphere, time, and level of influence God assigned to him, satan is defeated toothless loser!

Culture

Years ago, while caught up in a vision, God revealed an interesting vantage point to me with regard to the goings-and-comings of man (Matthew 18:18)... This vision involved the concept we know as or call "culture." This is what the Holy Spirit shared with me... Culture is man's dance with the resident sin legally dwelling in his area. When sin is committed, but not properly resolved through repentance to receive forgiveness from God and man – sin's existence remains eternal and legally authorized to dwell in that place where it was originally committed, until it is atoned for and its binding power is broken through the blood and name of Jesus Christ (Colossians 1:10-14; Hebrews 9:22). The existence of any unresolved sin in a given physical or spiritual arena becomes a foundation upon which satan can build a stronghold of darkness due to the legal right that sin extended to him based on God's immutable laws. All unresolved sin within us acts as an open door into our lives functioning in a manner similar to our giving a deed or title to another with governing authority over that portion of our life within which the sin was committed. This fact makes satan a perfected lien holder in our sphere under such conditions. So legitimized, satan has the right to enter, dwell, and exert dominion over that area or territory for which he gained legal title. This positions both him and his dispatched minions as immovable residents in one's life. Let me try to paint you a better picture from yesteryear...

As kids, we sometimes went to arcades that were filled with all type of people, games, and pinball machines... There were bright lights, lots of noises, friends laughing, and games untold to test one's skill in beating the odds. When it came to pinball machines, the one playing pulled back the plunger, a ball was loaded into the launch channel by the machine, and the player let go of the plunger, firing the ball into the machine's game field where it encountered and rebounded off bumpers. When a pinball hit a bumper, it bounced off in an opposing direction (reaction) to hit either a side rail or another bumper on its way through the game field toward the discharge chute. If that player were superhuman and able to stand and play that same machine for weeks, shooting 100,000 balls through it, a numerical pattern of response would develop in the way the balls bounced off and charted their course toward the chute. This same numerical certainty has been observed in another device known as a random actuator. A random actuator is merely a vertical wall with a series of symmetrically positioned pins protruding from its lower vertical face just above the bottom. To use this device – thousands of rubber balls are dropped downward through the pins below to bounce off and accumulate in stacks within vertical channels in a consistent and reproducible pattern.

When fixed obstacles (strongholds) are encountered by moving objects (people) in a given area (hometown) literally thousands of times in repetitive fashion – observable patterns of response emerge and become visible to the eye.

When people come to live in an area (hometown) inhabited by different types of unresolved sin evidencing strongholds in the spiritual realm within or over that sphere, the pattern with which they bounce off those unseen spiritual strongholds in daily life becomes what we have learned to call "culture" (Luke 4:24-27). That is why gateway cities like Seattle, San Francisco, New Orleans, Jacksonville, Washington DC, and New York to name a few – are known for their very distinct cultures, whether liberal, unbridled, demonic, oppressive, or violent... This truth reveals itself in these settings because each city was founded by different people, who committed varied sins which erected unique strongholds that were subsequently inhabited by corresponding spiritual powers or principalities. Hence, resident sin or strongholds (bumpers) which exist in a given region (hometown) for those people residing there to encounter and unknowingly react to (dance) in daily life – do exist. With all resident sin or estrangement from God, a level of corresponding delusion (blindness) co-exists with the stronghold to obscure it from human view or detection (2 Thessalonians 2:9-12). This is similar to trying to look at a yellow car through yellow glasses, thereby making the yellow car much less visible.

Through research, you will also find that most gateway cities throughout the world have convergent weather patterns over them as well because those cities represent entry points for multiple and conflicting cultures, philosophies, and religions. These churning weather patterns exist over geographical locations because the spiritual clash between these opposing cultures, philosophies, and religions in the spiritual realm precede their physical manifestation on earth. The presence of these clashing cultures, philosophies, and religions create open doors between the spiritual and physical realm through which satan is permitted to perpetrate his evil influence upon the earth. Because God authorized satan as the spiritual ruler over the kingdom of the air (atmosphere), he then has and exerts dominion over those dark spiritual forces he commands and the distortion (filters) their presence creates within that realm to affect people's physical world perspectives. Since people live in the atmosphere surrounding the earth which God gave satan dominion over, people's perspectives are filtered through those distortions the enemy creates.

Over the years, I have found these portraits of culture, convergent zones, and portals to be identifiable and at work all over the world. So, now that we're a bit more enlightened on the above subjects, it's time to take a leap of faith deeper in enemy territory... Please understand, however, that there simply is no easy way to talk about things that challenge people's lives. In light of this chapter's opening story – one can only cinch the straps on their parachute a bit tighter, donning the weaponry of facts and reason before jumping out of the plane feet first into unpredictable enemy flak... In my leap from high altitude thinking onto earthly foundations impacted by God's kingdom authority and dominion – I hope to rip heaven's cord between eternal truth and fleeting deception without being shot for treason by compatriots claiming allegiance to my King. So, please hold your fire as I do my best to illuminate your path and lead you through darkness into a familiar prisoner of war camp under an independent demonic deception way too close to home...

In their well-intentioned...but, ultimately misguided colonial quest to escape human injustice...freedom-minded idealists from all walks of life distanced themselves from oppressive rule to discover new frontiers and express their personal liberties in an expanding world. Following the preceding onset of European colonization of the Americas in 1492 by Spain, England, France, and the Netherlands, punctuated by the voyages of Columbus and Ponce de Leon laying claim to territorial ownership and ensuing government – principled men, later-to-become founders of the United States traveled their own life journeys from imposed despotism toward the promise of freedom to leave their mark on human history... After establishing the original thirteen colonies between New England, Chesapeake Bay, and the lower southern regions between years 1607 and 1732, operating under the extended auspices of Britain's crown, Continental Congressionalists tagged traitors entered the Revolutionary War in 1775 before officially exerting their bid for independence from British tyranny on July 4, 1776. The Revolutionary War between Britain and thirteen New World colonies lasted until 1783, ultimately growing into a global conflict between other European nations. Freedom's price would only later be realized through the serendipitous discovery of previously misunderstood and invisible consequences generated by asserting liberty that disregarded authority's institution (Romans 13:1-7; 1 Peter 2:13-21; Titus 2:9-10). Due to perspective, circumstance, and the authoritarian response of Britain's King...avoidable spiritual realities well-described in Scripture sadly came to bear on America's citizenry in ways most have yet to comprehend...

Revolutionary War Sign US 117 Halifax, NC - 1st USA Walk – 2002

Smithsonian in Washington, DC on Repent America Walk – 2002

Since early in its existence, America has been presented to the world-at-large as a sovereign nation rising to a stature eventually becoming known as the home of the brave and land of the free – in principle. However, this poster child image of implied philosophical unity and righteous governmental motivation has been skewed in its portrayal through both unintentional and agendized human deception rooted in spiritual blindness. In truth and to a substantial degree, America's social and spiritual picture has been painted with the collaborative brushes of entwined human idealisms and promoted by founding fathers compelled by diverse intellectual, religious, moral, and political beliefs and aspirations. Our founder's combined physical, mental, and spiritual collateral is represented and declared in America's legally binding foundational documents as they endeavored to chart our course toward enlightenment and unhindered freedom. Yet, the bible clearly tells us that mankind will travel a different path toward a one world system before its demise, making it obvious why both our great nation's founding language is portrayed as divinely inspired and yet – possesses a brushed-over ecumenical framework, inciting compromise and decline when entrusted to fallen human nature. This blurry snapshot of distorted ideological, spiritual, and moral unity within American patriotism displayed before an on-looking world, has converged to reduce social accountability and legitimized wayward governmental aspiration at the expense of both those governed and the very Judeo-Christian God America claims to represent...

If America was truly founded on Judeo-Christian values as revisionism champions, our founders would have made it their primary goal to build and declare our nation's foundational creeds upon the Chief Cornerstone Jesus Christ Himself as history's greatest champion of freedom (John 14:6; Ephesians 2:19-22). Yet, the name of Jesus Christ is nowhere stated, identified, or declared in America's three foundational documents including: (1) The Unanimous Declaration otherwise known as the Declaration of Independence – 1776, (2) The Articles of Confederation – 1781, (3) And, the Constitution of the United States of America – 1789 as openly affirmed and signed by 143 signatures representing 118 different signers (Matthew 10:32-33). This fact seems unbelievable in consideration of historical reports stating that our nation's framing documents were debated, drafted, and signed by highly intelligent, religious, and ethically-minded pastors, sons of clergymen, deists, theists, and otherwise – socially upstanding men. Additional signers comprised of lawyers, doctors, merchants, and those involved in education also left their ink on America's governing documents as well.

Remember however, that nobility is not established based on human intent, intellectual assent, or adherence to any idealism or creed – true nobility is credentialed by God the Father through Jesus Christ His Son, alone (Matthew 28:18-19). Like all people, America's Founding Fathers were noble men by human standards as they openly professed and stood for their high philosophical, moral, and spiritual principles at great personal cost in their passion to lead others upward in life. The error housed within the inner rooms of their human misunderstanding of an incomprehensible God however, unwittingly left the doorway to human decline standing wide open to evil's assault as revelation-based spiritual authority rooted in Christ failed to be exercised due to flawed spiritual belief and awareness. It is wholly irrelevant whether one's inactivity or error is based in ignorance, complacency, or rebellion... what matters is...innocent people suffer when leadership bypasses strategic Christ-centered responsibility entrusted to them by God in Scripture. At this juncture in my writing, many will ask how someone like me can assert such a view while in the shadows of former statesmen of worldwide acclaim and valor. Simple... One must merely compare the verbal and moral integrity of leadership's established written declarations from which they govern those in their charge...to...God's eternal character, truth, and heart revealed through and exampled by His Son Jesus Christ in Holy Scripture...

Though religionists, secularists, and noteworthy biographers champion a generic God as the source of man's unalienable rights...that America's founding documents reveal sentiments of divine intent and inspiration...and that those document's signers were in fact agents of supernatural providence in the hands of their Creator – as men, human leaders are still required by God to identify and declare their dependency upon Jesus Christ if they're to properly establish God's involvement in and dominion over our nation (James 2:19). This central issue carries extreme governing weight in God's tone of intervention within the affairs of men... Unless America's relationship to "Thee Holy God" of Israel through the person of Jesus Christ is absolutely established through open declaration as the Chief Cornerstone of our nation and society...we lack the foundation upon which to build our claim of being either Judeo-Christian or possessing the right to call upon Him based on biblical principle when in need (Psalms 11:3). Without the name and declaration of Jesus Christ...using the word or making the claim to be Christian is misguided and meaningless as it falls from our lips to the ground void without foundation. It is much easier to understand the above-described dilemma when one grasps that approximately 90% of America's founders were members of intellectually-based Christian denominations who depended far more on head knowledge and experience, than on miracles or spiritual revelation their theologies dismissed. The concept of "revelation knowledge" was widely downplayed by seventeenth century British philosopher John Locke, whose writings and principles of "Empiricism" heavily influenced Thomas Jefferson's (deist) composition of America's Unanimous Declaration. We must gain an accurate grasp of our founding leader's religious views if we are to rightly butter the stones of America's foundation with truth's mortar. Please consider the following non-exhaustive definitions:

Deism

A religious philosophical view that one's perception of the physical world and reason alone are adequate, without the help of a religious system, to establish that the universe is the work of an all-powerful creator. Deists believe that the creator does not alter human affairs or bypass natural laws governing the universe. Though deists believe in one God...they do not typically accept miracles, prophecy, the Trinity, or the inerrancy of Scripture. Deists usually assert a belief that God designs and constructs the universe, letting it run on its own once He has set it in motion (Clockwork Universe Theory).

Theism

Theism holds to a doctrine relating to the nature of monotheistic

God and His relationship to the physical universe. Likewise, theism attributes a personal nature to God through which He intervenes, governs, and defines the natural world and universe. In an over-generalized contrast, theists believe God builds the clock, starts the clock, sets the clock in place, and occasionally comes back to rewind the clock. Deists on the other hand, believe that God does not come back to adjust the clock in any way once He starts it.

Agnosticism

Agnostics believe one cannot determine or know whether God exists or metaphysical claims are true or not. Agnostics divide themselves over the differences between belief and knowledge, holding that human reason is not able to establish adequate basis to prove or disprove whether God does or does not exist. An agnostic does not believe or doubt the existence of God.

Atheism

Atheism generally rejects the existence of even one God.

Empiricism

Empiricism is a theory that knowledge most often comes through sensory experience, evidence, and observations associated with the natural world as they simultaneously minimize the value of either intuition or revelation knowledge.

Now that we more clearly understand the above belief systems, let's continue ...

America's foundations were originally erected as a republic, which is a form of government designed to strictly and morally control the majority in a manner that protects an individual's God-given, unalienable rights as a member of any minority, as based on law. American's have been systematically taught that their republic's governing law was heavily based upon and inseparably-linked to God's eternal and immutable laws governing His kingdom on earth and beyond. Tragically, America has been silently converted to a democracy over time by default through diminished reference to its republic, bypassing God's immutable eternal laws, and agenda-driven politics seductive to those who are uninformed, unconcerned, or uninvolved among its governed. Meanwhile, our country's increasingly-deviant leaders now invade to impose governmental controls based on majority rule that affords no protection against unlimited majority power to those who qualify as legitimate citizen-based individuals or minorities. In reality...the open-ended language contained in America's founding documents through declaration of an undefined God has allowed our nation's guaranteed freedoms, purchased by the blood of its people on both foreign and domestic battlefields...to be exercised in a manner that destroys the freedom we have. When a society loses its anchor in truth, it has been cast adrift on the sea of misfortune. As a fourth generation farmer and traveling preacher...based on evidence and Scripture...I find it difficult to believe the above historical saga was either enlightened or prudent since it was reported to have been presided over and ratified by some of history's greatest minds... America literally means "freedom." And yet, based on the unprecedented rate of decline revealed in America's current unraveling social, moral, spiritual, and financial culture, we are anything, but free. Let's go even deeper behind enemy lines to see why...

Independence

Had America's forefathers openly declared and tied themselves inseparably to Jesus Christ as the Chief Cornerstone in our foundations...Christ-centered benefits and blessings without sorrow would be evident in our nation today rather than – disintegration (Proverbs 10:22). One's concept and application of governing authority obviously has potential to produce opposing outcomes as it plays a pivotal role in lasting relational and spiritual stability within the lives of those it governs. Sadly, our founding fathers unwittingly opened the door to the spirit of independence over our nation, unaware of its future consequences. An independent spirit opposes unified peace. Why? The essence of independence implies "being under no governing authority," free from influence, guidance, or another's control making it impossible for those dominated by its power to agree with one another productively. Independence and infidelity are synonymous in God's eyes based on scripture, with unfaithfulness to one's partner, being at their core...

Based on Scripture, "being under no governing authority" is prideful, rebellious, inconsiderate, and in direct competition with God's rightful position as Lord over His creation. Because we are individually created by God as members of His Creation, our independence defies His dominion. The spirit of independence mirrors the same heart attitude that caused God to cast satan out of heaven (Isaiah 14:12-15). It is absolutely imperative that we draw a clear line of demarcation between one's act of establishing physical autonomy through biblical principles of righteous and agreeable separation...versus...the act of wrongfully exerting independence based on principles of pride and rebellion with binding power to erect strongholds and limit freedom due to the evil spiritual forces it unleashes. Though our founding fathers gradually separated from tyrannical rule, taxation, and religious oppression through a series of what appeared to be biblically righteous pleas...ultimately, their actions rebelled against God's divine institution of authority (Romans 13:1-7; 1 Peter 2:13-21). The final decision and methods used by our forefathers to cut ties with British oppression based on misguided human versus divine deliverance...reveals the existence of an embedded attitude of "self-rule" within them wholly inconsistent with God's heart and Christ's example (2 Chronicles 20:15-30; Matthew 26:36-56). Had they chosen to exercise humility and patient submission to authority, relying on God to deliver them in His time...He would have liberated and exalted them in due season, and with it, bestowed blessing (Romans 13:2-5; 1 Peter 5:6-7). Because they chose to effect their own emancipation from perceived tyranny however, they were labeled rebels, charged with treason, and incurred the assault of authority's disciplinarian action known as the Revolutionary War...

Moravians

In contrast to the approach taken by America's founding leaders – a potter named John Leonard Dober and a carpenter named David Nitschman, both in their early twenties, skilled in their professions, and known as noteworthy speakers – left Copenhagen to become the first Moravian missionaries to the West Indies where an unbelieving British owner held between 2,000 and 3,000 slaves in 1732. The slave owner was determined that no preacher or the like would ever stay on the island or talk to anyone there about God. In Dober and Nitschman's eyes, the slave owner's vow left as many as 3000 slaves trapped in the jungles of Africa on an Atlantic Island unable to hear about the love and liberty of Jesus Christ. When both men learned of the atrocity...they personally sold themselves to this same British slaver and used the money gained from their sale to pay for their ocean passage to the island. On the day their ship left the dock, other Moravians came to see the two young men off as they embarked with little hope of return. These selfless and love-driven men sold themselves into a lifetime of slavery, not a short term mission trip. It was reported that one of the men left his wife and children shattered and weeping on the wharf as he found himself unable to deny God's heart toward the West Indie slaves by choosing his own freedom and comfort – instead. As the ship left the pier, both men cried "May the Lamb that was slain receive the reward of His suffering." Both Dober and Nitschman wanted to obey God at any cost while armed only with the knowledge that He Who called them would grant the courage, grace, and anointing necessary for them to do what He called them to accomplish.

The Moravian Movement was originally founded by Count Nicholas Ludwig von Zinzendorf as a refuge for Christians in papist Europe, but soon became a place where those who desired intimacy with God through prayer and outreach could come. Count Zinzendorf and other community leaders began a 24/7 day-and-night prayer meeting that lasted over 100 years, eventually seeing God's power break out and overwhelm them one Sunday morning with testimonies as many were baptized in the Holy Ghost accompanied by other signs and wonders. Methodist Church founder John Wesley visited the revival more than 10 years later... While there, he had a deep encounter with God that ushered in and altered his own relationship with Christ in a manner that radicalized his own evangelistic reach to a dying world from there forward. It was this very cross-tension in prayer and intimacy with Christ that birthed Dober and Nitschman's insatiable hunger for God. As a result of them selling themselves into slavery's tyranny, lives were ever-changed and the kingdom of God, advanced. This obvious contrast in attitude between two bold-yet-surrendered young

Moravian missionaries and America's founding idealists reveals an undeniable, yet pivotal difference between self-preservation at the expense of others...and...self sacrifice so others may live.

In truth, America has been bound by a spirit of independence since its official inception. Though its citizens and other individuals can experience a level of personal freedom and proper dependency on Christ in their response to authority, they will remain spiritually bombarded and their freedom diminished to varying degrees. This truth will never change "until" the spirit of independence is identified, confessed, and renounced in Jesus' name by leaders who actually hold governing offices which possess adequate corresponding levels of authority specifically required to dismantle any specific issue or entrenchment. America's Unanimous Declaration was ratified by presidential and upper level officials, thereby requiring that those holding these same offices or levels of authority shoulder the burden, make remedial declarations, and affect proper revisions to sever the destructive power of independence over their people. Without exception, the spirit of independence loose upon the earth is at the heart of all divided marriages, friendships, partnerships, churches, organizations, governments, countries, and fragmented individuals, because independence cannot submit one-to-another out of reverence for Christ in its effort to achieve complete unity (Matthew 18:19-20; John 17:20-23; Romans 8:6-8; Ephesians 5:21).

Again, Jesus Christ is the ultimate Champion of and propelling power behind pure unadulterated – freedom. Had our founders declared God as the Father of Jesus Christ and recognized their proper dependence upon Him...religious, moral, and personal freedom would have gained its greatest opportunity in human history to be fully exercised with unhindered liberty. "If" religious freedom was truly one of several core reasons our forefathers fled British tyranny..."if" so many genuinely enlightened pastors among founding signers truly grasped the nature of God represented within the bulwarks of Christianity..."if" moral accountability to that holy God and eternal truth were genuinely sought as the enduring anchor of our society – then, Jesus Christ would have been openly declared over America – without question. While subsequent generations continue to be indoctrinated with the intrinsic value of a fallen moral philosophy, history proves that our nation's founders actually instituted a flawed social and spiritual foundation rooted in a form of godliness, thereby denying its power (2 Timothy 3:1-5). Sadly, our nation has perpetuated this same fallen lifestyle and form of democracy all over the world, assuring that each nation who embraces its philosophies, will run their own gauntlet of sorrow pummeled by difficulty and demise much akin to ours (Romans 1:28-32). Only truth can set us free (John 8:32). Yet, an illusion of truth remains a lie, shrouds us in darkness, and imprisons our souls... In light of human nature and ongoing religious practice, we have a tendency to think we are extra special and extraordinarily benevolent when we help someone, provide them quarter, or give uncommonly, when in reality, we are commanded by Christ to do so as evidence of His presence and Lordship in our lives. How have our social and spiritual cultures collided and combined at a level of purported faith, in which we openly disobey Christ in our expression of love to others, and still believe we qualify as His disciples? It's as though we believe we can go our own way and maintain access to heaven, simply because we feel we are entitled to spiritual validation and subsequent entrance into His presence, because we feel we have sacrificed to bless another equally created in God's image...

As an American...my citizenship affords me freedom to cite my own country's foundational formation as an example of how easy it is to become merely religious, driven by good intent and still...miss it in God's eyes, as evidenced by the moral, social, and spiritual decline in our own lives and land. Many have risen in their quest to return to America's foundations, rejoining the path of her forefathers as though it will fix everything now obviously amiss. Once again however, America's bedrock of belief is shaky ground since Jesus Christ was never officially set in place as the Chief Cornerstone upon which to build. Returning to America's foundations will fix nothing – it will merely reproduce the same crumbling chaos we already have... Remember, the definition of insanity is doing the same thing while expecting different results. People's belief that patriotism's rediscovery of our roots, while neglecting to identify existing flaws in

Freedom's foundation, are simply being duped by a different face of deception destined to leave them dismally detoured, dismembered, and dead outside the grace of God. And yet, America is not alone in her unbridled justification of misplaced autonomy and the destructive spirit it embodies and has unleashed over our nation. Other countries have likewise forged ahead to exert independence, act in rebellion, struggle against tyranny, and to wrongly establish fallen-self-rule in lieu of Christ's Lordship. All who have taken such detours, travel a pathway of pride and defiance trying to find elsewhere that which only God the Father and Jesus the Son can provide – lasting life, love, and liberty (1 Corinthians 10:1-11:1). Do we really want to be free as individuals, as a nation? If true, we will do what it takes in both our personal and corporate lives to conform to Christ's likeness (Romans 8:28-30). If not true, we will do what we have been doing – and die. It seems that Paul's challenge for us to show our faith with action...not empty words...is relevant here (James 2:18).

The practice of ancient mysteries God held against Israel throughout history, as displayed in their spiritually adulterous love affair with foreign gods and corresponding immoralities, still run rampant today within many cultures upon the earth. The relevant question is not if these godless and adulterous mysteries still exist, but rather, how their expressions among men have changed? No matter how they manifest, such godless flirtations are rooted in a lie that destroys all who embrace and practice their demonic principles. No one is immune...no one! God's principles are true, functional, and productive, consistent with His character whether applied by those saved or lost...they are immutable and produce results for those who apply them. When applied in accord with God's heart...they bring life. When God's principles are rejected, neglected, or distorted...they cause death. Those ancient mysteries referred to above, which incited God to anger toward humanity, began in the Garden of Eden when Adam and Eve cooperated with satan's lie at the expense of unhindered fellowship with God. These same mysteries reared their head at the Tower of Babel...became foundation for religions rooted in darkness...erected economic empires supplying masons and materials to Kings David and

Solomon...re-emerged elsewhere through Druidism...expressed themselves during the Crusades...operated through religious Catholicism...pervaded pre-colonial Britain...landed on the shores of America...resurfaced in Nazi Germany...declared themselves on cemetery gravestones around the world...and still champion their cause boldly today through American experience in concert with a wayward world... Evidence does not lie...only those who evade its reality do...

Some historians and religionists promote a belief that the aforementioned pagan rituals associated with ancient-to-current-day elite or behind-the-scenes societies bent on global conquest through human exploitation and domination are merely a recent occurrence. Yet, this evidence-refuting belief is inaccurate, pervasive, and life-threatening to those who subscribe without wisdom. Paganism's rituals were designed, practiced, and delivered onto history's ever-emerging stage disguised in the re-painted and re-packaged human façade obscuring hell's agenda. The character traits of God and those of His antithesis, the devil, will never change. One must only ponder the nature, chart the course, and weigh the likely outcome of a given trend with common sense found in the mind of Christ, in order to rightly identify that agenda's true origin as coming from either heaven or hell. The belief that satanically-driven, conspiracy-based agendas only recently existed in post-modern governments, is simply untrue... Conspiracy is not a ridiculous theory as the willfully ignorant allege. Instead, conspiracy is eternally real, relentless, and ruthlessly rooted in the hellish heart of an evil adversary named satan who pits the unwitting, unsaved, and unredeemable from among men against God's people whom He knows are His (John 17:6-26; 2 Thessalonians 2:8-12; 2 Timothy 2:19). Humanity's downward spiral toward an eternal choice between spiritual life and death is inevitable. Meanwhile, satan remains diligent in his efforts to hide his deceptive entrenchments in people's thinking, while blinding them to truth and raping heaven's power so tragically missing in their practice of faith in Jesus Christ. This truth grows more visible within the contrast between lifeless religion that knows a lot about God, versus, experiencing dynamic personal relationship with Jesus, knowing God Himself (John 14:12).

According to Jesus...if the truth sets us free...we are free indeed. Yet, American culture has acquired a view of truth and freedom built on an incomplete...and therefore...inaccurate foundational portrait polluted and systematically re-directed by the distortions of revisionism. Sadly, such skewed national pride only serves to seduce and fuel people's insatiable appetite for more as their emboldened self-indulgent reach for that which destroys traps them in a mirage. Yet Truth remains unchanged in a person named Jesus Who is not subject to a recited religious or moral creed quoted, but never lived (John 14:6; Hebrews 13:8). It is this Truth...Jesus the Living Christ... that will free only those who recognize His existence, confess His Lordship, experience His liberation, and humble themselves under His Almighty hand to love Him with all their hearts as they love others like themselves.

Throughout Scriptural history, one's spiritual authenticity before God has been weighed on one scale alone, that which hangs in His sovereign hand to find its balance and validate its burden based on one's conformity with Christ. If any group, company, organization, government, country, or institution comprised of individuals, marriages, partners, churches, cities, states, or alliances are to experience deliverance from evil and rise to radiance in God's eyes...ground zero within those individuals or entities must be purified and rightly reconstructed upon Christ's sure foundation for God's house to stand (2 Chronicles 7:14; Psalms 11:3, 127:1; Matthew 7:74-27; 1 Corinthians 3:10-14; Ephesians 2:19-22; 1 Timothy 3:14-16; 2 Timothy 2:19; Psalms 127:1). If God designed each human being to be a temple of the Holy Spirit, to join together as part of His corporate temple (Church), and for His temple to rise without spot or wrinkle as His radiant Church (bride) built upon the foundation of the Apostles and Prophets with Christ as the Chief Cornerstone, then building God's way matters (1 Corinthians 3:16; Ephesians 2:20-21, 5:21-32)! Rising from such imagery, I find it interesting that King Solomon commanded his stonecutters to cleave large...quality stones...to provide a strong foundation for God's Temple that he was commissioned to build (1 Kings 5:17-18). As Christians, we are commissioned by Jesus to do the very same in our reach to the world around us (Matthew 28:19-20). It seems that building both our personal and corporate Church foundations on Christ alone as we define and declare our public identities has – foundation (Deuteronomy 32:15-18; Isaiah 44:6-8; 2 Samuel 22:1-4, 32; Psalms 95:1).

In retrospect, one can easily envision the different levels of harvest produced by the opposing motivational seed sown by the young Moravian missionaries versus those planted by America's founders... The seed sown by Moravians spurred a harvest leading others to eternal life, while America's seed produced an ever-increasing harvest of the very tyranny our forefathers fled. One's unyielding affair with sin always destines them toward destruction (Deuteronomy 8:1-20). If you found the Moravians noble and inspiring, yet inadequate to move your inner constitution, please immerse yourself in following story, asking the Holy Spirit to drive God's reality home...

Many years ago...a young woman was caught off-guard when she was contacted by a wealthy father from a distant country who told her that he would like to deliver his unborn child into her care at the time of birth. Such a challenge could not have come to her during more difficult circumstances than those plagued by social, economic, and spiritual oppression at the hands of an abusive leader and regime who governed her daily world. Though this unknown father whose fame, power, and authority preceded him provided little information regarding all involved in assuming such parental responsibility or the unborn child's true identity...the unnerved young woman agreed to accept and raise the child as her own though she was yet unmarried. When she told the man she hoped to marry all that the unborn child's father shared with her and what she had agreed to do...he grew troubled by the most certain shame that would accompany such a sensitive situation sure to cause trouble with his noble family, local synagogue, and home community. He knew those in his town would assume the child had been conceived out of wedlock and start a scandal bringing shame on him and his family because of his religious affiliations... Struggling to think beyond himself, he came to the conclusion that he loved her and did not want to cause heartache by leaving her in time of need. So while sleeping that night, he tossed and turned during a dream that gave him peace to walk through the ensuing birth-related process by marrying her and taking the yet unborn child as his own to silence public disgrace when the father-from-afar delivered the babe into their hands...

Amid social unrest, this now uncertain young couple felt drawn to return to the husband's place of birth some distance away for refuge. Upon their arrival there, they searched for a place to stay quickly being thrust into a downtrodden area for shelter where they remained because they could find nowhere else go. Not long thereafter, the wealthy father's son was born and delivered to the expectant couple as promised under the veil of secrecy to avoid giving away the child's location. Despite the father's efforts however, news soon got out, dispatching government agents to search for the child with intent to harm him if found. Concerned for his wife and son's welfare, the husband gathered his family and launched out for another country under the cover of night, arriving and staying there for some time until they believed it safe to go home... When word came that their hometown was relatively peaceful again, the couple set out for their country's capitol to have their son consecrated to the Lord at the temple by man of faith who mightily blessed the child before they returned to their hometown. As years passed, their once small boy grew in size and ability, learning many skills from his father who ran a local business. It was customary for the couple's entire family to take an annual trip to their nation's capitol, where they took part in services and celebrations held in the temple. On one such occasion after leaving the temple activities on their way home, their son lingered behind without them knowing he was missing for several days because they traveled with such a large family with many members. Retracing their steps immediately upon their discovery, the couple returned to the temple where they found their son talking to people just as they had left him days before... Obviously, his parents were not happy with the commotion their son had caused, but found themselves amazed at how mature he had become as they listened to him speak to others gathered around him... They pondered their son's passion for the things of God as they collected him and headed toward their home...

As time slipped away, their young son grew toward manhood, gaining more skill and business knowledge, before one day deciding it was time to shift his focus in daily life to eternal things. Now an articulate young man driven by passion for God's house – he charted a new course in life, leaving family behind to embrace God's call, strengthen his resolve, develop his message, and spend time with a fast-growing circle of new acquaintances both in town and at the beach. More time passed with his passion gaining intensity in its challenge for people to stop chasing meaningless things in life to become world changers instead... Controversy erupted everywhere he went as people from all walks of life either got in his face to shut him out...or responded to his call and left everything to join his cause. Day-by-day, local religionists grew more concerned about the young man's uncanny ability to incite ordinary people beyond the ordinary to challenge oppression as He authorized them to follow in his footsteps. Running out of options and pursuing access into the young man's inner world, a local leader invited him and others to dinner at his home. While there, the fiery young orator quickly found himself being judged by some there for letting an unsavory woman from the community get too close, give him gifts, and propel his purpose. More time passed with the young revolutionary's influence growing to such a degree that regional governing officials began to impose policies and station law enforcement throughout cities, waiting for young man's arrival so they could arrest him. To their embarrassment, no one was able to lay a hand on him as he repeatedly eluded those bent on his capture...

Everywhere he traveled, this dynamic young leader gave himself to help the downtrodden, consort with underdogs, hug the unacceptable, feed the hungry, and restore the fragmented with peace. Enraged by his skyrocketing popularity, religious leaders were gripped by fear that their scattering congregations and dwindling offerings would be plundered if the young man's ever-rising tide of momentum growing between himself and those chasing him was not soon stemmed. Tensions grew, plots deepened, stakes increased, and battle lines were drawn as unexplainable events surrounding the young man as he radicalized everyday people wherever he went.

Without informing anyone, this mighty messenger-of-the-hour turned toward his nation's sacred city to stand against oppression while making his greatest bid to enlighten those misguided and enslaved by religious or political lies as his followers lined the streets. While crowds stood by, onlookers were sure he would soon be ambushed or apprehended for chasing money-grubbers out of the synagogue or for speaking boldly against the establishment during public festivals at the nation's heart... Yet, to their amazement, he escaped unharmed time-after-time, slipping into the crowds without a trace... Now, embittered by their inability to catch him... local leaders met in secret to devise even more sinister plans...to quench the fire fueled by this young agent-of-change. With local cross-tensions at fever pitch, the young leader held a dinner party for his close friends to set an example...letting them in on what was about to happen...and to mention that someone close to him would let him down...

Now several years into his mission to "change" that which destroyed, his cause was coming to a predetermined head as weariness and turmoil invading his quest often called him to withdraw to solitary places for rest and refocus. Zeroed in on soon-to-occur strategic events while hammered by non-stop bombardment, the young zealot made his way to a secluded garden accompanied by close friends asking them to hang back...before he walked deeper in to seek God's guidance and settle his course through prayer... Emerging from his silent sanctuary with vision clear and purpose cast, voices converging on his location echoed in the night. Now, confronted by an armed band of enforcement sent by religious leaders threatened by his influence...this time-seasoned champion of freedom yielded himself to his soon-to-be captors...led by a once-close friend whose actions now set the long-planned outcome irreversibly in motion. Suddenly, his friends scattered, leaving him in his darkest hour as others led him to where he would later be scourged by authorities determined to cement his guilt... Within hours, destiny's agenda deferred liberty's voice as submission to higher purpose dragged freedom's champion before those in authority who questioned integrity, rejected humility, accused ruthlessly, dismissed reality, penalized unfairly, and inflicted brutality – without mercy...

From the cradle of a once displaced child sent from royalty's presence into the arms of uncertainty, injustice, and destiny – arose a Son whose example others were predestined to follow... Yielding silently as a friend-turned-traitor sold Him into political and religious persecution, sealing his demise for thirty pieces of silver, He sacrificed his life so those who are selfish, willful, and unfaithful – could live. When asked by those granted power to condemn or free...He made no reply, not a single word, as He was led away to be tortured and forced to tread an upward trail of disgrace, nailed to hell's savagery, willingly abused and...utterly alone. As life bled away amid agony's suffocating hush, Jesus said, "It is finished" as He bowed His head, humbled Himself under His Father's almighty hand, and loved those who killed Him, beyond tyranny...

If we want to see our world, country, churches, homes, and individual lives experience true freedom...eternal truth remains the only key able we have to unlock hell's oppression (John 8:32-36, 14:6). If truth remains the only key, Jesus Christ as Living Truth must be accepted, submitted to, and His example applied personally in the way we live and love those with whom we associate. For the person of Jesus Christ to actually become our life's foundation either individually or as a country – we must identify ourselves with His name and declare Him as Lord before men publically (1 Corinthians 3:11; Romans 10:9). So, if you want to be a Christian who lives with power and experiences life, prove it! Otherwise, admit your faith is a lofty illusion and be what the spiritual condition of your life choices represent to God and man based on both visible and internal reality – lost. If watered down truth did not protect our nation, it will not protect those who remain determined to go our own way, either. It's time to choose, declare, and rise or...get out of heaven's way! While our forefathers fled tyranny's crown of gold and greed fueled by a spirit of independence steeped in self-preservation, the Author of Life bowed to be beaten beneath tyranny's crown of thorns in silence so those who abused Him, could live. I rest my case...

Whether you are a president or simply an American...a governing leader or general member of any other independent republic or democratic society...a tyrannical ruler or impoverished subject beneath oppression's third world fist...or just an everyday man, woman, or child upon the earth crying out for life – Jesus Christ reigns supreme as either Loving Lord or Holy Judge over us all forever! In His glorious light, I challenge you to renounce the "spirit" of independence that estranges your individual life from God and to re-declare your "proper dependence" upon Jesus Christ as both Lord and Savior without limit or condition. Doing so will empower you to become Christ-centered Christians and citizens capable of praying for governing leaders with power from a position of righteous humility (1 Timothy 2:1-6). God will use your humble submission to Him as permission to transform your hearts, minds, and spirits as He resurrects you to become victorious fathers, mothers, husbands, wives, leaders, followers, and children, capable and qualified to rightly govern in all spheres starting with self and extending, to nations.

Until we willingly submit ourselves to God's institution of authority, thereby making ourselves properly dependent upon Jesus Christ alone for our timely deliverance, we cannot pray effectually (James 5:16). It's time that we let Jesus bring life-giving transformation to our marriages, relationships, churches, businesses, communities, governments, or nations through rightly-established authority openly declared and founded upon Jesus Christ. He is Heaven's Bridegroom, and we, as believers in Him...are His bride called to rise out of rebellion and into radiance as we make ourselves ready to meet Him (Ephesians 5:21-33; Revelation 19:7-9). If we will not declare His identity or submit to Him in our relationship with Him, we will never be capable of loving in other relationships either as proof of our true fidelity toward God and man. Many want to retrace history's steps and return to America's foundations believing that doing so will overturn our nation's demise. Yet, without exception to this very day, freedom is still purchased with blood through flowing from the only answer capable of healing us... Jesus Christ and Him crucified...

Jesus Story References

Genesis 1:1; Isaiah 7:14-15; Matthew 1:18-2:23, 3:1-4:25, 10:5-42, 17:1-23, 20:17-19, 21:1-17, 26:1-75, 27:1-44; Mark 1:9-20, 11:1-19, 14:1-65, 15:1-37, 4:1-30, 9:14-30; Luke 1:26-38, 2:1-52, 7:1-50, 18:15-30, 19:28-20:8, 22:1-23:46; John 1:1-5, 4:1-42, 4:43-6:70, 12:1-19, 13:1-38, 18:1-19:30.

Sunrise in Washington, DC at end of first USA Walk – July 4, 2002

White House in Washington, DC at end of first USA Walk – 2002

Chapter 7

Clothed With Christ

"So let us put aside the deeds of darkness and put on the armor of light...clothe yourselves with the Lord Jesus Christ and do not think about how to gratify the desires of the sinful nature" (Romans 13:12, 14 NIV).

While on my way home from walking across America and deeply engrossed in making "moving sale" signs to liquidate possessions for an indigent widow I had been helping who was losing her home due to family victimization – I was pierced by injustice that is so many times imposed by the strong upon the weak... In the meantime, the other side of my noodle was pondering the next subject I was preparing to write as I gave a sigh of relief, knowing I was nearing the end of this book. Suddenly, reality slapped its cuffs on my wandering thoughts as my phone rang; it was a dear Louisiana friend...who had just test read and digested this chapter's prior draft...on the other end of the line. He said, "Great chapter, best one yet!" "Thanks" I said. "Wonder if it may be even better broken into two parts, going from general in the first to more detail in the next," He mused a bit under his breath. "Deep stuff...true stuff...wow!" He added. I polled him for more input, chatted for a few more minutes on other things, and said "Chat with you soon" as I hung up and resumed making my last sign for the next morning's sale. "Where should I split the chapter and what story should I use to kick off the second one?" I asked myself as I scurried about getting ready for the next day...

Before I finished the thought, my phone rang again as I answered saying, "Good morning, this is Greg...what can I do for you?" "I'm calling about the lawnmower you have advertised," the voice on the other end of the phone replied. "What would you like to know?" I asked. He ventured his questions and I gave my answers as we bantered back-and-forth amid a few chuckles to boot... Before I could finish the call, another gentleman who had called several days earlier arrived to look around and pick up something that'd originally caught his attention and that he requested I save for him.

As the man walked through the house, went out the back door, and rummaged through items diverse...my call with Chuck continued.

After a few moments, the man who dropped by finished looking, asked prices on a few gadgets he'd gathered, pulled out a couple of twenty-dollar bills to pay, filled his arms and headed toward his car with the first load before coming back to get the rest. As the man headed out the door, I said, "Chuck, I need to help this guy load his stuff...I'll call you back." Chuck replied, "Save the lawnmower, I'm on my way." "I'll be waiting for you...I'll see ya when you get here," I replied as I cut the call, stuffing my phone back in my sweatshirt pocket – again. Finally, the man finished loading, shook my hand, thanked me, and drove away, giving me a chance to think through my friend's chapter feedback that rolled in by phone only moments before. Wandering the corridors of my mind, caught between this world and the one beyond, I thought, "Lord, I need another story to kick-off this new chapter if I'm going to split the original one in two...please send me someone with a story to tell." As I bustled about in the driveway, I noticed a beige sedan slip past the rear of my RV out-of-sight... Standing at a crude plywood table next to the white fence erected by the widow, around her rose garden, a spry gray-haired man caught my eye as he rounded the rear of my motor home on his way up the drive. I said, "You must be Chuck." "Guilty as charged," he replied sticking out his hand to shake...

"The lawnmower's inside...let me bring it out so we can fire her up." I told him as he planted himself awaiting my return. I backed the lawnmower out the door, spun it around, and rolled it across the concrete to a stop in front of Chuck. I bent down, flipped the choke, gave it a yank, and...it came to life. "Sounds good," Chuck said as I let go of the handle so it could die. It was a beautiful southern California day with temps in the 60's. Shifting gears in subject matter Chuck said, "Nice motor home." I replied, "Thanks, I've been on the road for 14 months walking, meeting people, and preaching my way across America...it's been an adventure to say the least." "I'll bet...long walk for sure," he said. "Walking was the easy part," I replied through an easy grin. I mentioned that I was trying to conclude the widow's affairs and finish my book before heading home over the next week. He inquired what I was writing about, giving me an opportunity to share a bit... So, I declared my book's subject, offered a few snippets, and hit the high spots of George's story of navigating two submarine tours in Korea, re-upping as a fighter pilot over Vietnam, going to work as a fighter test pilot, and having his plane disappear around him at 28,000 feet while on a test flight... "So, what do you do Chuck?" I asked. "I was an engineering test pilot for the major aircraft manufacturers for years." My mind shot back to my prior conversation that morning with my buddy concerning chapter layout issues as Chuck launched into a few stories of his own...

"I started flying as a test pilot at age 26...most of the other pilots were in their late 30's early 40's," Chuck said. "That's pretty young," I commented. "I came in with a degree in aeronautical engineering that most of the other guys didn't have," he replied. "I flew for one company in Wichita for number of years flying one project after another from beginning to end. If you started a test project on a plane, you flew through to the end before starting a new one. I remember the company I worked for wanted to break into the fighter business to get military contracts, so they developed and built a new model different from most. Because my company had never had a military fighter contract, they needed a test pilot with fighter experience to conduct the testing. I was in the middle of project at the time, so they had to hire from the outside even though I was qualified. They found a guy working for another arms manufacturer, got him approved by the military, and sent him to Florida where the new prototype he was to fly had been shipped. When he arrived to the airfield where the new fighter was housed... he grabbed his gear and headed for the flight line to kick the tires and take a walk around the plane. After he circumnavigated the fighter a time-or-two...he took his chute...laid it across the wing and said, "I'm not flying that plane...I quit," refusing to conduct the test. I simply scratched my head wondering why he refused when I heard about it." "Some people are hard to understand," I said. "About then," he continued, "the plane I was testing needed to be re-instrumented, putting my project on hold for a few months...so, I became available. My boss called and asked me if I wanted to take the new fighter for a spin and I accepted...I needed something to do. I jumped a plane for Florida a few days later, landed, grabbed my gear, strapped in, pointed her down the strip, and took off. It was just like any other plane...you push forward it goes down, pull back and it goes up, lean right it goes right...you get the picture. I never could understand why the other pilot wouldn't fly it...it was a good plane."

"Who knows...people chart their course through life based on fears and vantage points...right or wrong. It's amazing how many live far below the greatness God designed them to have," I responded. "I had a hard time getting along with my boss at the first company, so finally took a position flying for another arms manufacturer," Chuck said as he continued. "The second company tested planes, retrofitted them with weaponry, and worked the bugs out for final production. One day, I was scheduled to test fly a twin-engine jet attack bomber that had been retrofitted with a gun turret by another manufacturer just ahead of the tail rudder. The company I went to work for had a bit of an issue because their runway was too short for take-off according to military safety standards. The government made them self-insure in case of mishap. So, I gathered my gear that day, made my way toward the plane, strapped in, and ran down my pre-flight checklist. I eased the throttle forward, taxied toward the runway, and pointed her down range. About half way down the strip as I gained speed lifting my nose wheel, the rudder pedals began to jump and shake. I couldn't abort because I was out of room – I had to go! Once I got off the ground and gained speed and altitude...things smoothed out and went back to normal. I knew it was an aerodynamic issue. When I landed and sat down with my engineers telling them what happened, they were convinced the hydraulic system associated with the new gun turret had issues. I told them I thought it was an aerodynamic problem that we could figure out by using a simple test. But they wanted to call in the turret manufacturer's mechanics to tear down the hydraulic system, saying the plane wasn't safe to fly...

I persisted, telling the engineers that we could station a few short lengths of rope up the tail rudder and capture their activity on camera for analysis. They told me it was too dangerous... But I said the plane flew once – it will fly again. They finally took my advice and we affixed the rope segments up the rudder and proceeded. Once airborne, they came alongside in another plane taking pictures of the rudder at different speeds and altitudes. When we reviewed the pictures, we learned that there were turbulence issues because of the new gun turret. The company that installed it said they ran a wind tunnel test...but...no way." "I'm amazed by how many people or companies cut corners...there's no integrity any more...it's all about money," I mentioned. Then Chuck said, "I was always different from other pilots. If they didn't like a plane, they cut the flight short, and gave meaningless reports...what a waste of time and money. What good is it to know you have a problem and then not take time to figure it out? That's where my engineering background came into play," Chuck said. "Just listening to you, I bet you are a visionary who sees in pictures," I said to Chuck. He replied, "Yes, I do." "It took me years to realize that not everyone can see things that way," I said.

Over the next few minutes, I shared several experiences in which my vision and ability to see things made other people uncomfortable. Chuck nodded his head showing that he understood... We loaded Chuck's newly acquired lawnmower in the back of his sedan. As he prepared to take off, we expressed our mutual pleasure of meeting, having time to chat, and agreed to try to resume our conversation early the next week before my departure. "How old are you Chuck?" I asked as he turned toward his car. "87," he replied. "No way," I thought to myself as Chuck folded himself into his small sedan and drove away. Walking up the driveway, my mind retreated to my earlier prayer asking God to send me a story to kick-off the new chapter segment my buddy suggested I write... "God, You're hilarious...what are the chances of me meeting an 87 year old retired colonel-slash-test pilot thirteen months earlier at the onset of my walk...me deciding to use his story as an intro on the chapter draft my friend just called me this morning over a year later to comment on...me asking You to send me just the right intro story to split my original chapter into two segments...and having another 87 year old test pilot the same age as George walk into my world while helping an out-of-state widow...at precisely the time I need it to meet deadline? Unbelievable!" God's timing and attention to detail are amazing...

With the first half of my original chapter draft being general in nature – George simply knew his plane disappeared from around him without warning at 28,000 feet, never really knowing why. Yet, Chuck's mode of operation asked the hard questions, identified elusive answers, and stayed the course until victory was won... Now that we generally understand how America was founded and shaped...it's time to dive a bit deeper into the detailed inner workings and outward expressions tied to the spirit of independence and other issues that hinder our intimacy with God...

Many historians bent on defending the purported foundational righteousness of American society overlook an unavoidable reality governed by the immutable eternal laws and principles of God's kingdom. As these same historians quickly point out...while building their case, citing revisionism as a qualifier...America's founding document, entered into by our forefathers, was called "The Unanimous Declaration" – not the Declaration of Independence. In this light, said history buffs adhere to an erroneous belief that America did not technically declare independence, thereby wrongly concluding that our nation is, therefore, not subject to the spiritual consequences of rebellion. Yet, one must only read the document itself to see the obvious existence of an independent spirit within its language and intent. Whether overt declaration or covert intent, the same governing spirit and heart attitude inhabits both... It doesn't matter if it's a hard-hearted pharaoh...a burning bush leader...a shepherd become king...a prophet gone AWOL... an agent of betrayal...a Pharisee brought low...a misguided noble statesman...or a citizen cast adrift – God still opposes the proud and gives grace to the humble based on our attitudes and declarations (James 4:1-7).

In this light, it's crucial that we remember that our forefather's spiritual eyesight was somewhat diminished and distorted by their deism, theism, and empiricism, denying God's primary spiritual mechanism of human enlightenment. After all, how can God actually intervene in the affairs of men if His primary mode of spiritual communication with mankind, through miracles and revelation that are rooted in His divine nature – are largely erased by those who lead others? Due to their perspective's resulting shortsightedness, they were incapable of seeing the downside-spiritual repercussions associated with their supposedly noble declarations and actions. As a result, they unwittingly released a spirit of independence over our nation rooted in delusion's ignorance, foolishness, and defiance, unwilling and unable to submit to heaven's authority (Romans 1:18-32, 13:1-5; Ephesians 6:5-9; Colossians 3:22-25; 2 Thessalonians 2:9-12; 1 Peter 2:13-25, 5:6-7).

Before we take a look at some of America's founding language, however, there are several issues we must consider as we converge from varied vantage points, waiting for God to clear us for landing on heaven's page of understanding... First, both God's institution of authority and marriage are similar in structure, function, and purpose – releasing God's design, disseminating God's order, and fulfilling God's plan. Both institutions only succeed when they function based on mutual respect and submission one to another. Authority must respect its subjects and submit by providing those they lead with righteous leadership in order to inspire their allegiance. Conversely, subjects must respect those who lead, submitting to their governance to inspire that authority's righteousness and benevolence. Second, we must realize that intimate, cooperative, and mutually-beneficial relationship between authority and subject are the primary goal. When both authority and subject focus on the benefit of the other, unity that develops intimacy occurs. Conflict comes when authority gets wrongly focused on its right to exert dominion and subjects lose perspective and demand their rights – both attitudes are fueled by selfishness. When self rises above others, defeat is imminent. Third in our considerations is the issue of our selfless determination to consider others better than ourselves as we serve those around us (Philippians 2:3-5). Our individual emulation of Christ's character empowers unity, intimacy, and victory (John 17:23). In addition to breaking down and understanding the inner workings and expressions of independence, we must also ponder other factors that either empower or prevent our being clothed with the Living Armor of Jesus Christ in this life (Romans 9:6-8, 13:14; Galatians 3:26-29)...

Living Armor

Whether we were first introduced to Jesus when we were knee-high to a grasshopper, a young whippersnapper, emerging young lady, a star on-the-rise, a shattered divorcee, an imprisoned thief, a premature widow, or a retired professional – most of us have heard or been told to put on our spiritual armor before we brave the world each day... Typically, we are hauled to the book of Ephesians and repeatedly instructed to stand firm with the belt of truth around our waist...with the breastplate of righteousness in place...our feet fitted with the readiness that comes from the gospel of peace...to take up the shield of faith...the helmet of salvation and the sword of the Spirit known as the – word of God (Ephesians 6:14-17). Sadly, most of those chanting such mantra over our spiritual development only know the mechanical principles in part through intellectual theology as they blow by the deeper realities that actually give armor its protective power... Why? These well-intentioned professors of life and faith simply never gained God's revelation on the matter by chasing Him with whole hearts to seize supernaturally powerful face-to-face kingdom realities, themselves (Jeremiah 29:13; Daniel 10:12-14; John 6:45, 14:26, 16:8-15; 1 Corinthians 13:12; James 1:5; 2 Peter 3:3-7; Revelation 1:1-3). Why am I making such a big deal out this seemingly insignificant and ill-timed issue in view of the more lofty subjects already tabled before us? Simple...

First, what good is armor if it doesn't work? Most warriors don their armor to stay alive in the fight, not to hang tin trash from their necks. Whether we leave our armor back at the castle on the shelf (dusty bible)...it does not fit (unqualified use)...or, it has gaps between its plates (underdeveloped) – it still leaves us dead on the battlefield when it doesn't work. So, it seems logical and wise on our part, for us to pull out heaven's instruction manual to update our qualifications and re-configure our armor so we can win... The most technologically-advanced equipment does not make us a soldier...just as...gear does not make us a football player... fishing poles do not make us a fisherman...tools do not make us a mechanic...tights do not make us a ballerina...books do not make us a scholar...declarations do not make us a noble...Hebrew does not make us a theologian...church does not make us a Christian... words do not make us a witness...knowing does not make us faithful...and wishing does not make us saved – only obeying God does! Therefore, it seems a wee bit relevant at this very moment, to shuck our idealisms and get down to reality, God's way!

Scripture uses imagery to establish the person of Jesus Christ as one-of-three unique inseparably-linked expressions or manifestations of Christianity's monotheistic, Triune God. It does so by describing the different trinity-based roles of God as The Father, The Son, and The Holy Spirit. On this basis, we find that Jesus personally incarnates, embodies, or somehow personifies all seven components on heaven's list of spiritual armor found in the last chapter of Ephesians. Jesus is the belt of truth as He declares Himself to be the way, the truth, and the life (John 14:6). Likewise, He is the breastplate of righteousness as God's wisdom for us who is our holiness, righteousness, and redemption (1 Corinthians 1:30). Jesus is also the Prince of Peace upon which the gospel of peace is founded (Isaiah 9:6-7). Just as Jesus is known as the Author of Life...we find that He is also the Author and Finisher of our faith (Acts 3:15; Hebrews 12:2). Next, we find Moses, Isaiah, Simeon, and John the Baptist declaring and preparing the way of the Lord as God's salvation to them and the world-at-large, as His mighty arm works salvation (Exodus 15:2; Isaiah 12:2, 59:16; Luke 2:30, 3:6). Moving on, we discover Jesus is the coming Messiah known as the Word God Who is spiritual in nature and came to dwell among men (John 1:1-5, 4:24). And finally, we find Jesus is the ultimate prayer warrior as He ever lives in Spirit to intercede for His people (Hebrews 7:25). So, as you can see, Jesus Christ is – Living Armor (Hebrews 7:23-25).

Why settle for a mechanical misfit, when you can have the real deal? We can put on and wear God's Living Armor twenty-four hours-a-day, seven days-a-week without fret-or-worry, knowing we are always protected night-and-day wherever we go...if...we do our part. What is our role in the equation? Easy! We must live blamelessly before God through unconditional love, forgiveness, humility, submission, obedience, and faith in Jesus Christ! Easy to understand...a bit challenging to live at times along life's path... What does blamelessness mean? Being blameless is being willing to repent before God and man for every sinful thing we do in word, thought, or deed which the Holy Spirit convicts us of. Repentance simply means that we identify and confess our sins... seek forgiveness from God and those we wronged...and that we turn away from that sinful behavior to do things God's way instead. When we repent...it puts our sin beneath the blood of Jesus Christ and makes us clean and – blameless in God's eyes. How many times have we tried to live life based on an endless list of religious do's and don'ts only to land on the skids defeated? The potential benefits or risks we experience through either the fleeting qualities of intellectually-based mechanical armor...or...the radical rest, peace, and assurances we received through being clothed in the Living Armor of Jesus Christ – are literally worlds apart – physical versus spiritual. Intellectual armor relies on fallen human nature and effort, while Living Armor stands ever-victorious in the Living God from a position of rest (Hebrews 4:1-16)...

The Holy Spirit began speaking to me about becoming a "Warrior or Rest" years ago, rather than being a driven disciple. When we battle from a position of human effort – we grow weary, war-torn, and lay our weapons down, yielding to defeat as the enemy advances in our slumber amid the darkness. Yet, when we war from a position of rest...our armor remains intact, weapons stay on task, and victory stands its ground as God fights on our behalf. Though putting on God's armor seems simple enough – it will cost you submission to God's will and way... The process of putting on God's Living Armor will enlighten our inspiration, re-direct our passion, inspire our submission, and purify our confession as we allow Jesus to indwell, dominate, and empower us with His unconditional love, forgiveness, selflessness, and sacrifice toward others in life (Matthew 6:14-15; Luke 19:10; 1 Corinthians 13:7-8; Ephesians 5:21; Philippians 2:3-5). Now, that we have a clearer image of what it means, what is required, and what it releases when we are clothed in Living Armor – let's finish looking at the greatest barrier between ourselves and Jesus Christ – pride's spirit of independence. It is my hope that all prior inputs herein have properly set the stage to help you discover truth as you consider the principles and potentials revealed in America's founding language taken from the "Unanimous Declaration" quoted below:

Quote #1
"When, in the course of human events, it becomes necessary for one people to dissolve the political bands which have connected them with another, and to assume among the powers of the earth, the separate and equal station to which the laws of nature and of nature's God entitle them, a decent respect to the opinions of mankind requires that they should declare the causes which impel them to the separation."

Author's Comment / Quote #1
The above language from the Unanimous Declaration...though obviously focused on political issues...by principle implies, that when a relationship becomes challenged, its parties should declare and justify the reasons which urge, drive, or force them to separate from one another. Sadly, it does not communicate a corresponding countermeasure that also urges, drives, or forces reconciliation between the divided parties as prescribed in the bible. In principle therefore, the above declarative language promotes expression of differences without resolution, separation without reconciliation, and that allowing division to remain is acceptable. Hence, implied independence without submissive accountability to God or one another is clear.

Quote #2
"We hold these truths to be self-evident, that all men are created equal, that they are endowed by their Creator with certain unalienable rights, that among these are life, liberty and the pursuit of happiness."

Author's Comment / Quote #2
The language in this portion of the Unanimous Declaration speaks to an obvious truth that all men are created equal before God

in their right to live, be free, and pursue happiness. In this text the word "life" obviously refers to the state of being alive and able to live. However, both the words "liberty" and "happiness" are subjective terms based on the view of the one defining them and the circumstances governing a given individual's ability to exercise their unalienable rights. This distinction is critical because exercising one's right or freedoms must be done in a manner that does not limit or damage another person's equal right to exercise their freedom. The simultaneous expression of freedom by two individuals requires the existence of mutual selflessness and submission, not selfishness...which also communicates a biblical distinctive. If very different definitions of liberty or happiness exist in the perspectives held by two separate people, unity between them can only be achieved through discussion, compromise, and mutual submission to one another...if...a lasting unity adequate to preserve peace – is to exist.

Quote #3
"That to secure these rights, governments are instituted among men, deriving their just powers from the consent of the governed. That whenever any form of government becomes destructive to these ends, it is the right of the people to alter or to abolish it, and to institute a new government, laying its foundations on such principles and organizing its powers in such form, as to them shall seem most likely to affect their safety and happiness."

Author's Comment / Quote #3
Quote #3 holds the most independent language of those cited herein. Please review and consider the enclosed issues addressed in the author comment sections. Likewise, please remember that biblical Christians believe that "unadulterated kingdom government" rests upon God's shoulders alone through the person of Jesus Christ (Isaiah 9:2-7). If America were truly the Judeo-Christian nation it believes itself to be...its founders would have declared Jesus Christ as the ultimate champion of freedom and Chief Cornerstone of their newborn government and society...and unfortunately...He was not (2 Corinthians 3:12-18; Ephesians 2:19-20). Since God's institution of authority mirrors His divine institution of marriage

as portrayed through the imagery of Heaven's Bridegroom (Jesus) coming back to join His radiant bride (Church / Ephesians 5:25-27)... please consider how well the stance American forefathers took on civil and governmental relationship would work within the context of your own marriage and home...

First, you will notice that the opening sentence of quote #3 eludes to governments which are instituted among men, draw their power from the consent of those they govern...not God. Next, we find the second sentence in quote #3 clearly revealing that those people governed have the right to alter or abolish their government if they deem its oversight destructive to their safety or happiness. Furthermore, the language in quote #3's second sentence also extends freedom for the governed to start a new government based on whatever principles they determine most effective in achieving their subjective definition of personal safety and happiness. In light of marriage...how is this any different than a disgruntled spouse coming to their mate saying, "I don't like the way I'm being treated in our relationship, so I'm going to alter (separate) or abolish (divorce) our marriage covenant?" Without mutual submission drawing its strength from Jesus Christ as the Eternal Truth with humility...how would such a relational situation have any chance of resolution? In truth, the language contained in quote #3 proudly opens the door to the unbridled expression and manifestation of an independent spirit otherwise known as revolution or rebellion devoid of humility, accountability, submission, or unconditional commitment as the bible portrays through the life of Jesus Christ... To further exacerbate the problem, this self-based, non-reconciliatory attitude is fully rooted in the wayward whims of people – not eternal truth. To grasp the scope and impact of our forefather's actions...we must understand the nature of independence and submission's companion role in agreement.

Please note that independence is exclusive in nature and fully incapable of allowing or extending liberty toward others in order to express equal freedom, power, or ownership as demanded or exercised by oneself. By nature, the spirit of independence proudly exerts its freedom, demands its rights, lays its claim, sets its course, and imposes its desires on God and others without concern, compromise, or compassion. Simply put, the spirit of independence is sin-based, anti-Christ, and cannot please God (Romans 8:5-8; 1 John 2:22-23). The spirit of independence is selfish, competitive, indifferent, and defiant toward God's divine institution of authority. Independence prevents those who hold rightly established leadership positions from administrating their authority over its rebellious nature due to an excluded, but absolutely necessary factor in the equation of biblical agreement known as – submission (Matthew 18:19-20; Romans 13:1-5; Ephesians 5:21).

The ingredient of submission rises out humility to bridge the gap between two individual human or corporate wills set in prideful opposition toward one another. Submission cannot operate or co-exist in the same heart, soul, mind, spirit, or realm as the spirit of independence. For submission to co-exist and operate within the same location...one's declaration of and proper dependence upon Jesus Christ as both Lord and Savior must pre-exist submission's free expression. Any individual, marriage, home, partnership, church, business, organization, or government dominated by a spirit of independence will find it impossible to escape turmoil, achieve unity, experience peace, or enter God's rest (Hebrews 3:7-19). In short, the spirit of independence unwittingly unleashed by founding father deism, theism, or empiricism-based spiritual blindness continues to demoralize present and future American liberty, spirituality, and society to an ever-deepening degree (Romans 1:21-32). It was this very competitive character trait that caused satan to be cast out of heaven for aspiring to make himself like God Most High (Isaiah 14:12-15).

Open declaration (confession) of, submission to, and reconciliation with Jesus Christ through repentance, is our only hope to escape from the tyranny embodied within the spirit of independence, because it was Jesus' death on the cross which removed the dividing wall of hostility between Himself and mankind (Matthew 10:32-33; John 14:6; Romans 10:9; 2 Corinthians 5:17-20; Ephesians 2:14-16). Tyranny is a cruel, oppressive, and evil perversion, and antithesis, to the righteous government of all things which rests solely on

God's shoulders in Jesus Christ (Isaiah 9:6). If God requires open confession, submission, and reconciliation with Jesus Christ from and individual person in order to solidify salvation...then, He will also requires these same things from a nation comprised of those individuals in order to qualify as a Judeo-Christian nation. The fact that our forefathers did not publicly declare and identify our nation with the person of Jesus Christ bound our individual and corporate lives as members of an autonomous nation to a path promising our demise if not corrected. As a result, American culture has both re-created the environment for and is now living beneath the very tyranny represented by the seventeenth and eighteenth century British Crown our founding fathers fled. How could this happen? Simply put...the tyrannical spirit is tethered to and in league with the independence previously unleashed over our nation, government, and people by those lacking spiritual foresight. The enemy of our souls finds more-than-creative ways to invade and rob our lives of fruit that lasts...

I remember an old neighboring farmer in our area that raised some of the best peaches around. He worked hard to grow his crop on one of the nicest southern sloping parcels of ground in the valley. As peaches began to ripen and harvest ensued...he would take his daily pick of peaches into his old shed, cover them with a heavy cloth, and lock the doors at night to protect them from theft before leaving each day. To his chagrin, he found bite marks across the top of his peaches each morning when he removed the cloth covering the stack. Stumped – he leaned back against the bench, tipped his hat back on his head, and chewed on the stem of a piece of orchard grass as he pondered what happened. Snapping back to attention...he looked all over the building and discovered that the culprits causing the problem were – rats. Fueled with frustration, he jumped in his truck and rolled on down to the local farm store to buy some rat poison to rid the building of the pesky critters before they destroyed more of his hard-to-grow peaches...

When he got home, he poured out several piles of rat bait in around the inside of the building before covering the current day's peach pick and leaving for the night. Fit to be tied, he found more bite marks the next morning after removing the heavy cloth covering the boxes. By now, he was furious...but without a clue as to how the rats were getting in. So, he started looking around to find their entrance...but without success. In the middle of the day, he suddenly had a vision of what to do... He would cover all the windows, turn out the lights, and look for where light was coming in, certain that it would reveal what he was looking for. After a bunch of huffin'-and-puffin', he finally got his windows covered and flipped off the light switch waiting for his eyes to adjust. Slowly, he turned around looking for any sign of light, but found nothing. Yet, as he turned toward the last corner, he spotted an ever-so-faint glimmer of light. Making his way through the dark in the light's direction...he almost maimed himself as he ran into a pile of something without warning... Giving his wife a yell he said, "Turn on the lights" finding himself toe-to-toe with a stack of half-worn truck tires coming into focus through light-blinded eyes. If that were not enough...there was an old truck fender, ice chest, a set of antlers, and a few boxes of Christmas lights stacked on top too. After clearing off the top of the pile and rolling the final truck skin out of the way...he discovered the bottom 12 inches of one of the barn's side boards had either rotted or had been gnawed through. Now, it all made sense... Looking at the trail, it was clear that the rats had been scurrying in-and-out through a hole in the wall hidden beneath a pile of clutter at will, doing their damage to the farmer's peaches. Though he had used all at his disposal to save his crop, he failed at protecting his esteemed fruit. How? His unawareness of an established entry point (sin) hidden beneath a pile of familiar everyday stuff, was being used by his avowed enemy (satan) to destroy him from amid the darkness, causing him to suffer the consequences... In this light, please consider the following example from American patriotism as one of the primary ways the above spiritual principle functions in our culture to maintain its grip in our lives and country...

Strongholds spoken of in the bible represent spiritually binding patterns of thought rooted in deception and dwelling within fallen human thinking (2 Corinthians 10:3-5). Based upon our American forefather's reduced level of spiritual enlightenment and those religious views they acted upon in their efforts to build America's philosophical foundations...the devil was given a foothold through which he established a fortified entrenchment in American perspective. Again, I am speaking specifically about the spiritual transaction and corresponding repercussions associated with the issue of independence, not about the physical or historical nobility of America's founding statesmen. In a nutshell, those spiritual forces of wickedness operating within and exerting control over American perspective needed a mechanism to legitimize, cover, and maintain that stronghold's right to exist within the hearts of its citizenry and the land-at-large. To do so, satan's ability to uphold that stronghold's right to exist required that the recurring declaration of spiritually binding vows be spoken by those bound beneath its dominion in order to reinforce his dark entrenchment. Let me describe how this has happened in American culture and what was and is still being used to do so...

America's original three founding documents including the Unanimous Declaration, Articles of Confederation, and Constitution of the United States of America established the original stronghold which released the spirit of independence over our nation. Next, Americans celebrate "Independence Day" every Fourth of July commemorating the philosophies, commitments, and actions set forth in the afore-mentioned foundational documents. And, the Pledge of Allegiance has been repetitively recited at the opening of local to Congressional level governmental meetings and by other public and benevolent organizations to include public schools, Order of the Elks, Knights of Columbus, Royal Rangers, Boy Scouts, Girl Scouts, Fraternal Order of the Eagles, Rosicrucians, Freemasons, Lions Club, Rotary Club, and many other groups since the pledge was adopted by governmental leadership. Please consider two noteworthy issues concerning people making this binding pledge... (1) That the one pledging places their hand over their heart...and also (2) what they are specifically pledging their allegiance to... You may find it of interest that America's original Pledge of Allegiance was penned by Francis Bellamy, a Christian Socialist, in 1892 and that it was subsequently and officially adopted by Congress as our country's national pledge in 1942. In its current form, America's

Pledge of Allegiance reads:

"I pledge allegiance to the flag of the United States of America, and to the republic for which it stands, one nation under God, indivisible, with liberty and justice for all."

Please notice that those reciting this pledge are declaring allegiance to the "flag and republic" of the United States of America while placing their hand over their heart – the wellspring of life – not to Jesus Christ as Christians are admonished by Scripture to do (Proverbs 4:23; Romans 10:9). This follows form with and compounds the afore-mentioned consequences as not declaring the name of Jesus Christ in our founding documents. It does so as the one reciting it declares their allegiance to an inanimate object and to an earthly government, not to the Lordship of Jesus Christ... Likewise, please note that this same pledge declares allegiance to a "generic" God rather than God the Father of Jesus Christ. And finally, this pledge affords liberty and justice to all without defining boundaries or controls that uphold spiritual integrity, thereby leaving the door open to moral decline and ultimately, failure without recourse. All of these oversights, in effect, cast our culture adrift on the sea of relativism now unraveling our nation at an ever-increasing pace... Though some may oppose my view, it is obvious that the foundation and governmental system erected at America's inception has been unable to stem the tide of decay as leaders rip their power out of the hands of a misinformed and misguided populace... This dear friend, is nothing more than a rerun repercussion akin to the fallout Israel experienced when they rejected God and asked for a earthly king (1 Samuel 8:1-22).

The real issue embodied in ratifying foundational documents devoid of Christ or one reciting any creed or Pledge of Allegiance to anyone or anything...invokes a biblical principle...wherein making a vow built on a decision of human will spiritually binds its declarer to the terms of that vow (Numbers 30:1-2; Psalms 66:13-14; Proverbs 20:25; Ecclesiastes 5:1-7; Jonah 2:9). Had the Unanimous Declaration, Articles of Confederation, Constitution of the United States of America, or Pledge of Allegiance openly declared the name and governing supremacy of Jesus Christ – America's citizens and nation-as-a-whole would have bound themselves to scripturally-sound behavioral principles capable of producing life and freedom. As it was written and ratified however, founding document and subsequent pledge language denying clarity on the rightful position of Jesus Christ over our nation...spiritually bound America's citizens to declining morality and spirituality now delivering us to the brink of destruction. Therefore, it seems relevant to elaborate on those ties that bind...

Binding Vows

A binding vow is very simply one's verbal declaration of any decision of will they have made in their mind, heart, and then acted upon. When we say, "I will or will not do anything," we are making a binding vow that holds us fast to what we have just declared. That vow will remain in place until it is renounced in the name of Jesus Christ by either ourselves as the one who declared it or...by those holding proper levels of spiritual authority over us to renounce what we have declared on our behalf (Numbers 30:1-10). The positive power of binding vows is enforced by heaven in the salvation transaction that sets us free from sin when we declare Jesus Christ to be Lord of our lives with our mouth (Matthew 10:32-33; Romans 10:8-10; Hebrews 13:15). Why is the binding power of a spoken vow so important to God? Simple, verbal declarations evidence the posture of one's heart before God (Proverbs 18:7; Luke 6:45). Throughout history, we have both observed and experienced the positive or negative binding effects of spoken or written vows in situations involving salvation, marriage, contracts, courtrooms, and government. As I previously mentioned, God's kingdom is built and operates based upon legally binding eternal principles He established to govern both heaven and earth. The binding power of these principles find their basis in God the Father's holiness, which by essence, is absolutely just and without compromise. It is because of the unswerving nature of holiness embodied within God the Father, that He sent His Son Jesus Christ to earth as His divine advocate in the form of a man who was ordained to spill His blood on a cross to pay the price for sin...as His reconciliation of fallen man to God the Father personal sacrifice. Binding vows carry eternal weight. One can only find release from their binding effects by renouncing them in the name of Jesus Christ in one's appropriation of freedom through the liberating redemption of His blood (Hebrews 9:22). Please let me tell you a story of an encounter I had on one of my walks across America that reveals how binding vows enter one's life and gain unhealthy dominion over them...

One night after speaking at local church along my walk path, I lingered near the front of the sanctuary and visited with those in the congregation who came to talk with me one-on-one. First, one lady offered encouragement. Next, a young man shared how God spoke to him through my message. And then, a number of others stopped by who either wanted prayer or had a story to tell. Bringing up the rear of the line however, was a dear ole' gent named Fletcher who immediately caught my attention, tugged at my heart, and asked if we could sit down and talk a bit more. When my time inside the church concluded, I invited him to visit at my RV parked next to the building. He headed to get his car on the other side of the church as I walked toward my RV arriving there before him to turn on the lights and put on a pot of tea... Moments later, Fletcher knocked at my door and labored his way up my somewhat steep entrance steps and came to rest in my leather recliner just inside. As we chatted back-and-forth, I began discerning an all-too-familiar spirit I had encountered many times over the years, emanating from this dear m an. Finally, I politely asked him if he was or had ever been involved in the Masonic Lodge to which he replied, "Yes, I am a thirty-second degree Mason in the Scottish Rite and also a Shriner." I said, "I could feel your involvement when we met, thanks for letting me know."

As we continued visiting, we shared more about our personal lives while greatly enjoying each other's company. Fletcher was quite the historian as a member of several organizations focused on preserving and returning to the roots of Americanism. If I would have had time – I could have listened to Fletcher's stories for days – he was amazing! Mid-stream in our conversation he offered, "I suffered a heart attack about four years back and a stroke two years ago. I use to have such an excellent memory, but it's been a challenge sometimes as I wait for thoughts to gel. I just want God to use me for His glory in the time I have left!" I replied, "I'm sure God has a lot in store for you yet." Then I asked, "Have you ever renounced your vows to the Lodge?" He replied, "I demitted from both orders several years ago just before my heart attack and stroke that came later." The deeper we continued into our time together however, different strongholds surfaced in beliefs Fletcher held, terminology he used, and responses he had to typically-dismissed historical facts and bible passages I shared with him. With each subsequent Scriptural principle I shared in context with known historical distortions, one could see the light turning on behind Fletcher's eyes. Soon he said, "You're enlightening me...you are enlightening me." Then he asked me, "Where did you get your education in theology and history?" I replied, "Chasing God in the bible, on my face in prayer, and studying history that fits His call on my life." He said, "I've been involved in mainstream societies and reading about history most of my adult life...almost 50 years...and you're revealing things I've never heard, but know are true based on what I do know to be fact." He continued, "No one has ever put these pieces of history together with the bible like this for me before...you're enlightening me" as he jotted down the Scriptures that had been flowing out of me like water for the past hour...

By now, the hour was late and Fletcher slid his elderly frame to the front of his seat not wanting to impose and asked, "Can I buy you lunch tomorrow?" I said, "I'm trying to write as much as possible, so I could spend a couple hours Tuesday if that works." He said, "I'll pick you up at 12:00 noon straight up Tuesday, figure out what you want to eat." He rose, turned, and made his way down the steps to land on asphalt with me right behind him heading toward his car where we spoke a few more minutes... At this point, the Masonic Lodge came up again and I asked him a question to which he replied, "I can't answer that after being raised into the third degree." I said, "I know, that's why I asked it...to hear that you had been raised into the Order." I continued, "The bible says there is only one baptism Christians are to experience, not two" (Ephesians 4:5). Then I asked, "Do you understand why?" He said, "No." "Let me explain," I said continuing, "The bible admonishes us to be raised with Christ and warns us not to be deceived by hollow and deceptive philosophies that subject us to two masters or cause us to be double-minded. When you were raised into the third degree, you allowed the enemy to fragment your life between two masters through a descending series of binding vows you spoke over yourself." He was taken back again... One could see the wheels turning behind his eyes as he said again, "You're enlightening me" and he shook my hand, turned, got in his car, and rolled down his side window. I looked him square in the eyes and asked him, "Can we continue this conversation about the Lodge? I believe God is trying to liberate your life." He said, "I would love to." as he waved and he drove away into the night...

The next morning, Fletcher called just to visit a moment as his stories began to roll once again... Our call ended an hour later and I resumed writing, eventually burning the midnight oil that evening only to rise early to commence again Tuesday morning... Losing track of time lost in penning this book, I snapped back to reality when Fletcher's knock came at the door to haul me off to lunch for a couple hours before I was scheduled to return and keep writing. I jumped in his car and down to the local Chinese buffet we went. Once we had our food gathered and stationed ourselves at our table, our conversation picked up where it left off the day before by phone. It was as if we were on a path of unfolding thought heading to a pre-planned destination... Again, the subject of Masonry surfaced with Fletcher saying, "A dear older friend of mine who is a thirty-third degree Mason in the Lodge keeps tugging at me to enter the final level like him." I responded, "I believe you have not had peace or been allowed passage into the thirty-third degree because Jesus has been preserving your life due to what that degree requires of you." Then I asked, "Do you remember how you told me that you demitted from the Lodge several years ago and then got hit with a heart attack with a stroke coming two years later?" He replied, "Yes." Next I said, "Though you physically broke fellowship with the Lodge, it seems you never renounced the binding vows you spoke over yourself." He said, "No, I didn't." Then I told him, "When you demitted from the Lodge years back, you broke your vows to darkness and satan punished you by doing what your allegiance to him gave him legal right to do...hit you with a heart attack and then a stroke based on your vows. Until you renounce your vows to the Lodge and darkness that you have spoken over yourself and sever their power in Jesus' name, you remain subject to them." Another wave of revelation hit him as he said, "I never thought of that."

As our conversation deepened from there, what started as two hours for lunch turned into the rest of the day as God drew more Scripture and principles out of me to bring light to Fletcher's eyes... Within two and a half days of meeting, this dear man's entire belief system was undergoing surgery as God delivered him from one deception after another thrust upon him by the enemy of his soul. I could watch him change before my eyes... As our time together came to a close that day, I asked him if I could give him a list of bible verses to read and pray over asking for God's insight... He accepted them, promising to read them all very carefully. Over the next two days, I rolled up my cords and headed eastward as I continued toward my final walk destination... On my return trip, following the finish of my walk some time later, I was privileged to re-connect with Fletcher on my way by his town where I parked next to his church and spoke again. While there, he invited me to lunch the next day saying he would pick me up at my RV at 12:00 sharp, again. As promised, he arrived a few moments early, I jumped in his car, and back to the Chinese buffet we roared. While on the way, Fletcher said again, "You have enlightened me in ways I've never seen. Will you help me pray to renounce the vows I spoke over myself to the Lodge before we part company today?" I said, "Sure." During our time together that day, we prayed through all of his prior vows and set him free in Jesus' name! Here was a mid 70's-aged man who wanted to be used of God, was hungry for truth, was willing to do the hard work, and victory was gained. Again, he assured me he would continue to commit the Scriptures I had given him at the time we first met, to memory. When I left his town this time, Fletcher was a new man determined to help others likewise bound by darkness as he had once been, now discover more of God's light in Jesus Christ...

Many Christians today find themselves experiencing powerless religion, but not dynamic personal power-filled relationship with

Jesus Christ. Why? Like Fletcher, many have either negated God's rightful position in their lives or unwittingly entered into unholy alliances with darkness and have fallen beneath its dominion. Sadly, this oversight binds them to living in the "good" will of God at best, but never empowers them to identify and live in the "perfect" will of God with true freedom's irrevocable joy (Romans 12:1-2; 1 Corinthians 3:11-15). Though they are genuinely saved through faith in Jesus Christ, their misplaced faith experience will lack joy, hope, power, and victory only found within an intimate relationship with Jesus Christ necessary to both make disciples and change the world. As a result, their life efforts will only reproduce religious people like themselves, until they confront their internal strongholds with eternal truth, renounce the binding power of those vows in Jesus' name, and enter into the fullness of Christ with Him as their sole Lord and Savior. In western world culture, we find this reality manifesting itself in churches wherever spiritual leaders deliver messages focused on sin's symptoms, while never going to the root of the tree (Matthew 21:18-22; James 4:1). Why? This tether to powerless religion is due to the overshadowing affect associated with principalities of delusion hanging over America as a result of building on a flawed foundation legally dominated by independence and spiritual infidelity...

Ignorance Unacceptable

Just as ignorance or willful denial of truth with regard to God's existence, law, or sin does not release the offender from sin's penalty, one's ignorance of what they have vowed, with its corresponding bondage, does not release them from the binding power of that vow which inhibits their embrace of Christ, freedom, unity, and power. We are told all men are without excuse and that wisdom is free if we ask God (Romans 1:20; James 1:5). Again, the kingdom of God is based upon and governed by His eternal and immutable (unchanging) laws... When God's requirements are intellectually understood, verbally declared in the presence of human will, and subsequently ratified by either spoken or written assurance (contract) in private or before witnesses, God's laws bind those declaring them and also those under the auspices of their authority, to whatever was agreed upon within the framework of that specific declaration. Our founding fathers came from a varied human and spiritual origins with diverse vantage points in their mutual creation, acceptance, and declaration of America's founding creeds and documents. Despite their intentions, however, their self-perceived validity and spiritual unawareness regarding the level of dominion their associations and declarations unleashed, does not release them or those held fast by their legally binding vows, from the effects imposed through what they as leaders declared or signed on behalf of others. In America's case, the Unanimous Declaration becomes a primary legally binding authority over those who ratified and signed it, thereby imposing indirect limitations in the lives of those who live beneath their authority from that time forward throughout subsequent generations until renounced.

This said...those elected, appointed, or positioned to lead at any level must seek to fully understand the spiritual repercussions tied to their otherwise uninformed decisions...if we are to ever become a truly liberated individual, people, or nation... In Jeremiah 6:16, God's voice through His weeping prophet declared, "Stand at the crossroads and look; ask for the ancient paths, ask where the good way is, and walk in it, and you will find rest for your souls." Dear friend, what crossroad do you find yourself standing at in life? Are you willing to ask Jesus where the ancient paths and the good way are so you can find rest for your souls? As Moses said to God's people long ago – "I have set before you life and death, blessings and curses. Now choose life, so that you and your children may live and that you may love the Lord your God, listen to His voice, and hold fast to Him. For the Lord is your life, and will give you many years in the land He swore to give to your fathers (Deuteronomy 30:19-20). What will our decision be...Living Armor...or standing naked before God on that day without defense? The choice is ours...

Road to Freedom

If you are or have ever been part of any group, order, society, doctrine, or belief that distorts Scripture, imposes legalism, swears you to secrecy, or requires that you to declare vows over yourself in order to participate, you may need help. Please find a list of Scriptures below for your prayerful consideration. I encourage you to ask God for His insight necessary to liberate your heart, soul, mind, spirit, and future from bondage in Jesus' name.

Scriptural Foundation to Escape Bondage

- Life-Blessing/Death-Curses: Deuteronomy 28:1-30:20
- One Baptism: Ephesians 4:5
- Raised With Christ: Colossians 2:6-3:4
- Submission to Christ: 1 Peter 3:15:22
- Coming Into The Light: John 3:19-21
- Testing and Approving: Romans 12:1-2
- Identifying Spirits: 1 John 4:1-3
- Works of the Holy Spirit: John 14:26-27, 16:8, 13-15
- Commandments: Exodus 20:1-17 especially V.14; Matthew 22:37-41; Mark 12:30-31; Romans 13:8-10
- Jesus The High Priest: Hebrews 5:8-1; 7:26-28
- Deception - Delusion: 2 Thessalonians 2:8-12
- Counterfeit Righteousness: 2 Corinthians 11:13-15
- Idolatry - What Is True: 1 John 2:3-6
- Revelation: 21:8
- Two Masters: Matthew 6:24
- Friendship With The World: James 4:1-8
- Our Associations: 1 Corinthians 5:11-12
- Perfect Love: 1 John 4:16-18
- Godly Sorrow: 2 Corinthians 7:10
- Mercy: Luke 23:32-34, 40-43
- Dreams and Visions: Joel 2:28
- Ascension Gifts – Some People: Ephesians 4:11-13
- Gifts of Service – All People: Romans 12:3-21; 1 Corinthians 12:27-31
- Gifts of Holy Spirit – Situational: 1 Corinthians 12:7-11
- Our Job: Matthew 10:8, 28:19-20
- Our Example: John 14:6, 12, 17:1-26
- Our Reward: John 3:16, 14:1-4; Revelations 21

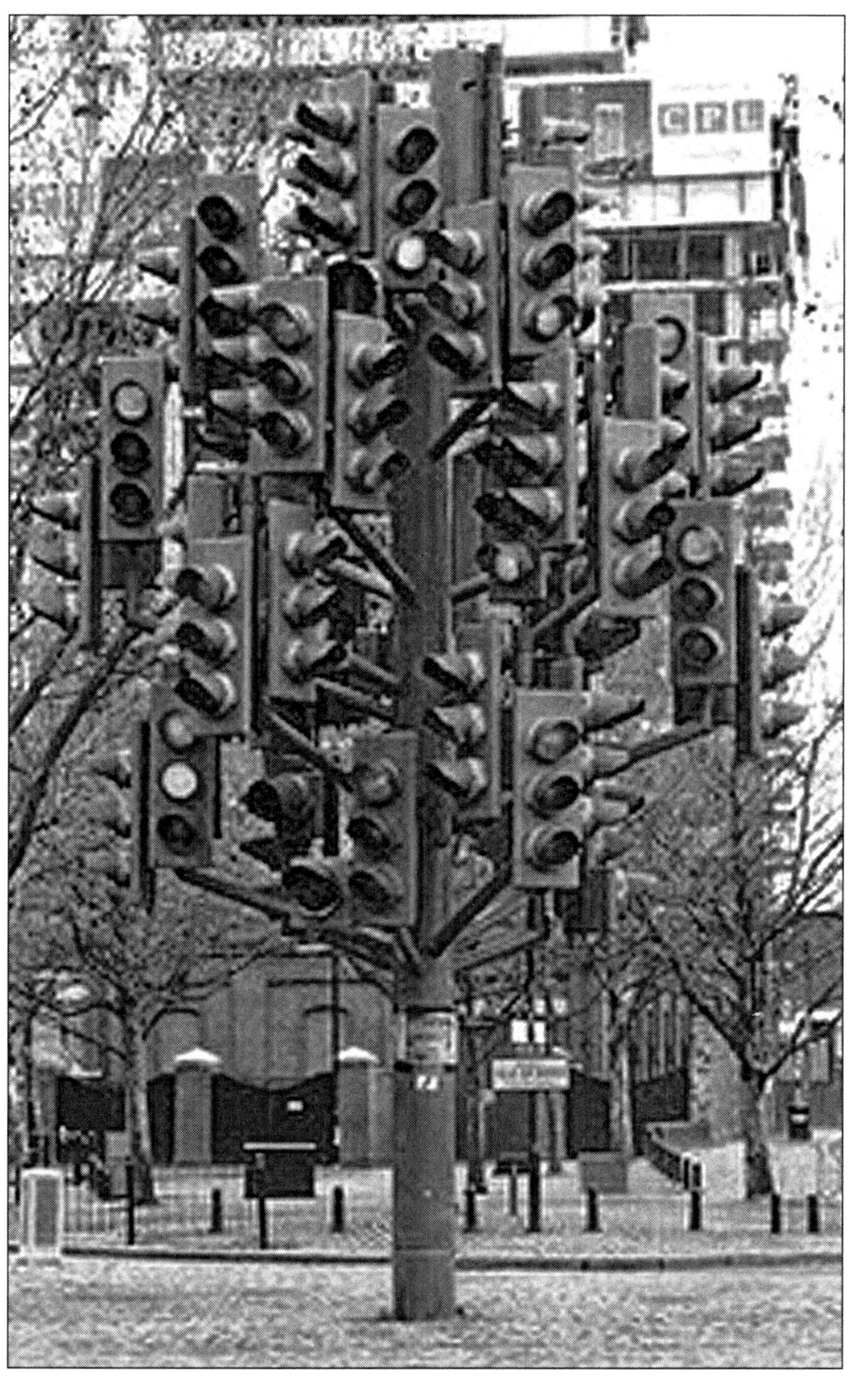

Confused by life's road? Call on Jesus the Navigator of your soul...

A gorgeous red rose of love...

Chapter 8
The Bridegroom's Table

"Let us rejoice and be glad and give Him glory! For the wedding feast of the Lamb has come, and His bride has made herself ready" (Revelation 19:7).

Years ago, my local farm community high school held an annual competition between classes to see who could raise the most money to fund class events and trips. As it turns out...my class was the only one since 1948 that won the contest all four years. The sky was the limit on what we could do to raise money. If we could dream it up and it was legal...we did it! We dug ditches, hauled wood, mowed lawns, washed windows, changed oil, picked apples, walked dogs, bucked hay, and helped old ladies with whatever they needed done for however much they wanted to pay. Close to winter each year, our school also held an annual smorgasbord open to anyone and everyone in an effort to raise more money used to send our basketball team, cheerleaders, and band to state tournament...a feat our school pulled off 25 times in 40 years. You should have seen the food: baked ham, roasted turkey, real stuffing, mashed potatoes, homemade gravy, buttered carrots, green beans, tossed salad, fresh biscuits, cranberry sauce, strawberry Jell-O, apple pie, peach cobbler, chocolate cookies, layer cake, and beverages...most of it made by hand.

People came from everywhere to eat their fill and go home stuffed. There were tall people, short people, thin people, fat people, old people, young people, parents, kids, policemen, mayors, and news reporters. They came for miles from all walks of life to escape fast food and eat the real deal... Almost everything we served was handmade and required the hard and dedicated work of people who cared about their kids, friends, and community. Many locals volunteered year-after-year to make food, set up tables, wash dishes, and work behind the scenes to fill the stomachs and touch the hearts of the world that walked through our doors. It was the end of an era when farming was still a lifestyle, families went to church in the same car, mom sat next to dad on a bench seat, weather held your future, and kids climbed trees, worked at age eight, rode their motorcycles, and shot their rifles without goggles, ear plugs, helmets, or supervision, wholly unprotected from themselves...what a life we had! People lived, loved, worked, and played hard to weave their thread into the community's fabric for the welfare of others. It was a time-now-gone-by when bringing a Store-roasted chicken, deli salad, canned apple sauce, frozen pie, or Wallmart cake was unheard of. In fact, people felt it almost an insult to sidestep the real to bring the fast food counterfeit that cost its bearer little time... One's investment of personal effort and time "were" the hallmark of being authentic and making a valuable contribution in the life of another... The offer of fast food was to the smorgasbord what empty words are to the hungry – meaningless.

Just as our local high school and community labored and loved to serve a meal beyond imagination to all who would come in... God has invited everyone to eat the greatest meal of all times on heaven's banquet table at the wedding feast of the Lamb. The meal was conceived in the heart of God, seasoned with His love, and prepared by those who heard God's voice, stood in faith, prayed for others, and gave their lives to glorify their King. There never has been, nor will there ever be, another meal like it throughout the whole of eternity. The difference between a meal and a "love feast" is found in the honor, hearts, hours, and hands of those preparing the meal... Though fast food cooks may zap and deliver a Big Mac...a great chef works to fill, taste, season, and stir the pot until it satisfies the hunger of those he serves. Jesus is both Heaven's Bridegroom and Heaven's Greatest Chef, filled with a passion to prepare and serve His bride the most extraordinary meal of all time. He shops with purpose, creates with kindness, cooks with passion, tastes with grace, seasons with mercy, stirs with patience, and serves the ultimate one-time supper to His bride with love as He becomes broken bread and poured out wine to feed His people... The Bridegroom's table will be set with life, joy, hope, freedom, peace, heaven's bread, and the new wine of His covenant. As believers in Jesus Christ, we are to do the work necessary to set the banquet table for those our King has invited to the feast (Matthew 10:5-39, 28:19-20; John 14:12). It's time that we stop serving a dying world religion's fast food that makes them die of heart failure – and start feeding them Heaven's Food that brings them life to help them become fruit that lasts, instead (John 4:32-34, 6:25-40). Please let me share the recipe God uses in preparation to set the Master's table on that day...

While walking across Texas several months ago, I was invited to preach at a local church where I had met a genuine, down-to-earth pastor. Here's how his invitation to speak at His church came... After lining out his work crew who was making repairs to a new Church building his congregation had moved into just months before, we retreated to his office where we talked and prayed before parting company. Upon leaving, I asked God to give the pastor vision if I was to speak in his church. I rarely pre-set my speaking schedule more than a few days ahead because I only want to preach where Jesus leads and confirms. The next day, I was drawn back to the pastor's parking lot a second time by the Holy Spirit. Meanwhile, he had been having his own conversations with God in my absence with regard to what he should do with a walking preacher like me who landed on his doorstep unannounced. Upon my arrival to his church that second day, we began talking in snippets between him directing workers and keeping his eye on renovations that needed to be finished before the upcoming Sunday Service two days later. Our conversation migrated from one subject to another, finally landing on the subject of Abraham Lincoln. As the former president's name rolled off my lips, the pastor looked at me and asked if I would speak the coming Sunday morning. After inviting me to speak, he told me that he had asked God the night before what he should do about having me speak...and then went to sleep. When he woke up the next morning, he saw a picture of Abraham Lincoln pass before his mind's eye for a few seconds... After the vision vanished, he told God that he would have me speak if I showed up at his church that second day. A few hours later...I rolled in. Both of us chuckled at God's sense of humor and set the date for me to chat with his people... Early on the morning I was to speak at his church two days later, I was still in bed reading my bible at 5:30 am just hours before I was to address his congregation. In a moment's time, God handed me a word picture from Scripture that portrays the four legs of and the chair to the Bridegroom's table being set for us at the wedding feast of the Lamb (Revelation 19:7). Please let me share the recipe the Lord showed me that we must eat to gain our seat at the Master's table on that day…

First however, please let me remind you that Jesus is portrayed in Scripture as Heaven's Bridegroom and His Church is portrayed as His Bride…that's us. All authentic, born-again believers in Jesus Christ are individual temples of the Holy Spirit who join together and corporately become the Church or, otherwise known as the bride of Christ (1 Corinthians 3:16; Ephesians 5:25-32). As we all know, today's church-at-large struggles with many sinful issues rooted in religion, judgment, pride, and immorality that pierce the heart of God. As a result, Jesus has been wooing His wayward bride (Church) to Himself for millennia as He longs to become one with her at the appointed wedding feast of the Lamb foretold in Scripture. Our ultimate reconciliation and subsequent reunion with God is cast in the imagery of a wedding banquet attended by those He has invited…not untimely or ill-prepared party crashers (Matthew 25:1-13). Scripture tells us that God is preparing history's most extravagant wedding celebration for His Son Who will dress Himself to serve His guests who recline at heaven's table (Matthew 22:1-14, Luke 12:37, Revelation 19:7-9). Hence, this is the basis for my word picture portraying the four legs of and the chair to the Bridegroom's table. The table's four legs of life are hewn out of truth, love, Spirit, and glory that Jesus spoke of in the book of John, chapters fourteen (14) through seventeen (17). I'll talk about the chair to His table a little later in the chapter… All four legs of the Bridegroom's table possess a common characteristic that I will likewise clarify along the way. So, let's take a walk around the Bridegroom's table and consider the qualities of all four legs…

<u>Leg #1 – Truth</u> (John 14)
Jesus is the way, the truth, and the life (John 14:6). Before anything of value or redemptive quality can be built within us…it must be founded upon truth. Jesus Christ IS Living Truth. Through our belief upon, acceptance of, submission to, and indwelling occupation by Jesus Christ…alone…we are saved and transformed from death to

life (John 3:16, 17:8; Acts 2:21; 1 Corinthians 5:17-20). Jesus is the bedrock of our salvation, or in other words, our faith's foundation (Psalms 95:1). His indwelling presence within us is essential to real salvation. There is no other way to God or foundation upon which we can build our rightful entrance into His presence other than personal one-on-one relationship with Jesus Christ. Next, we find that truth must be living and active in and through our lives, evidencing its existence as we emulate or do what Jesus is doing (John 14:12). Both Jesus and the Apostle Paul made it perfectly clear that simply being a hearer of the word without action means nothing (Matthew 7:24-27; James 2:14-26). Until our life takes on or walks in the unconditional and increasing character of lifestyle love, forgiveness, and service to others that actually meets need and changes lives as Jesus exampled...we only have a form of godliness and deny its power (Mark 12:30-31; 1 Corinthians 13:7-8; Philippians 2:3-5; 1 John 2:6; James 2:14; 1 Peter 1:3-8; 2 Timothy 3:5). Therefore, this first leg of the Bridegroom's table called "truth" requires our loving motivation, individual involvement, purposeful action, and selfless investment in others to evidence His presence in our lives at a level necessary to gain our seat at the wedding feast of the Lamb. Those who are proven to be mere hearers of the Word, who give lip service, make hollow promises, withdraw under pressure, put self first, manipulate the truth, and justify their own sin while judging others...will find themselves locked outside the wedding hall on that day. Now, let's turn our attention toward the second leg on the Bridegroom's table – love.

<u>Leg #2 – Love</u> (John 15)

I call John chapter fifteen the "if" chapter because it reveals that God will do His part in the equation IF we do ours. On a positive note, Jesus tells us that we will bear much fruit...can ask for and receive whatever we request...will remain in His love...and will be His friends who know the Master's business IF we remain in Him, His word remains in us, and we do what He commands (John 15:5-15). In fact, Jesus chose and appointed us to bear fruit that lasts (John 15:16-17). The act of bearing fruit, remaining in Him, retaining His word, and doing what He commands clearly shows that we must live out the behavior Jesus exampled to prove we are His disciples. Words alone mean nothing... On a less pleasant note, and in response to our doing what Jesus does...He also tells us that we will be hated...suffer persecution...and be ignored at the hands of the world which does not accept or believe in Him as their Savior (John 15:18-25). Once again, living beneath the tyranny of hatred, persecution, and devaluing indifference calls us to a level of action that responds like Jesus when opposed, oppressed, and overwhelmed. Truly possessing and walking out God's love in our interaction with Him and others has a supernatural character, specific look, and likely outcome. Jesus commanded us to love Him with all our heart, soul, mind, and strength and others as ourselves...not with mere words alone (Luke 6:27-31; Mark 12:30-31; James 2:14-26). Paul mirrors the vantage point Jesus holds on this pivotal matter by declaring that anyone who claims to love God but hates his brother...or who has material possessions while doing nothing to help another in need...is a liar and does not have the love of God within them (I John 3:16-18, 4:19-21). Obviously, God expects us to yield all we have to Him, to be aware of surrounding need, and to contribute whatever is in our power to give (Proverbs 3:27; Matthew 10:8; John 15:12; 1 John 4:19). Otherwise, we are religious, empty, unspiritual, and in danger of damnation. The next leg in the Bridegroom's table helps us understand, act with purpose, and overcome with power...

<u>Leg #3 – Spirit</u> (John 16)
I have listened to people say they do not know what God wants them to do since the time I was a small boy, it always puzzled me. I remember thinking...we have the bible, right (2 Timothy 3:16-17; Hebrews 4:12)? God promised to give us wisdom generously without finding fault, right (James 1:5)? The Holy Spirit is supposed to remind us of all Jesus taught us, right (John 14:26)? So then, how can we say we don't know what God wants us to do? It simply makes no sense... In truth, our rambling statement that claims not to know God's will really says we don't want to know what we're supposed to do...because discovery of our purpose imposes personal responsibility on us to do what Jesus does and give what Jesus gives to others when it hurts...as He did for us (John 14:12). The truth can only set us free if we both know and apply it

personally. If we know and have accepted God's truth...its presence within us should and will change how we live IF it genuinely resides in us. If we are truly saved with Jesus living on the inside of us, there is no way we can plead ignorance while being filled with Living Truth and being illuminated by the Holy Spirit Who testifies to the character of Christ. All Christians, especially in America, have been indoctrinated with empty religious form to varied degrees, rather than inspired by and held accountable to Spirit-led truth through willing imposition of self-discipline. Remember, all fall short of the glory of God and all are commissioned to go (Matthew 28:19-20; Romans 3:23; Galatians 5:22-23). As a result, most of us either did or continue to believe a level of hollow theologies which tell us we cannot be lost once we say the sinner's prayer (Matthew 24:13; 2 Peter 2:20-21). Likewise, many of us believe that the grace of God covers all, even when we're irresponsible (Romans 5:20-6:2). And, we're daft enough to think we can focus on ourselves at the expense of others as we ignore or refuse to meet the need of those around us (Luke 10:25-37; Philippians 2:3-5; 1 John 3:16-18). Simply put dear friend...that is over-spiritualized hogwash! Instead, Jesus did, taught, and bore witness to exactly the opposite through action as He modeled right behavior, enlightened hungry hearts through parables, and sent the Counselor to carry us to the next level (John 14:16-18). As genuine believers in Jesus Christ, we are without excuse as the Holy Spirit lives inside of us through the indwelling presence of God the Father and Jesus the Son (John 10:30, 14:9-10; Romans 1:20). How can I say that? Easy! Jesus asked His Father to send the Holy Spirit as "Thee Counselor" to instruct those of us who are in personal relationship with Him through five basic methods once we are saved: (1) To teach us all things and remind us of everything Jesus taught us (John 14:26)...(2) To convict us of guilt about sin, righteousness, and judgment (John 16:8)...(3) To guide us into all truth (John 16:13a)...(4) To reveal the future (John 16:13b)...and (5) To bring glory to Jesus (John 16:14).

So as my young boy curiosities once pondered, how in the world can we claim not to know God's will for our lives when God Himself is teaching, reminding, convicting, and revealing His heart to us as He glorifies His Son? When you couple the words of Jesus to those of the Apostle Paul who told us "...not to conform to the pattern of this world, but be transformed by the renewing of our minds, so we can test and approve God's good, pleasing, and perfect will...," how can we believe ourselves unable to know what God wants us to do? It's obvious He expects us to learn how to cooperate with His reach to the world around us (Romans 12:2; Ephesians 5:15-17)? Ignorance is a choice...not an acceptable excuse capable of stating its case before the Author of Life when we stand before Him on the day. Many have chosen and justified ignorance by praying God will send someone else, by writing a check instead of going to Zimbabwe, or getting caught up in misguided aspects of the prophetic, apostolic, deliverance, miraculous, or end times movements while ignoring the essentials of their faith. Thus far, we see that Scripture shows that the presence of truth, love, and the Holy Spirit in our lives calls us to action, not an armchair at Starbucks surfing the internet and ministering to those we are called to love – on Facebook. That said; let's take a look at the fourth and final leg of the Bridegroom's table – glory.

<u>Leg #4 – Glory</u> (John 17) – Isaiah 6
God's glory is a very misrepresented, misunderstood, mis-appropriated, and manipulated quality of God's nature within the Church and people's spiritual practice today. If we have been Christians for very long, most of us have heard the story of God hiding Moses in the cleft of the rock and covering him with His hand as His glory passed by. After His glory passed, God removed His hand and Moses saw His back, not His face (Exodus 33:22-23). Likewise, many of us have heard about God's glory filling or hovering above the temple when King Solomon dedicated it upon its completion (2 Chronicles 7:1-3). Additionally, we have likewise heard about the whole earth being filled with God's glory at the time Isaiah the prophet was commissioned for divine purpose before saying, "Send me" (Isaiah 6:1-8). And then, we come to what I believe, is the greatest reference to God's glory which is most relevant to us as individual believers...John, chapter seventeen. This passage reveals how God's glory relates to the work He gave Jesus to complete as it forges and reproduces divine character in and through our lives. Simply put, Jesus brought glory to His Father

by completing the work He gave Him to do (John 17:4). Notice that the glory Jesus reflected back to His Father was inseparably tied to doing the work He was assigned to do...the enlightenment and regeneration of those He was given to impact...and the redemption of mankind. What was included in the work God the Father gave Jesus to accomplish? In a nutshell, Jesus' work included: (1) Revealing His Father to those He had been given out of the world (17:6), (2) Giving the words the Father Had given Him to speak to those entrusted to His care (17:8), (3) Praying strategically for those God had given Him...not the world...but, only those He was given (17:9), (4) Protecting and keeping those in His care safe through the name He had been given... Jesus (17:12), (5) Sending those God had given Him into the world as His Father had sent Him (17:18), (6) Sanctifying Himself so those God had given Him could be truly sanctified (17:19), (7) Praying beyond the present time so He could extend His disciple's message to subsequent generations (17:20), (8) Reproducing His own glory, character, and unity with the Father in those He had been given and transmitting it to others who would believe through their message (17:22-23), (9) Knowing His Father... not just knowing or talking "about" Him (17:25), (10) Continuing to make His Father known to those He had been given so He could maintain His presence in them. So, as you can see...Jesus "did" a lot to accomplish His assigned task to bring glory to His Father! And, He calls each of us who have faith in Him, to do what He is still doing within the lives of those upon the earth (John 5:17, 9:4, 14:12, 15:14-16; 1 John 2:3-6). It will be a rude awakening on that day for many when they find that saying the sinner's prayer, giving empty lip service instead of love, and writing a few offering checks rather than going where God told them to go, is not enough to get through the door at heaven's banquet hall at the wedding feast of the Lamb (Matthew 7:21-23).

In truth, we as those created in God's image...who were told to be fruitful, increase in number, fill the earth, and subdue it...are His glory (Genesis 1:27-28). How can I say that? Simple, we are created in His image and – He is glorious! After Isaiah had his vision of the Lord seated on a throne high and exalted and the train of His robe filling the temple, we see the seraphs hovering above the disheveled prophet-to-be calling to one another saying, "Holy, holy, holy is the Lord Almighty; the whole earth is full of His glory (Isaiah 6:1-3 NIV). Though the temple Isaiah pictured God seated in represents His heavenly dwelling...we are individually temples of the Holy Spirit who become the Temple (Church) corporately as we join in Jesus' name (1 Corinthians 3:16-17). Please let me explain... As those created in God's image, we are designed to emulate His character qualities (Genesis 1:27-28). Our unsaved condition in which God's character has not yet been revealed, forged, or released in us does not portray His likeness as our fallen humanity and corresponding actions overshadows His divine nature. While numbered among those Jesus has been given out of the world, we are unwittingly drawn to God as He causes us to collide with His Son thereby inciting our redemption (John 6:39, 44-45, 17:6-19). When we run head-on into Jesus, acknowledge who He is as Savior of the ungodly, and submit to His Lordship, granting Him full dominion over our lives...we become new creations and represent the authenticated glory of God upon the earth through His indwelling presence and our expression of His character (John 4:32, 14:20, 20:28; 2 Corinthians 3:18, 5:17-20). In light of our original un-regenerated state...our surrender to God's dominion...His death-to-life transformation within us...and our resulting ability to operate with and demonstrate Christ's character in His name...God the Father's glory comes back to Jesus through us (John 17:10). What is this glory? It is the eternal image and character of God Himself being reproduced in us through Jesus His Son as our transformation into new creations reflects His heart, mind, and Spirit back toward Him and others. When we love and forgive God and His people unconditionally and selflessly...we become His glory that fills the earth (Isaiah 6:3). Jumping into the fire to become the glory of God will shake our temple's (lives) doorposts and thresholds as we realize we are ruined and unclean before the Lord Almighty and deeply in need of being touched by a coal from His altar before we can say..."Send me" (Isaiah 6:4-8). Even chasing the glory of God is hard, but eternally rewarding work...

Sadly, God's glory has been selfishly sought as an experience to include physical manifestations like gold dust falling out of thin air, perfect teeth being filled with gold, and myriad other counterfeit signs and wonders...not through doing the work necessary to be transformed into Christ's likeness (Romans 8:28-30). Though God has sovereign capability to display his wonders any way He chooses, even in the most frivolous of ways, He never simply splashes His power on the scene to perform supernatural feats to prove He can work wonders. Instead, He only exerts His intervening power to meet existing need, improve one's reality, and level the eternal pathway of one's soul for His glory and the fulfillment of His purpose. And yet, people proclaiming themselves to be genuine, born-again believers in Jesus Christ run from one meeting to another chasing glory clouds, heaven's fire, emotional highs, prophetic words, physical miracles, and sensational displays while never chasing God Himself (Jeremiah 29:13). This me-centric pattern of pursuing God's blessing rather than seeking His face is perilously rooted in darkness as it feeds on counterfeit signs and wonders Scripture foretold would occur just before His return in accordance with the works of satan (2 Thessalonians 2:8-12).

Worship – Chair to the Bridegroom's table – Romans 12:1-2
Self-validated segments found within global Christian culture... especially America...have twisted the responsibility-based, relational experience of knowing God face-to-face into a secularized, self-serving seduction, having a form of godliness while denying God's heart and power (2 Timothy 3:1-5). People run from pillar-to-post feeding their human desires at the expense of properly glorifying God through personal humility, sacrifice, and self-control (Galatians 5:22; James 3:17-18, 4:1-8). Though God enjoys our praise as we raise holy hands to him in musical worship...our personal willingness to lay our lives down for others as living sacrifices while saying nothing...declares our deepest worship toward Him through the extension of our surrendered hearts (Romans 12:1; John 15:12-17; Ephesians 5:21-33). Our lifestyle investment of love toward others brings joy to our Savior as His character rises in and flows through us for the healing benefit of those put in our charge. Our faith and deeds...words and actions...love and selflessness...generosity and giving must work together if they are to produce life in others and advance God's kingdom (James 2:14-26; 1 John 3:16-23). Our

understanding of truth, love, Spirit, and glory is worthless in the hands of God and the lives of others if it is not accompanied by a sacrificial attitude that puts the needs of others ahead of our own (Philippians 2:3-5). History's greatest example of worship toward God was expressed by Jesus His Son as He yielded in Gethsemane to brutality's blow that would nail Him to Calvary's cross, so we can live. Obviously, dear friend, our seat at heaven's banquet table will be awarded based on our attitudes and actions – not our theology's empty words... Please let me share a story with you...

On my return trip toward the west coast after completing my second Trans-American walk 2010-2011 in Jacksonville, FL...I was privileged to re-connect with Joe the soldier whom I had previously met and whose military experience I had written about herein. This once war-torn man strolled up to the table with a changed countenance, bible in-hand, and a journal filled with revelations that unlocked hell's dungeon to release God's mercy in his life. I was humbled to see the incredible transformation God had unleashed in his world following our encounter at Starbucks that day several months before... Now, while sitting with Joe for coffee a second time, he flipped the switch once again to play an entirely new life movie which portrayed his recent liberation from brokenness and unforgiveness to experience the very mercy he once declared did not exist. Prior tears of pain and torment had been transformed into the waters of freedom and joy... By now, Joe's re-oriented life path had caused him to meet and cement friendships with a number of people instrumental in keeping his appointment with destiny through Jesus Christ. Some of those he met immersed him in love, while others provided opportunity for him to help someone struggling to rise from the ashes of life. It was during this return-trip reunion with Joe that he introduced me to a dear young couple who had recently married, were bombarded by past's repercussions...and yet, were determined to overcome with God's help. My first introduction to Daniel and Paola occurred on the front steps of their apartment as Joe and I arrived just in time to find them on their way out for the evening. Short of time...we quickly shared a few words, exchanged names, shook hands, and mentioned we should get together again to learn more about each other's lives...

Two days later, following Sunday morning church service, we all stepped out into an adjoining seating area to visit and deepen our fellowship. One thing led to another and we quickly found ourselves engaged on an ever-deepening personal level. We bounced from current world events to theology and onward toward other spiritual subjects before delving into emerging issues obviously near to their hearts... Suddenly, after an hour flashed by, Daniel looked at his watch and said, "Let's go get some lunch." So, the four of us plus Joe's son jumped in our rigs and headed for a local Mexican restaurant to talk, after which, we would later retreat to their home where our conversation would resume where it left off... Meanwhile, secluded in the back story of the prior day, this couple had locked horns over past wounds arising from prior relationships, internal insecurities, and perceived infidelities now being thrown in their faces through one another's words and unwitting cooperation with the enemy of their souls... Armed with his newly revived faith, God's mercy, and heaven's tears...Joe wept and prayed through his appeal to them to set their impasse aside for the evening in order to regain a sense of composure before all was lost. Leaping forward once again to our prior story line...the four and a half of us found ourselves spending time that Sunday afternoon with one another on a level that revealed a divine appointment bathed in God's presence, was unfolding. Without warning...Joe's phone rang, he answered, and then he told us that he needed to leave. Before descending the stairs with half pint in tow...he asked me to swing by his house later when Daniel, Paola, and I were finished talking. As Joe left closing the door behind him...all three of us got up, stretched our legs, grabbed some water, and sat down in their dining room at what was soon to become the Bridegroom's table, set by God with a feast of love to liberate their marriage...

Imagine the scene...an empty, well-illuminated four-legged table with Paola and Daniel sitting directly across from each other and me seated to one side somewhat between them. From above... the picture of this seating arrangement formed a triangle with bridegroom, bride, and an advocate posted at its three corners. The room's atmosphere shifted from small talk and social façade to love's survival in a blink of an eye. Smiles vanished, nerves twitched, and tears welled up without warning... Questions went from superficial to gut level in a single leap as Paola breached the silence to make it perfectly clear that their new marriage was trapped in the crossfire of past failures, hardened hearts, and unbridled fears. Recognizing what was about to occur, I reached for their hands and prayed for God's love, truth, mercy, power, and healing to reign supreme before the ensuing storm gained momentum... Emotions were high, offense visible, and struggle to remain cordial obvious as I laid ground rules for disclosure and response. Once the grid for interaction was defined – I shared "Truth" as the first leg of the bridegroom's table... I told them Truth is both a person named Jesus and also the life-giving grid for reconciliation. I went on to explain that truth sets people free when offered in love and when focused upon the other person's best interest. By now, it had become glaringly obvious that both Daniel and Paola had much to say... And yet, they both struggled to open their hearts with the other based on fear of how their mate would react...

Finally, Daniel spoke and shared his heartache caused by not being trusted before Paola fired back..."Well, you lied to me and now it's hard for me to trust you." Tension shot to the surface as Daniel rose in self-defense, compelled to refute and clarify Paola's misunderstanding. Daniel's right jawbone flexed as verbal bursts threatening to volley like machinegun fire lurked behind his troubled eyes... Finally, I told them that Truth's purpose is to bring what is hidden into the light in God's effort to disarm satan's power...establish understanding...and restore lost freedom upon which real trust and unity can be built. I told them that love extends trust unconditionally before it is earned...not based on the other person's level of trustworthiness. Over the next hour...both of them stood in faith and shared their inner hearts, fears, wounds, and hopes through downcast, hopeful, enlightened, grieved, and tear-laden looks... Holding each other's hands across the table... doing the hard work of confession and reconciliation...they sought each other's forgiveness and took personal responsibility for their individual parts in growing and preserving their marriage. Without saying anything...my inner man reminded me that I was weary before the reconciliation process between them had begun...but, the joy within me in view of what God was doing in the lives of this dear young couple overcame my fleeting strength. As we finished the meal's appetizer, I turned their attention toward "Love" as the second leg supporting the Bridegroom's table...

As their advocate, seated in the chair to their side...I explained how many people claim to love each other based on words, but fail to prove their love is real based on actions. Anyone can say "I love you" when things are easy, but only real love stays in the game when it hurts. I went on to describe how we often fail to love when one dear to us tells us something about ourselves we do not want to hear. Then, I shared how real love...God's love...sacrifices self...thereby communicating value as it puts the needs of those we have been given to care for ahead of our personal desires, rights, reputation, and comfort to prove that genuine love exists. Next, I drove home the point that fear has no foundation and cannot exist in the presence of "unconditional" love. I told both Paola and Daniel that the existence of fear in our relationship with God or each other proves that we believe we will be cast aside, unloved, if we risk exposing ourselves for who we really are. Yet in reality, if we truly believe that God and our mate loves us, we risk being transparently real by telling each other the truth as we co-labor in our mutual quest to disarm hell's lies to let peace reign. Leaning back in my chair...I could tell it was time to take Paola and Daniel on a journey back into my own past where I had experienced the life-altering impact of my human weakness, bouts with sin, and one miracle story after another, testifying to how God redeemed my pulverized world. Once done with my tale, with tears dried and composure regained, Daniel and Paola glanced at me and then each other as they prepared to step into their second layer of reconciliation.

They reached for each other's hands and deep within their own hearts for courage to expose their inner doubts, entrenched fears, and resulting areas of unfaithfulness toward God and each other as their expression of newfound love... The atmosphere shifted as hell made its bid to retain its grip, while hidden sin and personal weakness rose from the shadows of their hearts and crossed their lips, bringing that which the enemy had used to bind them – into

God's glorious light. They had embarked on a common journey for lasting freedom...to become fruit that lasts for God's glory and each other's good. Eyes darted, lips quivered, tears welled, and voices broke as heartache emerged for a season before being swallowed up in victory and engulfed by Christ-centered love. Daniel's grip on his lady tightened as love's glimmer-for-her-man sparkled in Paola's eyes... Fear's hardness softened, sin's judgment fell, bitterness let go, and the ministry of reconciliation with God and each other did its work. I encouraged them to make it a matter of daily early morning lifestyle...to grab hands, look into each other's eyes, push through their fears, admit their weaknesses, and pray over each other with unconditional love to silence hell's lies in Jesus' name. Clouds parted, peace returned, and hunger for more rose as I drew them toward the Holy Spirit's work and the third leg supporting the Bridegroom's table...

Still seated in the advocate's chair, I began by sharing how God gave us His Holy Spirit to counsel us with love and reveal our shortcomings...to remind us of what Jesus taught us...to lead us into all truth...to reveal what is to come upon the world we live in...and to bring glory to Christ through our lives. Now several hours into our time together, with all looking a bit spent...Daniel and Paola's grip on each other tightened in tenderness as we continued... Then I said, "The Holy Spirit reminds us of everything Jesus taught us because He has the words of life that give us hope and the ongoing ability to overcome. The Holy Spirit leads us into all truth because God is all-knowing and has an answer for everything if we search His word in prayer. The Holy Spirit also gives us insight helping our eyes to see, ears to hear, and hearts to understand what He is saying, what is going on around us, and what is getting ready to happen in the days ahead so we can be ready. And the Holy Spirit brings glory to Jesus when His counsel within us is accepted by the hearer, results in changed behavior, expresses the love and character of God, and testifies to His presence in a dying world." Just then, we all grabbed hands to pray that God would shed His light upon us, within us, and through us by His Holy Spirit...to be willing to obey what He tells us...and to let Him flow through us as we love one another. I opened my eyes and looked up just in time to see both

Daniel and Paola looking at each other, forming kisses, and winking at each other as renewed love continued to rise... Though the night was getting late...we forged ahead to gain our grip on "Glory" as the fourth and final leg supporting the Bridegroom's table...

Stretching my arms, taking a swig of water, telling my groaning muscles to hush, and leaning back in my chair once again...I began by saying, "Too many people chase God's glory in the wrong way, wrong places, for the wrong reasons. We go to church, crusades, or national gatherings looking for smoke, gold dust, diamonds on the floor, or people's teeth being filled with gold...but, never chase God Himself. People go through their weeks, leave God in the shadows of their lives, repent for nothing, and come to church asking Him to bless them under the right colored lights, compelling music, fog machines, and technologies that tug at their emotions, cause them to cry, and send them packing after church, believing they touched God because they had...an experience. In many cases, God was not even on the stage...man was. Yet, God's glory is so much more than physical displays of power, warm feelings, and an extra lift in our step." Both Daniel and Paola nodded their heads as they remembered the type of situations I had just mentioned. Then Paola shared how difficult it had been to move from a more formal religion filled with ritual to one that relied upon an invisible God named Jesus, in faith. In response, I explained that we are God's glory because we are created in His image, called according to His purpose, and equipped to do His work as He lives within us to transform our lives. Likewise, I told both Daniel and Paola... who were still holding hands and flirting with each other...that God created us to bring glory to Himself as His character is reproduced within us and gets reflected back to Him through the way we live.

"So, how does that fit in our marriage?" they asked. "Simple, if you think about it" I said. Then I expanded on the matter saying, "Loving each other God's way is a choice. As you invite Jesus to do His work in you, individually giving Him permission to change you, His glory is revealed through you. If you focus on letting God change you...so you can love your partner better...the two of you will glorify God as He uses both of you to reproduce His glory in each other." "How do we do that?" they asked. I answered, "As you love and encourage each other with the attitude of Christ...you stir His character in the other person's heart. As you inspire the other one to feel beautiful and valuable...you are cultivating the glory of God in them. When your mate feels loved, attractive, and valuable to you...they will reflect the true character of God He designed them to have when He created them in His image. When that happens, God is glorified. Then I asked, "Can you see the difference between chasing God's glory in things, events, and sensationalism versus doing the work it takes to stir the glory of God in the life of one He has given to you?" "Yes," they replied. I continued, "Chasing God's glory in things is all about self. Yet, stirring the glory of God within your partner is about others. Jesus did not come to earth to glorify Himself... Instead, He came to glorify His Father by reproducing His heart and character in the lives of those He was called to save by completing the work necessary to transform humanity and reflect glory back to His Father. It cost Him everything to produce His glory in us..." This said, we finally made our way to the chair of Worship in which we're to sit as we take our place at the Bridegroom's table...

Before forging ahead...we all stretched again, cracked our weary smiles, and zeroed back in to bring all we had talked about together for clear understanding. Now 11:30 pm with everyone's eyeballs looking a wee bit weary and hair starting to stand on end, we launched into the home stretch... In my effort to make the truth, love, Spirit, and glory of God connection clearly understood, I had to bring the most important human element of all into the mix – one's choice to act sacrificially. First I said, "As God's people...we who have been entrusted with the ministry of reconciliation, are called to be His ambassadors to a dying world as the Living Christ in us makes His appeal through us to those who need Him. As God's ambassadors of reconciliation, we are called to give our bodies as living sacrifices as our act of spiritual worship to God by yielding our own lives, rights, and desires for the benefit of others." I stopped for a moment to explain...that Daniel giving himself at any cost for Paola's welfare and Paola giving herself for Daniel's sake, even when it hurts...is what it looks like and takes to be a living sacrifice within marriage. Just then, Paola jumped in and said, "But, if I tell him something he's doing hurts me or makes me feel bad and he doesn't stop, I feel unloved." Suddenly, Daniel rose up again, getting ready to defend and I gently stopped them both... I looked at Daniel and said, "If you want Paola to feel safe enough to be completely honest with you so she'll respect you...you must be mature and strong enough to take what she says, release it to God, wrap her in your arms, and care enough to pray for her in love...not defend yourself." Likewise, I looked toward Paola and said, "If you are saying something to your husband rooted in past that tears him apart in a flood of emotion and he says it hurts and you refuse to stop, you're not giving respect that inspires him to love you. Both of you must put your mate's feelings, needs, and welfare ahead of your own if...you Paola...want to be loved as a woman...and you Daniel...want to be respected as a man."

The endless circle of love that never fails – 1 Corinthians 13:7-8

They both admitted battling with this area as their smiles and love looks returned gazing down on their entwined fingers and now shimmering rings... Next, I explained that, "To be God's ambassadors of reconciliation...our lives must experience the transformational power of Jesus Christ within firsthand, so our changed lives can reveal God the Father to the lives we meet and touch each day. For us to experience transformation and reveal God's presence, we must let Him sanctify our own lives first if He's to use us to encourage others to be truly sanctified themselves. We cannot lead where we have never been nor reproduce what we have never gained... As we each walk through God's re-creation in our own lives in personal relationship with Jesus Christ...we will pray for, protect, and keep those we are called to love safe through committed relationship. Our devotion will be evidenced as we wait patiently to see God's glory in them reflect those things back to us, which our Savior equipped and compelled us to plant within them through selfless love. Our willingness to set self aside to enter the sacrificial process of standing for the welfare of others seats us as an advocate in the chair at the Bridegroom's table. Our willingness to be an advocate on behalf of others positions us as a type of the Living Christ in a dying world...whose lifestyle exercises our personal options, responsibilities, decisions, words, and actions with unified voice to declare true spiritual worship to our Lord and King." "Why is this important?" I asked rhetorically.

Answering my own question, I continued, "God created and placed us upon this earth as His glory to extend His love to those who He knows are His. So you see...truth found in John 14, love found in John 15, Spirit found in John 16, and glory found in John 17 are the four legs that support the Bridegroom's table upon which the wedding feast will be set. And our own sacrificial style of worship toward God and others – is the chair in which we will be seated before the banquet table at the wedding feast of the Lamb. When we live in this fashion before God and man as evidence we love Him and others...our intimacy with God is proven capable of becoming one with Christ on that day... Though I was weary before I entered the advocate's role on your behalf today Daniel and Paola, it has been my long-term commitment toward giving God access, yielding to His love, and putting others first that gave me strength, seated me in the advocates chair, stood for your marriage, and has now blessed me by getting to see the glory of God redeem."

There is a lot more to God's truth, love, Spirit, glory, and worship than the sinner's prayer, Sunday morning church, and having your ticket punched for heaven. A miracle was sealed that early morning as we grabbed hands, hugged, and said our goodbyes... Just before I made my way down the stairway on my way toward Joe's at 12:30 AM, I turned and said, "What God has done for me, He called me to do for you. Now, that you have freely received what God has done for you, give it freely to those He puts in your path as you do your part to love one another in Jesus' name." I finally got home at 2:30 AM... Both Daniel and Paola faced more struggles during subsequent days, but remained willing to do the hard work needed to stay in the game of marriage and win...

Marriage

God designed marriage to be an eternal, mutually-submissive, but structured covenant relationship between one man and one woman who operate with different relational role descriptions and levels of authority within the marriage (Genesis 3:16; 1 Corinthians 7:1-40; Ephesians 5:21-33; Colossians 3:18-21). He created both man and woman spiritually equal in His image and called them to co-exist with one another within covenant marriage relationship beneath His supreme authority and lordship as they both submit to Him and one to another out of reverence for Christ (Ephesians 5:21). To make this possible, God designed key differences into their individual marriage roles to accommodate the flow of love, truth, humility, unity, cooperation, order, and authority within both the marriage relationship and body of Christ-at-large. God gave man the role of responsibility to lead and protect his wife and children with truth, love, and tenderness in the same manner Christ gave and sacrificed His own life for His people, the Church. God will hold the man to a higher standard of accountability regarding the quality of leadership he expresses to his wife and family as the man operates as a type of Christ. Conversely, God gave woman the role in which she is to honor, respect, and surrender to her husband's leadership as his helpmate. God will hold the woman accountable for the quality of honor, respect, submission, and cooperation she expresses in her relationship to her husband.

Jesus is Lord

Though we know that no one administrates their roles perfectly in relationship, God calls both partners to put the needs of their mate ahead of their own as they submit to each other with kindness and respect. In this context, Jesus reigns over the man and woman in the marriage relationship as Lord of both individuals and the marriage covenant itself consistent with what the Bible teaches. Marriage is not a democracy with both partners contending for control. Instead, marriage is a Theocracy with Christ at the top over both partners in which the man and woman each fulfill their individual marriage roles based on Scripture. As both partners pursue personal relationship with Jesus Christ individually, they will automatically grow more intimate with each another on an emotional, intellectual, spiritual, and physical basis as they yield to one Lord. However, if either mate refuses to cooperate with God's marriage design, both will experience an associated negative impact within their marriage thereby suffering the consequences. God's design for marriage is a mirror image of His relationship with people, the Church, and the bride of Christ. Please let me describe a principle mechanism God showed me that will help you protect your marriage and live together with love, unity, power, and intimacy...

Heart Doors

Before marriage, each person has one SINGLE HEART with one heart door governed by one human will – their own. After marriage however, two people join their individual SINGLE hearts together into a ONE-FLESH MARRIAGE HEART with two heart doors governed by two human wills...and...no dividing wall between the two hearts that have been joined. Before marriage, both individuals were in full control of what they invited in or allowed through their heart's door, thereby making them the only one who would experience the impact of their decisions. After marriage however, both individual partners in the relationship become subject to the impact of their partner's choices. In marriage, both mates now share the responsibility to guard what they allow through their individual heart doors in the joined MARRIAGE HEART as they do their part to protect and bless their mate. Genesis 4:7 helps us realize that sin crouches at our heart's door waiting to break in, while Revelation 3:20 declares that Jesus knocks at our heart's door hoping to be invited in to spend time with us. Both marriage partners have an individual choice, yet joint responsibility to exercise their freedom for God's glory and the benefit of their spouse. If they both choose wisely using their freedom righteously, sin is denied access thereby allowing truth, love, and blessing to reign within their individual lives and marriage relationship.

Our Choice

If one or both partners exercise their freedom willfully and unwisely, however, the impact of their choices will permit sin to enter their heart door, provide it opportunity to cross through them, to impact their mate from the inside out, and both will mutually suffer the consequences of their individual choices. Though the ONE-FLESH MARRIAGE HEART exposes both mates to downside risk, it also gives both partners a wonderful opportunity to invite life and blessing into the marriage heart for their mate's benefit. How we administrate our choices and responsibility will determine the quality, fidelity, and intimacy of our covenant relationship with God and each other. Our relational future is in our hands and is subject to our choices. Please prayerfully consider the diagram below and the principle it represents shown below.

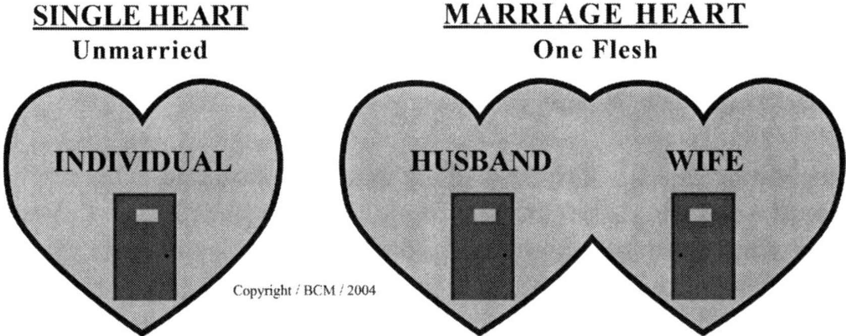

Jesus knocks at our door waiting to be invited in – Revelation 3:20
Sin crouches at our door waiting to break its way in – Genesis 4:7

Season of the Bride

During a 40 day fast ending the night before Easter 2011...God talked to me about the value and foundation of covenant. In short, God's people came through Old Testament covenant driven by duty's obligation to abide by God's law on their way into New Testament grace compelled by appreciation for all Jesus paid the price to give. Old Testament high priests offered incomplete, repetitive sacrifices for their own sin and those of their people, while Jesus offered a complete one-time sacrifice that satisfied all forever (Hebrews 7:23-28). For the most part, history shows that both Old and New Testament covenants are religiously structured, intellectually understood, and mechanically applied, thereby producing or evidencing little heart transformation due to people's limited understanding and lack of personal submission... Meanwhile, many leaders continue to preach "count the cost" as though we are to focus our lives on the element of sacrifice, rather than turning our hearts toward being intimately in love with God Himself through relationship with Jesus Christ. Until we fall in love with God at a level evidenced by our submission to His lordship, we cannot love ourselves or those around us. In truth, counting the cost of commitment was suppose to occur before we entered into marriage relationship with God or our mate, thereby allowing our honeymoon period to last forever. Sadly, more people step into salvation or marriage gripped by selfish desires, than those actually compelled to bless the one they love, selflessly. As a result, our relational honeymoon flies the coop as newness and novelty go out the window with them... Yet, once involved in the relationship, it becomes our individual personal responsibility to honor God and each other by doing whatever it takes to keep our vows to Him and each other fresh, tender, and life-giving as promised.

Anyone can quit... But, only those who love God and others with honor – can win. It's of interest to me that we typically pay a higher cost when intimately in love with someone than when we focus our attention on counting the cost... Yet, we simply don't care what price we pay when we're deeply and selflessly, in love. The honeymoon associated with both salvation and marriage was created to last forever, not just be a flash in the pan that disappears in a sea of selfishness never to rise again. So, if you find yourself frustrated and counting the personal cost, inconvenience, or injustice incurred in your relationship with Jesus or your mate...love has died and has allowed mere duty to step in. If you have encountered this empty place in your inner world, now would be a good time for you to ask yourself...IF...God's love for Him or the one you've married ever truly existed within you. If not, I encourage you to invite Jesus to do what He wants to do in you and through you toward another with unconditional love. As we prepare for Christ's return representing the "Season of the Bride" and...representing the final phase of insight He shared during my afore-mentioned fast...it's time that we jump into our love relationship with Christ and others headlong, armed with the faith of a child, without looking back if we're to truly, love our King. As leaders or lovers, we are called to inspire and reproduce intimacy in our wives, husbands, individuals, and others beyond in the world-at-large. Our hope in this endeavor will never be realized unless we climb out of religion's grid of infidelity to love others at all costs...

Love's fidelity and faithfulness is a choice, not a feeling. Our success in making that choice will be determined by our commitment to God, each other, and our level of personal spiritual transformation through Jesus Christ. We will either obey God to honor and put others first...or...we will choose self and dishonor all – including ourselves. King David said He would not offer to God that which cost him nothing (2 Samuel 24:24). If you claim to love God and others...prove it in the way you live and love! If you want to do life your way, be honest enough to admit it and go live like hell without polluting others with hypocrisy... Though people may wound and crush us at will, we choose our response. It's high time that God's people choose His way or their own without making excuses, being lukewarm, justifying sin, or pretending to be what they are not. Remember, God weighs the heart... Jesus is coming back for a radiant bride without stain or wrinkle – not a wayward woman. We must choose, get serious, and yield all without condition to be ushered to our seat at the wedding feast of the Lamb. Learning how the Bridegroom's table is built...how it applies to us...how we gain our seat...and, then making the required decision to live

God's way…is the only equation that empowers our rise to radiance (Ephesians 5:26-27). Every sin we commit estranges us from God, evidences our infidelity, and opens the door to hell's mistress, who stands defiantly determined to drive a wedge between us and the Lover of our souls. If we do not rise to radiance while blamelessly positioned in our relationship with Jesus Christ, we will find ourselves declared adulterers and turned away at eternity's door ceasing to be the glory of God…forever. What type of people are we called to be? Are we willing to pay the price to win the prize?

Greg drilling cliff for explosives 400 feet up sidewall – 1981

Chapter 9
Love Cries Out

"For God has not given us the spirit of fear; but of power, and of love, and of sound mind" (2 Timothy 1:7 KJB 2000) "God is love.... There is no fear in love..." (1 John 4:16-21).

Before I go any further, I must simply say...
Love is not a thing, feeling, gesture, or creed. God IS Love...Who came to earth in the form of a man Jesus Christ Who indwells us, re-creates us, and empowers us to love others unconditionally at the cost of our lives.

Two weeks before I spoke in front of an audience for the very first time many years ago, I found myself growing more uneasy with each passing hour as I prepared my message and time to speak grew closer. It was unnerving as the enemy reminded me that I was just a farm boy from a town of 400 people in the middle of nowhere, woke me up in the middle of the night to remind me of past failures, and asked what a guy like me could possibly have to say to help others. After working on my message for a week and arriving to the day before I was to speak, my thoughts began to scatter as realization of standing before a crowd the next day sank in. I navigated my day, forced myself to go to bed that evening, and woke up the next morning on that infamous day feeling like I was about to face a firing squad, though I had little basis for my fears. After re-checking my notes for what seemed like the three-hundred-and-seventh time, looking in the mirror again to see if I had corn stuck between my teeth, reaching into my pocket to be sure I had my arsenal of breath mints, and putting my bible, message, and coat next to the door to be sure I didn't forget them...the time came for me to head toward perceived slaughter. As mile after mile rolled beneath my tires, I was reminded of what other people who had been in car wrecks told me it feels like when everything goes into slow motion and one's life passes before them...

Rolling into the church parking lot two packages of gum later, my palms began to sweat as I turned just in time to lock eyes with the pastor. "I'm dead," I thought as realization that it was too late to escape penetrated to my core. Smiling back at him, I walked toward the entrance doing my utmost to muster confidence and appear cool, calm, and collected. The pastor and I sat and visited, joined in a time of prayer, and headed toward the sanctuary where people were already filtering in to take their seats. Making our way toward the front row, I took my seat next to the pastor where my stomach began to grumble and my vocal cords did their best to tie themselves in square knots. Without warning, the pianist began to play as the choir director trundled up to the podium telling the now-growing congregation coming through the doors to turn to page 187, Amazing Grace. As we lifted our voices, traveled our path through the hymns, bowed our knees at the altar in prayer, and the pastor took his place behind the microphone...I heard my name roll off his lips as the evening's guest speaker. I was a mess – visions of skyrockets, tidal waves, earthquakes, tornadoes, growling lions, and a few tangible aftershocks rattled my humanity just before the pastor's words, "Come talk to us Greg...the platform's yours" snapped me back to reality...

I walked toward the platform, climbed the steps, approached the pulpit, set my bible down, turned to the crowd, stared into the darkness lurking behind the glare of stage lights, and thought "So good so far." Have you ever gone to see one of those adrenaline-sapping catastrophe movies where someone survived a plane crash, the sun had just gone down, and they looked into the night only to realize they were surrounded by invisible, but obviously present, predators indicated by the big eyes of wolves looking back at them accompanied by low-level snarls on several sides? Once again, climbing out of my momentary review of mental movies in which I was the hero destined to die – the crowd, realization of my task, and the message on my heart pulled me back to center stage as I made my opening statement not knowing what to expect. Would there be tomatoes landing soon, a shepherd's hook reaching from the curtains behind me, men running at me with butterfly nets, or a verdict with my sentence "Guilty" being announced on my way toward the gallows, I felt uncertain? Yet, the next hour came-and-went without difficulty as I relaxed, settled into my stride, and delivered the message God birthed within me the best I knew how. After ending my message and opening the altar, praying with those who responded, and gathering my bible and notes before grabbing my coat – I looked around amazed that I was still intact. No one shot me, jeered at me, called me a heretic, or rode me out of town on rail covered with tar…

On my way home, I asked the Lord, "Why was I so afraid to get up in front of people tonight?" The Holy Spirit replied, "You're full of pride…you're more worried about what they think, than what I know. You are created in My image, according to My purpose, to complete My work, and answer to Me…not them." During the trip home after speaking that evening and over the course of subsequent years, God's immortal words spoken into me that evening never left me as I rose and spoke to crowd-after-crowd from that night forward. Were my speaking experiences always easy, painless, and free from fall-out – No? Did I suffer at the hands of religionists, theologians, and the downright ornery along the way – sometimes? Did anyone ever shoot, maim, or crucify me amid the emotion – not yet? Without exception – God has been faithful to inspire, empower, and deliver His message to churches, missions, prisons, schools, organizations, pastors, couples, individuals, soldiers, officers, leaders, consulates, and foreign presidents-to-be through my life while protecting me in His merciful and unconditional love… Yet, the journey has not been without its trials, testing, and testimonies as you can tell by reading pages gone-by…

Layers

In light of a message I preached one day entitled "Onion Dynamics," I have learned through personal experience that our destinies unfold like an onion rolling around in heaven's onion truck in life. On a day of His choosing, God snatches us our lives out of life's field and dirt as a dry scaly-looking onion and says to us, "I can make you shiny and new, but it will hurt a little bit." As He holds us in His loving hand and after asking us a few questions extending us freedom to accept or deny…upon our approval…he peels away our old rough skin to expose a brand new layer hiding just beneath our crusty exterior as we embrace salvation in Him. Once done, he gently sets us down in the back of heaven's onion truck bidding His driver to set destiny's course down life's highway... With each passing turn, approaching stop sign, take-off, and bump in the road – we roll from side-to-side, front-to-back, smacking a wall, or hitting a rivet in the floor leaving us cut, bruised, dry, and dingy much like that dry scaly onion He once lifted from the dirt in the field of life. Without warning and about the time we're ready to sell ourselves to hell's onion ring factory – God's loving hand reaches in, snatches us out of heaven's onion truck and says, "I can make you shiny and new, but it will hurt a little bit." Once again, He holds us in His loving hand, asks us a few questions, and proceeds at our permission to peel away our distress and expose another new layer hiding just beneath our wounded exterior. With each subsequent re-creation cycle and descending layer God removes with love – the issues He exposes in our lives become less obvious to the world around us, but more visible to Him...

When we first encounter Jesus Christ face-to-face, He peels off obvious symptom layers which everyone sees...like indifference, lying, drinking, sex, or drugs that rise from our carnal root desires planted deep within our hearts and souls. With each descending symptom layer He peels off – root issues like pride, independence, infidelity, bitterness, hatred, and rebellion...invisible to most passing casual observers...surface in heaven's light where they shake their fist and pierce God's heart. Though the behavior associated with each descending layer becomes less obvious to our peers while hidden beneath our now refined exteriors, those root desires destroying us from within grow more visible and serious to God as they break His heart in His longing for love relationship with us. Years later, while deep into an extended fast, I remember topping a mountain ridge weeping my way toward home on the freeway crying out to God from my core, for Him to make me more like Him... As I drove, wept, and prayed...I sputtered, "Lord, when You stood accused and condemned by those You love and Pilate asked you if You heard the charges being brought against You... You made no reply, not a single word – nothing!" And then I said, "Lord, when heartache gets so deep inside of me and those I love and care about cut me to the bone after I've given my all...I can't keep my mouth shut...please help me!" Not realizing what had just risen from my lips amid my own agonies into the presence of my Loving Savior, another dangerous prayer cried out for an answer as my emerging identity in Christ, fear of rejection, potential pain, and sense of isolation rose on my imagination's horizon...

God has continued to answer that dangerous prayer ever since as He directs my steps and crosses my path with those people, experiences, and realizations instrumental in defining and fulfilling my destiny in Him. Whether a minor symptom or a root desire – all wrongdoing is sin and reveals our level of estrangement from God (1 John 4:19-21, 5:17). Sin's existence in our lives exposes the presence of a mistress in our relationship with Him as we give evil desires, carnal inclinations, strongholds, and forces of darkness dominion over our lives and futures at the expense of side-stepping Christ's Lordship (Romans 7:7-25; 2 Corinthians 10:3-5; Ephesians 6:12; James 4:1-8). Based on God's word – we all struggle with independence, infidelity, rebellion, and fear's varied expressions whether we admit it or not – it is the fallen sinful human condition (Isaiah 29:13-16; Matthew 16:1-4; James 4:4-8). Whether we merely entertain sinful thoughts or desires in our hearts hidden away from the world around us, stir difficulty within ourselves, or cause problems for another through our actions – God sees it all. The question at hand is not "if" we struggle with independence and heart infidelity...but rather...what form it takes on within us, what attitude it releases through us, and what devastation it leaves around us...

Heart Infidelity

For any of us to claim that we do not face or battle heart infidelity within ourselves proves that we have defied God's Word, ignored God's voice, rejected God's love, forgotten God's forgiveness, and nullified Christ's example making Him out to be a liar (John 14:6, 12, 15; Romans 3:23, 8:28-30; 2 Peter 1:3-9; 1 John 1:8-10). Throughout history, God has rebuked everyone ever born for infidelity in their relationship with Him as exposed by their adulterous love affair with the seductions of this life and the world around them – everyone (Romans 3:10). We must understand that a moral standard and progression based on God's holy being, character, and His Upper Case Law of Love Law...is found within His creation and is confirmed both in the Ten Commandments and His Name – I AM (Exodus 3:13-15, 20; John 8:58). In God's hands, that moral progression leads to love and eternal life. In hell's hands however, our bout with its immoral manifest counterpart drags our lives through independence, infidelity, rebellion, adultery, shame, fear, rejection, anger, and death if allowed to run its course. Our only hope of survival in this life and the one to come rests in our entrance into personal relationship with Jesus Christ alone. Our independence separates us from God thereby severing our ability to discover and solidify our eternal identity and destiny. Until we our cement our identity in Jesus Christ within us, we will remain a fear-driven people who are hopelessly bound by our environment's inability to meet our unique, but very real, combinations of inner human need. Infidelity represents an unfaithful heart posture toward God and people created in His image, which wanders in the crossfire between raw human desire and Christ-likeness. Our level of victory against heart compromise gained by taking our thoughts captive and making all within us obedient to Christ – will determine how wide and how long we open our heart's door to the enemy's invasion (Genesis 4:6-7; 2 Corinthians 10:3-5; Revelation 3:19-22).

Fear

Once sin's compromise has authorized enemy intrusion into our inner worlds however, we will suffer fear's daunting assault against our lives, until we close our heart's door on God's terms. Fear is faith's antithesis or evil counterpart and emanates from satan, not from God. Where faith upholds and rests in God's unchanging eternal character of love, truth, and peace, fear forces its way into wavering human perspective to devour one's sense of God-given identity, destiny, and immortality with its lie-based distortions and delusions designed to destroy (Genesis 4:6-7; John 10:10; 1 Peter 5:8-9). Fear is punishment-based and incites a response rooted deep in self-preservation relative in magnitude to the imagined threat projected by that fear rising within oneself (1 John 4:16-18). Relative to one's spiritual development, fear's projected threat level has strong potential to determine whether one turns to run or stands to fight... For instance, I have been faced by having to push through the spirit of fear while writing this book, especially this chapter dealing with fear itself. This indicates that my efforts to communicate on this subject are exposing the devil's strongholds and inciting him to dispatch the spirit of fear against me in an effort to retain his hellish grip on the entrenchment yet outside the view of those he still controls, manipulates, and intimidates through witchcraft.

If our view of a specific threat confronting us supports our belief that we can outrun it, we will typically turn and flee toward safety. However, if we believe that the threat at our door possesses the ability to overtake or engulf us – we will be more likely to turn, stand, and fight in order to survive the physical, mental, emotional, or spiritual assault we perceive exists. Our corresponding reaction will either be based on faith's revelation of God's love and power, or fear's imagination. Our bout with intense or extended seasons of physical, emotional, mental, and spiritual bombardment will either increase our overall stamina, or reduce our resilience based on whether we carry the burden alone or release and share it with Jesus (Psalms 55:22; Matthew 11:28-30; 1 Peter 5:6-11). Our faith or fear-based perspective and choices will determine whether we gain victory or suffer defeat when faced with opposition. If we stand in faith, our stance will evidence that we have taken our thoughts captive by making them obedient to Christ as our actions reveal that we have placed our burdens in His nail-pierced hands (2 Corinthians 10:3-5). If we yield to fear however, our lack of faith opens the door of our heart and allows our imagination to run wild thereby pitting us against non-existent foes and realities known as – fantasy (Romans 1:18-32; 2 Thessalonians 2:9-11; Hebrews 11:6). We see this principle at work and spinning out of control all over the world within diverse creeds and cultures as uncertainties of all types grow, stability crumbles, and fantasy reigns above the Truth of Jesus Christ in people's faltering minds... If we yield ourselves to fear's assault and hell's lies, fantasy will be birthed within us and its detour will rob us of Christ-centered truth, identity, dominion, and power...

Power

Years ago, I sat down one evening to watch a Disney musical called "Newsies" with my wife and kids. The film was based on a true story and set on the backdrop of the 1899 Newsboy's strike in New York where thousands of street kids peddled newspapers for money and food while living in flop houses... Strikes were everywhere in the day as people got hurt, had no protection, and were fired from their jobs without income or options. The story revolved around non-unionized homeless kids who were being exploited by competing power-hungry media magnets Joseph Pulitzer and William Randolph Hearst...a 20 percent price hike in paper prices to the already squeezed paperboys...a 17 year old Manhattan newsboy named Jack with a dream to escape New York amid his own internal struggle between money and loyalty...and the paperboy's impoverished strike against power to gain voice, justice, and dignity. As the story unfolded, Jack and the newsboys enlisted the help and support of rival paperboys and other non-unionized child workers from other areas of the city to spearhead their attack against their oppressors and gain momentum. Along their path toward liberation, the newsboys decided to print their own flimsy newspaper to sound their cry for freedom on the surrounding New York street among crowds-at-large. As the story's tone intensified and stalemate declared...Jack, being older, charismatic, and adept at playing life's angles...was was chosen by his rag-tag paper crew to raise freedom's voice on their behalf against the unjust price hike and conditions that were crushing them...

As the plot thickened and the clash between money versus child slave labor came to a head, a scene in which the boys refused to sell papers until they were given a break from Pulitzer and Hearst, appeared. During the scene, Jack was ushered into Pulitzer's office where he took his seat across the desk from the hardened business tycoon. As they began to talk and their conversation progressed, Pulitzer tugged at Jack's dreams and insecurities as he sat squirming in his chair. Finally, Pulitzer offered Jack a position and new set of clothes as he tried to buy Jack's loyalties... Sitting up straight in his chair however, Jack retorted, "It's not about the money, Pulitzer!" In smug response, Pulitzer replied, "You're right Jack...it's not about the money...it's about the power."

Through one powerful, influential, and agenda-driven leader – the perspectives, choices, and destinies of millions can be re-shaped, detoured, and destroyed. Clearly stated – power is a faculty, quality, or an ability to do, act, or exert influence over someone or something else. Power can be used for blessing or curses, good or evil, life or death depending on its originating source and the inclination of the one who wields it. God designed power to love, heal, restore, direct, and to deliver people from that which destroys them. Those held in hell's sway however – use power to control, manipulate, intimidate, and destroy whoever and whatever they exert their power over as they operate through the building blocks of witchcraft. One does not have to look far in history to discover power's positive or negative expressions on humanity's stage. With investigation, we find sharp contrasts between the lives of figures like Egypt's hardened Pharaoh who oppressed God's people... versus...Moses who encountered God and his own call as deliverer in a burning bush before leading his people out of oppression through a parted sea. Looking further, we find those imposing slavery on their fellowman in America...versus...a common, but honest Abraham Lincoln who stood against oppression at the cost of his own life. Later, we find an emboldened Adolf Hitler who exterminated millions fueled by hate...versus...Mother Teresa who transformed the streets of Calcutta with her selfless touch of God's Upper Case Law of Love. Those empowered by truth and God's Law of Love brought life, while those driven by death's lower case law of hostility and deception, destroyed...

Power's Perversity

Deception or being deceived is a choice, not an inescapable condition. We have the power to exercise our personal freedoms to choose truth or deception, nobility or impropriety, love or hate – on our way toward personal regeneration. The course we choose will be determined by our source of truth, power, and its governing nature through which we either extend its righteous reach or impose its corrupt control. Jesus told us we can know the truth and it will set us free (John 8:31-47). Jesus is the Way, the Truth, and the Life and He liberates us from death's deception through our personal relationship with Him and emulation of His example (John

14:6, 12). This said and in light of God's majestic creation including flowers, birds, oceans, space, light, fruit, diversity, and all other things including people whom He created – we are without excuse with regard to Him because He has made His presence known to all (Romans 1:16-20).

Though declining in America – we still have relatively open access to liberty, libraries, travel, internet, experts, bibles, church, and other environments which permit free expression and interaction with God and others. Be warned, this same freedom is under fire at unparalleled levels and being actively curtailed as I write. If we work for the honor of the One who sends us, we are proven to be people of truth (John 7:18). If we work for our own honor however, we are pushing our own agenda and in bed with a lie (John 8:42-47). When we reject God's truth and act upon our wayward view, we subject ourselves to the spirit of lawlessness and put ourselves under God's powerful delusion causing ourselves to believe death's lie (2 Thessalonians 2:9-12). Please note that the preceding passage that was cited says that delusion comes to those who are "perishing." Perishing is NOT a mandatory either-or scenario in which we are simply in-or-out. In reality, it is proven that we are thriving in those areas of life controlled by truth and only perishing in those areas bound by deception. Anywhere we realize things are amiss within, indicates our pressing need for God's internal illumination, our deliverance, and change. This is the nature death, the impact of sin, the working out of our salvation, and the very process of being redeemed. Perishing is – the experience of being devoured (1 Peter 5:8). Though no one is perfect...deception, sin, and perishing are a choice...

Deception

Throughout history distorted or false information has been used by one person or group to deceive another for the sole pre-meditated purpose of gaining ungodly tactical advantage, control, and dominion. This self-serving tool is known as propaganda...and has been used to varied degrees by ALL people, cultures, churches, religions, nations, governments, and evil spiritual forces and is called, death's lie (2 Thessalonians 2:11 NIV). Propaganda is a by-product of sin and death released through the fall of man in the Garden of Eden and is used by those people who are bound by deception at a level which compels them to operate in witchcraft (control, manipulation, intimidation). Many may bristle at my generalized seemingly all-encompassing definition, but I will simply refer you to God's benchmark drawn in Jesus Christ and ask, "Where or when did He deceive or lie to anyone on any level...ever?" The hard part for us all is being willing to admit such deception is occurring through our own government, nation, religion, church, relationship, or personal life... Next, some readers may consider my vantage point to be "conspiracy theory" to which I will reply, "There is a conspiracy. The devil hates us, wants to destroy us, and uses people who are bound and driven by his deception, power, and dominion gained over them through sin – to carry out our destruction." We are all guilty of using different levels or types of propaganda at one time or another in our desire or effort to exert our will over that of another to our own advantage – to err is human.

The enemy of our souls (satan) seduces all who holds any position of power or level of authority – whether it be parent, pastor, or a President...to control others with demonically driven intent at the expense and risk of inflicting possible harm on those over whom

Sign revealing my surroundings on my 2nd USA Walk – 2011

they exert their power. The devil has one all-inclusive goal, to defy God and destroy people who are created in His image. The devil is a liar and the father of lies (John 8:42-47). His influence is found all over the earth and within our own homes, relationships, and souls as we choose our way over God's through our willing commission of sin. Our adversary carries out his evil agenda beneath a veil of secrecy and under the cover of darkness from behind old tires, closed doors, big smiles, empty promises, fancy titles, loose friendships, news articles, devalued monies, skewed theologies, and other special affects running rampant within governmental affairs and the polluted theatres of life... Propaganda by this definition, is one of death's magic arts which God hates and by which the destinies of those who practice them without repentance, are determined (Revelations 22:14-15). Our proper exercise of power can only be achieved when we believe and live out God's truth in daily life based on Jesus' example... Please, let me be direct...

As good stewards of what God entrusted to our care, every person born throughout history...at whatever level of influence they posses...has God-given responsibility to identify and promote governmental and religious leaders they believe live and represent the best level of moral example and leadership to their nation and people (John 15:12-17). Tragically, power's influence has been reduced to a commodity enslaved by elitism, brokered with belligerence, and garnered through greed. Political arenas and systems worldwide run wild in developed and semi-developed nations and have become one of the most corrupt and shameful displays of propagandized theatrics in the history of the free world. Upon this power-hungry politicized stage between supposedly upstanding, religious, and moral men and women of the world... debates are held, promises are made, victims are exploited, lies are told, characters are assassinated, scriptures are perverted, gods are invoked, and clandestine agendas are advanced at the risk of individuals, cultures, nations, and life for – palm grease and green. Citizens-at-large snag financial journals, grab news rags, and mount soapboxes to grind their axes and declare their cases, as God's Upper Case Law of Love's instruction Book sits atop televisions silenced beneath perversity's dust falling out of the philosophies their screens display. Social injustice, tax issues, personal convenience, campaign ads, retirement options, occupy movements, cruise catastrophes, cyber censorship, gas prices, and cow flatulence enrage the masses to hit deception's fan as the Lord of Glory weeps at our blindness... But, we're a godly nation...right? If that were true dear friend, decency would prevail and evidence would raise its own voice and fly its own flag (Mark 12:29-31; John 13:34-35; Galatians 5:22-26; 2 Timothy 2:14-26; James 2:14-26, 3:13-18). Do you see it...does it surprise you...do you care? Our response will reveal our answer...

Where have fruits of peace, kindness, goodness, self-control, and heaven's wisdom evidenced by purity, consideration, submission, mercy, and sincerity capable of producing righteousness or credentialing power – gone (Galatians 5:22-23; James 3:17-18)? As I said, the bible warns us of such decline in the last days... Meanwhile, as we go about living just as others before us did in the days of Noah while eating and drinking, marrying and giving in marriage, doing business, trying out oxen, or looking at new land oblivious to heaven's invitation and Christ's return...world-altering decisions, agreements, and events that shape nations, create wars, incite genocides, justify atrocities, and exploit people beneath oppression's hellish thumb are being made in secret without mention (Isaiah 54:14; Matthew 24:36-46; Luke 14:15-24). Behind the scenes, shadow technologies track and archive people's views, information, associations, affiliations, finances, and lifestyles on a tangled worldwide web to feed and impose godless agendas purposely hidden by those in power to their people's peril. We see patriotic celebrations of victory on one hand, and put those who lay their lives on freedom's line in combat on watch lists when they come home, on the other hand. Sadly, this same philosophical and idealism-driven battle for power occurs in homes, relationships, businesses, churches, organizations, governments, and countries from small to large all over the world each day...

The spirit of the age is upon us, has come out of the closet in force, and is pounding at our door with tyranny's fist (Isaiah 54:14; 2 Corinthians 4:2-6; Ephesians 2:1-10)... Tragically, miss-focused and misguided people of all persuasions are more zeroed in on fiscal responsibility, American Idol, pastoral appreciation, health care, Facebook friends, church names, marital redefinition, and ecumenical unity...all issues of varied importance...but still mere symptoms of an adulterous generation estranged from a holy and loving God. I recall God inscribed it in stone this way, "Thou shall not have no other gods before me" (Exodus 20:3 NIV). And yet, when mere men re-make God in their image, take His government upon their shoulders, denigrate people created in His image on any platform, push Jesus Christ into the shadows of human arrogance, and emulate a fallen angel who was cast from heaven to venture human effort and ascend God's throne through their egocentric competition with the Most High...men fall and nation's crumble (Genesis 1:26-27; Joshua 24:23; Isaiah 14:9-15). There is One worthy of honor, glory, and power...One Who is worshipped by heaven's angels, living creatures, and elders...One to Whom we will give an account and bow our knee as we confess Him to be Lord over the heavens and earth...and last time I checked...we are not Him (Matthew 12:36-37; 2 Corinthians 5:10; Revelation 4:9-11, 7:11-12). Power's deception is a choice...it is evil...and it devours everyone it touches...

The essence of Love protects, truth liberates, and – deception destroys. When we as God's people live among a supposedly free society that outlaws divine truth in the interest of not offending someone while risking moral devastation...a society who's culture is immersed in and defined by extraordinary affluence, perverse power, and unbridled indulgence – truth and those who raise its voice come under fire, are put on watch lists, are labeled enemies of the state, and truth itself...is in essence and expression...redefined, condemned, made illegal, and called unloving by a world-dying-at-large (Proverbs 11:1, 17:15, 20:23). Scripture warns us that we will face these very types of perilous times both inside and outside the Church just prior to Christ's return (Matthew 24:3-46; Romans 1:18-32; Timothy 3:1-5; 2 Peter 3:1-14). Have you taken time to find out what is "really" unfolding in the Middle East...what is drawing all Superpowers into centralized conflict...what underlying issues are at hand...and what the word of God says about it? Why not?

Without excuse, remember... If we believe what we have always believed...and do what we have always done...we will have what we have always had – hell knocking at our door. And yet, we are called to grow in God's love, truth, and character with increasing measure, to rise toward radiance, and to make preparations necessary for us to enter the wedding feast of the Lamb (Ephesians 5:1-33; 2 Peter 1:3-11, Revelation 19:6-9).

The Voice of prophecy grows louder, more insistent, and more urgent in its cry to a lost world each day through unprecedented events and those daring enough to remind us of all Jesus said. If events unfolding all over the earth do indeed indicated the season of His return, the potential heartache and catastrophe for many is staggering if they remain asleep in God's light (John 3:19-21, 14:27, 16:13; Revelation 19:10). I would rather be unpopular and save people who end up mad at me, than to be their best friend, watch them die, and know I could have stopped it if I had tried (Mark 8:34-38; Ezekiel 33:1-2). I am ever-aware that Jesus yielded His power, made His choice, and asked His Father to forgive those who made a choice to crucify the Lord of Glory. Real power, Love's power, God's power – sets self aside so others can live with freedom's power and sound mind...

Sound Mind

I grew up and farmed at the upper end of a high elevation 120 mile long farm valley nestled in the foothills of the Cascade Mountains on volcanic soils that lay in draws between boulder-covered high spots called rock buttes. Though the soil was rich and productive, farming next to rock piles was a bit challenging from time-to-time as mower blades or sub-soil shanks collided with one of the underground truck-sized monstrosities foiling my farming regularly. Dirt was over a hundred feet deep between the high spots and became shallower to almost paper thin as it met a butte's edge. Other farming areas enjoyed large expanses of land free from rocks making it much easier to grow orchard, but produced lower quality fruit. My small rural area of 400 people stationed in the foothills of Mount Rainier, though more difficult to cultivate, was known all over the world for producing superior high elevation apples and pears. And yet, rocks and machines simply do not mix...

After years of farming among the rocks and while on my belly beneath my brush cutter one morning looking rather forlornly at the entire blade assembly laying on the ground due to a rock-inflicted shattered shaft...I had one of those "moments" in which a great idea passes through one's being and grants them victory's assurance. In my case at age 23 (1979) – that was the day I gained vision and determination to start my third-of-three companies focused in the field of drilling, blasting, and rock removal through the use of controlled explosives. I had already been working with dynamite, blasting caps, and demolition cord for a couple of years alongside a licensed neighbor who also farmed rock piles. With only two other firms offering blasting services to the area and while surrounded by more than 25,000 acres of rock-infested farm land, I was certain there would be no shortage of work. With little delay – I jumped through the hoops, waded into deeper technical study, and later received my explosives licenses for blasting, transporting, and storing related supplies. During every waking opportunity – I studied explosives velocities, calorie-grams of power, time-delay systems, shot design algorithms, fragmentation, drilling technology, seismic movement, shock waves, structural dynamics, specific densities, and geology. The mental focus was intense as I acquired knowledge and assumed escalating responsibility, project sensitivity, and procured specialized equipment necessary to the task.

Over the next few years, I became one of two individuals in my state readily willing to do highly technical controlled demolition work in extreme liability situations next to homes, under buildings, along freeways, and other sensitive structures where noise and fly material were intolerable. My expertise was enlisted by construction companies, farmers, and prime contractors for drilling and blasting associated with site preparation, trenches, basements, pools, roads, quarries, wells, and aggregate production. Now, up to my neck in three business...often reminded of God's call on my life... stationed a few years before praying that first dangerous prayer... and being surrounded by life's back story – I pressed even deeper into gaining skills necessary for God's design and my future to unfold while I left Him watching from the sidelines...

As work progressed, job size expanded, technical detail grew, and industry recognition for my abilities opened doors…I became intrigued with the thought of becoming the third of three families in America who engaged in the technical art of dropping skyscrapers and hotels in metropolitan areas. I remember later going to watch buildings like high rises and Seattle's King Dome being reduced to imploded rubble as my kids and I looked on, or sometimes, going it alone on my way through life's process. Life was a constant run, opportunity was everywhere, and I was doing my best to build for my family's future… Without warning, it became obvious God's plan was taking me down a different path as I got sideswiped by life's back story in the aftermath of praying that first dangerous prayer, was granted new beginning, and made my way several years further down life's lane. By then, I was several years into ministry, in the midst of spiritual transition, and had moved out of state with my wife for extended education… After class one day while needing a break from brainwork – I jumped in my pick-up and headed toward home to 3075 Teardrop Circle. While on my way, I passed by a large open area and just happened to notice that several new-looking Ingersoll-Rand hydraulic track drills were boring downholes for explosives. Intrigued and thinking it offered the respite of distraction that my weary mind longed for…I spun a U-turn, hung a left at the light, made the spur road's dead end…and dodged into the field where I parked, got out, and leaned-up against my truck to watch…

A few moments later, a yellow company truck rolled up in a cloud dust, the door opened, and out stepped a middle-aged guy in a hard hat who strode up and asked, "Can I help you?" "I was just watching," I said. "This is a restricted blast zone closed to the public for liability reasons." "I understand," I said before offering, "Not trying to tell you what to do or anything…but, it seems your rock fragmentation and shot results would be much better if your drill pattern was two feet closer between holes in-the-row…two feet further apart between rows…and sub-drilled another 2 feet below finish grade marked on that survey stick over there. And, it would probably be best to configure your time delays to pull the shot to the right…start with your "zero" delay at the east end ascending upward in skip delays working westward and into the back wall.

That should muck everything into this bottom corner to minimize ground movement and fly rock," I finished. He looked at me, raised his hard hat to scratch his head, and said while setting it back down, "So, you know a bit about powder, huh?" "Yeah...a bit," I responded. "Where'd you learn?" he asked. "I had my own controlled explosives business for thirteen years before losing everything to a winter freeze after twenty years when God decided to stick me in ministry. He's always an adventure ya know!" I answered with a grin. "What brought you to Colorado?" he asked. "Bible College... my wife and I wanted to take in some classes," I replied. He stuck out his hand and offered, "My name's Jim." "Greg here," I shot back as I latched on and shook. "Well, we don't normally let people on-site during operations...but, it'd be okay if you want to stop by and watch...I'm usually around," he offered with a smile. "That's great...thanks!" I replied. "I need to go chat with my crew about that drilling pattern...," he said with a smile...lifted his hat...slicked his hair...dropping his lid waving as he trudged through the dirt to his truck. "See ya later Jim...thanks again!" I shouted after him in the din of drills... He got in his rig and drove away in a cloud of dust making a bee-line for his crew. It was time for me to leave as well...

As I headed home, pondered my encounter with Jim sitting back in my seat to unwind until my arrival, I began having a conversation with the Lord about the realities of being an almost starving Bible College student barely making ends meet. I rolled in the driveway, closed my pick-up door, and made my way inside where I found my wife doing housework. We talked about her day, her Bible College classes, and money realities related to our decision to attend school. Afterwards, I told her about the blasting project, meeting Jim, and how good it felt to be near the action again... She gave me one of those looks and said reassuringly, "We came here because God told us...even if...we're almost starving and our family's over a thousand miles away." "Yeah...I know," I replied as I saw the longing behind her eyes. Suddenly, the phone rang breaking our concentration and I bounded downstairs to grab it before it stopped. "Hello," I said as I held the receiver to my ear. "Is this Greg?" was the reply from the line's other end. "Yes...can I help you?" I asked. "This is Tom, I'm VP for the number two explosives company in the United States...I was wondering if you would like to come to work for us" he said. "I hear from Jim, that you're pretty sharp on explosives, delays, drilling, and rock...we need a lead shot design, loading, and implementation tech to drop rock in seven cement quarries from southern Colorado to southern Wyoming," he continued. "We're the company that pioneered the bulk-loading truck. We can transport explosives down the highway in their non-combined state before blending individual components on their way down the borehole on-site. Our drilling crews will punch the six-to-eight inch diameter hundred foot deep holes before you arrive...and your job would be to travel from site-to-site on a two week cycle, supervise loading, hang delay systems, push the button, drop a 150,000 to 200,000 cubic yards of cement on the floor, and go to the next quarry. Each shot takes from a hundred (100) to hundred-and-fifty (150) tons of explosives depending on conditions. We'll start you around $55,000 a year plus benefits, a truck, a phone, and laptop," he finished. "Are you interested?" he asked leaving me a bit stunned. "Give me a bit and let me talk to my wife...I'll get back to you," I replied. "Great...I look forward to your call!" he said as we both dropped our receivers in their cradles.

With my mind in high gear...I made my way back upstairs recalling the rush of saying "fire-in-the-hole" and thinking about my wife's longing...pressing bills...class loads...and God's call... "You'll never believe who that was," I said to my wife. "Who was it?" she asked me. "It was the VP of a big explosives company back east," I answered and told her the rest of the story leaving us both dumbfounded... As we talked over the offer and its possibilities for the next hour and what we knew God had already told us to do...we knew in our hearts and agreed...that the job was a distraction in disguise. So, I got up, headed for the phone, dialed, and Tom answered. After preliminary introductions, I said "I appreciate your offer Tom...but, after talking it over...taking the job would be a detour to God's call on my life... I'm sorry, but, I need to decline." "Well, sorry to hear that, but I understand. If you change your mind down the road...please don't hesitate to call me...I could use your help," he replied. "Thanks," I said as we hung up and parted. There my wife and I sat – 1,351 miles from home, in Bible College, pulling full class loads, short of money, unable to visit family, being offered an incredible opportunity…and in agreement…to stay our course God's way…

That choice was 17 years…three moves…multiple 40 day fasts…a first transcontinental walk…watching people being healed… nearly two hundred sermons…a fifty day fast…almost dying in a car wreck…praying at America's East-and-West Gates…radical transformation…seven years learning of coming tribulation… life's back story…400,000 driven miles…twice on-site in Europe-Afghanistan-Pakistan…days filled with heartache and brokenness… seeing untold miracles …closing a three year prayer loop at Israel's Wailing Wall…sleepless prayer-laden nights…growing 417,000 trees…a second transcontinental walk…encountering a wayward church…stepping into the impossible in faith…reaching into broken lives…turning down another high dollar job while on the road penniless…seeing many more miracles…being radically altered again…knowing God loves leads me…writing this book…and being pierced by the reality of His pressing return…

Sound mind calls us to desire, see, heed, enter, and complete the vision God grants us… The enemy of our souls goes to war with our hearts which were created to take on God's heart nature, our minds created to be renewed and take on Christ's mind, and our thoughts…which exalt themselves above the knowledge of God… which were designed to be taken captive and made obedient to do His will (2 Corinthians 2:3-5). Double-mindedness occurs when our lack of vision, faith, and commitment to Jesus Christ throws us on life's battlefield trapping us in the crossfire between heaven and hell to vacillate between God's will and our own (James 1:2-8). Though we have entered the battle at that point, we did so out of wimpy waywardness, not a choice to engage in warfare. Under such combat, our prize is imperiled with loss as we find ourselves pulled from the blood-stained dirt by the loving touch of God's angelic medics, but filled with hell's holes. Double-mindedness represents an internal mental and spiritual battle ripping our humanity between God and self, faith and fear, honor and reputation, victory and defeat, and life and death. Based on reliable sources – most trauma-related, environmentally-induced mental illness is believed to be caused by unresolved internal conflict between opposing idealisms, forces, and personalities which emerge as adaptive identities built on distorted truth, descending deception, and fragmented reality. Yet, as God's people, we have been given the heart of God to love others unconditionally and "Wired-2-War" against hell's lie armed with the mind of Christ as we don His Living Armor to fight and win (John 13:34-35; 1 Corinthians 2:6-16; Philippians 2:3-8; 2 Thessalonians 2:9-12). As His people, we are given authority over fear...called to exert God's loving power...called to set captives free...called to set our face like flint...and called to head resolutely toward Jerusalem, rise in radiance, and to be the Army of God (Isaiah 50:7; Luke 4:18-19, 9:51; Romans 13:8-10; Ephesians 5:1-33, 6:13; 2 Timothy 1:7).

Suffering

Standing our ground in faith is not always easy or fun...sometimes it simply hurts. As God's example to us, though not a popular thought, Jesus also learned obedience through suffering (Hebrews 5:8-9). You may wonder how He learned obedience through suffering when He was in fact, God. Yet, Jesus learned obedience through suffering when He faced and embraced circumstances or decisions with potential to either free or crucify His will, reputation, rights, freedoms, or life. This was proven when He was rejected by religion, denied by disciples, betrayed by friends, settled his Gethsemane decisions, stood before Pilate, subjected Himself to beatings, and liberated our destinies on Calvary's cross (Matthew 26:31-34, 27:13-14; Luke 14:36, 22:47-53; John 5:36-43, 6:38-39, 8:32, 14:6, 19:11, 21:15-19; 2 Corinthians 3:17-18). All Jesus said and did WAS His example, WAS His act of spiritual worship toward God His Father in heaven, and WAS God's PATTERN through His Son's life for His people to follow, including you and me (John 6:37-39, 14:12; Romans 12:1-2)

Following Jesus is not for wimps, whiners, or the wayward. Following Jesus is contact sport for those who realize their need for forgiveness, who grasp how much they have been forgiven, who appreciate what God sacrificed in love, and who are willing to forgive others freely in the same manner and measure they received themselves. When Jesus uttered the words, "Follow Me" to His sleeping disciples while being handed over to condemnation and crucifixion by one of His inner circle...after spending several years showing them how to feed multitudes, forgive adulterers, evict demons, heal blindness, cleanse lepers, restore life, confront religion, and do God's perfect will...evidence shows that Jesus knew His identity and purpose (Mark 14:32-42).

Judgment

It is human nature to become weary and war-torn amid the suffering we endure in the battles of life. No one is perfect, no not one. Yet, we are called according to His good purpose to do our best to emulate and extend the same type of love, forgiveness, mercy, and grace He first and freely gave to us as we reach to others freely with clear and yielded hearts (Matthew 10:8). We cannot pull it off if we stand in judgment of others. The very standard we use to judge others sets the standard by which we too will be judged ourselves (Matthew 7:1-5). It is common for fallen human nature, as often revealed in legalistic forms of religion that deny God's heart, to impose expectations on others it will not practice itself. Being in relationship with Jesus calls us to live consistent with His life example or pattern. God's character and resurrection power revealed in Christ's life on earth embody romance theology and personify His Upper Case Law of Love as His preeminent governing authority over-and-above our personal interpretation of Scripture. When our personal immaturity and theology pushes Jesus aside to justify our own views, cuts us loose from Living Truth, and grants us wide berth in our moral accountability – the existence of independence, infidelity, fear, and defiance toward God, others, and ourselves through miss-perceived injustice are proven to exist within us (James 4:1-8).

Dreams

Since I was very young, it has been commonplace and ongoing for me to receive vision from God regarding things to come well in advance of their physical occurrence. As I've tried to understand those things He shows me...while having no one but Him, His word, Christ's example, personal prayer, and trying to live in faith as means of discovering my question's answer – I've learned in the school of hard knocks. Sadly, doing my best still separated me from others I love because they did not understand or know what to do with those things God had shown me or called me to do. As a young adult, neither did I. People's typical choice of solution in such situations left my world less-than-desirable to say the least. Yet, amid the battles...God came close, became personal, granted mercy, extended grace, and never left me alone, ever. Otherwise, I would not have survived hell's assault in life and through others. Because God allowed me to learn in the furnace of affliction however, He has used my pathway and its corresponding trials, setbacks, and victories to encourage others and help them find their way while refining my character, developing my gifts, increasing my faith, purifying my discernment, and directing my steps at an unspeakable personal cost I'll never be able to describe in words... Eight (8) years after my 2003 fifty day fast which marked the beginning of the seven (7) year season God said He was going use to teach me about coming tribulation...after living out that hellish season in my world...and after leaving all behind to embark on my second walk across America – I met Daniel and Paola almost exactly 8 years after the onset of that fast...

At the same time as meeting them – I was actively approaching the end of my seventh (7) vision-valley-release-completion-vision cycle in life over the course of 40 years as I walked toward completion on the Florida Coast in Hannah Park September 28, 2011 where I would step onto the beach at sundown as Rosh Hashanah's (Feast of Trumpets) began. Before meeting Daniel and Paola, I had already begun telling people that I was leaving cycle number seven (7) in my life and that I was preparing to enter cycle eight (8) significant of new beginnings. Likewise, I told people that the September 2011 Feast of Trumpet's onset would be followed by an immediate increase in global chaos and unrest. That statement has become true in spades... In retrospect, I had traveled a pathway to Israel's Wailing Wall on my fiftieth (50) birthday nearly five years earlier, while mid way through the seven (7) year tribulation experience God used to teach me of future events...was heading toward my second transcontinental walk's completion in Florida on Hannah Beach between parking lots ten (10) and eleven (11) significant of walk start and end dates... and my fifty-fifth (55) birthday on October 26, 2011 was quickly approaching. Before walking onto the beach that day as evening settled in just before official sundown at 7:18 PM, I received a call from a widow the Lord compelled me to help over the prior 8 months and who had just received word of victory...

It was at this mile post, from this vantage point, and under these circumstances, that I was approaching walk completion and during which time I had met Daniel and Paola just two months before. After standing alongside and working through life challenges with them in their home that first night as related in chapter eight (8) herein entitled "The Bridegroom's Table"...after numerous subsequent calls and hours talking through issues related to their lives, marriage, and callings...after seeing who God had created them to be, watching the devil come after them with force, praying for them, and standing with them...after helping train their hands for battle, to recognize their created purpose, and to disarm the weapons the devil fashions against them – they were on the rise. Likewise, after navigating another enemy assault against them... after Daniel and I spoke the evening before while I was taking a break from writing amid sipping on an Americano at Starbucks, had met a wounded and recovering Marine...after Daniel had a dream "last night" in the early morning hours of today January 13, 2012...after the Holy Spirit led him to Isaiah 58:8-12 and he and Paola stood strong in their faith, marriage, and in prayer together... after God had just given me pieces and Scripture references for the completion of this chapter that I had already written down while laying on my bed...and after...I sent a text message to a friend for prayer while needing clarity – Daniel and Paola called me moments later on speakerphone so Daniel could share the following dream...

Daniel began, "Paola and I were walking around together in a foreign nation surrounded by European people. As we walked about, Paola was anxious and afraid before we arrived in front of a big church. I asked her to come in with me so we could pray, but she did not want to. Finally, I convinced her and we entered finding holy water there. So, I put some on her forehead and prayed over her asking

God to settle the fear, make her strong, and protect us both. She calmed, we left, and began walking again. As we continued down our path, we came to a second church and decided to go in. As we entered, I realized that I had a big flashlight in my hand. The church was full of people and the roof was supported by large pillars and columns. The column in front of me was the biggest one of all. As I stood there however, something did not feel right to me. So, I shined my flashlight on the column from bottom to top where I saw a crack that continued from the column into the ceiling. As I kept looking at the crack during my dream…I was able to see deeper into it beyond the ceiling, through broken rafters and beams, and out of a huge hole in the roof. As I continued to look, the crack in the column grew wider and deeper making me aware that the column was going to collapse and the roof cave in on everyone. So, I found an usher, showed him the crack, and told him everyone should leave before the roof crashed in on them. JUST THEN, my dream shifted scenes and I saw America's president pointing at his wife with disfavor as she stood near him. AND THEN, I WOKE UP.

After waking up this morning, I shared my dream with Paola, we prayed together, and God led me to Isaiah 58:8-12. 'Can you tell me what it all means?'" Daniel asked me.

In response to Daniel's question – I could see that the dream clearly applied to him, their marriage roles, people in general, the Church-at-large, America, Europe, and the world – warning of a coming crash that is imminent. Based on the Isaiah 58 passage God took him to, I could also see that the dream was a contrast between being real or counterfeit as mates, leaders, nations, the Church, and as individual people who are being faced with a critical life decision between God's Truth and deception's destruction. Again, the tone of Daniel's dream was imminent, implying soon. I shared the principle I believe it conveyed to them, their marriage, the Church, America, Europe, the World, and how it applied to me as it confirmed what the Holy Spirit had led me to write down just before they called me. As we talked through Daniel's dream and its implications, the Holy Spirit handed me the following contrast between Isaiah 58:1-7 – 1 Corinthians 13:7…and Isaiah 58:8-14 – 1 Corinthians 13:8.

<u>Contrast</u>: Isaiah 58:1-14 and 1 Corinthians 13:7-8 (authenticity, selflessness, obedience, action)

- Isaiah 58:1-7 – Man's selfish approach to God and others through death's lower case law of hostility.
- 1 Corinthians 7 – Reveals God's selfless character toward man through His Upper Case Law of Love.
- Isaiah 58:8-14 – Reveals God's benefits, outcomes, and conditions for us to live selflessly in love.
- 1 Corinthians 13:8 – Reveals Love always protects, trusts, hopes, perseveres, and...never fails.

I shared this unfolding story because it is reminiscent of many extended fasts and consistent with my entire life experience with God. When I say yield to God and step beyond myself in faith, it releases His personalized message-of-the-hour on-the-spot, and allows me to experience His miraculous power as I walk into the impossible each day. I also share this story for several other reasons...

First, I want to remind you that God is God...He has an unfolding ever-pressing plan playing out in light of humanity's current condition, global events, Scripture...and that He speaks through anyone filled with His Spirit who is willing to listen and obey (Matthew 24:1-51; 2 Timothy 3:1-5; Revelation 19:10). Second, I want you to see that God loves those who are His and obey His commandments (John 15:1-27; 2 Timothy 2:19). Third, I want you to see that God's plan directs people's steps...uses the struggling, weak, lowly, and despised to deliver His message to the wise, strong, and statuesque in this world, including you and me (1 Corinthians 1:26-31). Fourth, I want you to see that God gives wisdom freely to those who ask without finding fault...when they are hungry for righteousness, humble themselves, pursue Him with whole hearts, consider all loss, stand in faith, obey, and love Him with fervor (Jeremiah 29:13; Matthew 5:6, 6:33, 10:8; John 14:15; 1 Corinthians 2:6-16; Philippians 3:7-11; Hebrews 11:1-6; James 1:5; 1 Peter 5:6). Fifth, I want you to see that God is pouring out His Spirit at intensified levels on ALL people now and is using those who are willing to rise up, take risk, leave all, and stand in faith to do His bidding (Isaiah 60:1-5; Joel 2:28-32; Ephesians 6:13; Hebrews 11:1-6). Sixth, I want you to see that we are all created in His image, are His workmanship, are called according to His purpose, are seated in heavenly places, are granted access to His power, are all commissioned to go, and are all able to be useful in the Master's hand (Genesis 1:26-27; Matthew 28:19-20; Romans 8:28-30; Ephesians 2:6-10; 2 Timothy 1:7, 2:19-22). And seventh, I want you to see that God is Love…is faithful and just to forgive us our sins…will leave His deposit to seal us for that day…is able to do beyond what we think or imagine…has prepared a place for us…and is coming back to get us – SOON (John 14:1-4; Ephesians 1:11-14, 3:16-21; 1 John 1:9).

Dear friend, it's time we wake up from our slumber, rise from the dead, and make our way heavenward toward radiance to secure our seat at the wedding feast of the Lamb (Isaiah 60:1-5, Ephesians 5:14, 27; Revelation 19:7 NIV). Our preparation and path toward revelation, transformation, and resurrection is illuminated by God's glorious light as we enter His presence, renew our minds, become living sacrifices, love our neighbor, obey His commands, and do what Jesus is still doing (Matthew 22:37-40; John 3:19-21, 14:12, 15, 17:26; Romans 12:1-2, 13:8-10; Ephesians 5:21-33). Love's call to us comes through the Law of Love after Paul's image of authority's institution…after his discourse on resurrection…and "before" his portrait of the institution of marriage (Romans 13:1-11; 1 Corinthians 15:1-34; Ephesians 5:1-33). This order seems fitting because we must surrender to God's authority, be motivated by the God's resurrection power, and administrate our high calling without fear while armed with sound mind within the beauty of marriage to win the prize. Why? GOD IS LOVE and reveals Himself in HIS Creation, Law, Son, Word, Way, Truth, and our individual lives. He is our Savior, Lord, Friend, Messiah, King, and heaven's Bridegroom now reaching to His lady during this dark hour…as… Love cries out! Are we listening?

Age 55 at the foot of Kerrville's Cross on 2nd USA Walk – 2011

Chapter 10
Dancing with God

"Do not think that I have not come to abolish the Law or the Prophets; I have not come to abolish them but to fulfill them" (Matthew 5:17).

While deeply engrossed in writing down all the Holy Spirit was saying to me, I asked God to give me just the right word picture to start this chapter. Every time I ask, I'm always amazed at how He provides on-the-spot, real time situations to draw from... Two days ago, my schedule was re-directed by events tied to helping someone navigate their unraveling world. Yesterday began with what was to be a few-minute call, but became over two hours of spiritual interchange. When I finally returned a second call that came in during the first conversation, I found myself similarly immersed in discussion when we jumped into the subject of Evangelical and Jewish viewpoints toward keeping the Sabbath. Our conversation was light-hearted as we brought our personal thoughts and experiences to the table looking for common ground relative to our individual backgrounds, callings, and spheres of influence. Though my own long-term relationship with Christ carried me deeper and deeper into His rest and my communion with Him...on this day...I made a conscious choice to rest for the remaining Saturday hours of the Jewish Shebat. I was curious if I would discover that I had been missing something, while planning to resume writing afterwards. This was the first time in my life that I made a conscious decision to observe Sabbath based on form, rather than freedom in Jesus Christ.

As the sun went down and Shebat, I grew prematurely tired and could not motivate myself to resume writing as planned. Before long, my entire day and night slipped through my fingers. So I went to bed without writing a single word... Before going to sleep, I set my glasses on the night stand where I usually park them for the night and dropped off to sleep not long thereafter. The next thing I knew, my alarm was going off and it was time to get up. Being early Sunday morning, I climbed out of bed and launched out for a walk to pray and think... As I caught my stride, I noticed my eyes were watering and that I was experiencing blurred double-vision. I wiped my eyes, glanced at my glasses, and noticed that they were dirty. So, I turned back toward the house to clean them and to try a few eye drops before re-starting my walk. Upon my arrival...I put in the drops, blotted my eyes, and cleaned my glasses thinking all would be well. Yet, when I looked at my computer screen on the way out or at things a bit further away as I began walking, I still was unable to see clearly. So, I started looking at street signs, overhead electrical wires, and other objects both close and far away, and discovered my vision was still blurry. When I glanced over the top of my glasses however, my double-vision went away. I wondered, "What happened to my eyes last night, or is the enemy just messing with me?" When I asked the Lord what was going on, He led me on a merry chase through 2nd Corinthians 3:14...then verse 18...then to Ephesians 2:14-18...then to Galatians 5:1-26...and finally Colossians 2:6-23. Immediately, the Holy Spirit convicted me that my prior day's decision to observe Shebat based on religious form rather than freedom in Christ – placed me back under the law regarding that specific issue and veiled my vision[1] because it was a step backwards in my personal relationship with Christ. So, I resolved it in Jesus' name and my vision started to return. Meanwhile, I sent a text message to the friend I had discussed the Sabbath with the day before and shared my experience...

Still unable to see with full clarity, I asked Jesus for wisdom and direction. He compelled me to find a local optical shop, to drive there, and ask a few questions. As I walked in the store and made my way to the counter, I was greeted by a great young man named Jason. I told him what happened and he invited me to take a seat opposite of him in the fitting booth. "May I have your glasses for a moment?" he asked. "Sure," I replied handing them to him. He got up, went into lab, and held them up in bright light and marked the fields of vision with a dry erase pen before coming back to take his seat. "Please put these back on," he said. So, I did as he checked to see how my pupils lined up with the marks he had drawn on the lenses. "How's that," he asked. "A little better, but still a bit doubled," I replied. "Cover one eye and read this," he said putting

1 2 Corinthians 3:14; Romans 9:30-33; Galatians 5:7-8

a magazine down in front of me. I covered my left eye and vision was better. Then, I covered my right eye and things still looked blurry. "Please let me have your glasses again," he said. I handed them to him, he adjusted the shape of the frame, and handed them back to me. I put them on again and said, "That's better, but still not like it was yesterday...I can't imagine what could have possibly changed since last night." He took my glasses again, adjusted a bit more, and handed them back to me a third time. "Ah, that's better!" I said. "Let me go clean them for you now," he told me. So, I handed him my glasses and he disappeared through the door. He returned a couple moments later and handed me my glasses to try on again. "Great, I can see crystal clear again!" I said. "I've been wearing eyeglasses for forty-nine years. Nothing like this has ever happened to me before...ever! I went to bed last night and everything was fine...put my glasses aside...never touched them again until this morning...and then could barely see this morning. So, I cleaned my glasses, put in some eye drops, tried moving my glasses up and down and nothing took away the blur. "I've been writing a book and asked God to give me a story and I think He may be showing me something," I told Jason. He replied, "Could be... Sometimes, one or both lenses move and the two fight each other rather than working together as a team to see clearly..."

As I left the optical store - I thought back on all I had written about God's Law, Creation, and the institution of marriage herein. Likewise, I pondered the passages of Scripture God had given me during my vision challenges while being very aware that eternal principles were on the table, not theology or opposing views. As I considered it all, revisited my friend's response to my earlier message about my vision issues, and sat back to listen to God's still small voice – this picture materialized before my eyes...

Like many, I have a seeing condition known as an astigmatism, which means that one eye is farsighted and the other is nearsighted. As a result, both eyes have a distorted view of the same object thereby causing them to fight each other due to their conflicting views. Because no one is perfect and all see through eyes dimly in this life...we are all deceived to some degree... The first thing the Lord set before me in light of the vision situation I had just encountered was regarding the Gentile's distorted view[2] of privilege, exclusion, injustice, and hope when they consider their relationships with God, Israel, and others. Next, He showed me Israel's distorted view[3] of His Law, being His chosen, observance of man's tradition, and their lacking extension of mercy to non-Israelites. As I listened the Lord, He reminded me that Gentile Christians who were once far off and Israel who is near are at opposite ends of the religious scale, rarely work together...and yet, both have access to God's presence through the one Spirit[4]. As I sat at the optical store with Jason only moments before and he made individual adjustment to both lenses in my glasses, clarity of vision improved...

Next, the Lord showed me that when corrective lenses are prescribed, each eye is tested and corrected individually so both eyes can look more clearly at the same object, unify their focus, and benefit in combined vision together. The Lord made it clear that both sides (eyes) must seek His help individually and personally if their sight is to be restored and their relationship reconciled in Jesus Christ as members of the true Israel who enter God's presence through the Promise[5]. Next, the Holy Spirit whispered that everything done by either Gentiles or Israel – must be directed by Christ alone and be motivated by freedom, faith, love, and mercy[6]. Just then, I recalled how attentive Jason had been upon my arrival to the store...how he recognized my condition from the onset... how he knew just what to look for and how to correct it...that he offered his help gently with a smile...and then sent me on my way seeing clearly and filled with life. Next, the Lord spoke to me about the blindness and lifelessness of law's fallen religion and how it's built on hollow intellectual philosophies rooted in human regulations, teachings, judgment, and mechanical observance. Likewise, He

2 John 4:21-24; Romans 11:17-32; Galatians 5:13-15; Ephesians 2:11-13

3 Exodus 19:5-6; John 19:7; 2 Corinthians 3:13-14; Ephesians 2:14-15; Colossians 2:8, 16-17, 22-23

4 Ephesians 2:17-18

5 The promise: Abrahamic Covenant found in Genesis 15:18-19; Mosaic Covenant found in Exodus 19:5, 24:1-18

6 Galatians 5:1-26: Freedom v.1, 13; Faith & love v.6, 13-14; Christ v. 7-8; Mercy v. 14-15, 22-23; 2 Timothy 2:23-26, James 3:17-18.

showed me that human tradition, festivals, and Sabbath days are merely shadows of what will become reality in Christ and that freedom, love, and unity come through Him alone[7]. As I said, all of us are deceived somewhere because we are not perfect and our hearts deceive us[8]. As I made my way back to resume writing, I thanked God for allowing me to pass through my temporary vision challenges so He could help me see...

In a nutshell dear friend, we all need to make our way to Christ, our spiritual optometrist, so He can correct our vision and help us see Him and others face-to-face with love. Roughly four weeks ago, the Lord launched another chain of events and situations to help me better describe the differences between His Upper Case Law of Love and death's lower case law of hostility. The adventures and revelations along the way have been many...

Perspective

The following principle reality was revealed to me during this book's composition. God granted me deeper insight as an unfolding by-product of discussing (Midrash) His Law and the subject of boundaries in light of Scripture and our unique individual experiences with Him and His Love. This principle crystallized within me as I read all references to "law" found in Matthew, Mark, Luke, and John. This is not an attempt to create new terms. Instead, it is my attempt to portray how already established terms actually manifest themselves and function in and around our lives... What you are about to read emerged from my hunger-based search as I encountered the Lord... It was in this place, during this process, from this perspective, and in this Light – that God graciously shared His heart regarding His Upper Case Law of Love with me. Therefore, please read carefully and consider your view of God, relationship with Jesus Christ, and your fulfillment of His purpose for your life...

God's Way

"For your thoughts are not my thoughts and my ways are not your ways," declares the Lord. "As the heavens are higher that the earth,

---

7 Colossians 2:6-23.

8 Romans 3:9-31; Jeremiah 17:9

so are my ways higher than your ways and my thoughts are higher than your thoughts" (Isaiah 55:8-9).

We must first realize that there is only one Lawgiver – not many (James 4:12). Next, what is it that makes God's thoughts higher than our thoughts and His ways higher than our ways? He embodies Holiness, Love, Truth, Light, and Life...God never changes...God IS. Man on the other hand, was created in God's image and likeness pure, untainted, mortal, and without knowledge of good and evil at the time of his creation. As part of God's Love plan to share eternal reciprocal Love-based relationship with man however – man fell into God's Love mechanism through sin and became imperfect, polluted, and wayward after exercising his first uninformed sovereign freewill choice on behalf of posterity, thereby binding the whole of humanity to a lower fallen nature rooted in death. Man's first choice was uninformed in that he lacked awareness, knowledge, and experience related to things other than God's way. Man had no grasp of what a consequence is or what type of consequences could possibly follow his world-changing choice. Hence, God's thoughts and ways are higher because He knows all and His being emanates unending Life, Love, Light, and Liberty. Likewise, God's ultimate eternal position of spiritual and moral dominion over all creation...IS...superior in all ways to man's earthly spiritual and immoral position of limited dominion in the sphere he dwells...

<u>God's Upper Case Law of Love — death's lower case law of hostility</u>

The terms "God's Upper Case Law of Love" and "death's lower case law of hostility" refer to two (2) diametrically opposed positions and states of: being, purity, enlightenment, capacity, authority, dominion, location, motivation, and reality. In addition, these new descriptive terms represent a moral contrast between theologies, ideologies, philosophies, and methodologies – not people, races, cultures, or religions. This is, in fact, a contrast between God's eternal Law of Love filled with life and liberty through personal relationship with Jesus Christ versus man's sin-distorted religious perspective, misguided practice of all God entrusted to his care, and all God created him to do.

This contrast between God's Upper Case Law of Love represents a God-characterized, God-promised, God-inspired, Scripturally-sound, and humanly-attainable redemptive "Bridge Theology" instrumental to God's restoration of people's spiritual eyesight. Likewise, this contrast has potential to remove hostility's dividing wall within us...make one man out of two previously divided...and reconcile both in Jesus Christ as He lifts us out of death...draws us into salvation...carries us through Love's Promise (Covenant-Messiah)...and ushers us into a place of eternal intimacy as we become one with God Himself (Matthew 25:1-13; Luke 14:15-24; John 6:44, 9:35-41; Ephesians 2:11-22; Revelation 19:7). In brief, God's Upper Case Law of Love empowers those who are His with the loving, constructive, and redemptive intent of His Law of Love that brings life. Conversely, death's lower case law of hostility devours God's people with the judgmental, legalistic, distorted, and destructive "letter" of the law thereby imposing death on those created in God's image.

The following contrast emerged through Scripture when I noticed that references made to "Law" by Jesus in the context of presenting God's intent were capitalized, while those references made to "law" by writers and religion's description of God's love were in lower case letters (Matthew 5:17-20, 12:5-8; Luke 24:44; John 18:28-30, 31-32, 33-37, 19:1-5, 6-7, 8-17 NIV). Some exceptions to my observation were found in cases where writers referred to the Law of the Lord or the Law of Moses...in other places where religion's leaders came asking Jesus asking about the qualities of His Upper Case Law of Love...and when Jesus pointed out to them that they already had the written truth which testified to Him – underscoring their blindness (Matthew 22:36; Luke 2:22-23, 10:25-27; John 8:17 NIV). I find it interesting that Paul re-stated the intent of God's Upper Case Law of Love immediately following His Romans chapter thirteen discourse on God's institution of authority illuminated by overtones which indicate having to do with the last days just prior to Christ's return (Romans 13:1-14). Here is what the Holy Spirit gave me...

<u>God's Upper Case Law of Love</u> unconditionally and eternally exists,

upholds, declares, portrays, extends, offers, models, empowers, inspires, represents, and realizes the absolute purity, love, truth, and authority God embodies and thereby imparts to those He loves as He sees and gives Himself to ALL Creation. God's Upper Case Law of Love is represented in, expressed by, and heard through God's eternal voice declared by Jesus Christ, the Holy Spirit, and His Creation (Romans 1:16-20). God's Upper Case Law of Love reveals and expresses God's being, character and sees face-to-face as it upholds, bestows, and restores Life (1 Corinthians 13:12). God's Upper Case Law of Love is creation, character, command, and compassion-based.

God's Upper Case Law of Love is three dimensional (3-D) and empowered by the Love, Truth, Spirit, and Life (John 14:6, 6:60-65; Romans 8:2, 1-21; 2 Corinthians 3:6; Galatians 5:16-26; 1 John 4:16). Life is the force that fills that which is not yet living in its absence (Genesis 2:7). Without re-birth in Jesus Christ, we have not been born again, indwelled by Him, filled with the Holy Spirit, or become recipients of life. Death represents an unfilled void which exists and cries out to be satisfied in the absence of life (Proverbs 30:15-16). Life and spiritual illumination represented in the Spirit of Life are the third and essential dimension of God's Upper Case Law of Love... and DO NOT inhabit man's fallen expression of death's lower case law of hostility which is almost devoid of Holy Spirit illumination. Life and Holy Spirit illumination are inseparably-linked, represent the glorious "radiance" of God needed by heaven's bride before marriage, and are found in one's relationship with Jesus Christ alone (Isaiah 60:1-5; Ezekiel 10:4; John 5:21-26; 2 Corinthians 3:12-18; Ephesians 5:27).

God's Upper Case Law of Love is only able to be spiritually discerned, recognized, and applied by those saved through Jesus Christ and thereby filled with the Holy Spirit (Romans 8:6-8; 1 Corinthians 2:14-15, 6-16; 2 Corinthians 3:4-18). God's Upper Case Law of Love IS the mind of Christ toward God, people, and the whole of His creation. Those who have rejected Jesus Christ are under God's powerful delusion, bound by lifeless religion, blind to revelation, and are wholly incapable of recognizing, possessing, or operating in God's Upper Case Law of Love until they repent, bow their knee, and confess Jesus Christ as Lord (Isaiah 45:21-25; Philippians 2:9-11; 2 Thessalonians 2:9-12).

NOTE: God and His Upper Case Law of Love remain eternally pure and unchanged. It is man's reduced fallen capacity to perceive and administrate the qualities and power found in God's Upper Case Law of Love that have been diminished and perverted. Therefore, all negative qualities associated with death's lower case law of hostility clearly refer to man's polluted perception and demoralized capacity to rightly administrate God's Law of Love. God IS pure, holy, and loving.

Next, we find that <u>death's lower case law of hostility</u> is only two dimensional (2-D) as it conditionally and humanly tries, believes, breaks, imposes, twists, denies, eludes, devours, discourages, misrepresents, and <u>distorts its expression</u> of God's absolute purity, love, truth, and authority. As a result, the birth of God's character within and through those created in His image is hindered. Likewise, death's lower case law of hostility is represented in, expressed by, and heard through satan, fear, judgment, and a blinded and disobedient human race who's misguided nature proliferates death's destruction in God's Creation and people (Isaiah 6:9-10, Matthew 13:10-15; Roman's 11:30). Also, death's lower case law of hostility reveals and expresses death's character because it only sees through darkened eyes dimly (John 18:31, 19:7; 1 Corinthians 13:12). Additionally, death's lower case law of hostility promotes infidelity, estrangement, bondage, and damnation because it is judgment, perversion, boundary, and destruction-based. Finally, death's lower case law of hostility IS the evil antithesis to God's Upper Case Law of Love and acts as a counterfeit, deceiver, devourer, and destroyer in and through satan, sin, fallen man, and those who wield it. Therefore, death's lower case law of hostility stands exposed in us all when we choose our way over God's commands.

God the Father gave His Upper Case Law of Love to man in the Garden, at Sinai, and in the foreshadowing of a coming Messiah thereby revealing it through the example of Jesus Christ who lived out the Bridegroom's Table built on Truth, Love, Spirit, Glory, and Worship (Chapter 8). Man's commission of sin and God's act of veiling His face subjected mankind to only seeing life through the eyes of death's lower case law of hostility virtually unable to perceive the Holy Spirit's presence, radiance, and illumination (Genesis 3:6-19; Exodus 32:8, 34:29-35; 2 Corinthians 3:12-18). Therefore, death's lower case law of hostility is blind-eyed, head-based, and judgment-driven religion that brings death through the letter of the law as it did when it crucified the Author of Life (John 4:21-24; Acts 3:14-15; 2 Corinthians 3:6, 9).

Clarity

The above glimpse of God's pre-conceived mechanism of Love... and death's distortion – were essential to man seeing Jesus through lower case eyes so that who were those religious were unable to recognize God standing before them in the flesh, in the person of Jesus Christ, as they condemned Him. If Christ had not been crucified as redemption's central element, God's reciprocal love-based relationship with man could not occur. So, it was in this state of God-imparted blindness...through this perversion of Love-based Law...and through this misperception of Love-based thinking – that fallen religion sentenced God to death, ordered execution, carried out crucifixion, established justification, incited resurrection, and propelled emancipation necessary to man's redemption through love. That dear friend is called a plan – a pre-conceived chain of events that lead to a pre-determined destination. Therefore, God's Plan, a plan ever-existent in His foreknowledge founded on His desire for intimate relationship with mankind was implemented with His love-based purpose...conducted with His love-based Law... supervised with His love-based compassion...and fulfilled with His love-based mercy. Soon, God's plan will be completed with His love-based consummation...confirmed in OUR reciprocal love-based marriage...and shared as we rule and reign with Him forever! That's the greatest plan ever made, the greatest gift ever given, and the greatest love story ever told...because...it's HIS-story!

God's foreknowledge and physical creation of man in His image and likeness...represents the onset of <u>God's selection of</u> humanity to be

His eternal partner in reciprocal love-based marriage relationship (Genesis 1:26-7). God presented history's original sovereign freewill choice to man through the serpent just following man's creation and before his fall into love's mechanism (Genesis 3:1-5). The devil's reversal of truth (death's lie) in his question "...Did God really say, 'You must not eat from any tree in the garden,'" presented a choice to man with potential to reverse his nature's direction from life to death and ultimately caused man to fall in love with God (Genesis 3:1-5). Within man's first choice, he unwittingly sacrificed his only experience with true sovereignty...and reduced his decision's character to mere free will choice. Man will not re-experience true sovereignty again until he becomes one with Jesus Christ on his way to the wedding feast of the Lamb.

Please understand that man was sovereign at the time of his creation in that his lack of knowledge of good and evil and his unawareness that he could exercise God-like freedom, left his sovereignty without expression. In truth, man was only commanded not to eat from the tree of the knowledge of good and evil (Genesis 2:17). Had he known that he was able to exercise his first sovereign freewill choice to touch and eat from the Tree of Life – doing so would have made him immortal like God. Sadly, man would have missed intimate relationship with the Lord by obtaining immortality prior to the fall and his subsequent salvation from sin through Jesus Christ.

God presented a second freewill choice to man when He offered His Upper Case Law of Love at Mount Sinai through Moses when it was verbally accepted Israel as a nation. This event marked the end of God's selection process and the beginning of man's betrothal to Him (Exodus 19:1-20:21). Next, God presented a third freewill choice to man through salvation in Jesus Christ, thereby marking the end of betrothal and entrance into the sealed marriage contract by those who are willing to drink from the first shared cup of marriage to appropriate Christ's saving forgiveness through His blood (Luke 19:10; John 5:24-27, 6:37-39, 15:1-27; Romans 10:9). Baptism, repentance, and one's transformation represent the second shared cup of marriage between themselves and Christ. It is on the heaven side of one's salvation choice, that God reverses our life's direction again turning us from death back to life as He leads us into Love Itself through a process Scripture calls the working out of our salvation (Philippians 2:12-13).

ALL God foreknew, desired, created, did, allowed, or effected relating to man in the whole of eternity...as displayed in man's creation, choice, estrangement, toil, reconciliation, resurrection, and consummation with God Himself...IS...and was done in Love. God's Love plan had purpose as salvation began with the Jews... was shared with the Gentiles...and will return to the Jews again as God reconciles ALL to Himself in Jesus Christ and allows us to emerge as members of the true Israel (Acts 28:17-31; Romans 9:1-11:36; Ephesians 2:11-22). Over the years, I have been privileged to live and listen to the Lord both before and during this book's writing based on God's Upper Case Law of Love though I have never known what to call it – before now. Amid rampant human decline, increasing prophetic activity, and related events around the world...this revelation of principle reality is for a time such as this when we find ourselves in need of a Savior Who is still knocking...a transformation that's still unfolding...an intimacy that's still missing...and a Bridegroom Who's still waiting, weeping, and wooing His bride to Himself as He cries out from within His mansion's wedding chambers during history's eleventh hour. When, will His Father dispatch Him to collect His bride? Have you made preparations...are you ready to run to Him without delay... have you risen toward radiance without stain or wrinkle...have you kept yourself blameless as you await His approaching day?

Now that we better grasp the heart behind God's Upper Case Law of Love, let's take a step back in time to consider Creation through our now more enlightened eyes...

Love's Plan – Creation

God is Love...God has a plan...Love's plan is...to save man. God's foreknown plan to save man from sin represents a journey beginning at physical Creation and travels through sin's entrance, man's fall, love's reconciliation, intimate union, eternal marriage, and our ultimate co-habitation with Him (Ephesians 1:4-13). God designed Love's plan to operate with Love's mechanism to incite Love's attraction. Love's plan paints history's greatest picture of the selection, betrothal, and marriage process with all its allure, courtship, improprieties, consummation, estrangement, reconciliation, and renewed joy in a framework of eternal covenant. Love's plan is both a studio in which we learn and eternity's stage upon which we will share our wedding dance with God. How well our dance unfolds and the afterglow it leaves depends on the partner we choose, rhythm we set, lessons we apply, and the submission we yield as we follow His lead. Just as ballet and the waltz take effort, time, and passion to learn – we must be willing to get our toes stepped on, led back to the center of God's studio, and begin anew in His love...if...we're to enter heaven's banquet, present our hand, and dance with our King...

In brief, here is the basic chronology of God's creation of the heavens, earth, man, and the mechanisms through which love, choice, freedom, estrangement, redemption, and intimacy participate in the greatest love story ever told...

On Day 1
God reveals His pre-existent, present, omniscient (ALL-knowing), omnipotent (ALL-powerful), and omnipresent (ALWAYS-present everywhere) qualities at the onset of creating the physical heavens and earth, man, and the remainder of His creation (Genesis 1:3-5). Through Scripture, God was later revealed as I AM , Love, Light, Word, Son, Way, Truth, Life, Priest, First, Last, Beginning, and End (Genesis 1:1; Exodus 3:14; John 1:1-5, 5:16-30, 14:6, Hebrews 7:23-28; 1 John 4:16; Revelation 22:13).

Days 2 thru 5
We see God speaking Light into existence separating it from darkness calling the Light day and darkness night...creating expanse called sky between the waters on and above the earth...defining, separating, and establishing land and seas upon the earth before letting the land produce various types of vegetation and seed-bearing plants and trees that bear fruit with seeds. During this same time juncture God created lights in the heaven to separate day from night and

serve as signs to mark out seasons...made two great lights with the greater (sun) governing day and the lesser (moon) to govern the night...made and set stars in the sky to give light on the earth, to govern the day and night, and to separate light from darkness before letting the water teem with living creatures, let birds fly across the sky, created great creatures in the sea, blessed them, and said be fruitful and multiply to fill the waters and to increase on the earth (Genesis 1:6-23).

Day 6
God let the land produce living creatures including livestock, wild animals, and creatures that move along the ground....revealed Himself as the Trinity saying, "Let us make man in our image, in our likeness...both male and female..." blessing and telling them to be fruitful and multiply...to fill the earth and subdue it...to rule over all the fish, birds, creatures in the sea, birds of the air, and living creatures that move along the ground...giving man and woman every seed-bearing plant or tree upon the earth for food (Genesis 1:24-31). Man was given dominion over the earth, told to fill it, subdue it, and to rule over it. Yet, God retained dominion over man and the whole of His Creation.

Day 7
God rested from His work, blessed the day, and made it holy as history's first Sabbath (Genesis 1:24-2:3).

Romance Reaches
Because God the Father is holy, sin's presence in our lives separates us from Him. As a romantic act of His love and mercy, God the Father sent Jesus His Son and His Holy Spirit into the physical world as our Advocate and Counselor to build a bridge between ourselves and Him... Sin is anything and everything we do, say, think, omit, or commit in word, thought, or action that knowingly and willfully breaks or violates God's Law, Christ's example, and Their Living or written words. Sin is not accidental. Sin must be done on purpose with foreknowledge of right and wrong to be sin. When we commit sin, we are acting in direct opposition to our design and violating God's holy, moral, just, and loving character toward Him and within ourselves.

Falling In Love

We first see and become aware of God's existence by virtue of His obvious presence prior to His commencement of physical creation of the heavens, earth, and man. Though not revealed until later in humanity's redemption story, it is apparent that God's plan to save man from himself emerged out of divine foreknowledge and a passionate desire to share eternal love relationship with those created in His image. It is likewise apparent that for such relationship to exist, reciprocate, and flourish eternally...it would require: (1) man's exercise of freewill choice, subjection to death's dominion, and result in estrangement from God, (2) that such estrangement would require God's selfless expression of unconditional love and forgiveness toward man, (3) that man's receipt of God's love would inspire him to express love and forgiveness back toward God to make it reciprocal, (4) and that the existence of such a reciprocal love relationship would require man's submission to God's authority, emulation of God's character, and dependency on God's faithfulness...even when man himself is faithless...if his relationship to God was to be eternal. Please keep these things in mind as you consider the following observations and perspective of God, man, and the motivation compelling Love's plan...

Love's Cast

Love's plan required a cast of characters created and equipped to play specific roles in history's ultimate love story. This said, I believe death, satan, and sin were all conceived in God's foreknowledge, embody His antithesis, and personify evil's assault to incite and perfect His love relationship with us. The existence of these evil entities presented man with an opposing option to God's loving nature which was necessary for man's choice to exist and be exercised. The existence of this opposing option laid the foundation upon which man became aware, considered, and exerted his original sovereign freewill choice which ultimately caused him to fall in love with God (Isaiah 54:16-17; 2 Corinthians 12:7-10). So in reality – the existence, roles, and impact of death's dark spiritual forces in our lives and process of redemption are an act of God's love. It is the tormenting presence and activity of death, satan, and sin which God uses to reveal our fallen nature, while purifying us from unrighteousness and reconciling us to Himself in love through the cross (Galatians 2:17-21; Ephesians 2:14-22; Colossians 1:19-20; 1 John 1:9). God is love and everything He IS, thinks, says, does, and exerts is a method of and motivated by loving His people (1 John 4:16).

Love's Mechanism

Now, let's take a peek at Love's mechanism of creation, freedom, estrangement, reconciliation, and consummation. Within Love's mechanism – please consider the "fall" which estranged God and man from each other. In God's story, the fall is identified as the entrance, first commission, and impact of sin and death upon man's existence, destiny, and relationship to God. From our fallen perspective as observed through eyes which only see in part – we have viewed the fall of man as an act of God casting us out of his presence "after" Adam and Eve committed the first sin (1 Corinthians 13:12). From man's distorted and diminished viewpoint – it appears as though God got offended, judged mankind, erected a barrier, and threw him out of the Garden and His presence with good justification – He's God. On the flip side – man's misguided reaction to the fall reveals that he judged, blamed, and resisted God based on death's lie because of sin's characteristic deception, pride, independence, and binding effects released by man's own decision. However, I believe it relevant for us to consider the principle which governs symptoms and root causes found in Jesus' encounter with an unproductive fig tree (Mark 11:14, 20-21). This principle paints a portrait of a long-known dynamic called cause-and-effect, action-and-reaction, and root-versus-symptom. Within this principle exists the very reason for humanity's distortion and ongoing hostile reaction toward who God truly IS.? Please let me explain...

Original Man

In reality, man was created holy in God's image except that he did not possess the knowledge of good and evil or immortality at the time of his creation thereby making man neutral (n) (Genesis 1:26-27, 2:17, 3:22). Likewise, man was created in "into" God's presence in the afore-mentioned state fully inhabiting both the physical and spiritual realm simultaneously prior to sin's entrance, appearance, commission, or subsequent impact which resulted in man's exit from God's presence and the Garden. At the onset of and during this pre-sin segment of time from creation's onset to man's first commission of sin – man roamed freely in God's presence and Garden without fear or shame. It was not until sin entered, was committed, and opened man's eyes to good and evil – that fear, shame, and nakedness were revealed thereby causing man to hide (veil) himself from God (Genesis 3:10). Though technically guilty of disobeying God's instructions, man was no less created in God's image at this point simply because he made a bad choice in history's first decision. Man did however, possess a new-acquired ingredient as represented by his new-found knowledge of good and evil inseparably-linked to his life through the choice he had made. This inseparable link to the tree of knowledge of good and evil rooted in death thereby bound man to deception, rebellion, and hostility represented in and flowing through that graft union. His graft into the tree rooted in death was authorized by acting on his freewill choice and would remain binding until broken by atonement of sin through the blood of Jesus Christ on the cross. It was likewise through this destructive graft union – that death's evil emissaries of fear, shame, and deception entered man's life and body thereby distorting his perception of God, others, and his basis for all decisions thereby affecting his existence and future.

Love's Redirection

The onset of man's exit from the Garden and God's presence began... specifically...because of man's newly-acquired knowledge of good and evil which elevated him to God-likeness with potential to live forever, but polluted by death's nature (Genesis 3:22). Man's departure from the Garden resulted from his choice...NOT...God's exclusion. Man's exit from the Garden was not due to a boundary drawn by God or a conflict between the two of them as beings. In simple terms, man's post-fall nature was now incapable of standing in the presence of a loving and holy God (Exodus 3:5-6, 20:18-21, 34:29-35). God did not throw man out or reject him – man made an uninformed freewill choice which unwittingly drew him into Love's plan. In a nutshell, and as a result of man's decision, God and man possessed two diametrically opposed natures...Love versus judgment...peace versus turmoil...Life versus death. It was this clash between opposing natures...not between God and man...which precipitated man's life re-direction and fall into Love's mechanism. Because Love always protects, trusts, hopes, and perseveres...it cannot co-exist with violation, fear, suspicion, and death. In man's exercise of choice and unwitting elevation to God-likeness with the knowledge of good and evil...he inadvertently put himself in competition with God's sovereignty and dominion. For the picture of marriage to work between them, man's acknowledgment and submission to God's ultimate authority and dominion were essential.

Death's Estrangement

The effective differences in nature expressed by Love's exertion of pure moral character...versus...death's exertion of impure immoral character are in direct conflict with each other. Their opposing expressions during the time preceding man's original awareness, consideration, and opportunity to exercise freewill choice when faced with options for the first time – resulted in his "amoral perspective" upon which he assessed, based, and exerted that original choice. Though his decision was necessary for God to carry out Love's plan, man's original choice did indeed shackle the whole of humanity to death's deception, disobedience, and dependency upon God's love, intervention, and redemption (Isaiah 6:9-13; 29:10-30:26; John 12:39-41; Acts 15:12-21; 28:17-31; Romans 11:8-32; 1 Corinthians 2:10-16). As a result, sin's perversion of man's perspective and heart motives activated by his freewill integrated him with death's judgment and nature. As a result, man took on a skewed sense of injustice thereby inciting him to justify self, condemn God, and to enter into his ongoing expression of sinful independence and infidelity. Seeing self, God, circumstances, and his future through fallen eyes – man then projected his own self-inflicted sin-based views, failures, and compromised character qualities on God showing that man had become driven by competitive jealously in pursuit of God's position and power. It was through man's transitional fall from God-likeness into Love's mechanism that he believed, penned, adopted, and acted on his hellishly immoral nature I now refer to as death's lower case law of hostility in defiant reaction against God's Upper Case Law of

Love. It was this vantage point and heart attitude which surfaced again during Israel's worship of the golden calf and later made it impossible for Christ's accusers to recognize God standing before them in the flesh as they rejected and crucified the Author of Life (Acts 3:14-15).

Due to God and man's opposing natures (polarities) and man's distortion in viewing his own immorality and sin as god-like righteousness...man's fantasy-based self-perception caused the two diametrically-opposed natures to compete for the same moral position with man seeing himself like God. If God's positive Love nature (+) would have come near man's negative sin nature (-) to occupy the same space – their differences would have fused them together with each other's opposing nature thereby integrating with the other. If this had happened – God's embodiment of Life and Love would have been corrupted by death, His holiness would have been polluted by sin, His peace would have been diluted by fear, and – He would have ceased to be God as He presents Himself. I find basis in the whole counsel of Scripture to believe that God chose to personify evil in and through satan who was subsequently dispatched amid Love's plan to present man's original freewill choice...and...to draw man into acting upon that decision. In light of a second option in addition to God's prior directives to him, man simply chose something new and different without evil intent because he had been created holy and in God's image prior to sin's original commission. Man's unawareness of consequence and his subsequent interaction with the tree of the knowledge of good and evil simply presented him the opposing option which ultimately brought sin to bear, sealed man's need of redemption, and granted opportunity for love's expression necessary for God's relationship with man to result in marriage – not simple co-existence with others like Him. This distinction is essential for us to grasp if we're to truly understand that everything God does or allows is an expression of and motivated by love...

If man had been able to indulge in the Tree of Life and had gained immortality prior to the fall – that single event would have circumvented God's original purpose for Creation – sharing eternal marriage-based love relationship with man. As a result, God's creation of man in His image would have merely increased heaven's population of eternal God-like clones devoid of love. In a nutshell, God would have found Himself alone in a crowd... In reality, God and man would have separated after the sin transaction based on opposing natures alone because it was their embodied differences that separated them – not will, decision, or lines in the sand. We see this dynamic at work in the natural laws studied in physics. Man was not drawn to God prior to sin because he had God's nature without knowledge and immortality. This left God positive (+) and man neutral (n). God is Love and Love's nature was drawn to man as the object of God's creation, but man lacked the opposing polarity or magnetic potential in his neutrality thereby generating zero drawing or repelling forces between the two. This is why I said earlier that God designed Love's plan to operate with Love's mechanism to incite Love's attraction. For attraction to exist, both objects must possess what the other is missing. In God and man's case – God's Love remained pure and moral (+) after man's fall, while man's post-fall condition took on an impure and immoral negativity (-). Hence, attraction between the two was born. It is in fact, this very positive (+) versus negative (-) magnetic attraction that draws a Loving God to his wayward Creation and sinful man to his Loving God...

Love's Attraction

I thought this small aside may help illustrate my point through the principles of magnetic attraction based on polarity. In magnetic attraction, when one positive (+) pole and one negative (-) pole are thrust together, they attract each other and cement their bond magnetically. However, when two positive (+) or two negative (-) poles are thrust together, they repel each other aggressively making self-adhesion impossible. So what? Well, let's make an application to our relationship with God. When we acknowledge the difference between our dependent negative (-) sinful nature and His sovereign positive (+) holiness, our need for forgiveness and redemption attracts His desire to love and save us causing us to bond in complete unity through Christ (John 6:44, 17:20-26; Colossians 1:9-23). However, when our pride blinds us to our independence and our negative (-) unrepentant deceived nature believes that it is actually positive (+)…when it is not…we then find ourselves trying to be God (+) in our relationship with God (+) and our pride pushes us out of God's presence (Isaiah 14:9-15; 2 Thessalonians 2:9-12). Since only man's nature changed in the fall, man must assume responsibility for any strife between himself and God. Scientists have recently discovered that this same dynamic separates oil and water. By changing oil's polarity, the two will blend. Even Creation's natural laws attest to God's Love and character. So, what did God do to fix it?

In God's infinite wisdom and foreknowledge – Love's mechanism dispatched a Trinity-based expression of God Himself, Who being in very nature God, took on the form of a servant in the person of Jesus Christ making Him the only 200% being Who was the only 100 % God and 100% man ever to exist (Philippians 2:3-11). God designed the person of Christ to function as a dual polarity (+/-) Bonding Agent with bi-directional filtering qualities capable of blocking death's pollution from corrupting God's nature, while still allowing Love to pass through to transform man's fallen nature, thereby preserving and reconciling both to one another simultaneously (1 John 4:16-21; Romans 12:1-2). This part of Love's mechanism is the saving grace God uses to destroy the dividing wall and remove the lower case law of hostility between Israel, Gentiles, and Himself (Romans 6:8-10; Colossians 2:15).

Moral Dilemma

Humanity's standing dilemma could only be truly resolved and re-directed on an individual basis through one's experience of Holy Spirit conviction of immoral behavior, through a Savior's example, and through God's exerted drawing power (John 6:44). Man's potential deliverance from death, restoration to God-likeness, or opposing potential for death-bound damnation hangs on his…now informed…freewill choice and being numbered among those God knows are His (John 17:6, 9; 2 Timothy 2:19). Love could only effect its outcome through God's foreknowledge of Christ's role and pre-authorization of Christ's dominion over death…Christ's purpose to lay His human life down…Christ's sacrificial atonement for ALL sin...Christ's power to resurrect Himself as the Son of God...Christ's purchase of man's pardon on death's tree of the knowledge of good and evil...and Christ's extension of God's unconditional love, forgiveness, and restoration as the Tree of Life toward man (Fruit that Lasts) (Matthew 25:31-46, 28:18; John 6:44, 10:17-18, 14:6; Romans 13:10; 1 Corinthians 13:7-8; 1 John 4:18).

Motive
Though created in God's image and fully equipped with free will and choice – man had never faced, been made aware, been given reason, or held opportunity in his control to choose between opposing options prior to the fall. As a result, man had never been given opportunity or means to exert his free will, possess knowledge, or gain experience with consequences... In forty years of chasing God, I do not find evidence in the creation account or the whole of Scripture to substantiate that man's original exercise of sovereign freewill choice was pre-meditated, defiant, or in pursuit of God's power prior to making that choice. I am firmly convinced based on biblical text, observation, and extensive personal experience with the love and mercy of God – that everything embodied within the context of physical creation, sin, satan, free will, man's fall, law, authority, marriage, and man's redemption are rooted in only one thing – God's Love.

Spiritual Blindness
When man left the Garden due to his newly-acquired sub-standard nature – he blocked his own ability to see God face-to-face...to perceive God's presence...to see into God's spiritual realm...and to save himself from death's lower case law of hostility without the help, advocacy, or deliverance exerted by a Savior. Man's original choice made from a position of personal purity while in the presence of God, moved him from his position of purity, and dislodged him from history's only grip on innocent human independence. On the fallen side of man's first choice – he was subjected to death's invasion where he became blind, disobedient, and godless in his expression of wayward human independence bound by sin (Roman's 11:30). It was from this position that man perceived, adopted, redefined, and applied death's lower case law

of hostility toward God, Jesus Christ, others, and self. This reality, in conjunction with man's blind administration of lower case law, represents the primary reason why many do not want to know God and His people. Love in the person of Jesus Christ is man's only hope. Consequently, how Jesus looks when He lives in and through us has an impact on the unfolding of Love's plan... We are called to give freely that which we received for free (Matthew 10:8).

Never Left

Though man's free will actions removed him from God's presence within man's own perception – man never really left God's presence because God WAS, IS, and ALWAYS will be within the infinite scope of omniscience, omnipotence, and omnipresence making Him impossible to elude, leave, or escape. In reality, Adam's choice on behalf of mankind only severely damaged humanity's face-to-face perception of God and the spiritual realm due to sin's characteristic blindness. Man's fall into Love's mechanism only served to bring about God's ordination, designation, and validation of deliverers, priests, seers, prophets, and people-at-large. Their ordination was based on covenant, lineage, purpose, or their individual position of moral standing through which God still entrusts visions, dreams, and prophetic words today (Exodus 33:11; Daniel 4:1-18; Acts 7:54-8:3; 1 Corinthians 12:1-11). Visions, dreams, and prophetic words are given for both personal and corporate edification, conviction, instruction, and illumination necessary for us to receive God's deliverance while estranged from Him in this life (Joel 2:28-32; 1 Corinthians 14:1-25). Prophetic voice is the very mechanism of access God chose to equip us with, so we can navigate this physical life empowered to commune with Him, share His Truth, and love others His way. Visions, dreams, and prophetic activity will increase in magnitude the nearer to Christ's return we get. These "glimpses" into the spiritual realm represent God's loving covenant reach through which He defines our pathway back to Him. Amid this urgent hour, we believers in Jesus Christ must exercise our freewill to make ourselves intimately ready to join Him at the wedding feast of the Lamb...

Early 2011 while walking across America, I entered another forty day fast in pursuit of God's insight regarding what is unfolding upon the earth during this perilous hour... The heavenlies were raging as I found myself parked in the rural epicenter of darkness amid the State I was walking through. While deeply immersed in a prophetic word pictures which God had already drawn me into, my spirit was astir as I shut the door on life, poured through Scripture, and prayed all day and into the wee hours each night... The ebb-and-flows of brokenness, burden, awareness, revelation, victory, and battle were ongoing as I dug deep into God's foundations. When I did sleep, I was often roused only hours later during the third watch of the night compelled to pray for those caught in life's storm... On occasion, I attended gatherings of people who unwittingly manifested the spiritual realm through their perspectives and actions, thereby affording me opportunity to take eternity's pulse amid all God was revealing. My quest led me through several hundred chapters of Scripture from one end of the bible to the other. One night...thirty-nine days into the fast...I found myself at a home meeting where pastors and people who considered themselves deep walkers had joined for worship. As the music wound down, the host asked everyone to share what God had been saying to us. After an hour and a half, when everyone else relayed what God had placed upon their heart as others listened on intently...I was asked what God had been saying to me...

Standing to face the group, I said, "The Lord has shown me we are in trouble, the hour is urgent, and it is time to make ourselves ready. In the Old Testament, man was under obligation to the law and driven by duty. In the New Testament, man was granted grace and was to be motivated by appreciation. Now however, we are entering the "Season of the Bride" and we are being called to deeper intimacy with our Bridegroom Jesus Christ. Both Old and New Testament perspectives were intellectually held and religiously structured, but lacked intimate relationship with Jesus. Importantly, the "Season of the Bride" will only be entered by those willing to put their trust in God's unchanging character, jump in with the faith of a child, and to fix their eyes beyond personal cost to love and marry their King. Most all of us have heard it said that we need to count the cost. Yet, counting the cost was to have been done "before" we married, entered salvation, and the honeymoon was to last forever.

Unfortunately, many gave their lives to God or another when things were new only to find themselves counting the cost once again as the honeymoon wore off of as a result. Since, many have grown selfish and are trying to convince themselves to stay married to their spouse or God for another day. Yet, when we're truly in love, we don't care if we drive an extra hundred miles, work twenty hours a day, or spend our last fifty bucks because love looks to the one it loves, not at the cost. In truth, we actually pay a higher price when we're in love than when we sit around to count the cost. The difference is, we simply don't care. Most of us are willing to let God bless us, but it's time friends that we focus on blessing God."

I continued, "We have also heard people quote Scripture and tell us that plans succeed through many advisors. Sadly, we tug on the shirt tails of pastors and people looking for answers, while rarely doing the work or falling on our face before God to seek Him with whole hearts and hear from Him in person. In truth, people cannot advise others how to go where they themselves have never been. Many have walked in Old Testament perspective and many through intellectualized New Testament grace. But, few in our day are willing to jump in and serve God at any cost while intimately in love with Him... The "Season of the Bride" is once-appointed and has never occurred before, nor will it ever occur again. It does, in fact, represent the long-foretold culmination of life as we know it detailed in Scripture. It's time we put off religion, drop division, put self last, and chase God with whole hungry hearts before it's too late... The hour is urgent...God's wedding invitations have been mailed...the armies of the earth are gathering...and Heaven's Bridegroom is reaching from His chambers. That is what God has been saying to me." As I finished, I turned, sat down, and gazed ahead...

Suddenly, an older gentleman rose out of his seat next to me, approached, and glared down at me thumping his bible against his other hand saying, "I'm so tired of you...you're so far back in the Old Testament...you're so twisted...what gives you the right to say stuff like that? You know a lot of Scripture, but little about God's voice." His tirade continued for several minutes in front of an entire room filled with motionless leaders and deep walkers, but no one upheld the love of God. When he finished, another woman said, "We need to lay hands on this brother, he's confused." She stepped up to lay hands on me and I said, "Pardon me I don't let just anyone put hands on me." She pulled back in a huff. Another elderly gentleman stood and said, "Son, we've all been where you've been...we're glad to see you're finally getting serious about following Jesus." I sat there in silence...

Finally, when all had said their fill and silence prevailed, I looked at the elderly gentleman who had just spoken and said, "Well sir, I've been chasing Jesus with all I am for over forty years...we've all been different places on this path called life." Next, I turned to the lady who wanted to pray and said, "Miss, I was not trying to be offensive, but I know exactly who God has called me to be, what He's called me to do, what He has spoken to me, and the passages which confirm it." And finally, I turned to the first gentleman who laid into me and said, "While you and everyone else shared what was on your hearts, I sat quietly and respectfully just taking it in without saying a word. And yet, as a pastor, you feel you have the right to stand, accuse, and defame because I spoke of our mutual need to fall deeper in love with Jesus Christ on our way to marry the King. It's a sad day when one gets crucified by brothers for encouraging us all to love God more. The whole bible is about marriage from cover-to-cover." Everything made sense however, when the original host stood and said, "We all know the last days are behind us and that we are no longer waiting for Christ's imminent return..."

Knowing God – Marriage

Many of us wonder how God's creation, salvation, and Love's plan works in our relationship with Him. So, I have done my best to paint you a picture of God's selection, betrothal, and marriage process below in basic terms. It's my hope that doing so will help you see how God composed the human marriage relationship between man and woman as a type-and-shadow portrait of His eternal covenant relationship with us. In cooperation with the God's Upper Case Law of Love, Creation, and man's redemption – the imagery of marriage reveals His very intimate and personal mechanism of love. Jewish marriage custom shows how God selected us in His foreknowledge and granted us freewill choice at the time of our creation. Likewise, the process of marriage reveals how God betrothed us, gave us opportunity to choose our participation in salvation's new start, and a way to separate ourselves from past through repentance (baptism) and His blood. And, marriage reveals how God entered the marriage contract ahead of us to make a way, to provide for our needs, and to prepare a place for us. As a result, it is our part to make ourselves ready for Him as a radiant bride who waits expectantly for His return as we long to become one with Him. Please keep these thoughts in mind as you venture ahead...

Selection represents the presentation of an opportunity to marry (Law-Sinai). In Jewish custom (Aleph, Bet), selection occurs when a Bridegroom's Father chooses a bride for his son, sends his servant to the prospective bride's parents to make arrangements (Aleph). Next, a price for the bride is established pending her acceptance or denial of the opportunity to marry at an upcoming betrothal ritual (Bet). This father's sovereign selection of a bride for his son in the marriage process is identical to what God the Father did when He selected us at the time of creation to be the bride for His Son Jesus Christ.

Betrothal represents the bridegroom and bride's formal entrance into a written covenant agreement to marry before physical union (Salvation). In Jewish custom (Gimel, Dalet, Hey), betrothal begins at an engagement party (ritual) when both bridegroom and prospective bride make a binding promise to each other, a cup of wine is lifted up, and the bride...if in agreement...drinks from the cup to seal betrothal (Gimel). Next, a written marriage contract is drawn up stating that the bride will be provided for and all her needs met by the bridegroom from that time forward. Then, the bridegroom signs the marriage contract in front of two witnesses and gives the signed contract to the bride and her father (Dalet). The bride's acceptance of betrothal is her statement of how intimate she wants the bridegroom to become with her (Hey). No physical union occurs during betrothal.

Marriage represents the celebrated covenant between bridegroom and bride from the time of sealed betrothal, through preparations, to celebration at the feast after physical (sexual) union occurs. In Jewish custom (Vav, Zayin, Chet, Tet, Yod, Kaf, L), marriage technically begins when both bridegroom and bride drink from the second cup offered in the marriage process as their mutual confirmation of the marriage contract. When they drink from this first "shared cup," their covenant is securely sealed and the bridegroom gives gifts to the bride and her family (Vav). This segment represents our formal acceptance of Salvation and God's gift of Himself to us. Next, the bride goes through a ritual immersion (i.e. repentance-baptism) setting herself apart from old things as she now begins new life with her beloved (Zayin). At this point, the bridegroom leaves his bride-to-be, returns to his father's to prepare a place for her, and makes a pledge of his return to get her (Chet). This mirrors Christ's death, burial, resurrection, and return to His Father's right hand. During this time, the bride prepares herself to be her very best for her beloved while she waits anxiously for him, is emotional at leaving family, doubts her own worthiness, and does not know the exact hour of his return. Only the bridegroom's father can approve the completion of his son's preparation of the wedding chambers and dispatch him to collect his bride and bring her home (Tet). Do you see the imagery?

When a Jewish bridegroom sneaks up to collect his bride in the middle of the night without warning while accompanied by friends...he gives a shout, sounds a trumpet blast from a shofar... and his bride must be ready to join him without delay. In strength and power, the bridegroom takes his bride to the place he prepared for her, and their marriage is consummated. At this time in the marriage process, the couple meets beneath the wedding canopy (Tallit) where blessings are spoken over them, they drink from a third cup of wine representing the second "shared cup" thereby sealing their marriage contract (covenant) a second time. Next, the bridegroom drapes his shawl (Tallit) over his bride in front of witnesses significant of what is about to occur in the wedding chambers, thereby beginning the honeymoon cycle or home-taking. Now, the couple enters their wedding chambers (Huppa) for seven

(7) days where the bridegroom gives his bride some of her wedding garments and covers her with himself as the two become one flesh sexually for the first time fully knowing and being fully known by each other. Then, their bed sheets with her blood on them are given to her family as proof and future assurance that the bride was pure at the time of their first union (Kaf). And finally, the couple emerges from their wedding chambers to join their guests at the wedding feast and celebration (L). The imagery in Jewish marriage custom clearly takes us through the entire invitation, salvation, transformation, and consummation with God process that will culminate at the wedding feast of the Lamb.

The Veil

What lingers behind the bridal veil? Though Jewish marriage customs concerning the bridal veil relates to purity, propriety, and protection as seen when Rebekah covered her face before she and Isaac were married...there are other deeply significant issues symbolized that are related to God veiling Israel's eyes...obscuring the life and spirit ingredients in His Upper Case Law of Love...and Moses veiling God's radiance from Israel's people (Genesis 24:64-65; Exodus 34:29-35; Isaiah 6:10; Matthew 13:10-17; Acts 28:17-31; 2 Corinthians 3:12-14). Moses veiled his face after his return from atop Mount Sinai with the second set of tablets revealing that Israel could not bear to look upon God's reflection displayed on Moses' face following Israel's worship of the golden calf (Exodus 32:1-10, 34:29-35). In this instance, I believe the veil represents Israel's inability to recognize or administrate God's character qualities of Truth, Love, Spirit, and Glory (Bridegroom's Table-Chapter 8). This fact was likely due both to God's plan to extend salvation to the Gentiles and because Israel's spiritual eyesight had been compromised through sin as they navigated the marriage process on their way toward intimacy with God. This is very similar to the scenario which occurred in the Garden of Eden, when Adam exercised man's original choice and his resulting sin obscured God's presence and spiritual realm from mankind's perception (Genesis 3:22-2). Just as Adam grieved God and removed man from God's presence in the Garden – Israel's sin grieved the Holy Spirit, dimmed their perception of God's Upper Case Law of Love, and caused them to encounter life and redemption through the eyes of death's lower case law of hostility. Based on Scripture, death's dominion over their vantage point and life experience would not to be broken until hostility's dividing wall would later be removed to fully reconcile their personal relationship with God through Jesus Christ (2 Corinthians 3:16-18; Ephesians 2:14, 4:29-32).

As related to marriage – the veil covers and protects the bride's purity, represents a barrier of chastity between a betrothed man and woman yet unmarried, and communicates that they have not yet consummated their union. In ancient Jewish customs, the bridegroom lifts his bride's veil just before the two become one in sexual union and he takes full possession of his bride forevermore. The unveiling which occurs at the wedding ceremony symbolizes the two are becoming one through words, vows, and speaks of their anticipation of what is soon to take place physically between them in their marriage bed.

As related to our personal level of intimacy with God – the veil represents what God pre-determined to do with Israel, so those among a Gentile world could be reconciled through salvation in Jesus Christ. The veil also represents the blindness that covers the eyes of those who are merely religious or yet unsaved. And, the veil represents that we have not yet experienced...nor do we comprehend...what it means to become one, to fully know, and to be fully known by Heaven's Bridegroom when we see Him face-to-face on our way to the wedding feast of the Lamb (1 Corinthians 13:12). Meanwhile, we who represent the bride of Christ have pledged to make ourselves ready, to rise in radiance with growing anticipation that our Bridegroom is coming to get us soon as we await His announcement at the trumpet (Revelation 11:15-19). Just as Jewish bridegrooms raise the veil to expose their bride's face at the end of the wedding ceremony to symbolize his anticipation of engulfing her and becoming one – our Bridegroom Jesus Christ will soon lift our veil, stare deep into our eyes, kiss our face tenderly, and draw us to Himself with passionate never-ending embrace as we become one with Him forever...

Jewish Origin

According to Jesus, our salvation comes from the Jews (John 4:21-24). Based on Scripture and God's Love Plan with man described in this chapter – salvation began with the Jews, was shared with the Gentiles, and will return to the Jews once again (Romans 11:11-32). Salvation's return to the Jews is being revealed as the dividing wall of hostility is removed from between Israel and Gentiles among those God foreknows are His...between God and those willing to accept, confess, and obey Jesus Christ as Lord and Messiah...and between this world and eternal life for those willing to pass through the covenant Promise unified with each other to become one with God (Romans 9:6-18; Ephesians 2:14, 11-22).

Tradition

Every person ever born has learned or been taught life values, customs, or thinking patterns by their parents or culture to some degree – whether good or bad. Salvation comes to the "true Israel" to whom God gave His Upper Case Law of Love (Torah) through Moses at Mount Sinai (Exodus 19:1-20:21). God's love is all-encompassing in nature and establishes His never-ending desire to have and share reciprocal love relationship with us. His plan to temporarily blind and harden Israel toward His Upper Case Law of Love as He reached beyond them to redeem Gentiles through the extension of salvation, will in fact, return the gift of salvation home to captivate and transform His chosen (Acts 28:17-31; Romans 11:25-32). This entire picture of selection, betrothal, and marriage relative to God's foreknown plan to become one with man in reciprocal love are well reflected in Scripture.

Three Covenants

Scripture also reveals three principal expressions of blood covenant between God and man within the imagery of marriage. These covenant transactions are represented in Love's plan toward man which is punctuated by four covenant cups of wine. The original covenant and its renewals have had very different circumstantial compositions and expressions. Adam represents God's original selection of man as His intended bride for Jesus Christ. God's secondary and subsequent selection of Abraham after man's fall in the Garden reveals God's first blood covenant-confirmed betrothal to man necessary for willing members of humanity to make their way toward being re-united with God...

First Covenant – 1st Cup

God's original blood covenant with man was established with Abraham, thereby known as the Abrahamic covenant (Genesis 15:18). God initiated His covenant with Abraham while he was still known as Abram, instituted it while Abram slept, confirmed it when Abram was ninety-nine, sealed it through circumcision, established its bearer as Abraham, and perpetuated it through Abraham and Sarah's son Isaac thereby granting future hope to mankind (Genesis 15:18, 17:1-22). The Abrahamic Covenant marks God's initiation and man's confirmation of the first marriage contract signed in blood, first covenant cup of man's redemption, and first betrothal cup essential to God's historical courtship-to-consummation-process in His love affair with humanity.

Second Covenant – 2nd Cup

The second blood covenant God entered with man was delivered to the nation of Israel through Moses at Mount Sinai and became known as the Mosaic Covenant (Exodus 19:5-8). After God declared that Israel would be His chosen people, they agreed to obey, sacrifice was offered, and Moses sprinkled covenant blood on them...it was then...that God called Moses to the top of Mount Sinai and gave him the first set of stone tablets (Exodus 24:3-12). The Mosaic Covenant was different than the other two in that its full transaction occurred through a series of revealing and purposeful events related to marriage following Israel's acceptance and confirmation (Exodus 24:3-12). In basic terms, these events relate to: (1) Covenant Acceptance. (2) Transition. (3) Covenant Renewal.

- Covenant Acceptance occurred when God declared His intent, identified Israel as His chosen, presented them with covenant terms, received their agreement, sealed it in blood, and He signed the marriage contract with His finger in tablets of stone (Exodus 19:7-8, 24:3-12, 31:18). This part of the transaction officially betrothed Israel to God as their entrance into the covenant represents the first "shared cup" in God's marriage process with man.

- <u>Transition</u> was revealed in this covenant's transaction in several ways and on several occasions. In short, it was during this transition period in Israel's covenant process with God, that we see their original transaction and resulting betrothal duly signed and sealed upon covenant confirmation followed by the first stone tablets (Exodus 24:3-12). Likewise, we see Moses' relationship with God grow more intimate, Israel's sin with the golden calf, Moses' self-sacrificial atonement for sin on their behalf, and God's elevation of His relationship to Moses through radiance followed by Israel's obvious fears (Exodus 24:15-18, 32:1-9, 32:31-32, 34:29-35). My discoveries related to this transition period represent some of the deepest, most penetrating, revelations God has ever given me regarding His marriage relationship with mankind. Yet, the Holy Spirit will not allow me to share more than I have at this time. Just know that those things I am not at liberty to share...radically altered the life courses of Moses and Israel, set them on vastly different relational planes with God, and were underscored by Moses' appearance with Jesus and Elijah amid God's voice in the presence of His Son's disciples during the transfiguration (Luke 9:28-36). Simply amazing!

- <u>Covenant renewal</u> occurred for Israel in the period between Exodus 32:33 and 34:35 as we watch Moses ask to see God's glory...Moses ascending Mount Sinai with a second set of tablets...seeking God's forgiveness on Israel's behalf...and spending a second forty days and nights inside God's wedding chambers alone with Him. When Moses emerged to descend Mount Sinai carrying God's second set of stone tablets (marriage contract)...it was at this juncture...that Moses' face was radiant, both Aaron and the whole of Israel were afraid to look upon it, and the veil of God between Himself and man was donned as death's lower case law of hostility was released in Israel's punishment, wandering, and toil...

Third Covenant - 3rd Cup
The third opportunity God gave man to enter blood covenant with Him was delivered through the life of Jesus Christ in what is known

as the Messianic Covenant. This transaction represents God's most intimate reach to mankind since the Garden of Eden. Why do I say that? In the Garden, man was simply created into God's presence without awareness or input. In the Abrahamic Covenant – God approached from afar, cut covenant on man's behalf, and operated through an earthly priest named Melchizedek (Genesis 14:18-24). In the Mosaic Covenant – God approached from afar, interacted with Israel, and operated through a deliverer named Moses and an earthly priest named Aaron (Exodus 18:-19:24). Yet, in the Messianic Covenant – God approached us personally in the form of a man through an Eternal High Priest Named Jesus Christ who saves, indwells, and empowers us with His Holy Spirit if we willingly exercise our freewill choice to enter personal blood covenant with Him (John 1:1-5, 14:16-20, 17:20-23; Romans 10:9; Hebrews 7:11-28, 9:22). In a nutshell, God's relational approach to man went from uninformed (Adam), to impersonal (Abraham), to friendship (Israel), and to courtship through Jesus Christ...

Final Cup

Now, what about the fourth covenant cup? Referring to Jewish marriage custom once again, the final cup of wine is shared after the wedding meal following prior consummation (Kaf, L). At the Last Supper Passover meal, Jesus offered both the wine and bread representing his blood and body. While offering the Messianic Covenant (third) cup at that historical meal, Jesus said, "This cup is the new covenant in my blood, which is poured out for you" (Luke 22:20). Just before this statement, He said, "...I will not drink again of the fruit of the vine until the kingdom of God comes" (Luke 22:18). In light of Jewish marriage custom...the fact that the kingdom of God is present for those who are in Christ...and that the kingdom of God will be physically established upon earth during Christ's literal return – we find basis for the fourth and final Cup of marriage that will be shared at the wedding celebration of the Lamb (Matthew 24:32-36; Luke 17:20-37; 2 Peter 3:1-14; Revelations 19:1-22:21). Remember, Jesus did His first miracle at a wedding feast in Cana of Galilee and He will do His last miracle in human history at the greatest wedding feast of all...

Moral Anchor

Though administrated through diminished perception, Jewish heritage is built upon God's Upper Case Law of Love presented in the Garden of Eden, at the burning bush, at Mount Sinai, and through the person of Jesus Christ. As a result, Jewish heritage technically represents an unchanging moral, social, and religious foundation upon which lasting life, relationship, marriage, spirituality, and culture can be built, sustained, and perpetuated. Because God never changes, neither does His eternal Upper Case Law of Love that was given to the Patriarchs as His Love plan designed to draw us all to Himself within the intimate structure of marriage relationship. It is my view therefore, that the anchoring qualities of Jewish heritage IS the very reason why so many proven-to-be evil leaders down through history – have made it their personal vendetta to displace, oppress, or eradicate Israel, the Jews, and Christ. As one tyrant said, "If you take away a people's heritage, you can lead them anywhere." Due to death's concerted effort to separate us from our Jewish roots—Gentile believers have become a social and spiritual culture drifting away from God while trying to build solid lives, marriages, and relationship with Him and others on the shifting sands of religious view without proper foundation.

Marriage Process

What does the anchor of Jewish heritage look like? In essence, salvation came from the Jews because Israel was the first nation of people to come after Abraham, Isaac, and Jacob...because God selected Israel to become His chosen people...because Israel represents the first nation and people to whom God offered His perfect Upper Case Law of Love...and opportunity's choice to both receive and reciprocate that love back to Him. In the process, Israel accepted God the Father's offer of betrothal through their agreement during the time before the first set of stone tablets came to be (Exodus 19:8, 24:1-18). Later, Israel joined God to drink from the first shared cup of marriage through Moses' atonement for their sin with the golden calf as he convened with God at Sinai (Exodus 32:31-34:28). In this instance, Moses functioned as a type of Christ who was willing to sacrifice his own life to save others. Meanwhile, as God's chosen deliverer for Israel, Moses accepted betrothal to God just after his burning bush encounter, joined God to share in the first shared cup of marriage before ascending Mount Sinai to received the first stone tablets, drank from the second shared marriage cup through atonement for Israel, and descended with a radiant face in possession of the second tablets (Exodus 3:1-11, 4:25-26, 24:15-18, 32:31-32, 34:29). It was at that time it appears, Moses took on the indwelling presence of God and was empowered to do even greater miracles, became fearsome to Israel, and covered his face with a veil symbolic of God hiding His face from His chosen. This was to portray the status of God's emerging marriage relationship to Israel and also in response to their unfaithfulness (Exodus 34:10, 30). Meanwhile, Israel who had already been betrothed to God prior to the first tablets, found relief through Moses' Christ-like atonement between sets of tablets, and joined God in the first shared cup of marriage while the second tablets were created.

Lifting the Veil

Both Moses and Israel were on concurrent parallel, but uniquely-directed, pathways stationed at different junctures within the divine marriage process substantiated by Jewish wedding custom. Unlike Israel, Moses was living a dual role simultaneously functioning in the types and shadows of God's deliverer, of Christ, and of a faithful bridegroom on one hand. On the other hand, he was simply another member of Israel who would join God's bride through the Promise. Because of Moses' dual role and as Israel's deliverer – He was consequently one step ahead of Israel's betrothal status with God, and as their leader, was already married to the Lord during the season between sets of tablets as evidenced by his time in the clouds with God and his gloriously radiant face when he finally emerged. The veil over Moses' face after the second tablets symbolized that the marriage preparation process between shared cups, before home-taking, and prior to consummation had been entered by mankind. God's face being symbolically veiled marked the onset of Israel's blindness and revealed that consummation between Heaven's Bridegroom and His bride was still yet to come. It was during this time frame, that man's perception and administration of God's Upper Case Law of Love was reduced to the practice of death's lower case law of hostility thereby preparing the way for salvation's extension to the Gentiles, for Christ's purpose to be fulfilled, and for Love's reconciliation to be released.

After thorough consideration of biblical accounts which reveal and define God's being, covenant Law, and commands concerning His Creation and institutions of authority and marriage...it is clear why Scripture counsels us to honor and bless the nation of Israel. Israel is God's chosen people, His firstborn son, the Gentile's older brother, and the protected keeper of God's antiquities (i.e. Genesis 12:1-9, 15:17-19, 32:22-30, 33:13; Exodus 3:4-15, 4:22, 19:5, 32:13; Leviticus 25:8-24; 1 Kings 8:52-53; Psalms 121:1-8; Isaiah 46:8-13; Jeremiah 31:35-37; Joel 3:16; Luke 1:1-25, 15:11-32; John 5:39). In Scripture, the firstborn operates from a heightened position of blessing and authority, thereby making it obvious that the younger brother should indeed honor and yield to his older brother's position. Therefore, there is a blessing granted to those who honor Israel and the structure of their Father's household.

Complete Reconciliation

Gentile-based Christianity has rarely been taught or tried to learn about God's foundation for "selection, betrothal, and marriage." Conversely, Israel or their Jewish Torah-based culture has rarely been taught or tried to learn about a present dynamic personal relationship with Jesus Christ and the Holy Spirit. Detachment from Israel paved the way for Gentiles to build life, marriage, and relationship with God and others without knowing, understanding, or possessing His foundation so typically passed down by Israel to subsequent generations. Many Gentiles are mercy-oriented without structural accountability (Matthew 9:12-13). Conversely, Israel is structurally sound, but lacking experience with Holy Spirit-illuminated grace only found in relationship with Christ. Consequently, most Gentile cultures have crashed morally, relationally, and spiritually. Though they have crumbled as mentioned however, many Gentile Christians have experienced a very personal relationship with Jesus Christ and the Holy Spirit on a more expansive level than most members of Israel.

We Need Each Other

Gentile Christians tend to be more unbridled, presumptuous, and cavalier in their posture toward God's mercy than their Jewish counterparts. Gentile experience with the Holy Spirit and God's Upper Case Law of Love is a cultural asset which could make a very valuable contribution to Israel if willingly received. Likewise, Israel's long-established practice of Torah has potential to afford Gentile Christians deeper understanding of the Law's imagery. Both Israel and Gentiles need each other's individual, but diversely separate parts, in order to rightly reconcile the two groups in Christ into one new man who enters through the Promise (Romans 9:6-9). In a generalized nutshell, the only things Gentiles have been taught about Christ (Yeshua), salvation, and His return to gather His people merely "reflects" the elements found in Jewish marriage structure – but lacks the Law's foundational truth. Conversely, Israel has been predominantly taught the Law and of the promised Messiah, but to a large degree, lacks personal indwelling encounter with God (John 3:9-21, 4:21-26).

Humility

We know Israel's hardening was part of God's Love plan, not a negative connotation toward Israel as a people or nation (Isaiah 6:9-10; John 12:37-50; Romans 9:14-18). Yet, until Gentile Christianity's non-accountable grace-based arrogance toward the Law is resolved through selfless humility – the dividing wall of hostility cannot be removed. Conversely, until Israel's jealous resentment toward Gentiles is resolved through selfless humility – the dividing wall of hostility cannot be removed either. And third, I believe dead religion's grasp of this revelation has potential to restore the very heart of reconciliation Paul alluded to as essential for the "true Israel" comprised of both natural and in-grafted branches to be gathered from all tribes and tongues throughout the earth during this critical hour (Romans 11:17-24). Both Israel and Gentile Christianity are in opposing ditches of extremism along life's road and must come to the middle in both Torah and biblical truth confirmed by Christ's example and the Holy Spirit if they're to be reconciled in Him. Both must come to the reconciliation table willing to give to and receive from God and each other.

Gaining a grasp on all that has been said and making it real in your own world dear friend – IS dancing with God...

Reality

In current history, based on Scripture, and colored by Jewish marriage custom, I believe we as God's people stand historically in phase number ten (Yod) in our marriage process with God. We must all determine if we have made ourselves ready, if we are waiting expectantly, and if we are ready to join Him with without hesitation?

As I pen this, I am soberly aware while being engulfed by revelation, pierced by realization, and humbled by love's intervention through tears as a man undone in His presence barely able to write amid my own waywardness... O God, forgive me...I am a man of unclean lips living among a people of unclean lips, and my eyes have seen the King... O Lord, listen...O Lord, forgive...O Lord, hear...O Lord, act and save us! For Your sake, O my God, do not delay, because we bear and carry Your Name to the nations...

This is dancing with God...

On the farm in my overalls, and ready to play – 1958

Chapter 11
Come Unto Me

"Come unto me all you who are weary and burdened, and I will give you rest" (Matthew 11:28)

Back in 1990 while rising out of one of life's whales twenty one days into a forty day fast straining for the hem of God's garment, He grabbed life's wheel unexpectedly and turned me toward my hometown health club for a workout... Though you may chuckle at what I'm about to say, this began a ten year season in my life in which the Holy Spirit would simply say, "Go to the hot tub." After all that happened during my first time in its waters that afternoon... when I heard those words within me...I knew God was getting ready to show me something amazing. I wondered for years why He sent a guy like me to that same pool more than a hundred times and several journals after-the-fact to simply speak with me face-to-face. I mean...why not at home during early morning devotions...while sitting on a rock overlooking a valley...kneeling at a church altar... or, face down on the floor weeping before Him? The only reasons I ever came up with for the Lord sending me there was the water's likeness to Jerusalem's pool of Siloam...and apparently...that I was a blind man whom He had chosen to help see (John 9:1-11). I only know that virtually everything He ever revealed to me while in those stirred waters came true – journals full of it...

During that particular season of prayer, circumstances and isolation were discouraging as God trained my hands for battle and gave me eyes to see. The war around me raged as people withdrew into the shadows of my world simply not knowing what to say or how to help other than promising to pray for me. I searched the bible, fell on my face before God, worshipped, journaled, and made my solitary trips to the tub at His direction time-after-time to convene with Him. It was surreal arriving to the athletic club, grabbing my pen and pad out of my gym bag, and heading toward the tub where I placed a folded towel on the surrounding tile next to the wall to set my things on so they'd stay dry. Then, I flipped the switch on the tub, jumped in, prayed for wisdom, leaned against the side with my head tipped back, eyes closed, and listened for the still small voice of God, for hours at a time. As the Holy Spirit spoke to me, I wrote down what I heard, left the club with several pages full of revelation each time, and walked into what He had shown me as I looked on in amazement and watched it come true. As days slipped away and opposition's assault grew, so did the detail and intensity of vision God gave me. People around me grew more distant by the day as I plunged headlong into the presence of God undeterred and determined to gain victory...

Now thirty two days in, I received a late morning call from my pastor who said, "Good morning...what are you up too...how are you doing today?" "Just jumped out of the tub and have been listening to the Lord...pressing in...and hanging on to the horns of His altar," I replied. "The Lord told me to be your prayer partner...can you come by my office later today?" he asked. "When," I responded. "Drop by around three this afternoon and we'll chat." He replied. "Okay, thanks. I'll see ya then," I responded before ending the call. So, I finished getting dressed, threw my pad in my bag, and headed toward my car with several hours on my hands before it was time to meet with my pastor. As I drove down the street, I became very aware of division on the loose in our local congregation spurred by the pastor's recent decision to change the name of our church. A year prior, he stood before our fellowship and said, "I believe God has shown me that we are to drop the denominational label off our church name to make us more inviting to those in the community. After talking it over my staff and praying about it for some time now, we have decided to make the name change effective over the next few months." I remember looking around that morning as people began to mutter, whisper to each other, eyes rolled, sighs could be heard, and one could almost hear the hair on the back of people's necks stand up. The pastor made no mention of taking a vote, seeking anyone's input, or needing the cooperation of his people...a dangerous place to tread for new leader who had only been in the saddle for under a couple of years. I'll never forget the buzz that day after church as people gathered in the hallway, out-of-the-way places, and in circles with arms crossed deeply engrossed in debate over the pastor's announcement. Over subsequent months –

pastoral complaints, back-biting, dissension, and gossip spread like gangrene as attendance and giving plateaued, began their descent, and battle lines were drawn deep within the hearts of many...

Several hours later making my way toward the church to meet the pastor, I rolled in and parked before heading inside. On my way across the parking lot toward the entrance, I felt the Holy Spirit nudge me as He compelled me to stay alert. I stopped by the reception area and asked the gal tending the desk to let the pastor know I was there for my appointment. She picked up the phone, rang threw to the pastor's office, and said, "Greg's here for his three o-clock." "Send him in," came the almost inaudible reply at the line's other end. She hung up and said, "Pastor told me to send you to his office." "Thanks," I said as I headed that direction. Arriving to pastor's door, it opened and he met me with a smile saying, "Come on in and take a seat." I made my way to the overstuffed chair opposite his desk and plopped down. He returned to high-back swivel and leaned back putting his foot on the edge of his desk. "Well, so how's everything going with you?" he asked. I brought him up to speed on all God had been showing me, shared how it had come true, and told him what I had just heard from the Lord that morning while in the tub...

He paused for a moment and then said, "Last night, the Lord told me to be your prayer partner. I know you've been deep in prayer chasing Him, but some people think you're going off the deep end... they don't understand the level of prayer you're in." "All I know Pastor...is God tells me things and they happen just like He says," I said. "Maybe you could tone it down a bit," he replied. "So, let me see if I understand what you're saying. You would like me to slow my pursuit of God in the middle of Him doing miracle-upon-miracle, so other people can be more comfortable...is that right?" I asked. Before he answered I said quietly, "I'll make you a deal...I'll keep chasing and listening...write down everything God shows me...and then I'll give you a copy of my journals. If what He tells me comes true...leave me alone and tell people to mind their own business. If it doesn't come true, I'll pull the plug on it myself." Looking at me over the rim of his glasses obviously perplexed he finally replied, "Okay, that's fair. Meanwhile, stay in touch and I'll be praying for you." "It's a deal...here's my journal...this is what God said to me this morning," I offered. Reaching across his desk and glancing at the journal as he took it in-hand he said, "Looks like He had a lot to say." "He usually does, now let's see what happens," I replied. We parted company a few minutes later and I hopped in my car and made my way toward home...

Over the next three days, everything I had written in the journal I handed to my pastor came true down to the smallest detail. When I called to tell him, he asked me to swing by his office the next morning by 10:00. That night as I lay in bed staring at the ceiling and talking to the Lord, He spoke to me about the church name change situation and told me to ask the pastor the next day for week-by-week church attendance and giving totals for the past fifteen months. Likewise, the Lord asked me to suggest a course of action for the pastor to take in his effort to resolve strife in the church. And lastly, the Lord gave me specific responses depending on the pastor' answers. "Father, Pastor is the first person during my entire fast that asked to be my prayer partner. Now, You want me to put him on the spot...I don't get it," I prayed. "It will be okay, go to sleep," whispered the Holy Spirit. A bit unsettled, I finally dropped off to sleep again waking up several hours later to shower and make my drive to the appointment. The closer I got to the church, the more uneasy I felt finally saying out loud, "Lord, please give me wisdom, humility, and the words I supposed to say...I really don't want to lose the only prayer partner I have." Again, the Lord said, "It will be okay, trust Me." A few minutes later, I came to rest in a parking spot at the church, navigated the reception drill and found myself seated across the desk from my pastor once again. After the opening pleasantries were satisfied he said, "So, you're telling me all these things have happened?" he asked while scanning down the page of my journal. "Yes, every single one of them," I replied as I elaborated on the unfolding of each one-by-one while he leaned back in his chair. An hour later, he had nothing to say...

Then, I heard the Holy Spirit whisper, "Ask him for what I told you to ask him for." I paused...looked at the floor...and mustered the courage amid my own brokenness to look my pastor in the eyes and said, "God woke me up last night and told me to ask you for week-by-week attendance and giving totals for the Church over the past fifteen months...I don't need names or personal information... just totals so we can chart a trend line." He looked back at me and asked, "What for?" "I think both of us are aware of the mounting tension over the Church name change. I believe the attendance and giving figures will reveal the date on which an event occurred that sparked offense and stirred division between you and your people. It's my guess that we'll find that attendance and giving were on the rise before you announced the name change, plateaued beginning the day of the announcement, and began to decline thereafter. Likewise, I believe we will find when the outbreak of dissension began. Ya know Pastor, this mess would be so easy to fix if we all just do our part. Just so you know...I really believe you heard God and that He told you to change the name of the church...it was the right thing to do. But maybe, you went about it the wrong way... The people are upset and the church is suffering. If you'd stand up in front of your people willing to eat a little crow and seek their forgiveness for not asking for their input on the name change before you implemented it...it would disarm the offense and everyone could heal. Some of these people are charter members who have been here fifty years. Sure, we know people get hung up on the wrong things. But as leaders, we're called to rise above and example what it takes to win like Jesus did. It wasn't what you did, but how you did it that offended them. If you'd just humble yourself and disarm the offense...it will turn the Holy Spirit loose to convict them of their own judgment, bitterness, and gossip. Otherwise, they'll see you as the offender...they'll be blind to their own sin... you'll be gone in a year...and your staff will go its separate ways. This problem isn't going away by itself..." "Well, I'm not at liberty to supply you with any information...it's their problem, not mine," he said a bit defensively. Just then, I heard the Holy Spirit whisper, "Enough." In response, I said, "Okay Pastor, I was just doing what God asked me to do...nothing more. Thanks for taking time. Just remember, since everything God told me came true, I'm going to keeping chasing Him with all I am like we agreed." As I rose to leave that day, something shifted...

As my fast came to a close, God granted me victory as promised. My prayer relationship with my pastor disbanded not long thereafter. Sadly, the pastor never sought Scriptural reconciliation with his people through humility and the offense was allowed to reign and destroy. Tensions over subsequent months during board meetings and throughout the church continued to escalate. Ten months after my meeting with the pastor, he announced on a Sunday morning that he was resigning to take another church out of state. Because no one from either side of the equation exercised Christ-like humility or spiritual responsibility in the matter, sin remained in the camp, and plagued both the parting pastor and local church members to varied degrees for years to come. And the staff...who had previously enjoyed long-term camaraderie in shared ministry environments... went three separate directions and remain separated to this day...

Offense

Offense is devil's weapon of choice for stirring division. If the devil is allowed to incite offense, it causes the one offended to leave the door to their heart open to enemy intrusion and deception. Based on the span of lag time between offense and resolution in which one's heart door remains open to sin, the scope and severity of damage inflicted within, between, and through the divided parties will be defined. When offense becomes the entry point in our armor and is allowed to remain unresolved, the enemy of our souls will intensify his assault and bombard us with ever-deepening deception, division, and destruction followed by heart infidelity, rebellion, fear, and anger until we humble ourselves under God's Almighty hand beneath the Lordship of Jesus Christ (1 Peter 5:5-11). Whether strife stands between a pastor and congregation...a Chaplain and an inmate population...a husband and a wife...or between wayward thoughts and truth...man draws pride's lines in hell's sand between God's Upper Case Law of Love and death's lower case law of hostility – God does not!

Anger

When people's sinful conduct gives the devil legal right to assault them with deception, rejection, and fear – a human reaction of self-preservation rooted in fallen human nature typically expresses varied forms of passive or aggressive anger in its effort to stem the tide of perceived threat. Many times, one's anger is rebellion-based defiance directed at an invisible God through attacking those created in His image. Yet, righteous anger can have a healthy affect when it emulates God's love-motivated protection of others suffering harm's injustice beyond their control. Scripture clearly shows the difference between righteous versus unrighteous anger, thereby challenging us to express our own anger without committing sin (Ephesians 4:25-27). In its raw unbridled human form, anger can be destructive (i.e. judgment, hatred, retaliation). Please note that hatred does not only refer to an emotion found in one ready to wipe someone out. Instead, hatred begins in our heart where God sees it as an aversion to or a wish to avoid God or someone equally created in His image as we are ourselves (Matthew 5:27-30). In principle – even if we only entertain the invisible qualities of hatred, independence, infidelity, or anger in our heart without physical action, we are still guilty of the act in God's eyes (Matthew 5:28). Please note that Jesus reveals this timeless principle in the prior Scriptural snapshot associated with physical infidelity as you consider this book's ongoing thread of marriage imagery linked to Heaven's Bridegroom and His wayward bride.

Though anger is fear and perception-based, it manifests in and through our daily lives in many ways. It can be overtly or covertly silent, withdrawn, outspoken, unforgiving, bitter, vengeful, evasive, deceptive, seductive, devious, dishonest, belligerent, vicious, and beyond at the expense of self, others, and God. Likewise, anger can be directed inward or outward at self, others, or God in a combination of two or toward all three at the same time. Anger's natural defense mechanism rises to protect...or offend... self and others in response to real or perceived threats, violations, injustices, or isolations associated with pain, neglect or suffering. Righteous anger protects others in the face of threat or injustice at one's own expense...or...can be used by God to offend ourselves and others in the presence of sin. Have you ever been angry with yourself for doing something wrong? Unrighteous expressions of anger, however, are driven by the presence and influence exerted by the spirits of control, manipulation, and intimidation around or within someone affected or bound by witchcraft.

Have you ever known someone who really has their act together in life personally, relationally, professionally, and spiritually...but, reverts to a five year old in one specific area of their life experience... have you experienced it yourself? Such an occurrence represents an area of arrested development indicating either unhealed past trauma or the presence of a corresponding spiritual stronghold – most times both. The subject, tone, style, direction, and magnitude of anger we choose to express is our choice and evidences our real level of faith, maturity, commitment, and submission to God, Truth, and others as declared and exampled by Jesus Christ. If we struggle in an area, it is our job to search out, apply, and secure solution within ourselves so we can do our part to live at peace with God and others (Romans 12:9-21). We naturally notice and judge the fears and anger we see in others based on our own superficial self-serving assumptions. Yet, often refuse to ask questions, gain understanding, or take responsibility for our own part in provoking anger's expression in a given situation (Galatians 5:16-26). If it were not within our grasp to stir anger in another, God's word would not have addressed the subject. Realistically, if we're rightly submitted to God as lovers of Truth – we will experience His conviction, pursue truth, take responsibility, humble ourselves, seek forgiveness, foster unity, and glorify God as we error on the side of extending grace toward others.

Please Forgive Me

My day had been busy to say the least, as I scurried all over town gathering doors, lumber, nails, tools, and other items for a home project I was up to my neck in. Please take a moment to realize that I'm the guy who can fix or build anything I can see in my head when armed with a good hardware store and tools. Growing up during the hay-day of the American experience – I grew accustomed to being able to buy just one screw of a certain type and size... a gasket for a specific part of an engine...an individual fan for my laptop...a broken bail of shingles for my roof...or, a missing plastic wheel for my seven year old forty-six dollar barbecue, inexpensively, rather than replace the whole thing. So, after a lifetime of doing just that, I had headed for town much earlier that day temporarily oblivious to the ongoing invasion of big-box stores, bubble packs, and progress which demands that we buy five of something when only one is required and the extras almost certainly get lost before their needed again. Now so enlightened and even though the major components of my then-current building adventure had been easy to locate...it seemed like the most common of minor items everyone-and-their- dog should have stocked oodles-and-gobs of were like searching Burbank for the Holy Grail. As my day wore on and sunlight critical to my forward progress threatened to duck behind a looming horizon...my patience began to wear just a tad bit thin...

Rolling into a gargantuan parking lot facing what seemed a day's trek from the door, I bounded out of my truck heading toward the interior of yet another bubble-pack bound big-box building center... Through the doors I blew as I passed shopping carts on a bee-line for the aisle affording the greatest probability of ending my quest. I rounded the aisle's end-cap, wove in-and-out of shopping carts, and glided by those sporting glossed over eyeballs giving silent testimony to the fact that ignorance truly is – bliss. Suddenly, my sights locked on the multi-drawer cabinet in which I was sure to find my final prize. I stepped up, gave the drawer a yank, and to my mortal chagrin found one empty compartment...you guessed it...the one I arrived to procure. To put it mildly, my emotional composure found itself rationally challenged. On my way toward the customer service desk passing by the doors just in time to see the sun fall behind the ridge like a rock, I screeched to a halt in front of the counter requesting the manager a bit impatiently. Standing there with my fingers tapping the counter, Sam trundled up to the customer service desk's other edge moments later and asked, "May I help you?" "Having inventory would help me much more than empty bins," I replied as I traveled down a troublesome trail. After more-than-adequately declaring my disfavor, I walked out the door toward my truck and I heard the Holy Spirit say, "Look what you just did to Sam." But, I kept right on walking as my spirit sank lower than a snake's belly before jumping in my rig and making my way home...

I tossed and turned that night finally waking up at 3:00 a.m. and the Lord had His say before I went back to sleep. I got up early the next morning, showered, and made my way toward town. I rolled in the lot, headed through the sliding doors, and arrived at the customer service counter asking for Sam. Moments later, Sam strolled up to the counter with a smile once again and said, "May I help you?" "I need to apologize for how I treated you yesterday," I said. "Oh, don't worry about it man...its okay," he replied. "No, it's not okay... and please let me tell you why it's not okay," I said back politely. "Yesterday, I was a jerk! The reason it's not okay is because I'm a Christian and I know better. But, what makes it even worse is...I'm a preacher and I preach better! So, please forgive me for the way I acted...I was wrong and out-of-line." He looked at me...paused...a smile began to rise...and he said with a grin, "Don't worry about it brother, we all have days like that. If you ever need anything...look me up." "Thanks," I said, "But, I don't deserve it..." as I waived and head toward home...

The heart of God is grieved when we act wrongly, but he's cares more about how we resolve our failures than he does about the failure itself. When we go back and clean up the messes we make in life, it proves that we have both experienced and responded to the Holy Spirit's conviction thereby revealing we are beneath the Lordship of Jesus Christ (John 16:8). But, when we sweep our informed and willful violations under life's rug as though they never happened and keep on walking...it says a lot about our character and the realty of our relationship with God. As Jesus showed us, anger can either be a tool or a torment as we look to Him for wisdom, strength, and humility. The choice is ours...

Anger can occur anywhere, anytime, and in almost any situation and affects our relationship with self, others, and God. Ultimately, our expression of anger will be consistent with our level of actualized submission to God's sovereign authority over our hearts, souls, minds, spirits, wills, thoughts, emotions, imaginations, decisions, actions, and destinies as revealed by how practically our attitude compares to that of Jesus Christ. If we reject God's rightful authority and dominion over our lives – our reception and expression of an independent spirit thereby commits the sin of infidelity which opens our heart's door to enemy intrusion, gives him legal access and right to dispatch fear, and subjects us to satanic deception, oppression, and our own regression – until we repent of our sin (1 Peter 5:6-7; 2 Peter 3:9) Our intercourse with independence exposes us to the enemy's invasion and occupation allowing him to devour our disobedient lives with isolation, delusion, and suffering (John 10:7-10; 1 Peter 5:8-9). When anger is rightly harnessed and directed beneath the Lordship of Jesus Christ – it stands against injustice to bring life (i.e. defending widows, children, downtrodden). Anger is a normal protective mechanism that rises within us to avoid or minimize perceived threat-based punishment, pain, and suffering before, while, or after it occurs. However, anger must stand against godless idealisms, not people if it is to remain righteous in God's eyes. It is important that we understand that it is both possible and commendable in God's eyes for us to bear up under the pain of unjust suffering for doing what is good and right. It is possible and commendable because we have set Jesus apart as Lord in our lives…because to this we were called…and because He suffered for us as an example and told us to follow Him (Matthew 27:13-14; Luke 23:34; 1 Peter 2:19-25, 3:15-17).

Suffering

As God's example to us, though not a popular thought, Jesus also learned obedience through suffering (Hebrews 5:8-9). He learned obedience through suffering when He faced and embraced circumstances or decisions with potential to either free or crucify His will, reputation, rights, freedoms, and life. This was proven when He was rejected by religion, denied by disciples, betrayed by friends, settled his Gethsemane decisions, stood before Pontius Pilate, subjected Himself to beatings, and liberated our destinies at the cross on Calvary (Matthew 26:31-34, 27:13-14; Luke 14:36, 22:47-53; John 5:36-43, 6:38-39, 8:32, 14:6, 19:11, 21:15-19; 2 Corinthians 3:17-18). All Jesus said and did WAS His example…WAS His act of spiritual worship toward God His Father in heaven…and WAS God's PATTERN through His Son's life for His creation to follow – including you and me (John 6:37-39, 14:12; Romans 12:1-2)

Following Jesus is not for wimps, whiners, or the wayward. Following Jesus is contact sport for those who recognize their sinfulness, their need for forgiveness, how much they were forgiven, and who are willing to forgive others freely in the same measure they freely received from God themselves...unconditionally. Jesus' words, "Follow Me" to His sleeping disciples as He was being handed over to condemnation and crucifixion by one of His inner circle...after spending several years showing them how to feed multitudes, forgive adulterers, evict demons, heal blindness, cleanse lepers, restore life, confront religion, settle Gethsemane, and do God's perfect will – proved that Jesus knew His identity and purpose (Mark 14:32-42).

Identity

People's fear-based expression of anger is often rooted in deception or distorted reality, rather than an act of willful aggression toward others as today's psychologized world teaches. When anger is focused on preserving self instead of protecting others in the face of perceived injustice or threat – it has potential to do harm rather than bring life if not mastered in one's intimacy with God through Jesus Christ (Genesis 4:6-7; Matthew 27:11-14, John 19:8-11). Sinful expressions of anger toward God or others are the direct result of usurping His sovereign authority, dominion, and sole right to attribute value and exert control over his creation including you and me. As God's people, it is our mutual responsibility to lovingly and submissively administrate His kingdom authority rightly in our relationships with each other. Any unrighteous expression of anger reveals our unnerving realization that we have lost control over our distorted reality and are making a futile bid to regain what we never truly possessed. It is our loss of God's vision, subsequent bout with fear, and deluded belief that we have the right to control the world around us that spurs the irrational thought we can rule over others like God. When we lose God's vantage point and our pride-based thinking spirals downward to become depraved outward behavior, infidelity in our relationship with God is exposed at that very moment to mirror satan's attitude which cast him from heaven long ago (Isaiah 14:9-15; Romans 1:18-32). During an extended fast many years ago, the Holy Spirit said it to me this way:

"When we live outside our identity in Christ, we strive to control and manipulate our world through fear-based anger in our attempt to muster the courage necessary to silence or avoid the idea or situation confronting us. Yet, when we embrace our true identity in Jesus Christ, we are empowered and released to walk as God's tender warriors who affect our world through our expression of gentle faith, surrender, trust, and obedience necessary to extend His love and mercy toward those entrusted to our care."

Perspective

When we step out in faith beyond our own capabilities wholly dependent upon God for our provision, protection, and power – satan confronts us with our weaknesses often, thereby making our firm grip on God's view and our own identity in Jesus Christ essential if we're to gain victory. Jesus clearly knew His identity and purpose – we must know ours too (John 5:17, 14:12, 18:36-37). Before we can truly discover and mobilize who we are in Jesus however, we must see reality through God's eyes in light of Scripture, the mind of Christ, and with the Holy Spirit's help (John 14:26, !6:8, 13-15; 1 Corinthians 2:1-16; 2 Corinthians 10:3-5; Colossians 2:8-15; 2 Timothy 3:16-17). Our grasp of God's reality arrests us through our knowledge of His word, through the Holy Spirit's revelation of Jesus Christ, through His indwelling presence within us, and through His intimate death-to-life transformation working out His salvation in the context of our daily life experience. Our ignorant indifference toward God or His word will gives the devil a foothold from which to twist the meaning of key terms in the bible which are central to our spiritual liberty thereby robbing us of God's victory (Ephesians 4:25-27). During another extended fast, the Holy Spirit explained several key terms and concepts to me this way:

"Imagination is the counterfeit to God's revelation just as fantasy is the counterfeit to God's vision (Colossians 2:18). Imagination questions and corrupts God's revelation, thereby opening the door for fantasy to undermine God's vision in us (Proverbs 29:18; 2 Corinthians 10:3-5; 2 Thessalonians 2:9-12). Satan uses this seductive mechanism to incite unbelief in our hearts and minds, which cause us to question God and abort His purpose in and through our lives. God's peace that surpasses understanding flows through His revelation – the devil's schemes bring chaos through vain imagination. Revelation is the seed bed of vision God uses to call us beyond human impossibility to experience miraculous reality. Christ-centered visionaries suffer more often than most as their perception of God and response to His call intimidates those who give more dominion in their lives to fear, than to faith in Jesus Christ (Romans 7:1-8:17). Vain imagination obscures hell's deluded denial of Christ, while in contrast...revelation declares truth and exposes hell's lie to set God's people free."

Primary Authority

When reasoning together over Scriptural truth and our inflexibilities regarding our intellectual stance on an issue are encountered thereby dismissing Christ's words, attitude, and example as merely secondary to our personal interpretation...a stronghold of delusion has been exposed (2 Corinthians 10:3-5; 2 Thessalonians 2:9-12). Once a stronghold stands exposed, satan launches his attack to protect, fortify, or regain his grip on the territory he believes is being taken from him. His assault under such conditions involves his dispatch of demonic spirits, weapons formed against us, and his evil schemes devised to undermine or destroy our clarity, composure, and courage (Isaiah 54:16-17; 2 Corinthians 2:11; Ephesians 6:11). In such cases, satan typically dispatches lying spirits of fear, deception, judgment, rejection, anger, unforgiveness, confusion, strife, and division against anyone in the discussion speaking truth in love consistent with Jesus Christ (Matthew 10:22, 24:9). The spirits of fear and rejection work hand-in-hand to form a foundation from which anger can rise if not quickly resisted in and rightly subjected to God's authority (2 Corinthians 10:3-5; James 4:7-10). When Christ's words and example are raised as the supreme governing authority between two believers over any issue Jesus took a position on...and one's personal interpretation of Scripture is cited over-and-above the position and authority of Christ to justify one's view or behavior...an entrenchment of independence, infidelity, rebellion, and fear has been laid bare thereby revealing demonic activity and dead religion – not surrendered personal relationship with Jesus Christ (John 5:31-44, 14:12).

Midrash

I was recently privileged to spend time with dear friends whom I had met just after the onset of my first walk across America back in 2001. They have been married, in ministry, and have contributed much to each other and the lives of those God had given to them for many years. Pre-ministry, he was an unsaved biker who collided with Jesus and found himself radically altered and on a new path. Conversely, his dear wife is a full-blooded Jewess who traveled her own path toward the Messiah. Together, they embrace and practice their faith in light of the Torah, the Bible, and through their love for God Himself in the life He gave them according to His purpose and good pleasure. Catapulting forward ten years, the Lord re-connected us just months before my second walk concluded, after eight years of silence, in response to one of those Holy Spirit tugs. Our resumption of fellowship occurred while I was reviewing my 2003 fifty day fast journal which carried me toward America's East and West Gates while studying unfolding global and prophetic events in light of Scripture and while penning this book. It was like we hadn't missed a beat when we came back together, shared life updates, and hit the ground running on a similar path of passion rooted in the Master during this eleventh hour. Based on our reconnection, unified passions, and God's word to us all…I was invited to their home during the Christmas holidays for a meal, fellowship, and lots of Midrash. As you can imagine, we shared a wonderful time of reminiscing and reasoning together over all that is currently being revealed on History's stage and indicates the imminence of Christ's return. Though our vantage points vary somewhat relative to our individual callings – our discussions of the Bible and Torah, or Midrash in Jewish terms, were helpful to us all in advancing God's kingdom with love, respect, and unity between us…

During prior weeks and while together for holidays, we found ourselves engaged in an ongoing discussion with regard to what is commonly referred to as a boundary. Once this subject landed on the table, we then found ourselves discussing the origin of boundaries and who really draws them. Many believe boundaries to be healthy based on what they have been taught and human nature justifies, but have spent little time investigating God's word and Christ's example on the matter. As a result, our psychologized cultural concept of boundaries has taken on a life of its own with many dissimilarities when compared to what Jesus lived. By now, the social buzz issue of healthy boundaries is probably screaming in your head or pounding on your mind's table as you rewind and review snippets of what you learned in psychology, through secularized Christian counseling, from intellectualized theologians, and your own internal quest to master selflessness. Yet, we are called to obey God's word as exemplified by the person of Jesus Christ – not as interpreted, distorted, or perverted by well-intentioned religionists, intellectuals, psychologists, counselors, or theologians (1 Peter 2:19:21). If we as Christians will not listen to The Holy Spirit Who as "Thee Counselor" reminds us of all Jesus taught and lived, what good are the opinions of human counselors stationed among men? Why do we by-pass time in God's word and presence on our way to tug on the hem of a man's garment for advice about spiritual things (John 3:9-12)? Easy! Because we want someone with skin on them to rubber stamp our doing exactly the opposite of what God already said and did in His word through Christ as our pattern and example. If we will blow God, Creator of the heavens and earth, off when we disagree...we will most certainly blow man's opinion off as well. So, it seems that "Romance Theology" has jumped into our laps once again on the issue of boundaries...

Boundaries

God said the whole earth is His, so obviously, man has been the one drawing lines, surveying territories, erecting fences, and declaring ownership over that which God already declared belongs to Him (Exodus 19:5; Psalms 50:12; 1 Corinthians 10:26). We were told to be fruitful...to increase in number...to fill and subdue the earth...and to rule over all living creatures (Genesis 1:26-30). God never told us that we own the earth or rule over each other. Ruling over man is His job. Unfortunately, we chose an earthly king instead of the King of Kings Himself and have paid the price in our mortal lives ever since (1 Samuel 8:6-22). I understand your mental dilemma as Scripture comes crashing in on today's easy-believisms, religious practice, and carnal Christianity – but, Jesus said and did what He said and did. And if that's not enough – He drew no lines, lodged no complaints, nor withheld a single redemption on His way to or while hanging upon the cross, not one. Later, Jesus bent down and wrote Love's Law and the character of forgiveness in the dirt as an adulterous woman stood before accusing religionists. Yet, the more He wrote in the dirt, religion's judgment walked away one man at a time aware of its own sin, thereby leaving a guilty adulteress free of condemnation. As she stood alone in the presence of God, Love pardoned and restored her in-full "before" she had left her life of sin (John 8:1-30). Obviously, Jesus did not draw boundaries with their removal contingent on right behavior. He extended love and set her free to live without limitation. So, what am I supposed to say, except what Truth Himself actually did as I do my best to live according to God's pattern alongside of you – myself (John 14:6, 12)? In God's reality, we either do things His way or ours…there is no middle ground. You may take issue with this statement, but I believe what we have been taught to know as or call "boundaries" in today's watered down version of Christian love or commitment…are in reality…man's justifications for rejecting God's declarations. Please let me explain…

A pattern is a model, sample, specimen, example, or type. Whereas a boundary is a border, frontier, or dividing line that marks a subject or sphere of activity's limit or confinement. These definitions simply demand that a couple of obvious questions be asked and answered before we proceed. First Question: How does one limit or confine the person, character, reach, activity, or dominion of an omniscient, omnipotent, omnipresent, and unchanging God Who ALWAYS WAS, IS, and EVER will be – and still believe that He is being extended freedom by His subjects to be God or assert His sovereign dominion over them? Second Question: How can we as followers of Jesus Christ validate our claim to be enlightened in His revelation… immersed in His salvation…changed by His re-creation…filled with His Spirit…infused with His character…motivated by His love…and submitted to His will – if our faith and deeds do not line up with His PATTERN of behavior and activity lived by Christ as our example of how to produce fruit that lasts (John 15:15-17; James 2:14-26)?

God the Father is "Eternity's Pattern" Who compels His Son Jesus to say and do what He hears and sees His Father saying and doing (John 5:19-30). Jesus is God's only Son Who says and does only those things He hears His Father say and sees His Father doing. And, the Holy Spirit IS Heaven's Counselor Who reminds us of everything Jesus taught us through His words, attitude, and example - telling us we will do what He is doing "if" we have faith in Him (Matthew 28:19-20; John 5:17, 19-20, 30, 14:12, 15, 23, 27, 17:3-26). Therein is revealed – the Holy Trinity Who provides creation's Ever-Supreme Example upon Whom we are to base and to Whom we are to subject our faith, behavior, and theology toward God and man. God's eternal and unchanging character traits of holiness, righteousness, redemption, truth, love, forgiveness, mercy, grace, joy, and peace...to name a few...fully embody His Law, define His Creation, and provide our moral pattern of being, belief, and behavior. So as you can see – God only provides a PATTERN that gives, goes, and gathers – unconditionally, selflessly, and sacrificially. It is man's ignorance, distortion, and rejection of God's truth and unconditional love that sets up boundaries that are fueled by independence...polluted by infidelity...driven by rebellion... immortalized by fear...enforced with anger...and corrupted by religion. In a nutshell, we were commissioned to carry our cross and make disciples each day, not draw boundaries or build fences...

By now, you may believe my view is misguided on what I have termed, "boundary theory." Yet, based on many years of painstaking study, observation, and personal experience – I am convinced that our intellectual, psychological, and spiritual understanding related to the existence and application of boundaries represents one of the devil's most pervasive strongholds destroying the expression of God's love to and through His people. Why? I believe that boundaries and their blatant misuse have erected a bastion of sinful independence, justification, unforgiveness, bitterness, and rebellion toward God that defies the heart and example of our merciful Savior Who forfeited His own self-defense and life to love the very humanity who killed Him...including...you and me. That said and after penning my original draft of this chapter – God stirred my heart, provided living word pictures, and has compelled me to write at a much deeper level on the issues addressed in this chapter than originally intended. As a result, I have been in my chair for more than 35 hours over the past two days putting ink to the flood of revelations God has given me. So, please sit back and join me for a deeper look into the foundations of boundaries...

Boundaries – Continued

God's Truth ALWAYS offends hell's lie in ALL places...at ALL times... in ALL people...even you...even me (John 14:6; Romans 5:20). Truth comes knocking as a tug in our guts, a question in our heart, a thought in our mind, a voice in our spirit, and a Person in our redemption when we feel troubled, afraid, rejected, angry, or alone – called conviction (John 14:6, 16:8; 2 Thessalonians 2:9-12; Revelation 3:20). CONVICTION IS God's love that reaches when we are lost...His nudge that reminds us He is near...His pull that draws us to His side...His touch that proves He cares...His word that says He speaks...His Way that leads us home...His Truth that sets us free... His Life that gives us time...His cross that grants us joy...His mercy that offers us hope...His light that sees our blindness...His Warrior who guards our heart...His King who governs our dominion...His Armor who wraps our weakness...and His Bridegroom who calls us toward radiance...

Man's Opinion

God's Law reveals His being, Love, and character to a sinful people in need of His loving redemption. Man's distorted view and application of God's Law and Love exposes his blindness, fallen methodologies, and ongoing bout with sin. Throughout History – religionists have re-defined, re-written, and re-directed God's Upper Case Law of Love re-creating God in man's image to wield and wave sin's scepter over God's creation, thereby unleashing infidelity's lust for God's throne (Romans 2:1-16, 13:8-10; I Corinthians 13:7-8; James 2:8). When we usurp God's role, authority, and dominion at any level – we invite death's lower case law of hostility to engulf us in hell's lie embodied in the fallen angelic father of lies drawing a boundary and casting ourselves out of God's presence (John 8:42-47; Romans 7:7-8:2). Sin entered the world at the same time we see the serpent's first appearance because satan...as Christ's evil antithesis...embodies, personifies, and administrates the law of sin and death against God's created – us (John 8:42-47; Romans 8:2).

One of the clearest examples of man being responsible for drawing all boundaries...not God...is found in religion's words, "We have a law, and according to that law He must die, because He claimed to be the Son of God (John 18:31, 19:7). Notice, they did not say God or Moses had a Law, but that they, as the religious, "had a law." I believe this observation shows an important difference in the way God and man view, embody, and administrate God's Law. God's Law, an expression of Himself, was given after sin entered the world (Exodus 20:1-17; Romans 5:13-14). God's Law is not a boundary. Instead, God's Law declares His dominion and reveals His being by exposing those attitudes and actions which violate His holy character subsequently personified, embodied, and exampled through the Life of Jesus Christ. God's Dominion, Being, Son, and Spirit define and inhabit His eternal and immutable Law. God the Father sent Jesus His Son inhabited by His Spirit (Trinity) into the world as the Living Word, Law, and Preeminent Standard to reveal God's character, to define God's reality, and to free God's people by conforming us to His likeness (Matthew 5:17-20. Luke 4:18-19, 20:17-18; John 1:1-5, 3:3-21, 5:16-30, 8:31-32, 14:6-14, 17:20-26; Romans 6:4,8:28-30, 13:8-10; 2 Corinthians 5:17; Galatians 6:1-2; Ephesians 2:19-22; 1 John 4:16-21).

Because God's being IS Love and embodies His Law that ALWAYS protects, trusts, hopes, and perseveres ...because Jesus Christ is identical to His Father...and because we are created in Their image and called to do what Jesus is doing – the words, attitudes, and example of Jesus Christ have absolute governing authority over ALL human theologies and interpretations on issues He addressed (Genesis 1:27; John 5:17, 14:9-12; 1 John 4:16). To determine if our stance or course of action is on track in God's eyes – we must identify, accept, and comply with what Jesus does. If He did not position Himself on an issue – it is typically insignificant in the scope of our salvation, regeneration, and eternity. Man is the one who wrestles to know the Hebrew, Greek, syntax, context, and present or past participles in a misguided effort to control others through deviant theologies. God, on the other hand...foreknew, predestined, and created us to conform to the likeness of His Son...not to the likeness of other bible characters who were equally created to follow His lead as well (John 17:1-26; Romans 8:28-30).

Conformity

God's method of conforming us to the likeness of His Son Jesus began before Creation when He foreknew and predestined destiny's blueprint in the lives of those He knows are His (John 17:6-10). God is eternal – ALWAYS was, ALWAYS is, and ALWAYS will be. He is I AM (Exodus 3:14-15). Because God is omniscient (all knowing), omnipotent (all powerful), and omnipresent (all present everywhere at the same time) – ALL of His being, character, concepts, thoughts, ways, and creations are eternal and existed within Himself before any of them became physical manifest reality. It was from this eternal omniscient, omnipotent, and omnipresent foreknowledge – God spoke the whole of His Creation into existence. So in progression – God physically displayed His dominion as He created the heavens and earth...made us in His image...allowed sin to estrange...foretold a Messiah...birthed a King...inhabited a Teacher...crucified a Savior...resurrected an Intercessor...commissioned a people...sent a Counselor...and impassioned a Bridegroom to love His wayward bride. ALL of these facets pre-existed physical Creation in the mind and heart of the Great I AM. Everything that occurs in humanity's physical existence after God's foreknowledge...even before physical creation...became the working out of our salvation known as... His-story (Genesis 1:27, 3; Exodus 20:1-17; Isaiah 9:2-7; Joel 2:16; Matthew 1:18-25, 25:1-13; 28:19-20; Luke 2:1-7, 4:18-19; John 3:27-30; 14:15-17, 16:5-15, 19:17-42, 20:1-31; Romans 8:28-30; Philippians 2:12; Hebrews 7:25).

God does not draw boundaries between Himself and man – He never did. He always knocks and walks through doors that are open before Him, until they close (John 6:37; Revelation 3:20). That is not drawing a boundary – closing the door was and man did it – God did not. People's concept of boundaries within relationship, society, and spirituality are an intellectually, psychologically, and legally-based fallen human attempt to relate to a Holy and loving God. People's concept, acceptance, and application of boundaries... are in essence...the very mechanism that creates the "God-in-a-box" scenario found in powerless religion that limits a LIMITLESS God from loving a dying world full of lost people. Boundaries are man's excuses for God's expectations. Simply put – God IS and eternally exists as the Great I AM Who declared both His dominion and being too His Creation, which includes us. God is just being Himself. God's Law describes what needs to be upheld and how the devil's evil antithesis or counterfeit of God's image will display itself (Romans 1:18-20, 8:5-8). God's Law merely exposes the devil's lie. Meanwhile, people like you and me...who are created in God's image...have been bombarded by and living beneath the devil's evil counterfeit as revealed through our commission of sin in a fallen world, thereby distorting our perspective, attitudes, and behavior.

It is sin's tyranny over, our commission of, and its impact upon our lives that separates us from God. Our separation from Him "does not" occur because of boundaries He drew, commandments He gave, or Law He imposed. Clearly stated – He simply revealed His Holy nature while willing to grant eternity's unconditional love to us as a polluted people who's sin insulted, disowned, and crucified His Son – the Author of Life (Acts 3:14-15). So in truth, it is man who erects barriers and closes doors in God's face as His Son Jesus stands outside knocking and waiting for us to invite Him back into our world (Revelation 3:20). We erect barriers through our ignorance, rebellion, and rejection of God's moral being and character. Since God's Character, Law, Son, Spirit, and commandments are an inseparably-linked extension of Himself, a violation against one is a violation against ALL (Matthew 5:17-20). Ignorance about God is an avoidable and unacceptable choice in God's sight as He continually makes Himself known through His entire Creation (Romans 1:18-20). Despite man's exclusion of himself from God's presence as he shackled himself to sin and death in the fall, we have remained in God's world though we pushed Him out of ours. Until we change our view of boundaries, we will never understand, experience, or extend the unconditional love and forgiveness of God to anyone, including ourselves. In the context of marriage, we cannot love each other until we first love ourselves (Ephesians 5:28-33).

Adam

The primary event cited by those subscribing to and applying "boundary theory" use to build their case about God drawing boundaries, is God's command for Adam not to eat from the "tree of the knowledge of good and evil" and the implication God expelled man from the Garden (Genesis 2:16-17, 3:21-24). Please notice, that man recognized his nakedness, covered himself, experienced shame, and hid from God before He acknowledged and declared man's commission of sin (Genesis 3:6-13). So, man viewed himself as excluded from God's presence, when it was in fact, it was sin that was unable to stand before God. Before I can respond to the Adam situation however, I must build a bit of foundation for you...

Please recall that God IS and His being IS omniscient, omnipotent, omnipresent, and He eternally foreknew us before our physical creation occurred (Romans 8:28-30). This means that He foreknew the fall of man was coming, that sin would enter the world, and about humanity's moral tendencies, choices, and subsequent need to be redeemed by a Holy God based on free choice "if" His relationship to us is to be rooted and established in love (Ephesians 3:16-21). Why? Remember, God created us for His good pleasure, not because He needed us (Philippians 2:13). He is the ALL-existent One – not dependent. So obviously, a holy God Who IS love desires to relate to His creation based on love to incite His pleasure (1 John 4:16). For Him to do otherwise would be a moral contradiction of Himself that would evidence change, undermine His character, make His Law no longer immutable, pollute His holiness, and destroy Scripture's inerrancy thereby making all of it untrue. This would, in turn, deny His claim to be the Great I AM who is the same yesterday, today, and forever and Who is sovereign unto Himself (Hebrews 13:8). Sovereignty IS because God IS and pre-existed ALL, thereby establishing Him as the one being Who gives account to no one (Colossians 1:15-20). Next, in the equation after God's moral and perfect being has been thus dismantled by man's futile thinking, love and forgiveness would no longer be unconditional (Romans 1:18-32). Misguided theological disassembly of God's divinity and character would present a very real problem in our motivation and ability to experience personal relationship with God through faith in Jesus Christ. Why? "Anyone who comes to Him must believe He exists and that He rewards those who earnestly seek Him" (Hebrews 11:6). For our faith to have foundation, God's eternal base nature simply cannot change or faith has no foundation (2 Timothy 3:14-17). Bottom line, one either believes God is entirely true or not. The moment we perceive that God ceases to be solely defined as He declares Himself to be through inspired Scripture... our faith has lost its anchor.

Adam-continued

Based on God being Love Itself...His richness in mercy...His desire for relationship...His foreknowledge of Creation...His planned human redemption...His enjoyment of pleasure...and His sacrifice of Jesus His Son as a love-inspired salvation peddler with the task of knocking on humanity's stubborn heart doors, His commandment to Adam to leave the tree in the Garden alone was Love being itself protecting man from the very sin that ultimately caused him to withdraw from God (John 15:14-16; Acts 2:23; Romans 8:28-30; Ephesians 2:4; Philippians 2:13; 1 John 4:16-18). God does not scratch boundaries in the very dirt of man's composition to separate Himself from His creation (Genesis 3:19, 23).

Babel

When the tower of Babel was being built, man laid one clay brick of human pride upon another exerting his defiance against God as he attempted to strong-arm his way into God's presence, while remaining both independent and unrepentant with regard to God's moral being. When the Lord saw what one people armed with one language unified by sin could accomplish – He confused their language, scattered them all over the earth, and stopped the city's construction (Genesis 11:1-9). It is interesting to me that the mortar used between the Tower of Babel's bricks was tar...black in color – like sin and darkness (Genesis 11:3). Those who subscribe to "boundary theory" say that God erected boundaries by confusing the people of Babel's language, scattering them, and halting construction. However, this assumption is untrue – God was simply being Himself again. Again, God is Love. Love ALWAYS protects. So, when God's Holy being was confronted by the invasion of sinful men in their yet independent, disobedient, and unrepentant state...God's nature being Love...displayed Himself in the presence of sinful man who fled in fear, shame, confusion just like in the Garden...because sin cannot stand in the presence of a Holy God who embodies Love. It was the sin represented in the perspectives, attitudes, and behaviors of Babel's people that incited God spelled LOVE to exude His moral holiness which sent man packing. So once again, man's sin excluded him from God's presence. God did not draw a boundary or erect a barrier – man did.

Jericho

When the walls of Jericho tumbled in response to the trumpet blast based on God's pattern and command – the walls fell outward. They were erected by men and collapsed by God revealing that He tears down barriers...not build them. Jericho's walls were built by misguided Canaanite people created in God's image due to their fear that other people equally created in God's image would bring them harm because of godlessness. Estrangement from God breeds fear...fear breeds suspicion...suspicion incites self-preservation... self-preservation incites the expression of anger. Remember, God is love. Those who subscribe to "boundary theory" say that Jericho's walls were erected to protect, not to silence fear. Protection is one of love's interwoven unconditional attributes designed to protect God's people. Yet, God instructed Israel to destroy Jericho because of ungodly inhabitants unwilling to obey Him, so He could give the Promise Land to His chosen people in covenant with Him. Hence, Jericho's walls were fear-based boundaries erected by men, not God-based protection.

Man's Line

Hence, my stance that it is man's sin that excludes him from God... not God's boundaries excluding us from Him. The difference between a boundary and a commandment is literally the difference between two kingdoms – light and darkness. Boundaries divide – commandments unify. Boundaries are built on fear and judgment – commandments are built on Love and promise (2 Peter 1:3-11). God's commandments are simply His merciful effort to communicate His immortal character to mortal man using flimsy words recognized by challenged-at-best human intellect. We use our confusion as to what really constitutes a boundary or commandment to justify our wrongful application of a distorted version of God's Upper Case Law of Love, while focused on excluding Him from our world, and as we stake our claim on heaven just as Babel did. In clear terms, a commandment is God's promise-based restatement of Himself to His creation so we can become like Him. A boundary is man's judgment-based restatement of his demand that God remake Himself in man's image.

When people remain religious at the expense of not entering dynamic personal relationship with God through Jesus Christ and the Holy Spirit, they draw a boundary between themselves and God Who communicates deeper revelation truth by His Spirit (John 6:45). When one remains intellectually based and religious knowing about God, but never wholeheartedly pursues personal relationship with God Himself through Jesus Christ, that person severely limits their acquisition of revelation knowledge from God just as happened during America's inception. This is why Jesus told us that God seeks true worshippers who will worship Him in Spirit and in truth because He is Spirit (John 4:23-24). And please remember, that our act of spiritual worship is to give our bodies (lives) as living sacrifices...holy and pleasing to God as we no longer conform to the PATTERN of our fallen world (Romans 12:1-3). Please notice my prior comments about PATTERNS above in this chapter. Why? Just as Adam was "...the pattern of the One to come" speaking of Christ, I portrayed God as "Eternity's Pattern" Who compels His Son Jesus to say and do what He hears and sees His Father saying and doing (Roman's 5:14). A pattern is a standard, something to copy, and the source of definition. Where-as, boundaries evidence the futile nature of understanding, religion, and situational love we were counseled not to lean upon or practice if we're to acknowledge God in all our ways with action (Proverbs 3:5-6; 2 Timothy 3:1-5). Please recall, knowledge puffs up, but love builds up in "Romance Theology" and God's Upper Case Law of Love (1 Corinthians 8:1-3).

Now, we are all confronted by absolute moral responsibility to love and forgive God and man unconditionally without limit or delay.

Love Himself is crying out to us trying to be heard SO He can love us... Unfortunately, we are so busy blaming Him for our powerless religion, frenzied difficulty, and lacking redemption – that we will not take personal responsibility for scratching a line, laying a brick, or dividing ourselves from Him. And, we love God...right? So, either I have established a solid case for man to own the sin-based boundaries he draws in his own strength which separate him from God...or I have built a very good case for atheism. The existence or non-existence of one's faith tips the scale. Whether bricks of pride, walls of sin, or attraction's force – every brick and every wall of sin will fall, when we make Jesus Lord of ALL...

God's call on our lives determines how He deals with us, so He can use us to deal with others as He ordains. Offense only has power to separate those already willing to be offended as their excuse not to live as Jesus taught them. Throughout history, man's anger has been more used to defend self, than to righteously fortify Love's power to protect others. Boundaries simply represent man-justified rebellion designed to erase God-created purpose. Until we're willing to walk far enough into people's brokenness to get dirty, our dying world will struggle to experience God's extravagant love. Until we are willing to set our faces like flint amid the resulting heartache on our way toward the New Jerusalem, we will never carry our cross in the shadow of our King. And, until we are willing to face crucifixion, the crowd around us will never experience resurrection. Just as Jesus granted unconditional love, forgiveness, and restoration to a yet sinful woman and freed her to live, we are called in His name to do likewise without condition...

Following God's call on my life to preach while kneeling at that church camp altar back in 1972, I let my fear of other people's rejection chart my course into life's emptiness on the same basis as Adam who worked his ground by the sweat of his brow in his own strength through diminished vision. I worked for years as God equipped my life and brought me to the realization that He had a better plan. In my response to His still small voice and his answer to my dangerous prayer, He carried me beneath baptism's water and resurrected me a man on fire implanted with heaven's eyes and willing to burn brighter each day at any cost... God made us masterpieces dear friends who have been individually hand-painted by the Great I AM. We are priceless originals inscribed by our King and destined to change the world in Jesus' name! But, we have a choice... We can either get back in the ditch, live beneath tyranny, and stand trapped behind hell's lines in the dark sweating amid downtrodden toil...or, we can rise up to be more than conquerors who are free in Christ Jesus, radiant with His glory, and filled with His peace as He whispers...come unto Me...

Daily road miles chasing Jesus on Repent America Walk 2001-02

The cry of warriors at the Wailing Wall – 2006

Chapter 12
Warriors of Rest

"Do not be afraid or discouraged by this vast army. For the battle is not yours, but God's...You will not have to fight this battle. Take up your positions, stand firm, and see the deliverance the Lord will give you..." (2 Chronicles 20:15, 17).

Dead reckoning life's battlefield, calculating our current position from established truth and reality, requires that we have a fix on our origin before we can chart our course and arrive to our assigned destination[9]. Navigating life, discovering purpose, and realizing destiny pulls us into the crossfire thereby bombarding our resolve's courage with the opposing ever-shifting winds of fear, hope, uncertainty, faith, defeat, and victory[10]. To overcome, we must enter the fire fight committed to our Commander, clothed in His armor, and armed with His weapons to demolish enemy strongholds, affirm our allegiance, take kingdom territory, and raise His banner[11]. Amid the warfare, we must never forget that we do not wrestle or battle against those around us, but our fight is against the rulers and powers of dark kingdoms determined to take us captive to do their will[12]. Yet, victory does not come to those fearful or faint of heart, but only those who do their Master's will[13]. If we're to win, we must put our hope and trust[14] in our King...

Jesus Rules

Two hours into the flight, my conversation with a Christian woman I had just met on the plane turned toward how God calls us to respond to those who have hurt us in life. We continued our discussion

---

9 Genesis 1:26-30; Jeremiah 29:11; Matthew 18:10-14; Romans 8:28-30; Ephesians 2:10; Hebrews 12:1-3; 2 Peter 3:9

10 1 Corinthians 13:7-8, 15:57; 2 Corinthians 4:7-18; 2 Timothy 1:7; Hebrews 11:1-6

11 Genesis 32:28; Song of Songs 2:4; Isaiah 61:1-11; Matt. 24:13; John 13:34-35; Romans 13:14; Revelation 2:26-29, 3:21-22, 21:5-8

12 2 Corinthians 10:3-5; Ephesians 6:10-13; 2 Timothy 2:22-26;

13 Deuteronomy 20:1-20, 31:6; Joshua 1:6-9; 2 Chronicles 20:15-19; Isaiah 41:10, 43:5-10; Matthew 7:21-23; John 14:1, 27, 15:13-17

14 Psalms 146:1-10; John 10:27-29, 14:1-3;

on the subject unwittingly crossing into what later proved to be uncharted spiritual territory for this dear woman. As we dialogued about love's reply through our lives to those estranged by conflict, it became obvious that her beliefs and practice drew more ammunition from man's opinion and her personal interpretation, than accepting and emulating what Jesus said and did. "Jesus never delayed or withheld love, forgiveness, and restoration from anyone in need from my recollection," I said. "Yeah, but people have to earn our trust back when they break it," she replied. "Do you believe that Jesus taught us to follow His example?" I asked. "Yes, but He gave us a brain too," she responded. "Okay, so using our brains to read the Bible and see how He loved people who eventually killed Him tells us what He thinks...right?" I asked. "Well, yeah..." she trailed off. "Can you give me an example of a time you saw or experienced God telling you or someone else to go away and come back later so He could think about loving, forgiving, or restoring?" I asked[15]. "Well, I know what I believe and we need to protect ourselves, so I don't want to talk about it anymore," she retorted. "Okay. But, for whatever its worth...I've simply never found an example or experienced God pushing me or anyone else away," I responded. "I need to get back to my reading," she said as she opened her heavily-underlined book on "Boundaries."

When reasoning together over biblical truth and an inflexible intellectual stance on an interpretative issue is encountered which dismisses Christ's example as secondary to our personal interpretation – a stronghold of delusion has been exposed[16]. Once a stronghold stands exposed, satan will launch an offensive to regain his grip on territory slipping through his fingers by dispatching a spirit of rejection against the one in the equation who speaking truth in love consistent with the words and example of Jesus Christ[17]. The spirits of fear and rejection work hand-in-hand to become a foundation upon which fear-based anger can rise if not quickly resisted and rightly subjected to the authority of Jesus Christ[18]. When the words and example of Jesus are raised as the

15 Matthew 6:5-15; John 8:1-11

16 2 Corinthians 10:3-5; 2 Thessalonians 2:9-12

17 Matthew 10:22, 24:9

18 2 Corinthians 10:3-5; James 4:7-10

governing authority between two believers on any issue He took a position on...and...one's intellectual view of Scripture is cited above His words, attitudes, and actions as justification for personal behavior – an entrenchment of independence, infidelity, rebellion, and fear has likewise been revealed. This revelation indicates the predominance of intellectualized religion, not dynamic personal relationship with Jesus Christ[19].

Love Trusts

Trust is the central issue of love. Without trust, love is not in operation and cannot truly exist. The existence of trust can only be proven by action which includes unconditional and unlimited love, forgiveness, restoration, and freedom. For true Christ-centered trust to exist, one must remain unconditionally vulnerable and grant others unhindered access thereby exposing oneself to potential suffering. I understand that what I have just said in the last four sentences has burrowed deep beneath the emotional saddles of many who are reading. Yet, my motive is not to antagonize. Instead, my motive is to liberate love's expression among God's people. There are numerous widely-accepted man-contrived blindly-applied psychological principles which have been perpetrated and unleashed by hell to rape God's people, plunder God's love, and to immobilize God's Church. Westernized Christian culture has become an intellectualized, demoralized, and marginalized system of dehumanizing idealisms, traditions, and regulations more dependent upon the basic principles of this world, than on Christ as they offer a hollow form of godliness without power[20]. If you feel my comments are too strong, please let me ask a fundamental question. If we are doing such a great job as believers called to change the world both inside and outside our homes – why are we steamrolled by fear, deception, immorality, divorce, greed, exploitation, and godlessness at unparalleled levels? Why is America, the world-at-large, and Christianity crashing in dire need of a Savior who embodies love? In a nutshell, we do not love, trust, and obey God on His terms with action to evidence our individual and corporate allegiance to Him. Every answer finds its origin in the person of Jesus Christ...

---

19 John 5:31-44, 14:12

20 Colossians 2:6-8, 20-23; 2 Timothy 2:24-26

Trust must be unconditional, merciful, faithful, and selfless exposing oneself to harm for the benefit of another to verify love's existence. There is one foundation for this answer...Jesus Christ. This answer is proven by what He did, not words. Here it is... Jesus came to earth in the form of a man with foreknowledge that He would suffer and die at the hands of those He came to love and forgive. While in the process – He withheld no love, drew no boundaries, exerted no demands, laid no guilt, inflicted no wounds, extracted no revenge, imposed no control, and asserted no rights. In return – He was judged, slandered, mocked, assaulted, exploited, betrayed, ignored, abused, and murdered. Just prior to the cross while standing before Pilate being openly condemned and falsely accused amid innocence, He made no reply in His own defense[21]. In essence, He traveled His entire ministry path surrounded by the undependable who slept as He sweat blood at Gethsemane, deserted Him in His darkest hour, and fished on the Sea of Tiberias as their dismantled faith silently called Him a liar[22]. In response to it all, He extended ongoing, unlimited, and immediate unconditional love, forgiveness, and restoration proving that He trusted the untrustworthy with His Life. Then, He told us that those of us who have faith in Him will do what He is still doing[23]. When we look within ourselves and get real, who among us is trustworthy? When did Jesus ever tell us that He needed to heal before He forgave us? When did He ever make us walk through a process of accountability, counseling, and restoration before giving us full access[24]? Never, that's when. So, why do we feel we have the right to withhold fellowship, demand trust be rebuilt, and give ourselves permission to kick God off His throne?

Simple...we're deceived, rebellious, and in sin...bottom line. You may feel my position violates what you learned in church, seminary, counseling, or theology to which I will venture one response in the form of a question. What did Jesus do? To a real Christian, nothing else matters...

---

21 Matthew 27:13-14
22 John 21:1-19
23 John 14:12
24 John 6:37-39

Getting Real

Winding through coastal island roads in 1998 toward the home of a man I had only met briefly by phone and in who's home I would be staying for the next week as I spoke in his church, I took in the lush fern and flower-infested backdrop highlighted by shadows cast in the late fall's afternoon sun. Making my way along, I prayed through similar twists and turns within my own heart, mind and spirit as I pondered what I would preach during the opening revival service that night... Arriving in town several hours early, I stopped by the still-almost-vacant church to catch up with Pastor Ben and pray through the sanctuary before continuing on to Doug's house where I would settle, shower, and get ready to speak later that evening. On my way out of Doug's lower level door a few hours later...I traveled the short mile to the church, parked my rig, and traversed the parking lot meeting Pastor at the door. By then, the sound man had arrived and music was playing in the sanctuary's background as we walked into the room. I took off my coat and laid it next to my bible in the front pew where I would later be seated when service began. Over the next half hour, people arrived one-by-one, in two's, and in three's to find their places. Sometime later, overhead lights dimmed as platform spots brightened and those who had gathered against walls or perched on pews to engage in conversation came to attention and took their seats. Pastor Ben stepped up to microphone and opened in prayer...

We joined in several hymns, heard the announcements, my introduction came, and I walked up the steps where I set my bible on the edge of the pulpit and turned to greet the people. I shared a bit more about myself, told a couple of light-hearted stories, and landed on my passion to help people become all they were created to be... For the next hour, we traveled a course through the bible in which we identified hurdles in our path as we do our best to run the race in pursuit of God in this life. Finally, the Lord gave me the closing point – I paused in silent prayer for a few moments and laid it before His people... "Sometimes you just need to tell God you're pissed off at Him!" I said pausing for my statement to settle over the crowd. I noticed one middle-aged lady to my left halfway down the aisle immediately sat up in her seat looking back at me as if insulted...an older gentleman to my right in the third row doing all in his power to keep his tie from rolling up under his chin as he stared back in wide-eyed disbelief...and a young man who remained seated quietly in the next-to-last row gazing as if asking a question... "About now, some of are saying to yourself you could never talk to God that way," I said. "Likewise, some of you are asking yourself why on earth you would even want too. And, some of you are thinking that he's a preacher and should really know better than to talk to God or in church like that. But, the bible tells us that God knows[25] everything we think or need before we say it or ask for it," I added and paused again...

"So, if God already knows who we are, what we think, what we feel, and who we blame when things aren't going our way...when He doesn't heal someone we love...or doesn't bail us out of problems as we yell at Him inside our hearts, but lack the guts to say what we feel to His face...who are we really hiding it from?" I asked. "Think of the best friendship you've ever had...why you love or feel loved by that person...and what makes you feel safe," I said and paused. "In truth, we feel most loved when we can be our real self, dump our junk on the table, and be gut-level honest without fear of someone judging, punishing, or throwing us away," I ventured. Silence was thick in the room as prior insult yielded in consideration, disbelief melted in realization, and question transformed into illumination. "The real issue is not how we talk to God. When we can be real with someone, it proves that we know they love us. But, when we hide behind carefully chosen words, warmed-over smiles, and bottled-up emotion or anger...it shows that we're not sure we can trust the one who's presence we're in," I said allowing the thought to hang in the air like balloon on a string. As I looked around the room... gazes had fallen to the floor as tears rolled gently downward...faces were buried in people's hands...and others knelt in the pews to pray. Then, I continued and asked, "Why can't we be real in front of God?" "The bible says God is love...that love always protects, trusts, hopes, perseveres, and never fails...that perfect love casts out all fear...that fear has to do with punishment...and that the one who fears has not

25 Psalms 139:1-5; Matthew 6:8

yet been made perfect in love[26]. Why?" I asked again. "The next time you find yourself caught in the crossfire between God's goodness and your perception of His injustice in life...get real and be real with Him. He knows anyway... Trials are going to come, heartache is going to happen, and emotion is going to rage. There is nothing you can say to God that will ever surprise Him, offend Him, or cause Him to leave you beaten and alone – nothing[27]."

As we traveled the week's services together, God did great work in us all. On the last evening, one dear gentleman came up to me after service and said with a grin, "You preach like a shotgun, you just shot every sacred cow in our Church this week...thank you!" "Well friend, I just preach what God gives me and calls me to live myself. Thanks for being here!" I replied. An hour later as the lights were being turned off, Pastor Ben and I headed for a local eatery, had a cup of coffee, said our goodbyes, and made our ways to the place we each call home.

Lifestyle Forgiveness

A number of years back, I found myself engaged in an extended conversation with a gal as the subject of forgiveness landed on the table. As we continued talking, it became more obvious that she struggled with unforgiveness in her own life. "How can you forgive people who abandoned you and destroyed everything you worked for and love?" she asked. "Well, the question is not how I can forgive them. Instead, the right question to ask is how I could refuse to forgive them when Jesus forgives me," I replied. "Yeah, but a lot of people say they're sorry and do the same things over again and again. I really trust people when I meet em' and give em' a real chance to win in my world. I'll even cut em' slack a few times when they blow it. But, if they do something to me over and over, I'll stick em' in another category to stop them from getting too close. That way, they can't hurt me. A lot of people just say their sorry to get things off their back, but they really don't mean it," she said. "I understand, but forgiveness isn't a choice...it's a lifestyle that we choose when we give control of our lives to Jesus Christ as both Lord and Savior.

26 1 Corinthians 13:7-8; 1 John 4:16-18

27 Deuteronomy 31:6

If we make forgiving people an issue of choice, it's only a matter of time before we find what we feel is a good enough reason not to forgive someone we perceive has hurt us. Once we open that door though, it'll be easier next time to come up with another excuse to withhold forgiveness again. That's why we have to make the decision to forgive ALWAYS – without exception," I responded.

"Honestly, we do not have the power to forgive within ourselves – only God does[28]. All we have the power to do is to obey and give Him permission to forgive someone through us. God commanded us to forgive others if we want Him to forgive us[29]. So, when somebody hurts us making it necessary for us to forgive them, we're just obeying God and letting Him do His work through us. Jesus is the One Who died on the cross to pay the price for sin, not us. We're just the pipeline God uses to extend forgiveness to others," I explained. "Yeah, but it's wrong to tell someone you're sorry after hurting them and never change the behavior. Anyone can say sorry, but it's a lot harder to actually do something about it," she inserted. "True, it's hard to change... But, have you ever struggled with a bad habit that's got you by the hair and it caused grief for another person time after time?" I asked. "Well yeah, but I was really sorry about it and tried hard to fix it. I use to do that to my dad a lot, but he loves me thank God," she replied. "How do you know if other people are trying as hard as you are or not? You have to be careful not to judge people, only God knows our hearts[30]. Maybe they really want to change, but haven't been able to figure it out. Sometimes, things are just bigger than we are and only God can fix it. Good thing He's patient...huh? You hit the nail on the head though, when you mentioned that your dad put up with your problems because He loves you," I said. You could see the wheels turning as she pondered my words...

"So, why is forgiveness such a big deal? If I put the people who hurt me off to the side and I don't have to see or talk to them anyway... who cares?" she asked. "Forgiveness is huge in God's eyes because

28 Psalms 49:7; Luke5:21-26; 1 Peter 1:18-23

29 Matthew 6:14-15; Luke 17:4; John 20:21-23

30 1 Kings 8:39; Romans 2:1-11

it is the core reason Jesus came into our world and died on the cross to save us. When we choose not to forgive someone who hurts us, we're rejecting the love and forgiveness God sacrificed His Son Jesus to give us. If you give somebody you love something really valuable to you and they just toss it aside, how do you feel?" I asked. "It hurts, makes me mad, and makes we want to ignore em'," she retorted as her cheeks flushed with emotion. "When you consider that God gave His only Son to save and forgive us...that we could never earn or deserve what He gave us for free...that we toss it aside for other things in life every day...and then grab onto for ourselves but won't give it to others...how do you think He feels?" I asked. "I get it now," she replied. "If we're honest, you and I fall short at something every single day in our attitudes, choices, thoughts, the way we treat people...somewhere every day. If God forgiving us depended on our performance, worthiness, or His choice instead of Love's promise, where on His green earth would we be?" I asked. "In trouble," she replied. "Bottom line, none of us really deserves forgiveness. But, God loves us unconditionally and forgives us no matter how bad we fail. If we'll simply admit to God and the one we hurt what we did wrong and call it sin, seek forgiveness from them both, and then do our best to change our behavior with God's help...we're beyond forgiveness wading in God's grace. That's called repentance[31]... God doesn't expect us to be perfect. And yet, that's not an excuse to do whatever we want. He only told us to be blameless[32] in His eyes," I told her...

"What's blameless mean?" she asked. "Blamelessness simply means we are willing to repent for any sinful thing the Holy Spirit shows us that we did wrong in God's eyes. If we repent, our sin gets put under the blood of Jesus Christ and God sees us as clean in His sight. None of us can be perfect, but everyone can be blameless if they are willing," I told her. "Please pray for me," she said. "I can pray for you, but only you can choose to give God permission to forgive through your life," I replied.

---

31 2 Corinthians 7:10; 2 Peter 3:9

32 Genesis 17:1; Philippians 2:14-16; Revelation 14:5

Unconditional

Our story is set in the Temple Courts of Jerusalem around 28-36 AD. The story's plot surrounds a woman caught in the act of adultery by religious leaders who haul her before Jesus publicly in a manner that challenges Him to pronounce sentence on her as they look on prepared to stone her. Within this story, we find one of the most vivid portraits of the opposing natures embodied within God's Upper Case Law of Love and death's lower case law of hostility. We come into the storyline when Jesus is surrounded by people listening to Him teach openly in the Temple courts and religious leaders enter the scene forcing an adulterous woman to stand in public disgrace before the crowd, declaring her crime, and demanding a verdict[33]. At this moment, religious leaders declared that their law required punishment for the immoral act the woman had committed and waited for Jesus to take a position on the matter[34]. In response, He crouched down and began writing in the dirt with His finger. It is my perspective that He was writing the nature of God's Upper Case Law of Love in the dirt to reveal that they were driven by death's lower case law of hostility. Next, Jesus stood up and told whoever was among those present and without sin...to throw the first stone at her. Then, He bent back down to resume writing in the dirt. On this occasion, I believe it possible that Jesus began writing their individual sins on the ground before them[35]. Slowly, her accusers left one-by-one beginning with the older ones, thereby leaving only the woman and Jesus standing there. It is during this pivotal scene that Jesus stood up a third time and we watch Love act to shatter religion's lie...

"Woman, where are they? Has no one condemned you?" Jesus asked. "No one, sir," she said. "Then neither do I condemn you," Jesus declared. "Go now and leave your life of sin," He finished[36]. Did you catch the amazingly real, unconditional, and immediate response to sin Jesus just taught with action regarding how love, forgiveness, and restoration look in the midst of fresh violation? The guilty woman was publicly accused and disgraced by others.

---

33 John 8:1-4

34 John 8:5

35 John 8:6-8

36 John 8:10-11

Those considered Godly and who judged her were willing to kill her based on their own legalistic religious justification without mercy. Likewise, those who condemned her were obviously convicted by what Jesus wrote in the dirt regarding their individual attitude, thereby bringing them to the realization that judging and condemning her to death made them subject to the same end. Then, they all walked away one-by-one as their public destruction of another person's dignity exposed their prideful unwillingness to confess their own sin. Though extremely significant, these facts are nothing in comparison to this story's punch line...

Let me set the stage before putting this story's primary message on the table before us... Please imagine yourself in the adulterous woman's shoes and think of a time when you were caught in blatant sin...were accused and disgraced by another you knew had hidden fault themselves, but was dragging your failure into the public eye willing to destroy you...and when you had no leg to stand on for self-defense, you were guilty. Then, think of how easy it would be for you to forgive the person who condemned you in front of everyone...how likely it would be that you would respond by overlooking their secret sin if you were aware of it...and how willing you would be to consider it all no big deal, put it behind you without condition, and hang out with them like old friends as soon as the crowd cleared. Okay, now let's look at what Jesus really showed us here about God's heart toward the extension of unconditional love, forgiveness, and restoration. First, the woman was guilty. Second, we are not told whether she admitted her guilt, was sorrowful, repented, or asked Jesus for anything or not. Third, Jesus did not confront her, did not condemn her, did not call her to account, and did not brow beat her. Fourth, He honored her, loved her, forgave her, and released her with total immediate unconditional freedom and full restoration. And fifth, Jesus left Himself absolutely accessible, drew no boundaries, imposed no expectations, made no demands, initiated no process, declared no timeline for healing, and only admonished her gently saying, "Go now and leave your life of sin." Is this sinking in...is this sinking in... is this...sinking sinking sinking...in?

In light of today's intellectualized, psychologized, secularized Christianity and what this story just portrayed...Jesus DID NOT teach, suggest, imply, command, or example that there was to ever be any need of or justification for an imposed elongated time process for the perceived victim to heal before expecting them to extend unconditional love, forgiveness, and full restoration to the offender immediately. Likewise, Jesus' absolutely bypassed all justification for maintaining distance, limiting fellowship, and making oneself inaccessible while expecting the perceived offender to re-establish trust, re-earn privilege, and live with reduced freedom. In a nutshell, Jesus showed us that love, forgiveness, and restoration are ALL unconditional, unlimited, immediate, full, and free if they are truly motivated by His heart and released beneath His Lordship. Is that the way we love, forgive, and restore people who hurt, slander, threaten, and violate us? When we harm someone else, what kind of love, forgiveness, and restoration do we expect from them? What is proven by our response to another person's sin in our daily reality?

Is the example of Jesus Christ truly our governing authority? Or, do we justify and bow to our personal theology, Scriptural interpretation, and self-will thereby revealing that death's lower case law of hostility has dominion within? Right here, right now...I ask God to remind and convict us all of every relationship that we have in our lives which is not 100% free to operate, grow, and flourish without limitation in Jesus' name. Likewise, I ask Him to inspire, empower, and mobilize us to do everything in our power to live at peace with all people[37]. As I showed in prior chapters, God does not draw boundaries or build fences between Himself and people. If He doesn't do it Himself, He does not approve or condone it among His people if they choose to do it, either[38]. Since Jesus came to earth as God's Living Word and Portrait of His Father's heart to show us how to unconditionally love, forgive, and restore people His way...we have no excuse...no justification...and no defense in His eyes to impose, withhold, or distance ourselves

37 Romans 12:17:21

38 John 14:12

from anyone. Love, forgiveness, and restoration are a command[39], not a feeling or a choice. To prove we love God, we are called to obey His commands[40]. Slow to obedience IS still disobedience. Disobedience does not reveal love for God. Without love for God... we're in trouble. Do you want proof God calls those who are truly His to obedience? Consider the cross[41]...

Whole Meal Deal

Thirteen miles into my day's trek during my first walk across America, I strolled into a rural Kansas community where I found a small independent charismatic fellowship on a side street across from the town square. It was a cool crisp November day and leaves were still blowing here-and-there as the wind eddied in-and-around storefronts nearby. I approached the church looking for the entrance only to discover it around the side between a couple lone evergreens posted like sentries on either side of the gray steel door. Stepping up on the porch, I leaned forward, gave the knob a twist, and pulled the door toward me curious as to what I would find on its other side. "Hello," I called as I wandered down the hallway looking for life. Just around the first corner immediately to my right, I spotted a small sign high on the wall dangling from an arm on chain with "OFFICE" routered in its wood. The door stood ajar with light bouncing off the far wall from an unseen source around the other side of the partition. "Hello," I said again a bit softer. "Hi, may I help you," came her reply. Just then, a kind looking lady emerged from around the wall sporting a warm smile and a glint in her eyes. "I'm Greg from BattleCry walking across America... I've been on the road for almost seven months. Is your pastor in today?" I inquired. "No, he won't be in until tomorrow...sorry," she said back. "Well, maybe I can come by again...do you have one of his business cards?" "Sure...but, tell me a little more about your walk before you go...can you?" she asked.

"I'm from Washington State, a fourth generation apple farmer, and have a passion to raise warriors in Jesus' name," I said. "My wife

39 Matthew 6:14-15, 19:3-8, 22:37-41; Mark 12:30-31; John 13:34-35, 15:17; Romans 13:8-10; Philippians 2:3-5; 1 John 3:17, 4:19-21

40 John 14:12-24, 15:14-16

41 Matthew 26:36-46, 27:13-14; Luke 22:39-44; John 19:10-11

and I have been on the road since April when we left the coast of Washington State. My great granddad was a seventeen year old German preacher who came to America in the 1880's to plant churches. There's five of them still going today and I'm the first in four generations to be back in ministry." I explained. "So, what have you found on the road along your walk so far?" she asked. "I've met a lot of good people, found a lot of dead religion, and a struggling Church across all denominations. People want more, but they don't know where to start. So many have no idea who God created them to be or what He designed them to do," I replied. "I've been restless in my own life recently. I've been asking God a lot of questions lately. I know there's more, but chasing God's hard work," she said. "True. That's why most people in America are willing to let their pastors do all the Bible reading, study, and prayer for them," I responded. "Would you give me little input on something?" she asked. "I'm not sure I'll have an answer, but I'll tell you what I know. I'm just a man, so be sure to test what I tell you against Scripture," I replied with a grin. "So, what's your question?" I asked. "Do you think it's possible for people to be filled with the Holy Spirit without speaking in tongues? "Absolutely," I said. "Really?" she asked almost amazed.

"God the Father, Jesus the Son, and the Holy Spirit are inseparable[42]. If you accept Jesus as Lord and Savior, you get the Whole Meal deal called the Trinity living inside of you. But, just because you get em' all at once doesn't mean you automatically know how to recognize or make use of their presence in your life when you're new at it. Do you remember the first time you tried to use a computer and had no clue how? All the software and capabilities were inside the machine when you pulled it out of the box and plugged it in. Yet, you didn't know where to start to make the silly thing work. When we first get saved, we're kinda like the guy with a million bucks in the bank that has no idea he can write a check to spend it," I told her. "Yeah, I see what you're saying. So, you're telling me it takes time to grow, to learn how God speaks to us, and to recognize how He acts before we know how to cooperate with Him," she posed

42 Genesis 1:26; John 3:5-8, 4:23-24, 10:30, 14:6-26; 16:8-15, 17:20-23; 1 Corinthians 12:3-11; Revelations 19:10

tenuously. "Yeah that's right. When we first meet someone or start relationship, there's a lot we don't know about em'. So, it's hard to be a team. Yet, ten years later in a marriage, for instance, we somehow know what each other person is thinking. So, working together gets easier the longer we know each other," I replied. "I've always been taught that I have to speak in tongues to prove the Holy Spirit lives in me. But, it sounds like you're saying that's not necessarily right," she said half questioningly.

"The bible tells us that there are nine gifts of the Holy Spirit and that they are all expressions of the same Spirit. It also says that the gifts of the Holy Spirit are given to us based on what God decides, not what man thinks[43]. So, if you experience any of the gifts listed in First Corinthians chapter twelve, it's proof you have the Holy Spirit and that you're saved," I told her. "Oh, so that means the Holy Spirit is working in me, if I know Jesus, even if I don't speak in tongues," she replied. "Exactly," I said. Then I told her, "Let's say you live in Chicago, give your life to Jesus, get baptized, and start realizing that your having words of knowledge that help people...and...you start speaking in tongues unexpectedly one morning during your personal devotions while praying. And let's say that you grow as a Christian, start leading a Bible study, and that you help all kinds of people find hope over the next ten years. But, one night you go to bed and have a radical dream about going to Africa and helping people in the jungle that goes to your core. The next morning, you get up and over the next few months you begin noticing your new ability to identify evil spirits, lay hands on people and heal them, and that you're filled with supernatural faith you've never had. But, at the same time, you become aware that you aren't getting words of knowledge much anymore or speaking in tongues like you use too. Based on what just happened and if you're convinced that you must speak in tongues to prove that the Holy Spirit lives within... you'll begin feeling as though the Holy Spirit is slipping away. Yet, in reality you just gained three new gifts of the Holy Spirit that are merely different, but all expressions of the same Spirit. If you read what the Bible says, you'll notice that God gives different gifts to

43 1 Corinthians 12:7-11

different people[44]. Does that make sense?" I asked. "Yeah," she replied. "Here's why it's important to understand how God assigns different gifts of the Holy Spirit to people. Just like the story I told you...when God re-directs our path to use us for His glory and the benefit of others outside our normal grid as He decides...He must be given freedom to re-equip us for the specific task He's sending us to do. If we demand that we speak in tongues to prove something our way, we tie God's hands and limit what He can use us to do. I mean, you don't give a brain surgeon a baseball bat to operate with or a concert pianist a base drum to play Beethoven's symphony... right?" I asked.

"No, that wouldn't make any sense," she replied. "Based on experience, God has a way of sending us places we never imagined. If we want to function well wherever He sends us, we must give Him freedom to equip us as He knows best able to fulfill His plan because He loves us. Where the Spirit of the Lord is dear sister, there is freedom[45]. It has always amazed me how often we give ourselves freedom to do whatever we want, give others freedom when we feel like it, and rarely give God freedom to be Himself in our lives. We tell ourselves that we want Him to use us, empower us, and bless us...but, we want it on our terms. In my own life, I tell God He can give me whatever He knows I need to do whatever He calls me to do...and I never look back," I explained as the light came on in her eyes. "I get it now! That really helps me! I've been so worried I'm not like everybody else or that others don't think I'm as a spiritual as they are. But, based on what you've helped me understand, I'm just different and God can do whatever He wants in my life if I'm willing to be available, give Him permission, and do my part," she said excitedly.

"Honestly, people spend so much time trapped in their heads being religious and trying to understand an incomprehensible God as they impose twisted theology on each other, that they miss who God really is and the adventure He wants them to live. People who believe everyone saved has to speak in tongues to evidence the

44 1 Corinthians 12:4-7
45 2 Corinthians 3:17

presence of the Holy Spirit get so focused on that minor gift, that they short-change themselves and rarely pursue the greater gifts available to them. As a result, they live far below all God created them to have and accomplish[46]." I finished. "Thanks for taking time, I feel better! Pastor will be in tomorrow morning around nine," she advised. "Thanks, I appreciate that! God bless you," I said as I made my way back toward the open road...

Love Stories

Standing in front of a display rack whistling quietly to myself inside the corner video store on Main Street in a hundred year old logging town, I overheard the clerk ask my wife, "May I help you find what you're after?" "I'm just looking for something decent to watch," she replied. "Boy, he's in a good mood," the clerk said pointing toward me. "Oh, that's just the way he is...don't pay any attention to him...he's off in his own world most of the time," she said back with one of those grins. As the two of us scoured the shelves for a good love story we had not yet seen, we found ourselves feeling as though we were coming up empty handed. Noticing our about-to-vacate-the-store look, the lady clerk came up to me and said, "You're sure in a good mood today." "That's what Jesus does," I said back enthusiastically. Without warning, the woman burst out in tears like a breached dam. Caught off-guard, I thought, "What did I say," before she answered my unspoken question for me without even knowing...

"Six months ago, I lost my job unexpectedly. I'm a single mom with three kids and only have my income to feed us. I'm a hard worker, so I started looking for another job," she said between sniffs and tears. "So, were you able to find one?" I asked. "Yeah, about two weeks later finally, but in the meantime, I thought I'd take a chance and stop to ask a church for help," she replied. "I only needed a week's worth till I could find a job," she added. "Did you find anyone to help?" I asked. "Well, I stopped by the first church, but it was locked and nobody was around. So, I drove down the road another three four miles, found a second church, pulled in the parking lot, and went in. There was a middle-aged lady sittin' at

---

46 1 Corinthians 12:27-31

the desk and I asked if I could talk to her pastor while kinda tellin' her why I was there. But, before I got far...she cut me off...looked over her glasses at me and told me the pastor doesn't see anybody without appointments and that he was already booked two weeks out. I just told her I'd lost my job and needed some help to feed my kids," she said. "What did the secretary say?" I asked. "She told me that was the best she could do and asked if I wanted to make an appointment. I was kinda discouraged, so I just told her I needed something before then, thanked her, and went on my way," she replied.

"What did you do then?" I asked. "Well, I drove all the way into town and finally found one of the bigger churches, parked, and thought I would try one last time. It was kinda late in the day and I caught the pastor on his way out. He said he had a few minutes, so I told him about my job and that I only needed a little help until I found something else to do in the next week or so," she said sounding as if she was reliving the experience. "What did the pastor say?" I asked. "Well, he asked me where I attended church. I hadn't been going since my divorce a couple of years before when my husband left. But, then the pastor asked me what version of the Bible I read," she said looking puzzled. "I have an old beat up American Standard I've had for years, but when I told him that he got a bit rude with me," she said. "What do you mean?" I asked. "He said that people who read anything other than the King James are being deceived. He told me the other versions are all full of mistakes and that people who read em' have issues. When I asked him why he was upset, he told me he can't help anyone who doesn't go to church and who listens to lies taught by other translations," she said. I looked at her obviously genuine brokenness and said, "Please forgive us for turning you away based on something so absurd and wrong," I pled. "Why are you asking me to forgive you...you didn't do anything... you weren't even there?" she asked. "Because I'm a Christian and a member of God's Church and my Jesus teaches me to love people unconditionally in His name no matter what...especially, when they're in need," I replied. "Please forgive us...that was so wrong," I added...

"I just needed someone to care...I felt like I couldn't measure up," She replied. "Obviously you made it through the process in spite of it all, but I can see it really hurt you. On behalf of God's people, I'm so sorry...please forgive us," I said feeling a sense of injustice rise within me on her behalf. "So many churches are locked and vacant... too many of God's people are too busy to love the people He sends to them...and to many are willing to judge others as they live lies themselves. But, Jesus promises we will be filled if we hunger and thirst for righteousness...it's a promise[47]. He also said He came to seek and save the lost...to reach out to the sick and hurting...and that He doesn't harm those suffering[48]. He told us to treat people the way we want to be treated...that we freely received and that we're to freely give...and that we're to love others as ourselves[49]. On top of that, the Apostle Paul echoed Jesus' heart when he said God's love always protects, trusts, hopes, and perseveres[50]. Paul taught that we're not to be selfish or conceited – but that we're to stop thinking just of ourselves, put the needs of others ahead of our own, and to do it all with the same attitude as Jesus[51]. After telling us what the two greatest commandments[52] are however, Jesus is the One that got real with us when He said our faith in Him will be proven if we follow His example[53]. So, both Jesus and the Bible are clear how His disciples are supposed to treat people in His name," I explained.

"Well, like you said, I made it through...God took care of us," she responded. "Yeah, but I need to say something about that whole right-and-wrong Bible version idea. In truth, that issue is one of the greatest weapons of deception and legalism the devil uses to divide, control, and destroy people. And honestly, it has nothing to do with God... Bottom line, Jesus is the Living Word of God...what He says and does goes over-and-above anyone's opinion...God gave

47 Matthew 5:6;
48 Matthew 12:15-21; Mark 2:17; Luke 19:10
49 Matthew 7:12, 10:8, 22:37-40
50 1 Corinthians 13:7-8
51 Philippians 2:3-5
52 Mark 12:30-31
53 John 14:12

Him all authority in heaven and on earth[54]. So, when it comes to having to read the right Bible to meet, understand, or know Jesus... there is simply nowhere in Scripture to support that as true. Like other things, the whole Bible translation issue is nothing more than man trying to control and manipulate others based on his own opinion," I told her. "I don't understand," she said. "Well, please let me explain," I said before continuing. "Jesus promised He would respond to anyone who really wants to know Him[55]. He also said that none of us can come to Him unless His Father draws us and that if we do, we'll be taught by God – not men[56]. For someone to tell you that you have to read the right version, wear the right clothes, or attend the right church before they can help...is a lie and rejects everything Jesus teaches. Religion comes up with all kinds of rules, but does nothing to extend God's love. But, our relationship with Jesus will show when we love people His way[57]," I said while grieved within. "Can I ask you a question?" I inquired. "Sure," she replied.

"What are any of us to do with a deaf, dumb, and blind person? Obviously, they can't hear God's word, speak God's word, or see God's word. So...does that mean...that God created somebody and set them up to fail?" I asked. "That doesn't sound like God to me," she replied. "Me either. If we really wanna know God, He'll write what we need on a fence post...side of a building...across the sky...or on the tablets of our hearts...He's God and He loves us. I've always been amazed at how so many people get hung up on the King James because it was authorized by an earthly King. Yet, twist the intent of everything God gave Israel at Mount Sinai before He said it a second time in person through the life of Jesus the King of Kings. Honestly, some translations go way deeper into the original writings than the King James does. But, ya may as well hold your breath when people are determined to prove you wrong as they prop up their own insecurity. Meanwhile, while they're wranglin' over stuff that means nothing, I'm gonna love people and help em' find hope," I ended. "Thanks for taking time to talk to me...sorry you never found the movie you wanted," she said. "Well, it seems

54 Matthew 28:18; John 1:1-5

55 Matthew 5:6, 11:28-30; John 6:37-40

56 John 6:44-5

57 John 13:34-35

to me that God just showed up and played a love story none of us have ever watched before...in person," I replied. Smiling she said, "That's true...have a nice day!"

Silent Treatment

On one occasion while challenged beyond words, I went to prayer and asked God what He would have me do. After several days pursuing Him, He reminded me of several specific people who made it clear that I was to contact them if I found myself in need while on the road. Because God compels me to walk out the very faith I preach, I can honestly say that have only asked for ministry support less times than I can count on two hands in the past twenty-two years. As instructed, I contacted each of the people in my effort to present my current and pressing need, made my request that they pray about what God would have them do, and then waited patiently for their promised response certain they would be sensitive to my time-critical situation. A week went by, pressure mounted, and progress slowed. Another week passed, pressure stormed over the walls, and my progress ground to a halt. As I asked the Lord how to respond, He led me to send each of them one brief follow-up note to request an update. Their responses were as follows...

<u>Encounter One</u>: In addition to the above dilemma, I had met this pastor sometime before at the time God had already called me into the deepest prophetic challenge of my life on behalf of another. This gentleman had played a pivotal role in prior decisions related to that challenge, which later proved essential to the message of the hour being forged within me. Now, while fully aware of my additional need...this pastor whom I had come to know and love as a result of his prior involvement...made an unexpected comment in response to my follow-up note after not hearing from him as promised. He wrote, "I prayed and believe I have given you unconditional love. I do not want to be part of your inner circle. So, take me off your list and stop contacting me."

<u>Encounter Two</u>: I had known this gentleman for many years and enjoyed sweet fellowship and one-on-one prayer encounters in which we both made ourselves extremely transparent with each

other for the purposes of prayer. Both of us had navigated life-threatening episodes in which we kept up with the other's progress and condition. I tell people my life is an open book and they can thumb through its pages at will. As customary between the two of us, he was aware of other challenges God had placed before me and had promised to pray as I occasionally received a call from him from time-to-time. Many years later, while walking the continent for my second time – I presented my need, waited for response, and sent my follow-up note as directed. In response, I received a list of things wrong with my life that had been previously acceptable and was offered no further contact.

Encounter Three: I met this couple along my journey. Immediately after preaching, they invited me to lunch thrusting a business card in my hand, and telling me how they would like to talk to me about supporting my ministry. Though we spent an appreciable amount of time together, got to know each other either in person or by phone over subsequent months, I left their level of support between themselves and God knowing He knew best. When the afore-mentioned pitfall pounced on me and spurred my reach to them at the Lord's direction, I was promised a prayerfully prompt reply. I waited...waited...and waited some more, until God nudged me to send them my follow-up note. Though I was planning to pass through their area, they did not show up at church the week I was there, never called me, and replied with not so much as a word.

Why have I shared the above experiences? Some may assume that my heart is askew for doing so. Yet, I love each of these dear people, would do anything for them, can look them straight in the eye, and hold nothing in my heart against them. I believe God is revealing the impact the spirit of the age is having on His people. Please realize I had already invested more than $75,000.00 in my walk that I made the hard way before my above inquiry for help was ventured. So, it is not as though I came up with a hair brained idea expecting others to fund it and then got miffed when I didn't get my way. Had I been the one who originally approached them, solicited their support, and pressed them for involvement – their withdrawal would have made sense to a degree. But in truth, each of them had initiated and made the effort to make their offer and invite my communication if I found myself in need. Had they never approached me, I would have had no basis for expectation, would never have assumed, nor would I have ever asked in keeping with my long-term practice.

So, what compels us to offer ourselves to others in Jesus' name, invite them to draw from us...and then...to break continuity, commitment, and communion with the one our actions incited to ask? Was our offer really about honoring God and protecting others...or... promoting self? Why do we respond to life, people, and God as we do? Are we operating out of confidence and peace rooted in our identity in Jesus Christ? Or, are we operating based on performance trying to earn our value, access to God, and those we desire to receive love from based on fear? In addition to these questions, the presence of the "silent treatment" in the equation is most disturbing as it reveals widespread insecurity throughout God's people. In truth...many choose to overlook that hatred begins in one's heart, where God sees it as an aversion toward or wish to avoid someone.

After all, I'm a big boy. I've been told "No" before and actually lived. And, I would have survived in the above instances too had God told them not to support me as proven by the fact that I'm still here and have completed the task. Yet, to be written off in silence and cast aside speaks of a much deeper and cancerous issue within today's Church-at-large regarding spiritual integrity. I've always operated from God's principle of not withholding help from anyone who asks with genuine need and it's in my power to give[58]. To guard my heart and to error on the side of mercy and grace – I give God standing permission to take away my ability to give, rather than making my own decision which requires that I judge another's heart. This is my safeguard to be sure I do not do wrongly withhold or withdraw what God has entrusted to me so I can give. In truth, all we have belongs to God, not us. We are just the earthly stewards of God's riches in glory[59]... Thankfully there are many upon whom He can call to propel my way as I simply trust and obey[60]...

58 Proverbs 3:27; Luke 6:30-31; 1 John 3:16-18; 1 Corinthians 13:7-8

59 John 14:12, 17:10; Ephesians 3:14-21

60 Matthew 6:31-34

Letting Go

I know that many believe life owes us a snack lunch fantasy which hands us trauma in bite-sized easy-to-chew and swallow morsels. But, that's not reality on any level... Instead, it's not uncommon for us to be thrown a little meat on a lot-a-bone. Most of us would rather have it be a cinch by the inch, than hard by the yard... Why? When we're up to our neck in life's alligators, it's hard to remember that our original goal was to drain the swamp. Our cool, calm, and collected exterior gets ruffled and tad bit wrinkled when things land on us without warning. It is under such conditions however, that God stretches us like spandex to grant us unique opportunities to see if we snap back looking like Jesus. But, when we look into the mirror of His Spirit amid the battle...we often discover, to our chagrin, that our reflection better resembles a jackass in tights...

Amid such carnality crushers, we learn who we really are in our raw humanity, how much we really need help, and how tenderly our Father in heaven loves us eternally. Still, that doesn't mean we like life's sucker sandwiches, humble pie, and bitter pills. In reality, troubles in life come to help us run head-on into ourselves, encounter a Savior, consider it all joy, and to overcome by the blood of the Lamb[61]. This journey we call life is nothing more than going to school for Jesus. We're born into this physical existence, thrust into an unfolding reality, confronted with faith's challenge, and ushered out the other end either destined for greatness or damnation based on choice. Our brief sojourn along the corridors of life merely represent God's preparatory plan through which we're called to redirect our rebellion, capture His character, and apprehend His ascension as we let go of this life on our way toward Him. As you can catch a glimpse of that which God has taught me while reading this book, it has likely become obvious that I've been no stranger to life's suspension and God's afterschool class...

Letting go of this life on our way to the next is similar to letting go of our children. Realistically, they were never ours to begin with. They were simply on loan and we are merely the caretakers of their destinies. As parents, we were granted the amazing privilege of participating in their creation, directing their development, fostering their adaptability, and transitioning their autonomy from

61 Revelation 12:11

our faith into the unknowns of their own...after...we have trained them up in the way they should go, so when they're old they'll not depart from it[62]. Please notice the passage does not refer to the middle time between our faith and their realization of their own. Our views and approach will either teach them how to assess this life accurately, define this life selflessly, hold this life loosely, and navigate this life productively, or...imprison their destinies. Either we will push and prod our children to personify that which we never attained as we try to live it out through them vicariously, or we will empower them to discover, embrace, and exemplify that which they were created to be.

When one removes the biological and emotional ties in the human relational equation which tethers us to our children, we find that our kids are merely people upon the earth who stand before a holy and loving God. It is this otherworldly biological and emotional tie which exists between us, that love weaves its thread into our family fabric in life. Though we will ever-remain their parents who love them, the scope and brevity of our parental expression steps back into life's shadows as they spread their wings, leave father and mother, and cling to their own mate[63]. Letting go of our children begins at conception and releasing this life begins at birth. How well we have learned, applied, and navigated the process will be revealed along the journey and underscored at the time of their or our unavoidable departure. Most parents and people struggle for balance in the spiritual process of letting go, letting God, and extending freedom to Him and others in faith. If we truly love God, our kids, and ourselves – we will release that which was never truly ours to begin with, gracefully, so He can carry us all to fruition.

We were created to be recipients and expressions of God's unconditional love for His glory and our good. When we hang onto this life bound by unrealistic expectations, raw materialism, moral demands, and temporal plans – we subject ourselves to a much more difficult process of being delivered from this life into the next. I've learned that God only asks for those things we hang onto, not for those we've already yielded to Him. If you don't believe me, try hanging onto something that hinders your availability, obedience,

62 Proverbs 22:6
63 Genesis 2:21-24; Matthew 19:4-6

or relationship to Him and you'll see what I mean[64]. In my case, I learned He loves me more than I can imagine and that it's far easier to hand Him what He asks for, than it is to wrestle Him for it and leave with a limp[65]...

Resurrection

Thirty years passage delivered me up to my waist in water looking through tear laden eyes over a sea of people as I said, "As an act of my own will...not another's decision...I publically declare that I give my entire life and destiny to Jesus Christ and grant Him permission to direct, use, and send me anywhere at any time to do anything at any cost[66]." I had made my decision to know Christ and the power of His resurrection knowing that I would fellowship in His sufferings to become more like Him[67]. I went under transformation's water[68] that night carried in the arms of a fireball preacher named Fletch... as a broken man who had been baptized as a young boy...a man called to preach at age fifteen, but wandered...a man who owned four companies and could do anything with excellence...and emerged radically altered, resurrected, and on fire to preach the Love, Truth, and mercy of Jesus Christ[69]. Though some said passion's flame would diminish, its fire kindled within me that night burns in my bones to this very day with ever-increasing intensity and has become an inferno within...

This fire...heaven's fire...truth's torch...burns me to dust whenever the word of God cannot pass through me... I am simply a man once undone who now sees the King and has become fully known amid the brush of angel's wings and been re-created, reeducated, redirected, and repatriated in a heavenly country of my own[70]. Since that life-altering reality-changing day in 1987 which brought me in on the world's side of baptism's water driven by mortal existence...I traveled birth's canal and broke forth from eternity's womb into

---

64 Exodus 20:4-5

65 Genesis 32:22-32

66 Matthew 10:8, 28:19-20; Mark 12:30-31; Luke 9:23-26;
John 3:5-8, 4:23-24, 5:17, 7:18, 14:12, 15:15-17, 17:3-26, 20:21-23

67 Philippians 3:7-10

68 2 Peter 3:18-22

69 Jeremiah 1:4-10, 20:9; 23:29; 1 Peter 1:3-9

70 Isaiah 6:1-8; Hebrews 11:13-16

God's glorious light[71]. Oh Lord, pour Your foreknown fuel on my fire, consume my driven dross, fill me with Your word, and conform me to Your Love's likeness this day[72]! So now, each day, and forever more...I forget what is behind, strain ahead, and press on toward the goal to win the prize for which God has called me heavenward in Christ Jesus my Master and my King[73]. Oh Lord, send me...

Choice

Today's out-in-the-open conflict between Judaism, Islam, and Christianity...conservatism, liberalism, and extremism is not a war between people, races, or cultures. Instead, it is a moral conflict between skewed opposing religious and philosophical idealisms being advanced by everyday people, who only partially recognize the other's violations toward God and man as they overlook their own wrongs. It is, in fact, upon this platform God will draw His people to Himself from all tribes and tongues in Love during these final days. Scripture tells us that we as God's people must have faith to please Him and that such faith must believe He both exists and rewards those who earnestly seek Him[74]. That said, it will be through these opposing religious and philosophical views, resulting conflicts, and divine interventions, which those who have opposed, disobeyed, or rejected God will be fully confronted. Everyone upon the earth will crash headlong into the reality that God exists[75]. Likewise, they will be given a final freewill choice to encounter, see, accept, and yield to Jesus Christ through revelation eyes on their way through salvation toward radiance or be allowed to stumble over Jesus the Stone into their eternal destruction[76]. Humanity's time to either choose or reject Jesus Christ is at hand on all levels. Meanwhile, those exercising choice in opposing directions are being identified and segregated by power brokers who are determined to scratch battle lines and build fences in God's sand[77]...

God's call on my life keeps me ever-in eternity's crossfire... Nothing I say or promote is ever aimed at anyone personally, but rather at

71 John 3:19-21
72 Isaiah 1:24-26; Malachi 3:1-3; Romans 8:28-30
73 Philippians 3:13-14
74 Hebrews 11:1-6
75 Philippians 2:9-10
76 1 Peter 2:4-12
77 Exodus 19:5; Psalms 50:12; 1 Corinthians 10:23-24

that which destroys God's desire to bring love, life, and liberty to His people. The battle we face in this life is not between people who merely embody and advance those misguided ideologies they subscribe too. Instead, the battle before us represents a physically manifest spiritual clash pitting God's all-existence character, kingdom, and creation against pervasive, malignant, and compelling evil forces. In truth, God's Love and institutions of both authority and marriage reign over man for His benefit and redemption. That said amid obvious human decline, my life passion is merely fueled by heaven's hope that we as His people will realize and internalize that we who fill roles within those institutions have not administrated either well. If we had – America, the Church, and the World-at-large we find ourselves part of just prior to Christ's return, would not be crashing in dire need of a reaching Savior Who embodies Love Itself...

Weariness

Weariness is real... To maintain our ongoing resilience and survival, it's important that we acknowledge our various types of fatigue and trauma, but not at the cost of disobeying God and His Law of love. If we must withdraw from a situation to regain our composure, perspective, and strength, it is ALWAYS best to obey God's known will prior to pulling back. Why? Obedience is the hinge point and release mechanism for God's grace to flow in our lives. The faster we obey the sooner grace comes to help us weather the storms we face[78]. Yet, if we remove ourselves from a situation prior to doing ALL God called us to do, His grace is not free to flow. When we return later to invest our part on our own terms, we often find that things have degraded due to our disobedience, thereby leaving our heart's door open to enemy invasion. So authorized, the enemy of our souls distorts, magnifies, and multiplies the battles we must fight... If we had only done our part up front as asked, our rightly-exercised retreat "after" we obeyed would have released grace, resulted in rest, and filled us with peace. Why does this matter? Grace is essential to receiving God's promised hope, help, and healing. When we delay our obedience, it turns what we could have received quickly from God...into an extended and painful process which leaves sin's residue hidden away within our hearts to hammer us when we find ourselves least able to stand under its assault...

78 1 Samuel 15:22-23; Psalms 91:14-16; Matthew 11:28-29

Warriors of Rest

Three and a half years into my seven year season in which God had hemmed me in to learn of coming tribulation, He spoke to me about becoming a "Warrior of Rest." I was deeper in the trenches of spiritual war than I had ever been in my entire life. My world consisted of driving 6,000 to 10,000 miles and talking 5,000 to 8,000 minutes on my cell phone per month, conducting business in three states, working a hundred plus hours a week, supporting several in over their heads in life, navigating associated challenges, driving three hours to church on weekends, standing alone in adversity, and listening to God in the midst of it all... At the point He coined His phrase Warrior of Rest, I honestly thought to myself, "Really God...are You serious...how?" The mire of tribulation He had planted me in for the purpose of preparation was so far over my head that becoming a Warrior of Rest almost made sense to my staggered humanity in some strange sort of way. Meanwhile, I had just received vision for making my second walk across the United States as well without being told the actual hour of approaching release. As you can imagine, my spandex was indeed a wee bit stretched providing opportunity once again to see in whose form I would snap back...

As days wore on, prayer deepened, and tribulation increased – I found myself becoming a Warrior of Rest by default within the context of engulfing circumstances whether I knew how to be one, or not. I understood in concept, but struggled to make rest an applied reality as I watched hell unravel everyone's world around me in addition to my own. Cancers were everywhere, companies were failing, churches were compromising, economies were wavering, homes were crumbling, moralities were degrading...and all considered abnormal was becoming normalized as God allowed me to see beyond... Finally, my only means of internal survival was to let go of everything...take my hands off...sit back for the ride... and simply rest in Jesus as He carried me across the battlefield training my hands for victory in Him. Though things around me looked impassable, He led me through in a manner which, in retrospect, still seems impossible as I sit and write about it this day... In a nutshell and without shame, my life has simply been a non-stop blur from redemption to revelation regarding human shortcoming, God's transformation, and love's radical expression on an ever-recurring cycle in sync with His plan. Some things can only be learned and refined in love's fire...

At the end of prior cycles in life during my earlier years, I sometimes made the mistake of thinking that I was fully aware and had finally arrived into the fullness of God's call on my life. Yet, before long I soon discovered that I had merely topped another step in the staircase of my destiny, thereby revealing the likelihood that I would soon step up yet again as God reached deeper, called higher, and stretched me further than ever before. And then, I gained revelation about compartmentalized life, how blindly we lay spiritual weaponry aside, learned of "One Room Theology" in which God lives to wield love's arsenal 24/7 on behalf of His people, and that our rise to spiritual battle on victory's level never allows the enemy to advance. From this position – we can swing the sword around the clock as we hope in the Lord...renew our strength... soar on the wings of eagles...run and not grow weary...walk and never faint as we dwell in the shelter and rest in the shadow of the Almighty[79]. But, with knowledge comes responsibility[80].... This dear friend is the nature of God, the classroom of enlightenment[81], and the process of growth. As a result of His mercy, God has granted me privilege to touch heaven, change earth, and fight the fight as a Warrior of Rest. We stop where we think we can go, but God always calls where He knows we can go...

Running or Resting

Jacob wrestled with God and emerged Israel, the namesake of God's chosen[82]. Yet, we as God's people were are also invited into His presence to enter His rest[83]. Though circumstance and stakes demand that we enter the battle and fight fiercely at times before God grants what we ask for, we must be sure that we wage war on His terms rather than our own[84]. Though God blessed Jacob, renamed him Israel, and through him birthed a nation – Jacob left the struggle walking with a limp[85]. As we rise through the ranks and

79 Isaiah 40:31; Psalms 91:1

80 Luke 12:47-48

81 John 6:44-45

82 Genesis 32:22-32

83 Joshua 21:43-45; 2 Chronicles 20:27-30; Psalms 100:1-5; Matthew 11:28-30

84 John 1:47, 5:16-30, 7:16-18, 14:9-27, 17:3-19

85 Genesis 32:22-32

procure our positions of destiny in the Lord's army, those injuries we acquire and struggles we navigate in the conflict possess potential to either become victory-reminiscent battle scars useful in the Master's hands[86]...or fatal wounds that leave us lifeless in war's aftermath eternally dead[87]. We are God's people! We must remain ever-aware that the battles in life belong to Him. We were given dominion over the earth and responsibility to love one another. Yet, it is God's job to rule over His people, not ours. We may not understand another person's path or relationship with God, but we can let go and let God because we know He's in control[88]. When we stop wrestling with God in our demand that He and others do things our way...when we get ourselves out of His way...then...and only then...will we enter and become Warriors of Rest...

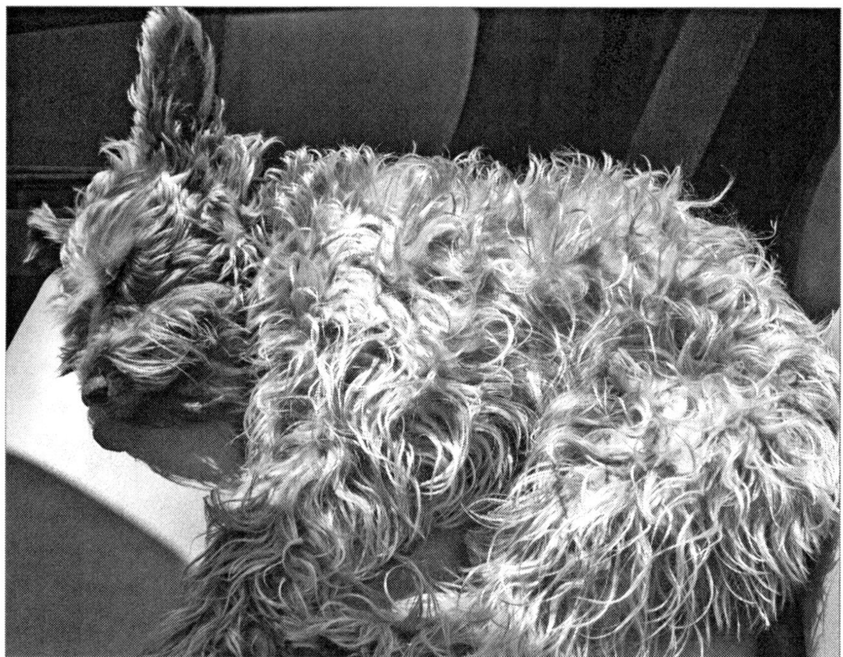

Amid life's hurricanes, even Bud became a Warrior of Rest

86 Romans 12:1-2; 2 Timothy 2:19-21

87 Matthew 6:14-15, 7:1-5, 19:3-8; James 3:13-18, 4:1-12; 1 John 3:16-18, 4:19-21; Revelation 21:7-8

88 Mark 4:26-27

The kid, a slingshot, and mischief in the making – 1962

In front of the 77 foot 7 inch tall Kerrville Cross on I-10 – 2011

Walking into the light of destiny on America's Gulf Coast – 2011

Chapter 13
Light Has Come

"This is the verdict: Light has come into the world, but men loved darkness instead of light because their deeds were evil. Everyone who does evil hates the light, and will not come into the light for fear his deeds will be exposed. But whoever lives by the truth comes into the light, so that it may be seen plainly that what he has done has been done through God" (John 3:19-21).

Throughout history, we find those responsible for life's greatest discoveries faced grueling setbacks during their vision-rich creative quests. To the casual observer still in the dark on matters needing illumination…a string of perceived failures by the inventor-to-be incites doubt in that luminary's capability or character before the public's eyes, not confidence. And yet, it is in fact, the encountered challenges, set-backs, and near-misses that revealed wrong thinking, exposed wrong methods, and re-oriented wrong actions, setting victors-to-be on a trail toward deeper enlightenment than those who sit in the dark convinced they know all. Please consider the following account drawn from the Smithsonian and other sources…

Thomas Alva Edison was one of history's most tenacious inventors. Every time you flip an electric light switch, you enjoy the fruit of an elusive victory that long evaded his grasp…the incandescent light bulb. Edison did not really invent the electric light – he simply refined it to better suit certain applications. Arc lights similar to today's street lights already existed prior to his efforts to create a better light bulb, but were found to be too bright for use inside people's homes. Most people typically used gas lights inside their houses, but the open and flickering nature of their flames made them both dangerous and undesirable. As a result, Edison waded into the equation to perfect indoor light… His greatest challenge to create a refined incandescent bulb came when he was faced with finding the perfect filament (wire inside bulb) capable of burning over prolonged periods. In 1879, after filling more than 40,000 pages with notes and testing over 1,600 materials including coconut fiber, fishing line, and human hair – he discovered the perfect filament…carbonized bamboo.

Though Edison did not technically invent the light bulb, his design improvements and arrangement of supporting light system components to include electricity generators, wires, fixtures, and more were accredited to his innovative insights. When asked by a local reporter one day how it felt to be a failure after trying unsuccessfully so many times to invent the light bulb...Edison was said to have replied, "I did not fail young man – I simply learned many ways a light bulb will not work." Edison was an inspiration to many because he leaned into his task with undaunted perseverance, until victory was gained. It is reported that Edison once said that, "Opportunity is missed by most people because it is dressed in overalls and looks like work." Due to one man's tenacity, light pierced the darkness in a new way and changed the world...

Anyone can give up, but only few will stand. In reality, all setbacks encountered in life anywhere between inception-and-victory are very simply – opportunities to learn. Failure merely represents fear's period punctuating the end of opportunity's sentence when concluded by – I quit. Being courageous enough to keep running the gauntlet of ridicule and condemnation while being beaten by the bitter and belligerent ultimately emancipates those who persevere and stay the course to overcome with joy (James 1:2-5). Anyone can cave in, withdraw, and hide in the shadows afraid to face life's many trials while hammered by those who lack the guts to risk failure, fall down, get up, dust off, and try again while everyone's watching (John 3:19-21). It's nothing new under the sun when those who judge our lives smile knowingly to our faces when we're looking and laugh behind our backs after we've gone. Though it hurts to our core, dear friend – that's just the way it goes rubbing elbows with those we're to love in a world dominated by rulers, authorities, and powers of darkness bent on our destruction. Yet in the midst of it all, satan remains a defeated loser...

When we choose to live surrounded by world tradition, social acceptance, and the status quo rather than in pursuit of truth at all costs, we are choosing to live far beneath all God designed us to be, do, experience, and contribute to the kingdom of God's expression on earth... Yet, it is within the fears, fires, and failures of life that we discover our weaknesses to a degree that grants us passage...if willing...into God's glorious adventure to become all He created us to be. Though faith has a way of calling us beyond discretion's role as the better part of valor – everyone who goes out on life's limb to reach for the impossible, falls out of the tree landing in a puff of dust dazed and alone sometimes. Sadly, when what seemed like a great idea earlier doesn't pan out to our liking – many of us refuse to look within as we scan the crowd around instead to find another upon which to cast our blame...

Sadly, when our prior valiant plan doesn't pan out as imagined – many lose perspective, lose courage, lose hope, and lose themselves if not nailed to Jesus Christ. Building our own house has a way of not working out so well for us or those nearby, when we sidestep the advice of heaven's architect (Psalms 127:1). If we will re-submit our self-guided plans to the Master Builder however... our misguided efforts will be overwritten, re-directed, and re-manufactured to become the mansion His foresight envisioned, His design empowered, and His love prepared according to His riches in glory (Psalms 139:13-16; Jeremiah 29:11-14; Ephesians 2:19-22; John 14:1-6). In this life we will face troubles many and bitter – but, God will restore our lives from the depths, increase our honor, and comfort us once again in the midst of those who need what our experience and transformed hearts have to offer (Psalms 71:20-21; Matthew 10:8). Though some will hang onto every perceived mistake we have ever made or sin we may have committed – others needing courage to brave God's life re-creation in their own world will recognize obvious insight and watch our backs as they benefit from where we've been because God gives grace to the humble...

In our individual quests to lay hold of those things dear to us in life... we often fail most miserably at that which we long for deep within. And yet, in the midst of failure...we are confronted with ourselves, experience redemption's fire, encounter a Savior, and rise from our ashes reborn – if willing. It is from within the failure of our rough-cut humanity as we acknowledge God, that He makes our path straight beyond our own understanding (Proverbs 3:5-6). Likewise, it is on this path, heaven's path...that we are truly re-created and equipped to realize that for which we were destined and have longed...God's way...and can win. Based on personal observation and experience, it appears that many fortunate enough to travel a less volatile pathway than those of us who are called to engage in "Black Ops for Jesus," miss out on God's intended message more often than not. Please understand that I am extremely thankful that many do not face or feel the level of trauma my journey has encountered. Yet, God's loving direction punches a tunnel through life's torment to enlighten, purify, and deliver my inner constitution from death to life empowered by God's love...

As believers in Jesus Christ, we are faced with a choice between love or hate...forgiveness or judgment...freedom or bondage...blessing or curses...life or death (Deuteronomy 28-30). In light of the two greatest commandments, we are called to love God and love people with all we possess (Matthew 22:37-41; Mark 12:30-31). As I have said, God writes our story line and forges His unique message within each of us according to His purpose...not ours. Consider Jesus' disciples for instance – a rag-tag bunch of misfits-turned-zealots like tax collectors, smelly fishermen, doctors, prostitutes, doubters, adulterers, lepers, Samaritans, thieves, and Pharisees – to name a few. People's pathway is not about sin, failure, or social acceptability...it's about heaven's heat, refining fire, and the connected human process of testing and approving the perfect will of eternity's Holy God and obeying Him (Romans 12:1-2). We are called to run the race marked out for us according to the rules in light of God's purpose while working out our own salvation with fear and trembling to change the world, starting with our own (Philippians 2:12-13; Hebrews 12:1-12; 2 Peter 1:3-11). Running that race requires that we identify our course while beating through life's brambles. Amid our journey, we must keep our eyes on Christ because people judge the external...while...God weighs the invisible. Likewise, people crucify the teachable, while God opposes the unacceptable...chase the material, while God purifies the corruptible...and marry the temporal as only God offers the unalienable.

When we live in a blind-eyed fashion putting our lives in the crossfire between opposing forces or philosophies, thereby polluting or estranging ourselves from both to varied degrees...we can no longer be faithful to either – especially God (Matthew 6:24; 2 Thessalonians 2:7-12; James 4:1-8). Faithfulness toward God is rooted in Jesus Christ alone Who has become our wisdom, holiness, righteousness, and redemption (1 Corinthians 1:30). Wisdom, holiness, righteousness, and redemption become a reality rising from within us through our "blameless" Christ-centered expression of purity, fidelity, and unity toward God and others. Though we all struggle, stumble, and stray in our hearts through our daily deeds to some degree...being blameless before God simply means that we remain willing to identify, confess, and turn from sin as we pursue forgiveness from God and the one who we wronged in our quest to honor Jesus, as Lord. As we stay in the game and place our sin beneath the blood of Jesus Christ...we are made blameless in God's sight...not sinless. Only Jesus was tempted in all ways that we are and remained without sin... So, when our decisions and lifestyles separate us from Him at any level, our ability to do things with eternal worth and impact is diminished relative to our level of separation (John 15:5).

When our selfish desires drive us to make-and-act on wrong decisions which harm God's heart and distance us from Him, we have for all intents and purposes, become unfaithful and adulterous in His eyes (Isaiah 29:13-16; Ezekiel 9:8-10; James 4:1-8). Anything we place more importance on than our relationship with Jesus Christ becomes a mistress in our relationship with Him, making us unfaithful (Matthew 6:24). Though you may consider it irrelevant – how many of us have traded church for golf, ignored another's need, broken our commitment, or withheld love's touch...all because of our personal flirtation with a sunny day, new car, investment plan, ball game, personal judgment, busy schedule, inflexible view, unforgiving heart, or God's call on the other person's life? At whatever point we put self, things, or behaviors...ahead of...our selfless devotion to and lifestyle love toward God and others, the world's mistress just strutted through our heart's door in life (Genesis 4:7; Revelation 3:19-22).

The presence of any "mistress" in our relationship with God or anyone else proves we are either thinking about or actively cheating on Him, giving evidence to the existence of prideful independence within us (Isaiah 14:12-15; Ezekiel 28:1-10; Matthew 5:27-28). If we are cheating or being unfaithful to the one we claim to love through our unbridled thoughts, words, or deeds, we are not emulating or acting in God's love (1 Corinthians 13:7-8). When we neglect our reciprocal expression of authentic love toward Jesus who is the Living Truth...we make our lives both vulnerable and receptive to satanic deception subjecting ourselves to hell's delusion found in the enemy's lie (1 Corinthians 13:7-8; John 14:6; Romans 1:18-32; 2 Thessalonians 2:9-12). If we subject ourselves to the powerful delusion God sends when we reject truth refusing to be saved from ourselves on His terms...our ability to perceive Him, self, others, and our surroundings through His eyes, ears, and heart gets built on a lie. As a result and while oblivious to all, we become hell's willing partner in destroying ourselves and those God has given to us. This is adultery's consequence as the by-product of our independence from God as we prostitute ourselves with the world around us... After all the romance, after all the sex, and after the honeymoon that was to have lasted forever has worn off...ultimately what makes-or-breaks our marriage to Jesus and our mates...is our individual and combined philosophies of life, love, and God. Though adultery's voice will call from the shadows to seduce, reduce, and abuse – no one can steal the real deal rooted in Christ alone...

Independence is a false sense of freedom rooted in rebellion and ending in bondage. Our humility-based submission to God and others remains the only avenue toward real freedom in Jesus Christ that we have (Mark 14:36; 2 Corinthians 3:17; Ephesians 5:21). Independence and infidelity are one-in-the-same. Independence destroys biblical agreement and its power between God and man...members of one body...man and wife...and the members of one's household (Matthew 10:34-40; 18:19-20; Romans 12:4-8; 1 Corinthians 12:12-30). Therefore, it is critical for us as Christians to realize that personal unfaithfulness toward God or others withdraws value, creates jealousy, causes pain, imposes rejection, incites anger, and spurs revenge. Our own infidelities will cause other people to react or struggle with sin (Luke 17:1-4; Galatians 5:26). Spiritual prostitution is inseparably-linked to independence. Its by-product manifests as relational unfaithfulness which legally or legalistically justifies all levels of divorce due to the absence of unconditional love and forgiveness (Matthew 19:3-8). Are you now up to your neck and asking yourself why I've traveled this path to put matrimonial struggle and divorce on the table? Please let me explain...

If truly looking – we can easily see attitudes and events foretold in Scripture are playing out all over the earth right now at unprecedented levels! Jesus told us we could recognize the season of His return...look around...it's everywhere! Lies, hatred, selfishness, rebellion, greed, pride, abuse, exploitation, arrogance, defiance, and hard-heartedness roam our streets as our world is hammered by storms, earthquakes, disasters, famines, diseases, and wars spotlighted on television, radio, and the rags we read. Yet, we must realize that such attitudes and events are merely the back story to heaven's main feature. From cover-to-cover – the entire bible is about marriage. Heaven's Bridegroom is coming to marry His bride at the wedding feast of the Lamb. Why do I say that? Simple... Jesus Christ came to earth to be crucified dead, buried, resurrected, and restored back to right hand of His Father where He weeps, woos, and waits for His bride to rouse herself toward radiance in her preparation for Him. Within the imagery of marriage, Jesus reaches to romance His adulterous bride (church-us) back to Himself through unconditional love, forgiveness...to wash away her spots and wrinkles...to make her holy and radiant... and to fully prepare her to marry Him at the wedding feast of the Lamb (Ephesians5:25-27; Revelation 19:7). Therefore, we must identify, resolve, and overcome the central issues of infidelity and divorce within or around us if our hope, existence, and entrance into the presence of Jesus Christ is to occur. If we truly love God and others unconditionally just as He first loved us, we must bring our sin into the light on a practical level as proof of our authenticity before God and man (John 3:19; 21, 14:12, 17:6). Otherwise, we are destined to live at an address, in a neighborhood, and with a partner we will dread...forever (Revelations 21:8).

Both the subject and the ruling spirits of independence and divorce have long-separated God's people from each other, ministry, and intimacy with Jesus Christ above all issues! This said, I believe God has allowed the issue of divorce to deeply invade His Church as an act of His mercy with divine purpose over the past 63 years since Israel became a nation. Likewise, I believe this to be God's crowning effort to reveal what is not working between man and Himself as He gives us the undeserved chance to "get it right" before we find ourselves locked outside the banquet hall at the wedding feast of the Lamb (Matthew 25:13). Surrounded by overwhelming human, historic, and heavenly indicators – it appears very possible that His season of return is knocking at the door of our generation. If this is true, our rise to radiance and subsequent marriage to the King of Kings on that day is an issue of critical import worthy of our consideration!

Whether a smelly fisherman-turned-apostle...a Samaritan woman-turned-evangelist...a blind man-turned-witness...a prostitute-turned-friend...a Pharisee-turned-writer...or a visionary-turned-light bulb inventor – God still uses the lowly, unlikely, unworthy, and undaunted to teach those who perceive themselves to be wise (1 Corinthians 1:26-2:5). In keeping with Scriptural pattern - it only makes sense that God would call, the devil would oppress, and man would discount those ravaged by divorce...as God's chosen vessels to which He would impart liberating revelation regarding what it takes to get heaven's matrimony right. Just because people live with only one partner under the banner of marriage in this life, does not prove their qualified grasp on God's one-flesh institution in their personal relationship with Jesus Christ adequate to secure their position in His presence in eternal life. As I've previously stated with regard to one's ordained purpose, message, and audience – it seems biblically probable that God would pull one through the fires of infidelity, divorce, heartache, brokenness, remarriage, and restoration with its persecutions – as He forges a message and prepares His people for eternal marriage with Him on that day (Exodus 9:16, 10:1-2; Daniel 3; Mark 10:29-31; Romans 9:16-26). We all know that our human flesh will die and return to the earth – it is the harvest that occurs as a conclusion to the birth, adolescence, adulthood, and old age cycle that mirrors God's immutable character, law, and plan. Yet, our entrance into the presence of God in the life to come is determined by those ordained governing principles and resulting character traits produced through the ongoing crucifixion of our old nature, not based on people's approval. Genuine love is rarely fun, easy, or convenient as it always protects, trusts, hopes, and perseveres with another in need or who is in way over their head in life (1 Corinthians 13:7-8). In most cases, obeying God and loving others is challenging at best as He calls us from the ordinary to beyond-the-accepted to touch others for Him. Please let me share one of God's greatest love stories to His people…

Heaven's epoch spins into action around 750 B.C. surrounding the governmental reigns of Uzziah, Jotham, Ahaz, Hezekiah, and Jeroboam II near the end of Israel's prolonged season of peace, abundance, prosperity, and blatant sin prior to its eventual fall in 722 B.C. Named to mean "salvation or liberation," Hosea found himself called of God to live out a heart-wrenching living portrayal that would cast his life under scrutiny's feet to declare heaven's message-of-the-hour to a wayward people. Though Hosea's mission unfurled during a time of perceived prosperity…Israel's northern kingdom was led by corrupt leaders and overrun by family instability, unbridled immorality, social division, open idolatry, and impoverished people. Israel acknowledged Jehovah to a degree, but refused to forsake their increasing worship of foreign gods that spurred His heart to jealousy, anger, and retribution toward His unfaithful covenant partner. As God's lower-key warnings went in one ear and out the other, man's sinful posture forced Him to turn up the heat on His communication method of choice. Time for talk was over and action was required. Therefore, God dispatched Hosea to enter a social situation that would pierce Israel's façade of declared moral uprightness by taking a prostitute for His wife in full view of the world. Can you imagine the outrage sweeping America's wayward body of Christ today if God were to call a well-known leader to marry and love a prostitute unconditionally in full view of the church by faithfully attending and sitting in the front row each week as though nothing were out of the ordinary? In God's eyes, that was the point… Both then and as it would be now, it is always easier to point our finger at perceived sin in the life of another than to look within ourselves…

Returning to Hosea's story, we see that Gomer eventually bolted to resume her evening trade after bearing him three children. But, God blocked her path with thorn bushes and confused her way so she could not find her old lovers. Likewise, He exposed her perversity, lack of appreciation, and drew her back toward her husband. After God laid her bare, stripped her of her options, and brought her to the realization of what she really had within the love of her husband...he sent Hosea to go and show his love to her once again and bring her home. Imagine the scene...Hosea arrives to the brothel...goes in to get his wife actively involved in adultery... lays his money down to buy her...looks deep in her eyes amid her elevated breathing and perspiration after she just left a lover...and tells her that she needs to come home, stop being a prostitute who is having sex with other men – and that she is to come live together with him for the rest of their lives. Within the confines of your own understanding and experience in marriage, can you imagine how Hosea felt? Really...can you? Had God set Hosea up to fail...incited him to sin...and then cast him adrift on the sea of eternity without redemption? To the contrary, God chose to portray His sovereign purpose, love, forgiveness, and promised restoration to those who least deserved it through Hosea's life and love to an unfaithful woman. God was using Hosea's life to portray the unconditional nature of His covenant with his wandering people who were ever-bent on chasing foreign lovers... Does any of this strike a chord in current reality as you consider America or within your own soul? Please remember that the entertainments of our heart that wedge themselves between us and our Loving Savior declare us guilty (Matthew 5:27).

Most of us think or believe we want God to use our lives to do something noble or world-changing... But, at what cost do we pull the plug and draw the line on where we will go in Jesus' name? Receiving God's vision and acting on His directives in a dying world extracts a have price. Clearly, vision without investment is valueless (Colossians 2:18-19). Heaven's vision within us is verified by obeying God's voice and staying in the game until victory comes like those who fought the good fight before us (Mark 14:32-42, John 14:12, 17:4, 26, 20:17; Acts 1:1-11). We love to listen to tales spun and adventure lived by those who see through God's eyes, step out, crumble in battle, and rise from the ashes to fight for victory on yet another day. If we had been near enough to observe the inner world of their war-torn trajectory toward triumph however...we would have likely judged them indecent, invalid, or insufferable... and become part of the jungle tribesmen killing them as happened to Missionary Jim Elliott or a member of a congregation rebuking them for misunderstood decisions (Acts 4:13-14)... Anytime we do God's in-the-trenches work, religion's judgment is waiting just around the corner to reduce us to hamburger – it's not a matter of if, but when (Hosea 9:8). Sadly, many who will benefit from God's word-of-the-hour will oppose the messenger to silence the message while never realizing that the one whom God sent was not an enemy, but merely one who had a different job description and was simply trying to obey Him for the benefit of others. Unless people press in to pursue God with whole hearts, discover their purpose, and keep their eyes on Him in the process, they will devour one another on the human plane to rob themselves of destiny. I have watched this reality destroy marriages, friendships, churches, businesses, and futures for almost forty years (Ephesians 6:12)...

Religion may rate sin on a scale from one-to-ten, when in God's eyes...all wrongdoing...whether by omission or commission...is sin and grieves His heart (James 4:17; 1 John 5:17). I've always been amazed how someone can go to prison for drugs, assault, robbery, embezzlement, and sometimes even murder...get radically saved while on the inside...and come out to be accepted as a soul-winning powerhouse. And yet, one can go through a struggle deemed by religion as socially unacceptable...and the weary warrior is excluded from religion's ranks as though they have committed the unpardonable sin... Unless we walk a mile in someone's shoes, we lack the experience and depth of understanding that person gained while in the furnace of affliction (Isaiah 48:9-11; Daniel 3). Every great or celebrated figure in history ventured out, fell in defeat, weathered rejection, and experienced isolation until they pushed through to victory – every one of them. It was on their defeat-to-victory trail that they suffered scorn, encountered death, experienced burial, and rose into new life capable of helping others while the less tenacious around them, later enjoyed the arm-chair version of that warrior's trauma without personal risk or cost (Hebrews 5:8-9; John 14:12, 17:3-19, 24-26; Acts 1:1-9). Now that we've traced a path together through prior centuries, heritage, childhood, buttercups, motorcycles, God's call, high school, orchards, warehouses, relationship, parenthood, business, catastrophe, America, Europe, Afghanistan, Pakistan, Israel, and the lives of some I've encountered along the way...please sit back as I bring more of my own back story into the light...

Ever since I was young, I have always been a love-based relationalist compelled to meet, know, embrace, and help the downcast and struggling of this world known as "underdogs" in life. Though understanding and making godly application of its efforts would take me on a journey of trial and heartache to grasp, I learned to appreciate its value. As a little guy, I sat in church leaning across mom's lap so she could rub my back. I enjoyed smiles, liked hugs, and loved how it felt to know that I was accepted and at peace with those important to me. I remember eating lunch on the front lawn of my first grade girlfriend's house after church one Sunday afternoon many years ago... I was happy, liked everybody, and just wanted to be friends. And yet, my efforts to understand and integrate with others grew more challenged the older I grew. It seemed that I was either misunderstood, in trouble, or on the outside isolated from those around me for reasons that were simply beyond me as I did all in my power to get along... I had no clue why fourth graders came across the school yard to give a second grader like me grief...why my third grade teacher took her home life out on me...why I was so fortunate to be silently elected the class idiot...why the cool crowd laid me waste before girls I liked...or why the school tough guys considered me the one worthy of their testosterone-driven torture as I went out of my way to get along...no clue...at least then anyway...

Making my way through school's obligatory twelve year trek, I found myself to be an average athlete in most sports I played, being blamed for the jock's mistakes or robbed of glory when I made a good play. Landing in high school however, two significant things occurred in my life – I turned out for wrestling...and...fell in love with

Six point pin wrestling victory as High School senior – 1975

a girl who would later find God... I concluded that turning out for an individual sport would at least give me a chance to be rewarded based on my personal efforts and performance, not the ego-centric whims of others. I learned a great deal about the value of personal effort, focus, sacrifice, tenacity, commitment, self-discipline, relationship, and myself during four years of wrestling and getting to know the young lady I loved. When I gave all I had to give, I won within myself whether left the mat or situation physically victorious or defeated. But, if I coasted through practice or took the easy way out in circumstances, I lost on the inside despite the physical outcome because knew I could have done better. In retrospect, God was revealing the satisfaction associated with doing one's best...or... the corresponding setbacks when I chose to do otherwise... Please remember that I was called to preach at age 15...had chosen to avoid my buddies' rejection...had already started my first business during my sophomore year of high school...had entered the party scene... and had indirectly distanced myself from church. Meanwhile, my girlfriend and I had grown inseparable and were voted most likely to succeed in marriage by our senior year. Classmates rarely talked about one of us without referring to the other...

We got engaged following graduation from high school in 1975 eventually marrying over the next year though both sets of parents had diplomatically pre-suggested we slow down. Young love rarely listens to wisdom... Just prior to our marriage, my folks gave me 2 acres on one of our family farms where we established our first home just in time to move in once married. Young, losing a job due to drought in an agricultural area, starting a repair business, still mixed up in the party scene, and not attending church regularly – our marriage got off to a less-than-beneficial start as husband and wife. As days passed, business grew, parties continued, and communications between us took on a more impersonal tone. We began drifting apart while partially entwined in the back story of other people's lives. Due to mutually unresolved misperceptions and my poor decisions, misguided actions, and personal weakness rooted in me not yet fully knowing who God had created me to be, she went to stay with her parents. My heart was devastated as I found myself the lone husband of a couple voted most likely to succeed...

well known in my community…feeling devalued by her departure… too embarrassed to face friends…and ill-equipped to resolve my sense of rejection in a right manner due to my distance from God. So, I wallowed in my perceived loss, accepted defeat amid my crisis without reaching to my wife, partied more, called another woman I knew, and dove deeper into my selfish insecurities to medicate my carnal desires and need for acceptance. In retrospect, my actions proved that I was more concerned about protecting my cloudy self-image than looking out for my wife's welfare and being a good man. As the result of my being too young, lacking identity, situational commitment, selfish decisions, and wimpy reconciliatory efforts, our marriage ended. I continued unwittingly heavenward in my compromise and unfolding discovery of who God created me to be as a man, husband, and father called according to His purpose…

Subsequent months fell by the wayside in our new relationship as our unending parties, unbridled sexuality, and wandering spirituality seemed to chart their own course… Little did I know, that God's plan was unfolding around me as I delivered myself into His hands to encounter love, confrontation, discipline, and to be launched into heaven's experience of ongoing transformation. Still, our lifestyle continued making it almost impossible for us to really know each other as our lives hung beneath clouds of spiritual oppression. Our relationship was more connected by party schedule, than truly getting to know and love the person we were with. Eventually, we married in June 1979 in my soon-to-be in-law's living room with our first child on the way. During coming months, God began drawing and speaking to me again in prayer. One day, my wife and I re-connected with old friends who invited us to the church they were attending. Several weeks later while we were sitting in the living room talking I said, "We've got kids on the way, we have to clean up our act and get back to church." So the next Sunday, we took our friends up on their offer and went to church. On New Year's Eve 1980, I made the first and only New Year's resolution I ever kept – to stop partying.

As mentioned in a prior chapter…we got involved in church, had several more children, built onto our home, and kicked off additional businesses over subsequent years. As our heads cleared on the heels of the 1980 New Year's resolution, our true personalities emerged setting in motion an entirely new and unanticipated relational cross-tension between us that rose out of our unresolved pasts and opposing world views. She was a great stay-at-home mom who loved her kids – but up to her neck in young children, household duties, life aspirations, unresolved hurts, mounting frustration, and caring for a new husband whose life blueprint unintentionally antagonized her world at every turn. I was an innovative visionary called beyond the box to overcome the impossible and who worked like a dog to love and provide for our family, uphold our marriage, build our future, squelch my insecurities, and validate my undefined identity through achievement, not God's design. Though well-intentioned, my path was littered with mistakes, poor decisions, and associated repercussions in her life and mine.

Impasse became part of an almost daily routine as our efforts to communicate and resolve recurring issues left us at odds feeling hurt, devalued, angry, and increasingly detached. She longed for love as she hoped to escape discouragement and domestic demands...I longed for love, support, and peace within. We both felt empty, alone, and cast adrift as individual expressions of disfavor cut the other's heart in half... Unable to weather long hours, mounting responsibilities and the growing storm, I re-directed my early morning bookkeeping sessions toward bible reading and prayer as I looked to my only hope, Jesus Christ... Not long thereafter, I prayed that prayer, "God break me and make me yours..." Over subsequent months as portrayed in prior pages, the rest became history as her and our four children's departure dismantled my reality unveiling itself while I sat in an unlit living room in my recliner...alone. As mentioned, the meltdown precipitated my closure of four companies...working for a large client...chasing God with a whole heart...rebuilding my world through Scripture... and rising a new creation through the waters of baptism in 1987 impassioned to preach the unconditional love and forgiveness of Jesus that I had freely received (Luke 7:36-50; Mark 14:1-9). To my yet-to-discover dismay, even deeper trials lay ahead as God simply gave me more of what I had prayed for...

In June 1988, after surviving prior battles and rising from affliction's ash, I remarried, starting life anew with a dear woman who had likewise navigated her own redemption story riddled by heartache very different from my own. Though my journey had filled me full of God's word, carried me through several prolonged fasts, untold hours in prayer, and my bones burned with fire to preach – I was still a bit cloudy on how to fully embrace God's call on my life... Our marriage began with a 2,500 mile honeymoon, a series of unexpected earthquakes, buying a much needed van, and returning home to losing my job, a newly formed Brady Bunch of seven, and feeling forced to re-open two companies in our newly-convened mutual quest to survive. Our plan was to re-open my former diesel repair and commercial fruit tree nursery businesses, expand nursery sales...operate the diesel repair for cash flow while waiting for our first crop cycle...and to then close the shop and run one business for a simplified life. Sounds great in theory...right? So, I sat down with my long term lenders to discuss our business plans and gained their approval. My wife and I set our direction...embarked on our team-decision...and journeyed down the path set before us. We took on trade shows and boosted nursery sales more than 300 percent the first year – before a famous actress made an untimely comment about harmless plant regulators on Sixty Minutes that decimated the entire fruit industry around us. Death and life truly are in the power of the tongue (Proverbs 18:21). Now obligated to following through on a much expanded contract fruit tree production effort, cash flow fell to the ground dead buried in a staggered agricultural lending environment. As a result, our entire family worked like dogs to grow 180,000 new trees on a shoestring without help or financing before finally securing a new lender later that year.

Breathing a sigh of relief, we took on our second trade show armed with the largest single source of much-sought-after apple grafting wood in the USA boosting sales and tree prices again and feeling blessed! We prepared for our contract tree production and field grafting work over the next few months waiting for spring. Weather patterns were irregular catapulting us into the earliest spring on record in our area with three weeks of season vanishing into thin air, thereby putting us under the gun as plants exploded into action early. As March 1989 arrived and rootstocks were delivered, crews were assembled, and daily 200 mile round-trips to job sites were made with workers as we ran our planting crews 100 miles away by two-way radio. We were up at 4:00 AM and to bed by midnight six days a week over a 5 week period leaving us looking like bombed out barns barraged by dust... Meanwhile, we had cash in-hand to pay our operating line that was coming due, but had been given permission by the bank officer to use our funds to propel our planting efforts forward under extraordinary circumstances – being told they would simply roll our note to cover technicalities with all being fine. As a result, we trusted what we were told, used the funds, and protected everyone's interests except our own by completing the planting and grafting work on time amid brutal premature heat. When we finally arrived to the bank 2 weeks later to take care of the details – we were accused of misappropriating funds, their prior approval was over-turned, and the lid on our $300,000 operating line, slammed tight.

Now faced with farming 285,000 trees without financing or hired labor during the season to come, we and our in-home work brigade (kids) did what we needed to do while running ditch water, pulling weeds, snipping branches, and everything else entailed in producing the highest quality plants we had ever grown in my soon-to-be 20 years in business. As August 1989 came-and-went, I began a dialogue with the Lord regarding His call on my life, not knowing how to retreat from business to participate, and giving Him permission to make the unidentified but necessary transition His way. Several months after that prayer and over the course of seven days, the Holy Spirit whispered "You're going to lose everything in the winter." Not real thrilled, but aware that it was God, I told a few friends before heaven's voice slipped into the shadows later to land us in early December 1989 with prior winter lows that season still having not dropped below +17 degrees F. Thirty six hours later...plummeting temperatures were falling out the bottom of the thermometer at -37 degrees F accompanied by a 25-30 mph east wind. Our nursery was nearly destroyed at the hard cost of about $800,000, ripping us from growing national distribution to near homelessness within a matter months. We were the only nursery among those damaged in the US that year that refused to sell injured trees, thinking they would heal if not transplanted. Our bank closed in, long-term customers who believed in us paid off their contracts early to get us through...the bank took the money... and we farmed another season without funds while exercising an injury clause in our contracts. Early in the spring of 1990, as we did our best to get through to the end we ventured into youth ministry at our local church. A year later, we filled 92% of our orders and closed our doors with customers satisfied yet, ourselves bankrupt. With all of this happening during the first two and a half years of our marriage, I'm sure you can imagine the weight which descended upon two people already pummeled by life. When we pray dangerous prayers giving God permission to have His way, He speaks and things happen...

My wife and I remained involved in youth ministry as I went to work selling for a California-based nursery. Interestingly, I was told the job was given to another while I was standing in my mountain gear at the pay phone ready to climb Mount Rainier August 1991, before hanging up the phone saying, "Well God, me and You are going to climb this mountain" and I hit the trail. After making the climb and getting back to base camp, I called my wife who excitedly told me that the firm had called back to give me the brokerage position because the other candidate had declined. Several years later in 1995, I made arrangements with the nursery I brokered for, sold everything, and we moved to Colorado at God's direction through a series of miracles. It was at this time while in an extended fast, that the Lord compelled me to start BattleCry Ministries based on Jeremiah 4:19. Later, while on the dean's list at Bible College the Holy Spirit probed me as I sat doing my assignment for the next day. The still small voice of God asked, "What are you doing?" I replied, "Doing my work and going to school." A few minutes later, He nudged me again to remind me that He had called me to preach, not go to school. In retrospect, sitting in those classrooms was way easier than sitting in His... So, I withdrew from school and launched out to preach, that's another story all of its own. It was during our time in Colorado that I was prayed over and received my double-portion experience in 1997 spoken of in earlier chapters herein. Heaven's timelines, transitions, and tensions were escalating around us and between us...

In 1998, we moved back to Western Washington, worked, and preached revivals before returning to our Eastern Washington home town in 2000. Now, ten years after a forty day fast in which God told me I would preach across America...my wife had her best job...we navigated challenges between us...and I was called to pray over a sick friend in Colorado with an inoperable brain tumor. While there, the Lord used a woman playing and prophesying behind a piano to speak straight off the pages of my journals as the Holy Spirit once again told me things to come... It was obvious that God had zeroed in as she kept saying "Now is the time." So, I called my wife, shared what had just happened, and His prior mention of me preaching across the USA quickly emerged to become, what you now know as, our first Trans-American Walk which began April 26, 2001 near Washington's Pacific shores. As we walked through ever-changing principalities and territorial powers lingering over regions we entered-and-then left...spiritual crossfire around and relational tensions between us intensified as personal fears, weaknesses, and yet unrefined areas surfaced in and around our lives. Hell raged as we did our utmost to stand in the battle... I fell short along the way as both a husband and man of God in our mutual quest to survive...

Ten days before reaching Washington, DC – darkness and tension increased sharply...relational impasse occurred...wit's end was reached...the word was consulted...hope moved beyond grasp...I hit the road to walk...my wife re-entered the freeway...and I did not see her again for 6 months. I could not have made the journey without her – and yet the spiritual environment around us had sapped my administration of love as I set my face like flint to stay ahead of heaven's prophetic thumb in my back. My wife's courage and nobility melted away and our combined inability's to muster all it took to gain unified victory – unraveled. Over those next ten days, I entered another fast...almost died of heat stroke...was found lying next to the highway unconscious...was hauled to a hospital and revived...and increased my pace against doctor's orders to complete my walk into DC's American foundations several days later within 30 hours of divine deadline after 430 days on the road, broken and alone. Upon completion, I fled the city, preached my way home, and prayed until our marriage was restored. We re-established local residence...preached our way to the east coast and back again...agreed on a plan to walk more of America... traversed Northern and Southern California...returned home for a family reunion...enjoyed our most peaceful time in marriage in years – and then watched our relationship disintegrate without warning as hell walked in the house precipitating my 50 day fast in 2003. Once again, circumstance revealed two undeniable recurring realities in life that God uses repeatedly in my watchman's world – the vision-to valley-to-release-to completion-back-to vision cycle... and...that I was always alone during God's deepest lessons and task completions...

Then in 2003...some thirty-two years after God met me at a church camp altar in the Washington woods calling me to preach while kneeling next to a soon-to-become professional quarterback...I entered vision cycle number seven (7) in my life as my previously mentioned 50 day fast began in the wake of my wife's final departure... It was during this time on my face before God that He carried me to America's east and west gates to pray for God's people to return home to Israel...told me I would close the journey three years later at Jerusalem's Wailing Wall on my 50th Birthday.... and that He was hemming me into a seven year season to teach me about coming tribulation...

Over the next fourteen months, intercessors called to tell me that God was taking me into a prolonged season in which I would not perceive His presence, but that He was faithfully there to direct my path. The silence was deafening as I navigated life alone over those unfolding months... Challenge increased as the chaplain's jealousy blocked God's flow through me to imprisoned inmates...I met and loved an unsaved woman with severe health struggles...chose her salvation over marital reconciliation...fell asleep behind the wheel and almost died in a car wreck by hitting the back of a parked semi-truck at 63 mph...led her to Christ a few months later...and trying to survive the stacking pain within while navigating personal loss...watching someone I loved suffer severely...feeling helpless... encountering my own sin...losing work because of another's lack of integrity...being engulfed by loneliness...resuming prior business... working day and night...driving 6,000 to 10,000 miles a month... going to Afghanistan twice...praying at Jerusalem's Wailing Wall as promised...and shutting down emotionally over the next three and a half years finally stepping away from relationship, love, and pain's brutality because my health was crashing...grew 417,000 apple trees out of state...was attacked by a friend I helped after he'd lost everything...ran an impossible harvest operation alone...saw my affliction coming to a close...regained heaven's vision...prepared for coming release...exited my seven year hemmed-in-hell pulverized... encouraged...empowered...and watched God restore life to me again... Ink does not do this saga justice...

As God promised during my 50 day fast back in 2003 – I lived seven (7) years of tribulation – it was hell. Simply put, the above back story of my life reveals how God journeyed with me into depths of an ever-descending sequence of challenges, confrontations, and redemptions necessary to reveal my shortcomings...purify my heart...forge His character...and empower His message His way... all because I asked Him "To break me and make me His..." He not only heard that early 1980's prayer and its latter companions...He has continued to answer my cry ever since as He spends my life to love others in honor of my King amid my own shortcomings (I John 5:14). There are some things we can only learn, own, speak, and achieve after having been taught in and released from the fire...

As you can see, I experienced the devil coming in like a flood along the race marked out for me while...being humbled under God's Almighty hand...taking strongholds captives that exalted themselves in my own life above the knowledge of God...losing all important to me...receiving evil in return for good...encountering judgment's heavy hand...being crucified by those I love...being bitten by those I feed...being condemned by those I help...being hemmed in...being handed over to the magistrate...learning firsthand that authority bears a sword...that satan has dominion upon the earth...that invaded freedom is oppressive...that authority only has the power over me given to it by my Father in heaven...knowing what it means to rejoice when I suffer trials of many kinds...that God leads me where I do not want to go...that angels break off hell's chains...that God's grace is sufficient...that those who lose their life will gain it...that God restores our fortunes...that He uses my life to display His work...and that He lovingly and mercifully preserves those who are His...

After traveling God's valleys toward purpose...Jesus unleashed His love, deliverance, and restoration in my life overnight. The process was indescribably brutal, humanly unlivable, spiritually transformational, and eternally beneficial for me and those willing to receive what God revealed to one who is often viewed among the lowly and despised because of my journey (1 Corinthians 1:26-31). Though I had received vision for God's next mission in years prior, hoping maybe someday that He'll send me a text book rather than a tragedy to learn – He changes not... Since that time, I have walked and preached across America on faith a second time, extending His reach to a sleeping church, emerging warriors-on-the-rise, intellectual theologians, displaced widows, and to those dying without Christ in a staggered world during an urgent and culminating hour...alone...all because my Lord said go. Along my path, the Lover of my soul has ever-immersed me in heaven's soon-to-be-fulfilled story of marriage between the Lamb of God and His wandering lady-being-made-lovely...

So you see dear friend, Heaven's Bridegroom is crying out waiting for His bride to rise to radiance before it is too late... Maybe now, you have a clearer grasp of my world and what it looks and feels like to live ahead-of-the curve in one's calling as I go where most, including myself, do not want to go... Though being set apart for God's purpose can be thankless, He gives us the grace and guts to love others in His stead without ceasing. God's call on our lives is not measured in magnitude, approval ratings, and does not make us superior or above accountability with regard to failures found in our attempts to love rightly. Likewise, our accountability and perceived credibility before God and man is not verified on humanity's carnal scale of reigning religious oversight and resurrection robbing control. One's authorization to preach or right to be heard is instead, established when their spirit has been taught and transmuted in heaven's classroom by Thee Counselor Who inhabits purpose and voice (John 6:44-45; Hebrews 7:26-28; 12:7-12). If you truly hear His voice, you will likely recognize mine as well (John 15:18-27; Acts 4:32; Ephesians 4:1-16). Like others, my life operates on a different wave length, caught in the firefight between the physical and spiritual realms ...the abstract...making it difficult for others wired in more traditional ways to track with me though my devotion to them is undying... When one grasps that most of my daily life lives in the abstract realm with a God-given responsibility to introduce an otherwise obscure element into another's practical world providing them with new options – I am sometimes misperceived, though I love much deeper than most. The repercussions of my gifting are further intensified based on the spiritual and historical season we are entering at any given time relative to Christ's return. Unfortunately, these facts go right over most people's heads making their situational resolution of tension through judgment and separation easier than entering my world. This is the cost of being set apart to God's purpose and the cross we are called to bear in our extension of love to those around us in Jesus' name.

I have not written this book to legitimize, justify, or obscure my personal failures, sin, or contributions to relational impasse. Though many consider me courageous based on places God sends me and I'm subsequently willing to go, I do in fact, face my own fears, inadequacies, misunderstandings, and brush with self-preservation, when waters get so deep amid my genuine attempts to love and protect others cuts me in half without reason. I am not perfect... It is common for me to encounter opposition from those I care about due to their lack of understanding or inability to integrate with the unique characteristics that accompany God's call upon my life. I have had to make peace with ongoing loss by laying it at His feet along the way to survive... People typically try to eradicate what they do not understand and die because of simple things like cigarettes or alcohol they think they control. In the short term, it's always is easier to throw the misperceived away, than to invest the time and energy necessary to lay hold of potential benefits only found in one's undying pursuit of Truth (John 14:6). God created us all with divine purpose, gifts, and strength to stand through battles we encounter in completing our work for Him (John 17). Though none of us asked to be created, our lives will experience the repercussions of heaven's design whether we understand or cooperate with it – or not. Sadly, most people are more committed to personal opinion, than looking beyond their own agendas to honor God and love another. Most view scenarios of relational impasse as attitude, sin, or behavior based when in fact, they have everything to do with the created differences of design and purpose found within individual lives. Because people do not understand, mere differences are reduced to right and wrong, inaccurate judgments are made, offenses are taken, separation widens, and relational divorce occurs within families, churches, businesses, governments, and a fragmenting world.

In His great mercy, I believe God is confronting the spirit of divorce in His bride, Church, and people for several reasons: (1) To redeem what man refuses to forgive and liberate with humility based on Christ's example, (2) To purify our adulterous hearts because of our shameful prostitution with the world (James 4:1-8; Revelation 18:9), and (3) To lead our rise to radiance by the hand as He prepares us for the wedding feast of the Lamb (Ephesians 5:25-27; Revelation 19:7-9). Scripture clearly shows that it is both biblically sound and consistent with God's heart – that He many times teaches those He loves in the very fire consuming them (Israel)...that He loves us enough to let us wander through sin or its appearance to forge our message (David)...that He has a plan of redemption when His people color outside socially-accepted lines to fulfill His purpose (Hosea)... that there is only one unpardonable sin...and, that His purpose reigns supreme, not our dignity. Divorce happens for a number of reasons based on the individual hearts, wills, and decisions of those involved. Due to my own life journey pursuing God with a whole heart, I believe the issue of divorce and its eternal implications is much larger than most grasp or are qualified to teach. Though we know Malachi told us God hates divorce, I believe traditional religionists do not see both sides of the equation they impose on others (Malachi 2:16; Matthew 19:1-9). It is my well-studied and painfully-acquired view that God hates divorce for two fundamental reasons: (1) When it destroys a God-ordained Christ-centered marriage covenant between two believers due to their individual or collaborative sin, and (2) Because divorce represents the cost of sin incurred when one is forced to break ties with the world or another before they can unite with Jesus Christ. God loves us dear friend and hates to see us hurt...

By world standards, many people have remained married to one partner for life. Yet, many such individuals or couples have learned to play games, compromise, or ignore deeper issues as they superficially live and laugh inhabiting the same house at the expense of missing heaven's true intimacy... Sadly, many so-called pillars of matrimony stay married in this life only to die hopelessly estranged from God forever because they never truly entered personal one-flesh marriage relationship with Jesus Christ. So, how well did they really understand or succeed at the institution of marriage when their approach to it left them eternally divorced from God? Where are you in your rise to radiance...? God does not condone or wink at sin. Yet, He uses it and its transformation within the one bound by it to save man from himself. All I know is this, I could not have learned what I now know about the institution of marriage, covenant, divorce, and God's heart had I not traveled my path with God's help. In the journey, I have been confronted by my sin, granted repentance through Godly sorrow, gained a glimpse of God's unconditional love and forgiveness, and experienced radical transformation. As a result, Jesus has empowered me to love much as a result of all I have been forgiven (Mark 14:3-7; Luke 7:47). Had my life-long experiences been different, I would not now be better equipped to love and forgive people unconditionally...would not possess revelation understanding on God's central issue of infidelity against His people...would not possess a relevant message of hope and redemption at this eleventh hour in history...and would not be able to help you enter the season of His return as His bride prepared to meet Him...

I have brought my relational trials into the light to show how the spirits of divorce, infidelity, and independence invade and wage war against every human heart in hell's attempt to destroy our intimacy with Jesus Christ. Infidelity in word, thought, or deed on the human plane exposes our heart toward God on the spiritual plane. Because Jesus forgave our pasts and infidelities, we are called to forgive those of others (Matthew 6:14-15). Our situational unwillingness to love, forgive, and help people embrace God's power and purpose, is pride's ultimate expression and carnality's deepest cry of infidelity as it rejects the entire reason Jesus came to earth – to give unconditional love and forgiveness to those who could never earn or deserve it. In my own quest, I have discovered that most relational breakdown with God and others has far more to do with one' s undiscovered personal identity, undeveloped spiritual maturity, or unconsummated relationship with Jesus Christ, than people's daily life choices. When our identity finds basis in anyone or anything besides Jesus Christ, we have conjured up fleeting fantasies upon which to build our adulterous reality. Just as human struggle does not indicate or disprove the existence of sin, validate or disqualify one's spirituality, or delineate between God's purpose or discipline – struggle paves the path to re-creation (2 Corinthians 5:17-20). Likewise, struggle most accurately reveals that Jesus is reaching to develop our purpose, forge our message, and to apprehend our audience according to His plan, not ours...

None of us are lily white...no one is perfect...no, not one. Simply put, some come through the fire and some through the flood, but we must all come through the cross to be washed in His blood. We all have a story... But God can only use ours if we own and yield it to Him by sharing it with those who need hope as we often have needed ourselves. A story hidden is pride...a story distorted is a lie...a story lived is a testimony...and a story told is truth that sets others hungry for love, free. Many times, life's back story travels a road from hell to heaven pulling us from heartache's miry clay to set our feet on freedom's Solid Rock to stay, at a price. When we bow humbly before the throne of grace to let Jesus transform our lives into His likeness, our story becomes "His-story," that we were conceived, created, captivated, and crucified to tell for His glory and the benefit of others. What is your story, will you tell it?

Until we get involved in the lives of others deep enough to sideline our dignity, roll-up our sleeves, give our last breath, and suffer the brutalities lurking in the mire of their realities, we will never truly own the love of God in our own world...

I stand before you this day as a man naked, exposed, and undone... yet, redeemed. If we are honest, we all face struggles in life... Some of us battle alcohol, others greed, another gambling, and the next person, bitterness. Some people wrestle with lust, while others judge without mercy. Some face fear, others rejection, the next doubt, and many pride. All of these tendencies indicate one thing...pride's infidelity and its resulting blindness in our personal relationship with God. It does not make one person's sin more palatable or acceptable than another's in God's sight just because it wears a suit, teaches Sunday school, gives big offerings, can quote the bible, does not cuss and does not chew, or go with girls who do. Sin is sin because God does not grade on a curve... In response, we must all come through Christ and take up our cross daily, whatever that means in our world as we follow Him, if we're to be counted worthy to be His disciple (John 14:6; Matthew 10:37-39). Whether our life looks like an Abraham, Sarah, Moses, Lot, Ruth, Samuel, David, Hezekiah, Esther, Elijah, Jeremiah, Hosea, Daniel, Peter, Lydia, Mary Magdalene, John, Paul, or Timothy – God created all of us with purpose to travel the unlivable, to conquer the impossible, and to experience the supernatural in our reach to a dying world on His behalf...with humility.

Before I release it, I already know disclosing the back story of my life and publishing this book will land me in the firefight between heaven and hell on religion's battlefield. I am fully aware that many who read this book may not understand, agree, care, or continue to support the man they conclude me to be. I am likewise confident there are even more radical chapters, in which I'm already involved, that have been written for and are now unfolding in front of me to live out for my redemption, God's glory, and the welfare of those entrusted to my care. The religious or hard-of-heart will not understand those chapters either... Yet, true love for God and others calls us into the light and carries us to the cross even when nailed their by those we love. I'm at peace with that... But, for God's little ones long hammered by religion's gavel who are hungry for hope and heaven, Jesus will seat me in the advocate's chair before me to break my bread, give thanks, and feed His multitudes through my life again... I simply know that I was once a man ruined and of unclean lips whose mouth God touched with a coal from His altar to take away my guilt, atone for my sin, and send me to the masses as it leaves me facedown in His love each day. That my friend, is what it looks and feels like for some of us to build God's kingdom...

Now, you know the rest of the story... In reality, I have no control over natural disasters and the life choices of others. I can only respond to whomever or whatever crosses my path in life the best I know how with God's help. If I had been in control, and thank God I wasn't, I would probably be a spiritually-empty multi-millionaire with a large work force, entering early retirement based on my multiplying net worth, full-time employees, and recognition for excellence in several specialized fields I had already achieved by age 29. Thankfully, God knew the path I had to walk to gain what I needed to achieve what He designed me to do. I simply know that Jesus Christ came into the world to save sinners of whom I am one of the worst. To encourage others, He gave His unlimited patience to me as an example so they could find hope, believe on Him, and receive eternal life... Years ago, I was saddened as someone near-and-dear told me they could not be used in ministry until they got their own world in order. And yet, God dispatched me all over the world amid my own battles in life to encounter the unseen and enlist the unknown for His glory, in spite of me. If He can do it for me, He will do it for you. Whatever the cost...whatever the opposition... whatever the pain – I still know that those who lose their life will gain it and those who hang onto life and reputation will lose it...

Am I proud of my past? No... Would I live it again? Not on purpose... Yet, I would not trade all God has revealed, all I have gained, and all who will be helped because I lived it. Now, you must choose whether you will ask God if what I have said is true... As one old gent I met on my walk said about the people's response to what we offer them calling the analogy the 5-W's – "Some will...some won't...

so what...somewhere...some will." You may accept what I've said in theory only justifying to yourself and others why it does not apply to you to which I'll respond with an axiom from another pastor I met along my trail who says, "An excuse is the skin of a reason stuffed with a lie." In bottom-line truth, God has commissioned all of us to love Him and to disciple others...not just those of us who are crazy enough to pray dangerous prayers and go when He calls... The most common and second option exercised by many in such an uncomfortable situation as this, is for you to pick up and use the armor-piercing bullets I just handed to you about my personal life, thereby giving you opportunity to shoot the messenger to silence the message. Though you may be able to wound the preacher, Love's redemption's message will never die...

Journal Entry: Okay Lord...now where? Send me...

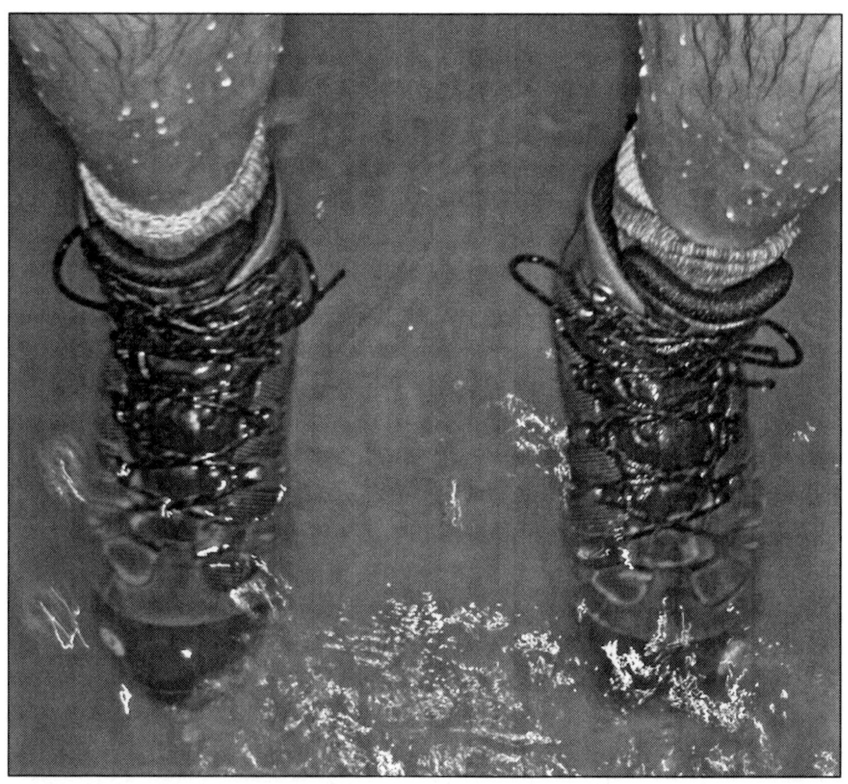

#2 USA Walk finish 7:18 pm Jacksonville, FL – Sept. 28, 2011

Radiance

"Arise, shine, for your light has come,

and the glory of the Lord rises upon you.

See, darkness covers the earth

and thick darkness is over the peoples,

but the Lord rises upon you

and his glory appears over you.

Nations will come to your light,

and kings to the brightness of your dawn.

"Lift up your eyes and look about you:

All assemble and come to you;

your sons come from afar,

and your daughters are carried on the hip.

Then you will look and be radiant…"

Isaiah 60:1-5

Epilogue

We live in an urgent hour in a troubled and fragmenting world based on events happening around the globe and within our own lives. It is urgent and troubling because Scripture plainly tells us what such events and human condition indicate... Whether we like it or not, we are all caught in the crossfire between God's love and hell's bid to devour our lives. Our opinion does not change God's reality, intention, or timeline...He alone is God.

Currently, we see widespread evidence of increasing global economic instability...potential for unparalleled multi-national military clash in the Middle East...radical nuclear weapon proliferation... regimes drawing battle lines in the sand...unveiled threats of overt terrorism...tightening populace control with technology limiting freedom...runaway political tyrants and power brokers driven by evil's agenda...world government's stage being set...fantasy and delusion out of control...plummeting morality and spirituality...a powerless Church...and the lives of people-at-large crumbling fast in societies cut loose from Truth's anchor...

Meanwhile, our holy and loving God is confronting ALL of us with a choice to open our eyes, bow our knees, release our sin, accept His authority, love our neighbors, and do life His way – or jump ship to our own peril. If we choose His rescue from life's tumultuous sea, we are assured that He will love, help, empower and deliver us safely into His presence forever. Conversely, if we go our own way, we are clearly told that our separation from God, those we love, and all forms of peace will be without end. Therefore, please remember that God made you a masterpiece, loves you unconditionally, calls you according to His purpose, and commissions you to change the world while giving Him permission to radically alter yours... In truth, we who have given our lives to Jesus Christ lock, stock, and barrel – are heaven's bride...

Thank you for your time, prayerful consideration, and walking into my life's journey in *Author unknown*. I pray God's deep-reaching love, greatest revelations, tender mercies, and extreme blessings upon you in the days ahead in Jesus' name. Now dear friend, join me as we keep our eyes in the East, rise in radiance, and await our Bridegroom and Soon Coming King...

Greg Benner - Steward
BattleCry Ministries

Walk Logistics

Almost everyone I meet asks me how the walk itself works as I trek across America on foot one step-at-a-time. So, to satisfy your curiosity, here's how it looks logistically in general terms...

RV and Tow Vehicle

I use an RV to live in and operate from while walking across America. Relative to my rate of progress, my motor home is moved forward from city-to-city every 50 to 120 miles based on how those cities are laid out along my route. Typically, I try to find a place that will permit me to park for a week to minimize the time and complication of finding another place. The primary source of RV parking spots is churches which let me stay in their lots while I'm in that immediate area. Most churches have varied types and combinations of electrical, water, and other hook-ups which allow me to exist while there. If I cannot find a church that is willing to let me stay in a given area, I then look for Walmart parking lots, private homes... and as a last resort...RV Parks. Because of my faith budget and not asking for support, it is always preferable for me to park for free in church parking lots, rather than pay for a spot in RV parks. Walmart and other alternative parking places do not provide power or water, thereby making my task much harder. In addition, I also tow a small vehicle behind my RV and disconnect it for use as a runabout in the area I'm walking through while my RV is parked there.

Parking Tow Vehicle

On a typical day while on the road alone, I drive my tow vehicle to either where I left off the day before or where I will end that current day. I never know which end of my day's walk path I will park, until I look and find a safe place for my rig to sit empty while I'm away walking. I have faith in God's protection, yet also try to apply wisdom. Once my day's parking place located, I hunt for someone able to give me a ride to whichever point I need to go. I find those who give me rides among people I've met at a church, along my route, through hitchhiking, or by calling a Taxicab. I've met some live ones behind the wheels of local Taxis. I never know who, where, or what will fill the bill that day, until the moment arrives...

Daily Walk Routine

This is generally how my walk routine looks on a daily basis. When I finish walking, I paint a mark on the road and record the nearest mile marker where I ended that day. Then, whoever picks me up returns me to my vehicle and I commence knocking on churches hoping to meet and pray with pastors, secure speaking opportunities, and locate parking spots. I drive as many streets in that area north and south and then east and west to find as many churches as possible on my way through. In general, I've cut a 10 mile wide swath across America twice to knock on every church I find in my path. There has only been two occasions where I have ever asked a church for anything more than a place to speak or park because the details are up to God. Remember, He always calls me to walk the faith I preach.

Actual Walking

Once I've dropped my rig at its parking place and have made my way to that day's walking start point, I take off stopping to knock on all churches I pass, to meet people of all sorts in all types of places, pray with them, drink coffee with them, cry with them, help them, and keep walking until my day's done. I typically walk from 12-20 miles per day 5 or 6 days a week depending on route, populations, and circumstances. My walk pace is approximately 4 MPH thereby allowing me to cover 15-16 miles in about 4 hours if not disturbed while en-route. I carry hand weights as I walk to stretch my stride increase my pace up to an additional half mile per hour...especially up hills.

Other Daily Activities

My usual day while on the walk consists of getting up early for devotions and prayer, traveling to destination, walking, knocking on churches, meeting pastors, helping widows, moving rigs, touching lives, writing books, preaching, uploading blogs, doing bookkeeping, managing personal life, doing laundry, connecting with family, hopefully getting to sleeping, and myriad other things associated with walking a continent alone. I rise early and crash late as my days are on the run for 16 to 20 hours each 7 days a week as I manage all that is required to accomplish God's task. I find my Sabbath rest amid the details as I keep my eyes on Him. Due to walk and ministry demands, I rarely stop for pleasure, stop at sights, or allow myself to wander off God's course set before me. That is a watchman's world...

Statistics

As of this writing, I've covered a bit less than 7,000 miles during two Trans-American walks (2001-02 and 2010-11). Along their pathways, I've cold called more than 3,000 churches representing 60 doctrinal stances, have sat and talked at length with approximately 1,000 pastors, have spoken in 23 or more denominations, have preached several hundred times...doing so in churches, youth groups, rescue missions, jails, schools, organizations, retirement communities, campgrounds, and have also been interviewed on local and talk radio, national television, and in numerous newspapers. And all of it was accomplished in faith without organized church or financial support, speaking engagements, or parking places having been set up in advance...except, on two occasions.

Bottom Line

So, whether I'm in front of thousands of people, an audience of one, behind bars speaking in a cell block, before a student body, or going out across the air waves – it remains all about Jesus on all occasions...

RV Parking Needs

- 20 to 50 Amps 110 VAC single Phase
- Clean water connection
- Waste water drain connection

Third Walk...?

As I seek God on where I go from here, it is possible that a third walk is ahead. I am not sure, but am praying on the matter as doing so would then encompass all 50 states. If so, I will walk Hawaii next to last in case I'm eaten by a Grizzly Bear crossing Alaska...

About the Book's Author

Greg Benner

History

Greg Benner lives in Washington State amid America's beautiful Pacific Northwest. He is a fourth generation farmer and also the first in four generations in his family to re-enter ministry since his great grandfather planted churches between 1893 and 1920 – several of which still meet. Greg still enjoys both parents Wally (79) and Laurel (78), being the only son and middle child between two sisters, being father to three girls and one son ages 26 to 33, and now being age 55 himself. God called Greg to preach at age 15 while kneeling at a church camp altar before taking an unwitting roundabout path to gain his life's practical message.

Amid the process, Greg raced motorcycles...started and ran four side-by-side companies for twenty years including contract tree production, heavy diesel repair, controlled explosives, and technical consulting. Likewise, he farmed with his father and became known in the industry as one on the cutting-edge. Along the way, Greg navigated divorce and remarriage, lost all to catastrophic winter weather, deepened his faith in God, and entered ministry in 1990. Since, he worked with youth, founded BattleCry Ministries in 1995, spoke in jails, walked and preached across America on faith two times, survived a near-fatal auto accident, traveled the war-torn Middle East, closed a three year prayer journey at Jerusalem's Wailing Wall, and met many of life's world changers through divine encounter.

Heart

God calls Greg to walk the faith he preaches, to engage prophetic tasks, to stay in the game while under fire, and to spend his life for the benefit of others at extreme cost. God's watchman-to-the-nations call on Greg's life catapults him ahead of the crowd to encounter, inspire, challenge, and help people-at-large dig deeper, stretch farther, and reach higher in their lives and faith. Due to his own journey and heartache – Greg reaches to the hurting, broken, fearful, and weak of this world in over their head in life as he helps them uncover and unleash their identity, destiny, and eternity in Jesus Christ.

Though Greg often leaps into life's fires, scales life's walls, plunges into life's valleys, and travels life's by-ways to find and restore hope to others...he's not religious, into theory, or tolerant of oppression. Instead, he is real, authentic, active, and armed with a smile in his never-ending pursuit of God's radical transformation in his own life and on behalf of others. As he often says to those he meets along life's way, "Unforgiveness lives in the past, fear lives in the future, and obedience lives in the now. I can't change where I've been or what I've done. But, I can do those things today which shape tomorrow as God transforms and uses me to change the world of others."

Greg Benner – Steward
BattleCry Ministries

30 days into 40 day fast on 2nd USA Walk at age 55 – 2011

Contact Information

BattleCry Ministries
Greg Benner

BattleCry Ministries began as the original BattleCry in the USA during an extended fast in 1995 while I was living in Colorado Springs. Meanwhile, God's call has given me opportunity to speak all over the United States to churches, youth, rescue missions, jails, schools, organizations, camps, and other groups in addition to being on television, radio, and in newspapers.

At God's direction, I make myself available to speak in any setting at any time under any conditions on a travel expense and love offering basis. My heart is to encourage, build, and love people...not to chase bucks. How God provides for me is His job, not mine. My part is to obey and let Him manage the details. So, if you care communicate, secure books, or schedule me for a speaking engagement, I may be reached at:

BattleCry Ministries
Greg Benner
P.O. Box 340
Cowiche, WA 98923
Web-site: www.battlecry.org
E-mail: info@battlecry.org
Phone: 509.678.0406

If you have further questions or needs, please feel free to contact me. Thank you and God bless you in Jesus' name!

With research scientists Peshawar, Pakistan – 2006

Money changers inside Old Jerusalem – October 26, 2006

Life’s highways and by-ways call us onward in Jesus’ name

CPSIA information can be obtained at www.ICGtesting.com
Printed in the USA
BVOW031428290312

286399BV00004B/1/P

9 781619 967465